Oxford Socio-Legal Studies

COMPENSATION AND SUPPORT FOR ILLNESS AND INJURY

OXFORD SOCIO-LEGAL STUDIES

Oxford Socio-Legal Studies is a series of books published for the Centre for Socio-Legal Studies, Wolfson College, Oxford (a research unit of the Social Science Research Council). The series is concerned generally with the relationship between law and society, and is designed to reflect the increasing interest of lawyers, social scientists and historians in this field.

Already Published

(By Macmillan)

J. Maxwell Atkinson and Paul Drew
ORDER IN COURT: The Organization of Verbal Interaction in Judicial Settings

Ross Cranston
REGULATING BUSINESS: Law and Consumer Agencies

Robert Dingwall and Philip Lewis (*editors*)
THE SOCIOLOGY OF THE PROFESSIONS: Lawyers, Doctors and Others

David P. Farrington, Keith Hawkins and Sally M. Lloyd-Bostock (*editors*)
PSYCHOLOGY, LAW AND LEGAL PROCESSES

Sally M. Lloyd-Bostock
PSYCHOLOGY IN LEGAL CONTEXTS: Applications and Limitations

Mavis Maclean and Hazel Genn
METHODOLOGICAL ISSUES IN SOCIAL SURVEYS

Doreen J. McBarnet
CONVICTION: Law, the State and the Construction of Justice

Alan Paterson
THE LAW LORDS

(By Oxford University Press)

Genevra Richardson with Anthony Ogus and Paul Burrows
POLICING POLLUTION: A Study of Regulation and Enforcement

P. W. J. Bartrip and S. B. Burman
THE WOUNDED SOLDIERS OF INDUSTRY: Industrial Compensation Policy 1833–1897

Keith Hawkins
ENVIRONMENT AND ENFORCEMENT: Regulation and the Social Definition of Pollution

COMPENSATION AND SUPPORT FOR ILLNESS AND INJURY

DONALD HARRIS
MAVIS MACLEAN
HAZEL GENN
SALLY LLOYD-BOSTOCK
PAUL FENN
PETER CORFIELD
YVONNE BRITTAN

CLARENDON PRESS · OXFORD
1984

Oxford University Press, Walton Street, Oxford OX2 6DP

London Glasgow New York Toronto
Delhi Bombay Calcutta Madras Karachi
Kuala Lumpur Singapore Hong Kong Tokyo
Nairobi Dar es Salaam Cape Town
Melbourne Auckland

and associated companies in
Beirut Berlin Ibadan Mexico City Nicosia

Published in the United States
by Oxford University Press, New York

British Library Cataloguing in Publication Data

Compensation and support for illness and injury. –
(Oxford socio-legal studies)
1. Personal injuries – Great Britain
2. Compensation (Law) – Great Britain
3. Sick – Legal status, laws, etc. – Great Britain
I. Harris, Donald II. Series
344.1063'23 KD1954

ISBN 0-19-827508-0
ISBN 0-19-827513-7 Pbk

Library of Congress Cataloging in Publication Data

Compensation and support for illness and injury.
(Oxford socio-legal studies)
Includes index.
1. Damages – Great Britain. 2. Compensation (Law) – Great Britain.
3. Social security – Law and legislation – Great Britain.
I. Harris, Donald (Donald Renshaw)
II. Series.
KD1949.C65 1984 346.4203 83 – 19310
ISBN 0-19-827508-0 344.2063
ISBN 0-19-827513-7 (pbk.)

Typeset by Oxford Publishing Services
Printed in Great Britain
at the University Press, Oxford

Contents

List of Tables ix
List of Figures xv
Preface xvii

1 Introduction 1
(1) The present systems: complexities and anomalies 2
(2) Objectives and functions of the different systems 17
(3) Research design 25
(4) Structure of the book 37

PART I COMPENSATION UNDER THE DAMAGES SYSTEM

2 Who Claims Compensation: Factors Associated with Claiming and Obtaining Damages *Hazel Genn* 45
(1) The problem of 'unmet legal need' 47
(2) The data used in analysis 49
(3) Characteristics of claimants and non-claimants 49
Demographic characteristics 51
Severity of injury 56
The importance of demographic and group characteristics 58
(4) The path to legal advice 65
(5) Trade unions and the importance of pre-legal advice 67
(6) Reasons given for failure to claim damages 70
(7) Conclusions 76

3 Claims for Damages: Negotiating, Settling or Abandoning *Donald Harris* 79
(1) Initiating the claim 80
The selection of lawyers 80
Recovery of damages without using lawyers 81
(2) The amounts recovered as damages 83
Legal rules and practice on the assessment of damages 83
Pecuniary losses 83
Non-pecuniary losses 85

The damages system in operation: the amounts actually received 86
The effect of contributory negligence 91
(3) Negotiations towards out-of-court settlements 93
Offers to settle 93
Negotiating strategies: the pressures to settle 97
Delay in consulting lawyers 104
Delay in negotiating a settlement 105
Reasons given for delay 109
Difficulties in negotiating: issues in dispute 110
(4) When negotiations fail 112
Court proceedings following the breakdown of negotiations 112
The decision to abandon a claim 113
(5) Damages: their use and adequacy 120
The use of damages 120
Views on the adequacy of damages received 123
(6) The solicitor-and-client relationship 125
Problems, disagreements, and complaints 126
Legal expenses 128
(7) Conclusions 132

4 Fault and Liability for Accidents: the Accident Victim's Perspective *Sally Lloyd-Bostock* 139
(1) The legal and psychological background 140
Common sense morality as a base for the tort system 140
Psychological reactions to harmdoing 141
(2) Research questions 146
(3) The data used in the analysis 148
(4) Results and discussion 149
Fault as a justification for compensation 149
The impact of legal norms 153
The relationship between victim and harmdoer 154
The accident victim's 'initiative' 158
(5) Conclusions 158

PART II OTHER SYSTEMS OF COMPENSATION AND SUPPORT

5 Social Security *Peter Corfield and Anthony Ogus* 167
(1) Benefits available 167
(2) Benefits obtained 174
(3) Administration and adjudication 182
(4) Difficulties with claims 185
Problems of legal interpretation 187
Demarcation problems 189
Administrative difficulties 191
An assessment of administrative standards 192
Conclusions 196

6 Criminal Injuries Compensation *Hazel Genn* 200
(1) The scheme and its rationale 200
(2) The survey data 203
(3) Characteristics of criminal victims 204
(4) Claims for compensation 204
(5) Non-claimants 208

7 Sick Pay *Peter Corfield* 211
(1) Receipts of sick pay 211
(2) Factors influencing receipt of sick pay 213
(3) Sick pay and the development of government policy 215

8 Private Insurance *Peter Corfield* 220
(1) Types of insurance available 221
(2) The private insurance policies held by victims 223
(3) Claims under the policies 224
(4) Problems associated with the private insurance system 227
(5) The amounts of benefit 229
(6) Competition 230
(7) Conclusions 232

9 Social Care *Mavis Maclean* 235
(1) Use of health and welfare services 240
(2) Use of local authority and community health services 243
(3) Informal support 244
(4) Patterns of service use 248
(5) Conclusions 252

PART III EMPLOYMENT AND HOUSEHOLD INCOME UNDER PRESENT SYSTEMS OF COMPENSATION

10 Employment and Earnings *Paul Fenn* 257
(1) Compensation and the economic theory of the labour market 257
(2) Time off work 260
(3) Labour market transitions following illness or injury 269
Retirement 270
Change of employer 272
Hours worked 273
Earnings 274
(4) Conclusions 275

11 Household Income *Yvonne Brittan* 281
(1) The household as a unit of production 281
(2) The data used in the analysis 283
(3) Results and discussion 285
The distribution of household income 285
The victim and household income 293
The wealth of the household 297
Sources of household income 300
Household adjustments in the labour market 303
(4) The contribution of a number of factors in explaining the household income 308
(5) Non-response and household income 311
(6) Conclusions: the impact of illness and injury on household income 312

PART IV SUMMARY AND CONCLUSIONS

12 Review and Prospect 317
(1) Summary of the main findings of the survey 317
(2) Allocation of compensation by cause of incapacity 325
(3) Proposals for future policy-making 329

Appendices
I Questionnaire for the screening survey 353
II Questionnaire for the Compensation Survey 357
III Solicitors' (postal) questionnaire 397

List of authors and government reports cited 401
Index 405

List of Tables

Table		Page
1.1	The main categories of financial support for illness or injury (1976–1979)	4–12
1.2	Screening survey: incidence of incapacity in relation to category of cause, sex, marital status, age, and socio-economic grouping	31
1.3	Numbers of respondents interviewed in the compensation survey in relation to categories of cause and weighting	35
1.4	Compensation survey: weighted sample of people interviewed, in relation to categories of cause of incapacity, sex, marital status, age, and socio-economic groups, and compared with the General Household Survey (1976)	37
1.5	Compensation survey: prevalence of residual disability in relation to sex, marital status, age, and socio-economic grouping	38
2.1	Types of accident suffered in relation to the classification of victims by the socio-economic grouping of the head of the victim's household	50
2.2	Legal outcome of accident in relation to types of accident	51
2.3	Legal outcome of accidents classified by sex and accident type	52
2.4	Proportion of accident victims obtaining damages classified by age and type of accident suffered	53
2.5	Legal outcome of accidents in relation to socio-economic group of head of victim's household	54
2.6	Legal outcome of accidents in relation to socio-economic group within accident categories	55
2.7	Proportions of accident victims obtaining damages classified by sex, employment status and type of accident	56
2.8	Proportion of accident victims obtaining damages classified by degree of residual disability and type of accident	57
2.9	Proportion of accident victims obtaining damages	59

classified by degree of residual disability and age group
2.10 Legal outcome of accident in relation to amount of time taken off work 60
2.11 Pre-legal advice in relation to victim's accident type 66
2.12 Reasons for not claiming (given by those who had considered the possibility of claiming compensation (damages)) 72
3.1 Amounts of damages recovered 87
3.2 Initial attribution of blame in relation to contributory negligence 92
3.3 Numbers of out-of-court settlements in relation to which successive offer was accepted 95
3.4 Number of offers in relation to the size of the final settlement 96
3.5 Number of offers in relation to the degree of residual disability 96
3.6 Offers expressed as percentages of the settlement finally agreed 101
3.7 Delay in consulting a lawyer, by outcome of claim 105
3.8 Delay between the date of the accident and the date of settlement in relation to time off work as a result of the accident 106
3.9 Delay between the accident and the settlement in relation to the degree of residual disability 108
3.10 Issues in dispute reported by those obtaining damages 111
3.11 Difficulties in negotiating reported by solicitors 111
3.12 Reasons given for abandoning claims 114
3.13 Use of damages 121
4.1 Whether anyone else at fault by whether anyone should pay compensation 149
4.2 Whether someone else at fault by whether any steps taken towards claiming damages 150
4.3 Type of accident by whether anyone else at fault, and whether anyone should pay compensation 151
4.4 Breakdown of who was said to be at fault 151
4.5 Type of fault by type of accident (work and road only) 152
4.6 Whether person at fault was morally to blame by whether compensation should be paid 157

5.1	The distribution of total amounts received in social security benefits	175
5.2	Social security recipients and the mean and total amounts received by the type of benefit	176
5.3	Estimates of future entitlement to some social security benefits for those victims in the Compensation Survey who were in receipt of the benefit when interviewed	179
5.4	The receipt of social security benefits in relation to employment status at the time of the illness or injury	180
5.5	Proportion of victims using savings in relation to the amount of social security benefit obtained	181
5.6	Number of applications for the various social security benefits in relation to the number of reported difficulties	186
5.7	Issues of a 'legal' character in the difficulties reported by social security claimants	188
5.8	An assessment of the standards of social security administration by the benefit for which an application was made	194
6.1	Cases where compensation was obtained, either under the Criminal Injuries Compensation Scheme or from the offender	205
6.2	Cases where compensation was not obtained	206–7
7.1	The distribution of occupational sick pay by total amount received	211
7.2	Receipt of occupational sick pay for all or part of absence and mean amount received by length of absence from work	213
8.1	Number of victims who held private insurance at the time of their illness or injury by type of policy	224
8.2	Number of claimants and the mean and total amounts received in claims under private insurance policies in relation to type of policy	226
9.1	Use of medical care in relation to cause of incapacity	241
9.2	Residual disability experienced in relation to cause of incapacity	241
9.3	Use of out-patient and general practitioner services in relation to cause of incapacity	243
9.4	Use of local authority and community health services	244

9.5 Use of informal support 245
9.6 Use of local authority services in relation to informal support 246
9.7 Duration and frequency of help with specific tasks by primary helpers 246
9.8 Relationship of helpers to victims 247
9.9 Percentage of victim population by cause of incapacity, residual disability, age, and recovery of damages in relation to the use of services (i) individually, and (ii) and (iii) in combination 249–51
10.1 Labour market status of all victims in full- or part-time work at onset of illness or injury 259
10.2 Time off work by length of stay in hospital for all employees with time off work 261
10.3 Time off work by residual disability for all employees with time off work 262
10.4 Time off work by cause of absence for all employees with time off work 263
10.5 Time off work by victim's characteristics for all employees with time off work 264
10.6 Time off work by receipt of sick pay for all employees with time off work 265
10.7 Receipt of sick pay by residual disability for all employees with time off work 265
10.8 Time off work by region, ranked in order of regional unemployment rate 266
10.9 Factors influencing the probability of return to work: employees in full-time work at time of illness or injury 268
10.10 Probability of retirement: male employees aged 16+ at the time of illness or injury 271
10.11 Probability of change of employer: male employees aged 16+ at time of illness or injury 272
10.12 Probability of reduced hours of work on return to previous employers: male employees aged 16+ at the time of illness or injury 274
10.13 Determinants of earnings at time of interview of full-time employees 275
11.1 A comparison between the Compensation Survey and FES populations of the number and percentage of households in each income bracket 286

11.2 A comparison of household types and mean household incomes for the Compensation Survey and for the 1976 FES population 287
11.3 Representation of socio-economic groups in the Compensation Survey and the General Household Survey 289
11.4 Mean household incomes for Compensation Survey and for GHS in relation to socio-economic group 290
11.5 Age distribution and mean household incomes in relation to the age of Head of Household for Compensation Survey and for FES 292
11.6 Work status of heads of households for Compensation Survey at time of interview and FES 293
11.7 Household income in relation to household status of victim at the time of the interview compared with FES 294
11.8 Household income in relation to activity status of the victim compared with FES 294
11.9 Household income in relation to existence (or not) of self-reported residual disability in victim compared with FES 296
11.10 Household income in relation to victims' registered disability with local authority and with Department of Employment 297
11.11 Compensation Survey household income in relation to type of accident/illness compared with FES household income 298
11.12 Household income in relation to whether any member of the household had to spend from savings or stop saving as a result of the illness or injury 299
11.13 Percentage of households reporting some income from each of the twelve sources at the time of the onset of the illness/injury and at the time of the interview 301
11.14 Percentage changes in the main source of household income from immediately before the onset of the illness or injury to the date of the interview 302
11.15 Percentage of households in each income bracket for Groups A and B, and FES for comparison 304
11.16 Main source of household income, at the time of the 305

interview for Group A households ('Victim no longer main earner')

11.17 Labour market adjustments as a result of the illness or injury made by victims who were previously the main earners 306

11.18 Labour market adjustments made by household members other than the victim as a result of his illness or injury 307

11.19 Logistic regression results for levels of household income 309

12.1 Summary of levels of household income (1976–77) 324

List of Figures

Figure		*Page*
2.1	The path to compensation (damages) of the whole accident sample	46
2.2	The path to compensation among different accident groups	62
2.3	The path to damages in relation to sex of victim	63
2.4	The path to damages in relation to age groups	64
3.1	Distribution of amounts of damages	88
3.2	The spread of offers in each category expressed as percentages of the previous offer	102
3.3	Successive offers shown as percentages of the amounts of damages finally accepted in all cases of settlements over £600 where the first offer was rejected	103
3.4	Delay between the date of the accident and receipt of damages	107
3.5	Relationship of plaintiff's legal expenses to damages recovered	129–30
10.1	Distribution of time off work for employees	260
12.1	The periods of time in respect of which present systems provide income maintenance for those of working age	331
12.2	Outline proposals: allocation of financial benefits	335

Preface

Victims of accidents and illness in England and Wales receive compensation and support from a multitude of poorly co-ordinated sources, with widely varying criteria of entitlement. The supposed goals and effectiveness of these various systems have been extensively debated amongst lawyers, economists, and those concerned with social policy. In particular, the tort (damages) system, whereby accident victims may sue for damages on grounds of fault, has come under widespread criticism as costly, inefficient, and inequitable in practice. The total abolition of the tort action in personal injury cases has been seriously proposed. The study reported in this book is an ambitious attempt to place these debates on a much firmer empirical basis. Our broad aim was to set the role of the tort damages system in the context of the many other forms of assistance in cash and kind provided by government agencies, local authorities, employers, and informally organized sources.

The possibility of major legal change in this area is made the more real by recent developments abroad – in particular, the abolition of the tort claim in New Zealand in 1974, which was replaced by a comprehensive state scheme to compensate *all* those injured in accidents irrespective of the place or cause of the accident; and the enactment in many states in the USA and provinces in Canada of 'no-fault' schemes to compensate all victims of road accidents. In England there has been growing dissatisfaction with the delays, expense, and other difficulties faced by potential claimants. These difficulties were brought to public attention by the controversies over the Thalidomide cases. The public and parliamentary outcry over these cases led directly to the setting up of a Royal Commission under Lord Pearson in 1974, to investigate the operation of the tort system in cases of death and personal injury. The work of the Commission was, however, constrained by its terms of reference to concentrate almost exclusively on accidents, with particular emphasis on road and work accidents. The Commission also felt political and economic pressures to limit its evaluation to proposals which were feasible in the short term. Thus, for example, the Commission was unable to consider the more radical proposals for a disablement costs allowance and a national disability income for all disabled people, irrespective of the cause of their disability, as put forward by such groups as the Disablement Income Group.

The SSRC Centre for Socio-Legal Studies at Oxford felt that the legal interest in accident compensation must be drawn together with these wider interests in the problems of support for sick and disabled people as a whole. Moreover, we felt that discussion of compensation systems seriously lacked reliable information on the experience of those affected by existing arrangements, and that there was a clear need for a comprehensive investigation of *all* systems of compensation and support, which studied not only the situation of the victims of all accidents wherever they occur, but also that of those who suffered similar kinds of incapacity through illness or congenital defects. The Centre was fortunate, as a Social Science Research Council unit with a multi-disciplinary staff, to have the resources to undertake a long-term project involving large-scale empirical work. With a special allocation from the SSRC, we were able to mount a national household survey to find a representative sample of victims who would be interviewed in depth about the legal, financial, and social consequences of their illness or injury.

The research team was led by a lawyer and included researchers from social administration, sociology, economics, and social psychology, as well as law. Each discipline brought a different focus to our common concern with the consequences of illness and injury. As a result, the individual chapters in this volume reflect the disciplinary background of those who assumed primary responsibility for them. Although the book is a collaborative effort, in that all the authors have taken part in the preparation of the whole book, we have indicated primary responsibility for individual chapters by the name or names shown against the chapter titles in the Table of Contents. In addition to those listed as authors, we must record the work of Anthony Ogus, formerly a Senior Research Fellow at the Centre, who not only commented on several chapters, but also himself contributed a section (on the objectives of social security) to Chapter 1, and several sections to the chapter on Social Security (Chapter 5), as is recognized by his name appearing as one of the two for that chapter in the Table of Contents.

The book is a general report giving a comprehensive account of the main findings of the survey. The issues discussed will be of interest to specialists in particular fields, but fuller treatment will be found in articles and monographs arising both from the survey and follow-up studies (see the references in individual chapters). A historical background study published in conjunction with the present volume is *The Wounded Soldiers of Industry: Industrial Compensation Policy 1833–97*, by P. W. J. Bartrip and S. B. Burman (Clarendon Press, 1983).

We hope to have ousted some myths and to have laid the empirical foundation on which future policies for compensation and support can be formulated. This foundation should be useful to any policy-maker, regardless of his political persuasion or preferred social philosophy.

A long-term and wide-ranging project of this kind naturally depends on the help and encouragement of many people. Several past and present members of the Centre's research staff besides the authors made a substantial contribution to the development and implementation of the project. We have benefited from the advice of many Visiting Fellows at the Centre, and from contributions made to seminars and conferences arranged by the Centre. On statistical and other technical matters we have received invaluable and generous help and advice from experts, and, in particular, from Social and Community Planning Research, who conducted the fieldwork for the surveys. We also wish to thank all those who have commented on earlier drafts of the book. It is not possible to mention individually the many people who have contributed in one or more of these various ways, but we must especially acknowledge the support of Monroe Berkowitz, Roger Bowles, Sandra Burman, Lucy Carpenter, Karen Clarke, Theo Cooper, Paul Griffiths, Anthony Hardie, Keith Hawkins, Graham Kalton, Peter Large, Philip Lewis, Clive Payne, Jennifer Phillips, Genevra Richardson, Colin Roberts, Seymour Sudman, John Utting, Ioannis Vlachonikolis, Philip Whittall, and Douglas Wood. We also owe a particular debt to the secretarial staff at the Centre for Socio-Legal Studies who have patiently typed many drafts of this book, in particular, Jennifer Dix, Noël Harris, Angela Palmer, Lorna Pollock, Beverly Roger, Ginny Rosamond, and Chris Storrar.

1 Introduction

This volume reports a survey of the ways in which the different systems of compensation and support function for the injured, ill, or congenitally handicapped and their families. The many systems which currently coexist in this country have evolved in a piecemeal fashion over the last century. New benefits have been introduced to meet the needs of particular categories of people, and the law has been modified in an *ad hoc* manner without any apparent overall strategy. The result has been much criticized as absurdly complex, as embodying serious anomalies, as inefficient, and as unnecessarily expensive to administer. Some critics have argued for drastic reform.

The study reported in this volume will certainly not end these debates, but we hope it will provide much fuller and more reliable information than was previously available about how the different systems of compensation and support actually function in practice. Much of the discussion and debate over compensation is carried on at a level abstracted from the actual experiences of those people they supposedly provide for, and relies on accounts of how various systems operate in principle, or on partial or anecdotal evidence which can give a very unrealistic and unbalanced picture. The approach we took in our study was, through a national survey, to collect information from the victims of illness and injury themselves about their experiences with all the relevant institutions. All types of illness, injury, and handicap were included if they prevented or restricted normal activity. Victims who met our criteria (or, if necessary, a proxy respondent) were interviewed in depth about the legal, social, and economic consequences of their illness or injury for themselves and their families, and about their experiences with legal services, social security, employers, local authorities and the National Health Service – as well as support from informal sources such as family and friends.

In this Introduction we first outline the main features of the present compensation systems and then discuss their supposed objectives and some of the central issues in debate where our survey results are relevant. We then present our research design and methodology, and incidence figures for the survey as a whole: these figures provide the basis for reports of the survey results in subsequent chapters. Lastly, we outline the plan of the rest of the book.

(1) The present systems: complexities and anomalies

Table 1.1 sets out the different types of financial support which were, during the main period of our survey (1976–9), available to various categories of those who were ill, injured, or disabled. The Table does not purport to be an exhaustive statement of the criteria for entitlement to payments: rather, it is intended to show the great complexity of the arrangements, and the many anomalies which occur in the rules for the different benefits. If each column in the Table is read vertically from top to bottom, the reader will see the different answers given to the same question by the rules of various categories: each has its own conditions for entitlement, its own method of assessing benefits, and often its own level of benefits and its own machinery for administration.

Column 1 in the Table gives a brief, general description of the coverage and purpose of each category of compensation and support. This column reveals a bewildering number of overlapping definitions and criteria, with such different terms as 'personal injury', 'accident', 'incapable of work', 'disabled', 'disablement', 'impairment', 'handicap', 'loss of physical or mental faculty', 'chronic sickness', 'illness or disablement', and 'unable to walk'.

About half the benefits in the Table depend on proof of incapacity arising in a particular contingency, or due to a specific cause, such as a work accident, a crime, or an accident caused by someone's fault (Column 2). The majority of social security benefits, however, and nearly all sick pay schemes ignore the particular cause of the incapacity, and look to the consequences – the need for financial support arising from the physical or mental condition of a person. The question of 'cause' in Column 2 is closely connected with that in Column 3 (which asks whether illness and congenital disability are covered). If no proof of a specific cause is required for a particular category of support, illness and congenital illness will be covered; but for some categories only certain diseases are covered (e.g. specified industrial diseases, or disease caused by war service). In our opinion, the accident/illness demarcation, as illustrated in the Table, is the most serious anomaly in the present arrangements. All recent additions to social security benefits for the disabled have followed the approach of the National Health Service in not limiting entitlement to those whose need arises from identifiable causes: the new benefits aim at social and financial consequences rather than at causes, and their enactment implicitly accepts that there is no social justification for giving preference to accident victims over those disabled by illness or other causes. The present study therefore focuses on the *consequences* of mental and physical disabilities, whether temporary or permanent. The population studied was defined, not in medical terms, nor in terms of the causes of the disability, but in terms of the extent to which a person's capacity to carry on a normal life had been damaged. We argue that, as a basis from which to examine the relative roles of the various compensation and support systems, the consequences mean more than the cause. The special needs of a man without a leg, for instance, are determined not by whether his disability was congenital or caused by disease or accident, but by the fact that his condition has serious implications for the life he can now lead. Our survey was designed (*inter alia*) to permit a comparison between the response of current social and legal institutions to the needs of accident victims with the response to the needs of those incapacitated from birth or through illness. We believe that in the past the policy-maker has failed to confront the fundamental question whether these institutions should continue to treat these two categories separately, and has, as a result, given preference to accident victims.

Column 4 points to the conflict between categories on the question whether entitlement depends on proof that the claimant is incapable of work. The fact that nearly all categories of income support in the Table (including sick pay) depend on this test reveals the overriding aim of protecting the labour force (both earners and potential earners). The data on age qualifications in Columns 7 and 9, discussed below, confirm this interpretation. Protection of those not in the working population comes from social security allowances for some of the extra expenses of disability, and from damages under the tort system. But protection of the working population is seldom dependent on payment of contributions by the beneficiary, as Column 6 shows. Only entitlement to sickness benefit (and its replacement for longer-term cases, invalidity benefit) depends on a contribution record; premiums, however, must obviously be paid for private insurance. Although all employees are required to contribute regularly towards the cost of the industrial injuries scheme, they become entitled to all benefits under it from the moment their

Table 1.1 *The main categories of financial support for illness or injury (1976–1979)*

Category of Compensation or Benefit		Main conditions of entitlement						
		Outline of the coverage and purpose of the category	Is it dependent on proof of a *specific cause* of the illness or injury?	Are *illness* and *congenital disability* covered?	Is it dependent on proof of *incapacity for work*?	Does it cover *partial disability* (i.e. if still able to work part-time or in a different job)?	Is it dependent on payment of *contributions*?	Are there *age restrictions* on initial entitlement?
		1	2	3	4	5	6	7
Damages	Damages at common law (as modified by statute)	Injury or illness caused by the negligence of another identified person (sometimes proof of fault is not necessary, e.g. 'strict' liability or breach of statutory duty)	Yes	Yes (but in practice they can rarely be proved)	No	Yes	No	No
	Criminal injuries compensation	Personal injury directly attributable to a crime, or suffered in crime prevention	Yes	No	No	Yes	No	No
Social Security (**Income support**)	Industrial injury benefit	Injury to an employee arising out of his employment	Yes	Cover only for specified industrial diseases	Yes	No	No	Employable age
	Disablement benefit	Loss of physical or mental faculty caused to an employee by an industrial accident or disease	Yes	As above	No	Yes	No	Employable age

	1	2	3	4	5	6	7
Special hardship allowance	Unable to work in previous occupation, as the result of an industrial accident or disease	Yes	As above	Yes	Yes	No	Employable age
Unemployability supplement	Permanently incapable of work, as the result of an industrial accident or disease	Yes	As above	Yes	No	No	Employable age
War pensions (and special allowances)	Disabled as a result of war service, or service in the Armed Forces	Yes	Disease covered if causally related to war service	No	Yes	No	Employable age
Sickness benefit	Employee or self-employed who is incapable of work because of illness or disablement	No	Yes	Yes	No	Yes	Working age
Invalidity benefit	Employee or self-employed who is incapable of work because of illness or disablement for a period longer than 168 days (when entitlement to Sickness Benefit is exhausted)	No	Yes	Yes	No	Yes	Working age
Non-contributory invalidity pension	People of working age who have been continuously incapable of work for 168 days, but who have not paid sufficient contributions for the (contributory) invalidity benefit	No	Yes	Yes (but from 1977 married women incapable of housework also qualify)	No	No	Working age

Table 1.1 *continued.*

		Main conditions of entitlement						
		1	2	3	4	5	6	7
	Invalid care allowance	People prevented from working by the need to care for a severely disabled relative	No	Yes (in the case of the relative)	Not the beneficiary's incapacity	No	No	Working age
	Supplementary Benefit	People over 16, not in full-time work, whose 'resources' are below their 'requirements' (according to scale rates). Entitlement is not restricted to sick, injured or disabled people, but the benefit provides a 'safety net' for them	No	Yes	No (But the claimant must normally either register for work or produce evidence of incapacity for work)	No (If the claimant is partially incapable he is expected to work and must register for employment)	No	Yes, 16 or over
Social Security (expenses)	Attendance allowance	So severely disabled for at least six months that need frequent attention from another person	No	Yes	No	No	No	Yes, 2 or over
	Constant attendance allowance	Needs constant attendance from another, and receiving 100 per cent Disablement Pension (as the result of an industrial accident or disease)	Yes	Specified industrial diseases only	No	No	No	Employable age
	Mobility allowance	Unable (or virtually unable) to walk because of physical disablement	No	Yes	No	Yes	No	(as at 1977) 5–60 (for women); 5–65 (for men)

		1	2	3	4	5	6	7
	The Family Fund	Discretionary payments may be made to relieve distress in families with a severely handicapped child	No	Yes	No	No	No	There must be a disabled child in the family
Private provision	Sick pay (from employers)	Employees' income is maintained, wholly or partly, during periods of incapacity to work (depending on the terms of the contract of employment)	Usually, No (but some exclusions are common, e.g. illness arising from pregnancy or maternity, or from abuse of alcohol or drugs)	Illness is covered (but sometimes incapacity arising from pre-existing conditions is excluded, e.g. congenital disability)	Yes	No	Usually, No	Employable age
	Private insurance	(Depending on the terms of the policy) 1. Personal accident 2. Loss of income (permanent health) insurance	1. Yes 2. No (all causes covered unless specifically excluded, e.g. self-inflicted injury; abuse of alcohol or drugs)	1. No, for lump sums; yes, for periodical benefits. 2. Yes (if no specific exclusion)	1. No, for lump sums; yes, for periodical benefits. 2. Yes, for full benefit	1. No 2. Usually, Yes	1. Yes 2. Yes	1. None 2. Employable age (normally 20–55)

Table 1.1 *continued.*

	The type of compensation or benefit								Administration	
Category	Is it paid as *periodical* payments?	Is the *period* of entitlement *limited* in duration?	Is it *earnings-related*?	Are there *ceilings* on benefits?	Are there special allowances for *dependants*?	Is there provision for *pain* and *suffering* (or loss of faculty)?	Is it *means-tested*?	Is it *taxable*?	What is the *source of the funds*?	*Agencies* to administer the benefit (a doctor's report is necessary in almost every case)
	8	9	10	11	12	13	14	15	16	17
Damages	No	No (the lump sum is assessed in respect of all future losses)	Yes	No	No	Yes	No	No (loss of earnings is assessed net of tax; and income from invested damages is taxable)	Liability insurance; or the assets of the defendant (normally the employer)	Lawyers; trade unions; insurance companies; the Courts
Criminal injuries compensation	No	No	Yes	Yes	No	Yes	No	No (but with the same provisoes as above)	General taxation	Lawyers; trade unions; a special Board
Industrial injury benefit	Yes	Yes (six months)	Yes (but only as supplement to Sickness Benefit)	Yes	Yes	No	No	No	As below	As below

Table 1.1 *continued.*

	The type of compensation or benefit								Administration	
	8	9	10	11	12	13	14	15	16	17
Disablement benefit	Yes (but lump sums for under 20 per cent disablement)	No	No	Yes	No	Yes	No	No	Earnings-related contributions from employers and employees; and a contribution from general taxation	Trade unions; the statutory authorities (insurance officers; local insurance tribunals; with appeals to the National Insurance Commissioners); the medical authorities (Medical Boards; and Medical Appeal Tribunals)
Special Hardship Allowance	Yes	Normally, Yes (but renewable from time to time)	Yes	Yes	No	No	No	No	As above	As above
Unemployability Supplement	Yes	Normally, Yes (but renewable from time to time)	No	Yes	Yes	No	No	No	As above	As above

Table 1.1 *continued.*

	The type of compensation or benefit								Administration	
	8	9	10	11	12	13	14	15	16	17
War Pensions	Yes	No	Yes (as special hardship allowance)	Yes	Yes	Yes	No	No	General Taxation	Secretary of State; Pensions Appeal Tribunal; the High Court
Sickness Benefit	Yes	Yes (not more than 168 days)	Yes	Yes	Yes	No	No	No	Contri-butions from employers and employees, and from general taxation	Statutory authorities (as above); the medical authorities (as above)
Invalidity Benefit	Yes	Yes (pension until retirement age; but no limit on invalidity allowance)	Yes (after 1978)	Yes	Yes	No	No	No	As above	As above
Non-contributory Invalidity Pension	Yes	No (it may continue beyond retirement age)	No	Yes	Yes	No	No	No	General Taxation	As above

Table 1.1 *continued.*

	The type of compensation or benefit								Administration	
	8	9	10	11	12	13	14	15	16	17
Invalid Care Allowance	Yes	No (it may continue beyond retirement age)	No	Yes	Yes	No	No	Yes	General Taxation	As above
Supplementary Benefit	Yes	No (at retirement age, it becomes Supplementary Pension)	No	Yes	Yes	No	Yes	No	General Taxation	A special commission; special appellate tribunals
Attendance Allowance	Yes	No (it is payable for life)	No	Yes	No	No	No	No	General Taxation	A special Board; appeals (on law) to the National Ins. Commissioners
Constant Attendance Allowance	Yes	No	No	Yes	No	No	No	No	Contributions from employers and employees, and from general taxation	The Secretary of State (no appeal)

Table 1.1 *continued.*

	The type of compensation or benefit								Administration	
	8	9	10	11	12	13	14	15	16	17
Mobility Allowance	Yes	Yes (until retirement age)	No	Yes	No	No	No	Yes	General Taxation	The statutory authorities (as above)
The Family Fund	No	Yes	No	Yes (in practice)	Not as such	Not directly	Yes (in practice)	No	General Taxation	A private body of trustees
Sick Pay (from employers)	Yes	Yes	Normally, yes	Yes	No	No	No	Yes (like earnings)	Employers, and (sometimes) employees	Employers
Private Insurance	1. Usually, lump sums; sometimes periodical payments. 2. Yes (periodical payments)	1. Usually 104 weeks maximum per accident or illness. 2. Usually until retirement age	1. No 2. Often, Yes	1. Yes 2. Yes	1. Normally, No 2. Normally, No	1. Often, Yes 2. No	1. No 2. No	Only after periodical payments have been received for one complete tax year	Premiums paid by the persons insured (or their employers)	Insurance companies; (occasionally, lawyers and the Courts)

employment begins. Another aspect of entitlement is means-testing: does the benefit depend on the level of the claimant's savings or his income from other sources (Column 14)? Only supplementary benefit is formally means-tested, but, in practice, the discretionary payments under the Family Fund take account of all the family's circumstances, including its means. Our survey investigated how many injured and disabled people are subjected to means-testing because they are forced to rely on supplementary benefit.

The issue of partial disability (Column 5) is whether any compensation or part of a benefit is payable to a person whose disability does not preclude him from earning, at least part time, or in a lighter job. The approach of the social security policy-maker has been to deny benefits to those with earnings from any employment, even part time. This 'all-or-nothing' policy prevents an injured person from taking a part-time job as a gradual move back to full-time work. The policy also excludes from any social security support those who are permanently but partially disabled, except in the case of war pensions, disablement benefit for industrial injuries, or the mobility allowance for a person who can earn despite being unable to walk. A major advantage of the more flexible damages system is that, although the amount is paid as a lump sum, it can be tailored to suit the individual case, including that where the victim is still able to earn, but at a reduced level; similarly, private insurance may cover partial disability.

On the question whether initial entitlement is restricted to certain ages, a glance at Column 7 shows that the majority of benefits are restricted to those in employment (of 'employable age') or of working age (which includes the self-employed). Column 7 thus emphasizes the concentration of existing resources on those in, or potentially in, the labour market; only damages and criminal injuries compensation ignore age criteria. Column 9, which asks whether the period of entitlement to benefits is limited in duration, shows that some benefits (industrial injury and sickness benefits) are designed to be short term, but that, of the long-term benefits, some (invalidity pension, mobility allowance, sick pay, permanent health insurance) terminate at retirement age when a retirement pension will normally be payable, whereas others are payable for life.

In Column 8 the question is whether the benefits are paid periodically. Sick pay, permanent health (disability) insurance, and nearly all social security benefits are paid at regular intervals, in the same way as salaries and wages. The only types of benefit paid as single, lump sums are damages, criminal injuries compensation (which is based on the damages concept), benefits for under 20 per cent disablement for work-related injuries, payments by the Family Fund, and certain types of accident insurance. Lump-sum payments suffer from a number of disadvantages: for instance, where the payment was intended to cover future loss of income or future expenses, it cannot be revised in the light of future inflation or future tax levels; and where a person's medical condition unexpectedly worsens, the payment cannot be reopened and increased. The different approaches indicated in Column 8 pose a serious question for the policy-maker – should loss of a regular income always be met by the provision of periodical benefits? Our survey provides data which bear on this question, e.g. information on how those receiving damages chose to use the money, and on whether periodical payments provide a disincentive to return to work.

Column 10 shows the various answers given to the question whether the compensation is related to previous earnings. Damages, in theory, are fully related to past and future earnings; sick pay and private insurance may also be tailored to the individual case, but only a few social security categories provide (usually on the basis of some earnings relation in contributions) for earnings-related benefits up to fixed ceilings. The Beveridge Report hoped that private insurance would be taken out voluntarily by those who wished for greater protection than flat-rate social security benefits. Apart from damages, all types of compensation have ceilings on the amounts payable (Column 11). But the apparent advantage of the damages system is restricted by the judges' use of a 'tariff' of regular levels of damages for the different injuries (supervised by the appellate courts), and by their refusal to allow for future inflation in fixing damages for future losses (expenses or loss of earnings). Social security benefits, on the other hand, are annually uprated to take account of inflation, but the increase requires legislative action, and is thus subject to the risk that a cost-conscious government might not keep them fully in line with inflation.

Column 12 asks which categories of benefit provide special allowances for dependants. The main purpose of the damages system has been to compensate the injured person himself: except in cases of fatal accident, the law of tort has been very slow to recognize that where one member of the family is injured, all members are affected. Some recent developments in the law now permit the assessment of damages to take some account of nursing services to an injured person provided by a family member who was not previously in paid employment. But the social security system takes a very different view: as Column 12 shows, all social security benefits designed to give regular income support are increased by allowances for dependants (normally a wife and children). Some benefits are especially designed to support the family: when a family member provides the nursing, the attendance allowance will be part of the family income; the invalid care allowance also encourages home nursing for a severely disabled relative – in the typical case it is paid to an unmarried daughter who gives up employment opportunities to stay at home to care for a disabled parent; the non-contributory invalidity pension is payable to a disabled housewife who is unable to work and do normal housework for her family; and grants from the Family Fund alleviate distress in families with a severely handicapped child. In line with the social security approach, we based our survey on the concept of the household as a unit.

The question of compensation for non-pecuniary losses, such as pain and suffering, or loss of the ability to lead a normal life (loss of faculty), is posed in Column 13. Most benefits in the Table give priority to meeting either the loss of income, or the reimbursement of the extra expenses incurred by disabled people. A few – damages, criminal injuries compensation, the disablement benefit for industrial injuries, and war pensions – do provide some money to assuage suffering or to give an alternative pleasure where the accident victim can no longer enjoy a particular activity. But this type of loss is covered by social security only in exceptional cases, and few people take advantage of the opportunity to buy private insurance cover against it. As the resources which society can devote to compensation are obviously limited, compensation for non-pecuniary losses cannot be given to all victims. Yet if only some are to receive this type of compensation, there should be a principle to establish their claim to priority; it is hard to reconcile the conflicting policies shown in Column 13 about the priority now given to some categories.

There is no consistency in the tax treatment of benefits (Column 15). A consistent approach might have been to make 'income support' benefits taxable, but to make allowances for extra expenses tax free. But most social security benefits are not taxable, even where they are intended to replace lost income; on the other hand, sick pay and income from invested damages are taxable, and periodical payments under a private insurance policy are taxed after the first complete tax year. In regard to expenses, until 1982 the mobility allowance was taxable, but not the attendance allowance. There is therefore considerable scope for rationalization in the tax treatment of benefits for the sick and disabled.

Column 16 shows the wide range of the sources of funds for existing benefits: some depend on the private sector (premiums paid for liability or accident insurance; sick pay from employers), while many depend on the public sector (taxation and compulsory contributions to social security). The same person may contribute through many different mechanisms, viz. as a motorist, an employer, a taxpayer, a householder, and as a private citizen. The use of several different mechanisms to raise money from the same source must involve extra administration and extra cost (see on Column 17 below). Some methods rely on a measure of risk relation: they attempt to reduce the number of accidents (or their cost) by making those who benefit from a particular activity bear the costs of accidents arising in that activity (as in the case of sick pay or liability insurance for motorists, employers, and manufacturers). But other methods ignore risk relation and spread the cost of compensation over wide sections of the community (e.g. contributions to social security, and general taxation).

Column 17 sets out the many different administrative arrangements under which the various benefits are paid. For some, a special agency – e.g. a Board – has been created for the sole purpose of administering one particular benefit; in one case, taxpayers' money is dispensed by a private body of trustees. But, even where there is no separate agency, almost all categories of benefit have their own set of bureaucrats or professionals to 'police' the boundaries of entitlement to the benefit, and to resolve the demarcation disputes which may arise between the categories. A claimant may often be entitled to several benefits in respect of the same incapacity, which means that officials from separate agencies may simultaneously be investigating the same case. Many categories have their own special machinery for reviewing decisions, or for appeals to special tribunals. There is an obvious need to simplify, to rationalize, and to integrate these procedures. One of the purposes of the present study was to find out how people cope with the complexity of the existing arrangements.

The Table could easily be extended to include comparisons of other conditions of entitlement; e.g. there are complex and inconsistent rules on the question whether a particular compensation payment or benefit can be accumulated with other payments or benefits from other sources which are payable in respect of the same illness or injury; again, the various categories have differing rules on the question whether the claimant's own fault or misconduct in partly causing the illness or injury is a ground for the denial of (or reduction in) a compensation payment or benefit.

The complexity shown in the Table often arises from the different objectives of the various institutions: we therefore offer some appraisal of the objectives which appear to underlie them.

(2) Objectives and functions of the different systems

A striking feature of existing systems is the absence of any consistent rationale or set of principles underlying them. This is perhaps to be expected when one looks at all the various systems together, but it continues to be the case when one looks at each system separately. There is no general agreement about the objectives of individual systems of compensation or support; nor about their functions and effectiveness in practice. This section outlines the objectives claimed for each system, and indicates the issues in debate where our survey is relevant: obviously we do not claim that our study throws light on all aspects of a wide-ranging debate on legal or social policy objectives.

Objectives of the tort system

The purposes of a judge-made set of rules, such as those on the civil wrong ('tort') of negligence, are seldom spelt out in a comprehensive way in any single judgment, but the following objectives may be gleaned from judgments and academic writings on the subject (e.g. Atiyah, 1980; Fleming, 1977; Winfield and Jolowicz, 1979).

(i) Compensation.

The most frequently stated purpose of the modern tort of negligence is the need to compensate persons injured in accidents. However, this is not pursued as the sole objective of the law: since the law wishes to protect the individual's freedom of action, liability to compensate those who are injured by his activities is, in general, imposed on him only where he was negligent. With a few exceptions, the law places the risk of injuries caused without negligence upon the potential victims of accidents, and transfers the risk to those causing accidents only if they can be proved negligent. Although this policy may well encourage people to engage in socially useful activities without fear of liability for causing 'accidental' harm to others, it is a policy which necessarily undermines the purpose of compensating the 'innocent' victims of accidents. It is obvious that only *some* victims will be able to satisfy the legal criteria, and that the others will receive no compensation through the law of torts. An important purpose of our survey was to establish, in the different categories of accidents, how many victims were able to use the legal system to obtain damages; how far the sums received were adequate; why the others failed to claim or to obtain damages; and how they managed to meet their living and other expenses. We were concerned to discover how the resources allocated to meet tort claims (particularly through compulsory liability insurance for motorists and employers) are in fact distributed among accident victims, so that social and political judgments could be made on how equitably the existing rules work. The statutory obligation to take out liability insurance, and the judge-made doctrine of vicarious liability (a doctrine which in practice is supported by insurance: under it, an employer must pay the damages if his employee commits a tort in the course of his employment) are primarily based on the objective of providing compensation for injured people. Yet the basic philosophy of the judge-made law on the tort of negligence is individualistic: the law seeks a justification for compelling one individual (the causal agent) to pay compensation to another individual (the victim) and finds it in the concept of negligence. If the question were removed from the level of individual liability to pay, we could then ask which criteria for eligibility should be met when an injured man seeks access to insurance funds for his compensation. The spreading of risks by insurance makes it possible to provide compensation for *all* accident victims, in *all* types of activity, without at the same time inhibiting the freedom of those who choose to engage in any activity: except for the cost of the insurance premium (which is a definite sum, known in advance), there need be no financial disincentive to avoid activities which could involve the risk of accidental harm to others. (It should also be remembered that the judge-made law does not itself actually provide the money for damages to compensate accident victims: it merely orders defendants to pay. The money is raised by potential defendants taking out liability insurance, sometimes under legal compulsion.)

In those cases where a person who negligently causes personal injury is held legally liable to pay compensation, the law on the assessment of damages provides very detailed and sophisticated rules on how the amount of damages is to be calculated in the individual case. Where the injured person was not himself partly at fault in causing the accident, the objective of the law is to provide 'full' compensation. Another purpose of our survey was to collect information on the actual amounts received by accident victims, particularly in the vast majority of claims which are settled out of court; only in the light of reliable facts on these amounts can any judgments be made on the 'adequacy' of the tort system of compensation. In the compensation debate it has been frequently claimed by many lawyers that damages are a superior form of compensation in various respects: e.g. in attempting to compensate for non-income losses, such as pain and suffering, or loss of enjoyment of life or of expectation of life; in covering cases of partial, as well as of total incapacity; and in having no ceilings on the amounts recoverable. Other lawyers, however, have been concerned with the practical difficulties facing the injured person in attempting to claim damages. We therefore also examined factors such as access to legal advice, lack of evidence, uncertainty about whether the evidence proves fault, difficulties in medical prognosis, and delay in the settlement process, to see whether they reduce the chance of recovering damages, or reduce the amount of damages recovered. Apart from these practical and procedural problems, we also wished to study the operation of one particular legal doctrine, called 'contributory negligence', under which the 'full' damages are reduced if the accident victim was himself partly at fault: to the extent that contributory negligence is a factor in reaching settlements, the 'compensation' objective fails to be achieved, because few accident victims carry 'personal accident' insurance which would cover accidents due to their own carelessness. (The social security system, in general, does not penalize the claimant in this way).

The tort of negligence is not the only system with the objective of compensating those who are ill or injured. As Table 1.1 shows, this objective is shared with other systems, in particular with social security, sick pay, and private insurance. In the last decade there has been considerable debate about the lack of integration between the systems, and the resulting complexities, anomalies, and overlapping. We planned the survey to show the actual results of the different systems, how far they were meeting their supposed objectives of 'compensation', and the extent of overlapping or 'gaps' between them. It is only in the light of these data on all systems, that the working of any particular system, such as the tort of negligence, can properly be appraised.

(ii) Deterrence of carelessness.

A second important objective of the tort of negligence is to deter people from acting negligently: many accept, as a matter of intuition, that the knowledge that the law will compel the negligent actor to pay for the harmful consequences of his negligence will have some general deterrent effect. However, the deterrent function of the law is blunted by various factors. First, it operates only if the carelessness actually causes harmful consequences, and even then, the amount of damages depends on the relative severity of the injury, not on the degree of blame attaching to the conduct which caused it: a trivial mistake can cause serious injury, while flagrant carelessness may cause only a minor injury, or none at all. Secondly, the law operates only if the victim can produce adequate proof of the actor's carelessness. Thirdly, the damages are normally paid, not by the careless person, but by his insurance company or his employer (under the legal doctrine of vicarious liability). Our survey was not designed to test the effectiveness of the deterrence provided by the tort of negligence, but we do not dispute that this may be an important role for the law. The policy-maker, however, must attempt to find a balance between opposing objectives of the law: if the objective of compensation conflicts with that of deterrence, one or other objective may have to be sacrificed or left to other methods – the deterrence objective, for instance, could be left to the criminal law, to the actor's fear of risking his own safety, and to a social conscience educated by publicity on accident prevention.

A limited role for deterrence, however, does affect the assessment of damages: if the victim was contributorily negligent, the damages will be reduced according to the proportion of his blameworthiness. (The deterrence objective in this way undermines achievement of the compensation objective.) The doctrine has an immediate impact on the amount of the victim's compensation and our survey provides data on its importance in negotiating out-of-court settlements; it cannot, however, tell us whether, in everyday life, the doctrine actually induces people to take care for their own safety.

(iii) Retribution.

It has been suggested that the tort of negligence meets the need to appease the injured person by some penalty imposed on the negligent person who caused his injury. Although nearly all tort payments for personal injury are made without publicity in out-of-court settlements by insurance companies, the payment is formally made in the name of the defendant, which may go some way to satisfy the victim's desire for the appearance of 'justice'. Some data in our survey throw light on this question, as we asked whom the victim blamed for his accident, and who, in his view, should have paid him compensation (see Chapter 4).

(iv) The need for an inquest.

Some writers have claimed that the tort of negligence provides the victim with the opportunity to use the courts to initiate a public inquiry into the cause of his accident, with a view to establishing whether it could have been avoided. Although the law may occasionally fulfil this role of publicizing the need for accident prevention, the achievement of this objective depends on the number of cases reaching a full hearing in court (our survey shows how few cases reach this stage) and on the independent decision of the Press to publish an account of the hearing. The 'inquest' purpose is further undermined by the ability of insurance companies to decide which cases to fight in court: the cases which are fought on the issue of fault are those where there is some doubt about whether the defendant was negligent, not the cases of flagrant negligence where the need for a public inquest would be the greatest.

Objectives of social security

The modern system of social security comprises a complex conglomeration of different legislative measures (Ogus and Barendt, 1982; George, 1968). The various segments have been derived historically from different traditions and principles and it is therefore difficult to analyse the whole in terms of a single objective. Our concern must be to provide a brief description of these traditions and principles. A fuller account of the specific legislative provisions available to support the victims of illness and injury is given in Chapter 5.

(i) The alleviation of poverty and need.

The aim of social security, as formulated by Beveridge (1942) was freedom from want, and the main strand in the tradition has been directed towards the satisfaction of need. One class of benefit requires affirmative proof of poverty: the claimant is subjected to a means test and is entitled to relief only where his resources are below a legislatively prescribed standard. The modern forms – supplementary benefit for those out of work, family income supplement for those in work with one child or more – have an ancestry which dates back to unemployment assistance between the wars, and perhaps even to the Poor Law. Rationalized as a residuary welfare system, the means-tested approach does not differentiate according to the cause of the need, except in the limited sense that controls exist to ensure that it is not self-inflicted. The other needs-based benefits are payable on the occurrence of a number of specific contingencies (disability, unemployment, old age, death). Here, it is assumed, in the absence of means testing, that the hazard gives rise to financial difficulties which may be divided into three categories: loss of earnings, loss of support for dependants, and the incurring of special expenditure. Historically, the various systems of support concentrated on the first of these categories; unemployment and sickness benefit and old age pensions provided a form of income maintenance, enabling the person whose earnings had been interrupted or lost to enjoy a standard of living at the very minimum. Additions for dependants were introduced in a piecemeal fashion, but, following the reconstitution of the system in 1946, became generally available with all income maintenance benefits. The household has become the accepted target for poverty relief, and the success or otherwise of benefit programmes is judged in relation to household income. The indemnity, or partial indemnity, of special expenses, particularly those arising from disability, was recognized relatively late. The principle played a minor role in the industrial injury scheme, but for those whose disability resulted from other circumstances, relief was not available until the 1970s when allowances were introduced for attendance and mobility.

(ii) Preservation of standards of living.

The traditional approach, as endorsed particularly by Beveridge, was hostile to the notion that social security should be employed to preserve the particular standard of living which an individual enjoyed before the occurrence of the contingency. This was both because the social solidarity motive behind social security was regarded as implying equal treatment for all and because the provision of welfare above the minimum was conceived to be the individual's own responsibility. These principles have been steadily eroded in the period since the Second World War. First, in 1946 an exception was made for the long-term disabled under the industrial injury scheme, primarily because it replaced the workmen's compensation system under which earnings-related compensation had been available. Earnings-related supplements for the general short-term benefits (unemployment, sickness, and maternity) were introduced in 1966, and, under the 1975 pensions scheme, earnings-related additional components were to be increasingly available for the period after 1978. These increases have never, however, aimed at more than a partial indemnity for lost earnings. Indeed, because the new approach complemented rather than replaced the traditional approach based on assumed need and containing, in particular, increases for dependants, it could hardly be otherwise.

(iii) Compensation for other losses.

The social security system has rarely ventured beyond the two objectives described above, and, in three specific respects, its scope is limited in comparison with tort compensation. First, it takes no account of an individual's economic potential: in so far as regard is had to earnings losses, reference is confined to an individual's performance up to the time of his illness or injury. Secondly, with the exception only of the industrial injury scheme, no account is taken of the partial loss of earnings: an individual must be wholly incapable of earning for the social security provision to be available. Thirdly, again with only a marginal exception under the industrial scheme, no compensation is payable for non-financial losses such as pain and suffering.

Social security does not exist in a vacuum; it has to be viewed in the context of current social and economic values. While it is clearly wrong to regard the system as primarily aimed at endorsing such values, nevertheless its principles tend to be formulated in such a way as not to be inconsistent with them. In particular, the issue of whether benefit levels present disincentives to work is the subject of a long and continuing debate amongst economists and policy-makers, and the rules surrounding eligibility for social security benefits reflect concern for such wider considerations of economic efficiency. The system may also be seen as endorsing some traditional conceptions of the family and sex roles. For example, dependency additions cannot be claimed for a cohabitee unless she is caring for a claimant's child; and no increase is payable for a husband except where he is incapable of self-support and, at the time of his becoming incapable of work, was being wholly maintained by his wife.

Objectives of sick pay and private insurance

Employers do not attempt to formulate in express terms the objectives of sick pay schemes. It is reasonable to assume, however, that they are designed to provide employees with an assurance of income support for periods when they are physically unable to perform their work. A sick pay scheme is like a group insurance scheme under which the employer 'pays' the premium by carrying the cost in his salaries and wages account; the entitlement is a fringe benefit for his employees and is therefore taken into account when levels of salaries and wages are fixed in collective bargaining. The most notable feature of sick pay entitlement is that the *cause* of the inability to work is irrelevant: an employee is normally entitled to sick pay whether he is ill or was injured in an accident (and, if it was an injury, whether or not the accident was connected with his employment).

In the field of illness or injury, the role of private insurance is twofold. First, to provide 'liability' insurance to enable defendants in tort claims to meet awards of damages made against them. Secondly, to give individuals the opportunity, on a voluntary basis, to buy financial protection against the risk of illness, injury, or premature death. Such insurance often takes the form of periodical payments to replace income lost through physical inability to earn, but it may also be in the form of lump sums payable upon specified events ; e.g. death, or loss of a limb in an accident. In relation to the field of our study, the main objective of such insurance is to provide financial support for a former earner who is no longer able to earn, or for the surviving dependants of an earner who died prematurely. Whereas employers' sick pay schemes tend to cover shorter periods of inability to earn, some private insurance policies (e.g. health protection, disability, or permanent sickness insurance) are designed to provide income maintenance up to the normal age of retirement.

Objectives of social care

The support offered to victims of illness and injury by the health services, local authorities, and members of the community (both through formal agencies and informally) functions independently from both the social security system and the tort system, and differs from them in that the primary objective is the concern with meeting individual 'need' with direct assistance, rather than with payments of money. Allocation procedures tend to be rationing devices, aiming at distributing scarce resources most effectively. The debates, or issues of concern about social care, are founded on the relative merits of various 'need groups' – such as the chronically sick, as opposed to acute cases, or the needs of the elderly, as opposed to those of children – and on the most efficient and effective ways of using scarce resources to help these groups; for example, on whether one form of support can substitute for another, or whether help in kind is more useful than help in the form of cash.

(3) Research Design

In order to collect information on the issues discussed in the earlier sections of this chapter, we needed to identify a sample of people within the general population whose activities had been limited as a result of illness, injury, or handicap, so that we could study the support from all sources received by the individual and his family or household, and the impact of ill health on their economic well-being. Surveys have previously been undertaken of the incidence and prevalence of various kinds of illness, and of disability, the most comprehensive being that reported as *Handicapped and Impaired in Great Britain* (Harris *et al.*, 1971, 1972), which was conducted by the Government's Social Survey Division. Other surveys in several countries have reported the extent to which the tort system was being used by the victims of one category of accidents, those involving motor vehicles.[1] The Royal Commission on Civil Liability and Compensation for Personal Injury undertook a survey in 1974 of the financial consequences of injuries suffered in all kinds of accidents (Pearson Report, 1978, vol. 2), but it did not compare the experience of those disabled through illness, and its emphasis was on support from the tort system. Our survey is the first to compare the experience of those injured through accidents of all categories with that of those disabled through other causes. Moreover, we examined all kinds of compensation and support which are actually received by the victims of illness and injury. Our data thus permit the response of any one institution, such as the tort system, to be assessed in the context of all institutions.

The survey was carried out in two stages during 1976 and 1977. First, a sample of the general population was interviewed to identify those whose activities had been limited as a result of illness, injury, or handicap, and who might therefore be expected to have needed compensation or support. Secondly, a sample of those identified as falling within our criteria was administered a full follow-up interview schedule about the compensation and support they had received. The follow-up Compensation Survey interview was carried out between six months and a year after the first, screening interview. A detailed discussion of the development and piloting of the screening stage is to be found in *Methodological Issues in Social Surveys* (Maclean and Genn, 1979); the present section briefly describes that work.

Screening techniques

Our decision to screen the general population for a sample of victims of illness and injury was taken only after alternatives had been thoroughly investigated. We looked carefully at the possibility of obtaining a sample through existing sets of records, but this did not prove feasible (Maclean and Genn, 1979, Chapter 2). As we wished to study victims of both illness and injury, records kept by those concerned only with accidents (such as the police authorities or the factory inspectorate) were inadequate. Furthermore, we wished to examine not only use of, but also failure to make use of, the various compensation systems. The records of any particular agency or organization would therefore not give us a fully representative picture. The only possible source which might have covered all the groups omitted by other records (particularly children and housewives suffering from illness) were the medical records of general practitioners. But the time and cost of securing permission for access to individual patients from a representative sample of general practitioners, together with the gaps to be expected in their recording systems once permission had been given, made this solution ineffective as a research strategy. We therefore concluded that we must obtain a nationally representative sample by a survey of the general population.

It was important that we should screen as large a sample as possible, since we expected that there would be a very low incidence of some of the subgroups of victims we needed to analyse separately. For example, the number of victims of a particular type of accident embarking on a legal claim would be a very small proportion of the general population. Several survey techniques were available which might enable us – given limited resources – to increase the sample size obtained at the screening stage. In particular, we considered asking each respondent screened not only about himself, but about others in the household; screening by postal questionnaire rather than by personal interview; and using the omnibus survey technique, whereby the researcher buys space on an interview which will cover a variety of topics for different researchers. After carrying out our own pilot work on each of these techniques, we found that only the first (proxy response) was acceptable (Maclean and Genn, 1979, Chapter 4), and that reliance on adult proxy respondents in our screening interview would not introduce undue bias. The use of postal questionnaires rather than personal interviews is commonly held to result in large cost savings at some risk to the quality of the data obtained. However, our pilot work indicated that in relation to our subject matter a postal survey could not yield accurate information, and, moreover, that the cost saving was negligible if we took into account the need for reminders and personal interviews to check the nature of the non-response (Maclean and Genn, 1979, Chapter 5). Pilot work also yielded an interesting finding in relation to the use of the omnibus survey technique. Although this technique is quick and cheap, we found that respondents were unwilling to agree to follow-up interviews after they had been approached in this way.

The size of sample we could screen was determined also by the sample design chosen.[2] The higher the geographical clustering of addresses, the lower the average amount of interviewer time taken in obtaining an interview will be. Savings in cost per interview through clustering can thus allow a larger sample to be covered within a given budget. A design involving dense clustering, of course, tends to have less precision than a similar design involving a large number of small clusters. However, for our particular purposes at the screening stage, a higher degree of clustering than is usual in national surveys was acceptable. With a short questionnaire, the gain in sample size with clustering becomes considerable, and as Kish (1965) shows, the optimum solution may involve quite large clusters. In addition, the adverse effects of clustering are much smaller when the aim of the interview is to identify a comparatively rare subsample – such as people who have had a particular type of accident – since even quite large clusters of addresses will yield only small clusters of a rare occurrence. In our survey the loss of precision resulting from clustering is therefore likely to be less for the subsample who were our main concern (i.e. those who would be followed up at the second stage) than for the initial sample screened.

A final source of possible savings in fieldwork costs lay in our choice of a survey organization to undertake the work, and this decision was in practice closely related to the choice of a sample design. We obtained a number of tenders, and were surprised by the variation in costs quoted. Organizations offered different advantages – speed, economy, thoroughness, and genuine interest in the research. We finally chose an organization which, although not the cheapest, offered us a close working relationship and relevant experience of social research. This organization suggested a highly clustered sample design which would enable us to achieve a high daily interviewer strike rate, thus cutting costs without creating unacceptable design effects (Maclean and Genn, 1979, Chapter 6).

After much piloting and investigation of alternatives, we therefore decided to use a personal screening interview, accepting certain adults as proxy respondents for the household, and using a highly clustered sample design to draw a nationally representative sample.

Screening criteria

One of the most difficult problems for the research team was to evolve and agree on definitions of basic concepts which could be worked into a screening instrument. Our interest in the legal, social, and economic consequences of illness and injury gave us an area of research rather than a quantifiable variable. It could be argued that the entire population suffer the effects of some degree of ill health – no household enjoys perfect health all the time – but we were not concerned with trivial problems. We needed to establish some criteria of seriousness, and focus our definition in such a way as to include those most likely to rely on some form of compensation or support. The problems were compounded by the fact that members of the research team wished to study different kinds of consequences of illness and injury. In designing our questionnaire we therefore aimed to maintain a high degree of flexibility. After lengthy debate, we agreed to build our criteria on the ideas of both some degree of deviance from the norm of ordinary activities of everyday life, and some level of consequent dependence on others.

We hoped to find a validated definition in recent work on defining health status and disability which would serve our purposes. However, definitions of disability, impairment and handicap, illness, and injury proved almost infinite in their variety: each had been developed for a particular purpose. It became clear that, with our concern to screen in, rather than to exclude marginal cases, and with the multi-faceted nature of our concept, we could not make direct use of any existing indicators of disability or impairment, nor of any straightforward combination of indicators. The most profitable line to follow seemed to be work on functional limitation, not in the physiological, but in the behavioural sense, i.e. we were more concerned with ability to perform the activities of daily living than with the motor capacity of particular parts of the body.

Having decided to use interrupted or permanently restricted activity as the basis of our criteria, we then had to decide on precisely which activities or functions, and which level of difficulty in performing those activities, as well as a minimum time the difficulties should have lasted to qualify as sufficiently serious (Maclean and Genn, 1979, Chapter 3). Similar functional definitions had been used in previous work, but none suited our particular purposes. After many drafts and extensive piloting, we produced our own screening instrument set out in Appendix I. We did not attempt to distinguish degrees of difficulty, but the problem had to have lasted for at least two weeks. The key question put to respondents, about each member of the household in turn, was: 'Over the last 12 months since —— (MONTH) 1975, has —— (PERSON) had any illness, injury or handicap which made it difficult or impossible to do any of the things on this card?' The card described activities in self-care, communication, mobility, housework, school and work activities. If this screening question produced a positive response, full details were taken of the cause of the problem and the duration and severity of the effects.

Two additional questions were asked in the screening survey. First, we needed to identify a greater number of the relatively rare road and work accidents than we could expect to find through the twelve-month recall period in the main screening question. We were particularly interested in accident cases where sufficient time had elapsed to enable a claim for damages to have been settled, which could take up to five years or more (see Figure 3.4). This was achieved through an additional question in the screening questionnaire, which said: 'Now, I'd like you to think back over the last five years since —— (MONTH) 1971. (Apart from what we've already talked about) has anyone had an accident on the roads, at work or at home, or been injured by anyone else?' (Question 4a, Appendix I). Answers to this question yielded 1,406 cases which were used in the subsampling for the Compensation Survey (discussed below). The sample of accident cases used in the Compensation Survey thus includes cases identified by questions relating to two different time periods, whereas the sample of illness cases arises only from one of these time periods (the twelve months before the screening interview). When incidence figures are used to make comparisons between the categories of illnesses and accidents (as in Table 1.2), only the figures from the initial twelve-month period are used – the accident cases in the previous four years are excluded. Elsewhere, however, where analyses are made *within* the accident category, or any subcategory of accidents, cases falling within both time periods are used.

The second additional screening question was designed to enable us to check our morbidity figures with those from medical sources (such as the Hospital In-patient Enquiry and the Royal College of General Practitioners Morbidity Survey). This question asked '(Apart from all the things we've already talked about) has anyone in the household any long term medical condition, a missing or defective limb or any similar condition?' (Question 5, Appendix I). This question yielded 3,526 cases which had not led to positive responses to the earlier screening questions based on functional limitations in everyday living; but these cases were not used to produce any part of the sample for the follow-up Compensation Survey.

The screening survey

Sampling and response rates.

The screening survey was carried out between April and June 1976. The sample design involved the selection of approximately 15,000 addresses spread over 200 parliamentary constituencies in England and Wales.[3] These 200 constituencies were selected randomly with probability proportional to electorate, after stratification by region, a measure of population density, and level of car ownership. Within each constituency, one ward was selected by random number, and within each ward, one polling district. A block of 158 consecutive names on the electoral register was then selected, the first name being selected by random number, and all addresses which were not

Table 1.2 *Screening survey: incidence of incapacity (lasting two weeks or longer during the previous twelve months) in relation to category of cause, sex, marital status, age, and socio-economic grouping*

Rates per 1,000 persons interviewed

	Accidents: Road[1]	Work[2]	Other[3]	Total	Illness[4]	Total for all categories	n
Sex							
Male	3.0	6.1	30.5	39.6	61.8	101.5	17027
Female	1.3	1.0	38.1	40.4	65.0	105.3	18058
Marital status[5]							
Married	2.7	5.8	33.1	41.6	71.1	112.7	17864
Single	1.4	0.8	22.7	24.9	40.2	65.1	13754
Widowed, divorced, or separated	1.7	2.0	88.0	91.7	116.2	207.9	3467
Age: 0–15	1.1	0.0	17.9	19.0	38.1	57.1	7982
16–24	1.3	1.6	23.6	26.5	26.3	52.8	5475
25–34	2.6	8.5	24.6	35.7	49.0	84.7	5036
35–54	2.6	7.3	27.6	37.5	63.6	101.1	7993
55–64	4.1	3.0	47.9	54.9	104.7	159.6	3697
65 +	1.8	0.2	84.5	86.5	129.7	216.2	4902
Socio-economic groups[6] 1	1.2	0.0	8.2	9.4	23.7	33.1	2570
2	0.8	1.0	26.2	28.1	50.8	78.9	4883
3	1.2	0.7	33.5	35.3	61.8	97.1	5889
4	3.0	6.4	36.3	45.7	75.4	121.1	11333
5	2.9	3.3	36.2	42.4	60.7	103.1	5521
6	3.6	8.7	47.8	60.2	72.0	132.2	1944
7	1.0	1.7	53.7	56.4	76.1	132.5	2945
Total	2.1	3.5	34.4	40.0	63.4	103.5	35085
n	74	122	1208	1404	2226	3630	

[1] 'Road' accidents include 'work/road' accidents, viz. those road accidents in which the persons injured were, at the time of the accident, engaged in their employment.

[2] 'Work' accidents exclude work/road accidents (see Note 1 above).

[3] 'Other' accidents cover all accidents apart from road or work accidents (such as domestic accidents, or at leisure or sport) and also include criminal assaults (see Table 2.1, Note 3), and industrial illness. (We accepted the respondent's definition of an industrial illness: the 12 cases reported are put with work accidents in Table 11.11).

[4] 'Illness' includes all illnesses except 'industrial illness' (see Note 3 above.)

[5] Figures for marital status exclude persons aged under 15.

[6] This classification of socio-economic groups is based on a 'collapsed version' of the grouping used by the Registrar General in 'Classification of Occupations 1970' (OPCS,

obviously institutions were listed. In most cases, each of the 14,769 addresses thus selected represented one private household. However, this figure was reduced by discrepancies in moving from issued addresses to private households with whom interviews could be sought; while measures taken to cover gaps in the register increased it. In all, 15,102 addresses were covered; of these, 14,566 were found to be in scope, and 14,866 private households were identified at these addresses. The interview response rate achieved was 82.6 per cent, i.e. 12,285 households. Of these, 12,217 interview schedules were successfully coded on to a computer file for analysis, and these schedules referred to 35,085 individuals.

Incidence rates.

Of the 35,085 individuals about whom information was collected in the screening survey, 3,630 reported some incapacity lasting two weeks or more in the previous twelve months, and arising from injury or illness. The supplementary question screening for further accident cases in the four years preceding that twelve-month period yielded an additional sample of 1,406 accident cases.[4] Finally, 3,526 reported some other long-standing medical condition which did not cause any functional impairment. Some individuals appeared in more than one of these three categories, and the total number of individuals in at least one of the categories came to 7,770.

The figure of 3,630 cases in the previous twelve months who had

1970), pp. x–xi. The collapsed version is found in *The General Household Survey 1976*, Appendix A, pp. 284–285, and comprises:

		Descriptive Definition	*Registrar General's SEG numbers*
Reference numbers used in Tables in the present volume	1	Professional	3,4
	2	Employers and managers	1,2,13
	3	Intermediate and junior non-manual	5,6
	4	Skilled manual	8,9,12,14
	5	Semi-skilled manual	7,10,15
	6	Unskilled manual	11
	7	Others (mainly those economically inactive, such as, members of the Armed Forces, and persons who have never worked (e.g. full-time students); but 7 also includes those whose occupation is inadequately described). (Note: this Group 7 is not itemized separately in *The General Household Survey* version.)	16; 17

experienced illness or injury leading to incapacity lasting two weeks or longer represents a yearly incidence rate of 103.5 per thousand screened, or roughly one in ten of the population. Table 1.2 shows how this rate of incidence is broken down by cause of the incapacity and by the demographic characteristics of the victims. We see that over 60 per cent of the interrupted activity is caused by illness, and that such illness is predominantly associated with older people. The overall yearly incidence of incapacity from road and work accidents is represented by rates of 2.1 and 3.5 victims per thousand respectively. Both types of accident are suffered mainly by men, and by those in manual employment (this is particularly so for work accidents). The likelihood of incapacity from road accidents appears to increase with age up to 64 years, but subsequently declines. By contrast, the rate of incidence of incapacity from work accidents is highest in the 25–34 age group. Incapacity arising from accidents other than road and work is far more common, with a yearly incidence of 34.4 cases of incapacity per thousand. These are principally accidents arising in domestic or leisure activities, and they tend to be distributed through the population in a way similar to illnesses: generally the victims are more likely to be old, more likely to be women than men, and to come from the lower socio-economic groups. These observed differences in incidence may be due in part to systematic variations in the risk of disease or injury, and in part to differing conceptions of 'normal' activity within the population. As a consequence of such factors, therefore, our screened sample of victims is demographically distinct from the population at large. (See Table 1.4 for a comparison between our sample used in the Compensation Survey and the sample used in the General Household Survey for 1976.)

The Compensation Survey

Subsampling and response rates.

The Compensation Survey interviews began in November 1976 and were completed by May of the following year. The minimum lapse of time between the screening and the Compensation interviews was therefore six months, and the maximum twelve months. Between May 1977 and August 1979 a number of postal questionnaires were administered, and further interviews conducted, in order to discover the outcome of claims for damages which were unsettled at the time of the first Compensation Survey interview (see Chapter

3). The questionnaire used in the Compensation Survey interviews can be found in Appendix II.

Excluding those cases of a long-standing medical condition which had not caused any functional impairment in the previous twelve months, a total of 5,036 cases were screened out of the initial sample. Our sample for the follow-up Compensation Survey was drawn from these, 2,226 of which were illnesses causing incapacity in the last twelve months, 1,404 of which were accidents causing incapacity in the last twelve months, and 1,406 of which were accidents causing incapacity within the four years before that.[5] The 5,036 cases involved 4,795 victims, since some were multiple cases. The Compensation Survey interview would relate to only one incident per interviewee, and it was therefore necessary to assign priorities to be used in these cases. Where more than one accident or illness had been reported for the same individual, we selected one incident as the basis of the follow-up interview according to the following criteria: accidents took priority over illness, and work or road accidents took priority over other accidents. If an individual had suffered both a work and a road accident, the more recent event was taken. As a result of this procedure, the number of cases which formed the basis of further subsampling came to 4,795.

The second step was to subsample from these in order to make optimal use of a limited number of interviews. We needed to conduct Compensation interviews with *all* cases of work and road accidents, of criminal injury, and of industrial illness. But for the larger subgroups, the victims of illness and of all 'other' types of accident, we decided that, having established their incidence in the population as a whole, we could conduct the required analysis on the basis of the information collected from a sample of one in two. (As some households contained more than one victim, we first selected a two in five sample, followed by one in six from the remainder, to avoid unrepresentative selection by household membership.) The total sample drawn in this way yielded 2,845 individuals for the Compensation interviews. After excluding individuals who at the screening stage had requested no further contact, and after reclassification by our researchers of some of the previously 'unclassified' accidents, we were eventually left with a Compensation Survey sample of 2,802 individuals. Of these, 252 were found to be ineligible because the potential respondent had moved or died, which left 2,550 eligible respondents; 2,159 interviews were conducted, and 2,142 cases successfully coded, which constituted an effective response rate of 84 per cent based on eligible addresses.

These 2,142 interviews produced the data for the analyses presented in this book: 1,202 were accident victims (including victims of criminal injuries and industrial illness), and 940 were victims of illness. Because of the differential sampling of the larger subgroups, it has been necessary for many of the Tables in this report to be presented in terms of a 'weighted' sample. That is, when the analysis requires comparisons between our sample and other nationally representative results, or between different subsamples, we have compensated for the different sampling ratios by appropriate weighting. This produces a weighted total (normally referred to in tables as $\bar{N}$) of 3,586, compared with the unweighted total (N) of 2,142.

Composition of the Compensation Survey sample.

Table 1.3 gives details of the weighted and unweighted totals of each accident and illness type. Although *all* victims of road and work accidents found in the screening survey were interviewed for the Compensation Survey, there is a small discrepancy between the unweighted and weighted totals in these accident groups. Similarly, although one in two of the 'other' accident and illness victims were interviewed, the weighted totals for these categories do not represent an exact doubling of the relevant unweighted totals. These apparent discrepancies have occurred because it was sometimes necessary, following the Compensation interview, to assign a new classification of cause. Victims were initially classified within the accident or illness categories on the information obtained at the screening stage, and the sampling procedure to obtain the Compensation interviews was based on this classification. However, on

Table 1.3 *Numbers of respondents interviewed in the compensation survey in relation to categories of cause[1] and weighting*

	Accident Category				Illness	Total
	Road	Work	Other	Total		Sample
Unweighted (n)	300	399	503	1202	940	N = 2142
Weighted ($\bar{n}$)	318	455	938	1711	1875	$\bar{N}$ = 3586

[1] The definitions of the various categories are found in the Notes to Table 1.2.

the basis of the additional information provided at the Compensation interview, we were able to record more accurately the cause of some accidents and illnesses. As a result, a number of cases were changed from the 'cause' category assigned to them at the screening stage.[6] These modifications enabled the analysis of the Compensation Survey sample into the different categories to be based on all the detailed information arising from both stages of the survey.

Table 1.4 shows the demographic breakdown of the final Compensation Survey sample after weighting, in comparison with that of the general population, which is based on the General Household Survey data for 1976. It can be seen that the Compensation Survey sample of victims tends to be older than the general population, and that, probably as a result, it has fewer single people and more widowed, divorced and separated. It has relatively more manual employees, but the difference is principally due to fewer intermediate and junior non-manual victims (socio-economic group 3); there are also many more skilled manual victims (SEG 4) in our sample than in the general population.

Prevalence of residual disability.

The Compensation Survey attempted to identify those who were suffering some lasting, physical effects of their illness or injury. All respondents were asked whether they were 'still affected physically in any way at all by [their] illness/injury or its effects' (Question 15b, Appendix II). If they responded positively, they were asked whether they were affected a lot at present, and if so, whether they were affected all the time, most of the time, or just occasionally (Question 16c, Appendix II). Table 1.5 shows the percentages of respondents who reported that they were 'affected a lot', broken down by cause (illness or injury, and type of accident) and by demographic groupings. As might be expected, the prevalence of self-reported 'residual disability', as we refer to this phenomenon, tends to be highest for older people: 63.6 per cent for those 65 and over, compared with an overall figure of 45.9 per cent for those under 65. Furthermore, illnesses and work accidents appear to produce more long-term effects than other accidents. This measure of the severity and duration of physical impairment following injury or illness is consequently an important element in much of the analysis in subsequent chapters, although we must stress that it is a *self-reported* measure: as such, it is sensitive to respondents' expectations and coping mechanisms.

Table 1.4 *Compensation survey: weighted sample of people interviewed, in relation to categories of cause of incapacity, sex, marital status, age, and socio-economic groups, and compared with the General Household Survey sample (1976)*

Percentage of weighted totals

	Accidents: Road	Work	Other	Total	Illness	Total percentage of all categories	GHS 1976
Sex	(%)	(%)	(%)	(%)	(%)	(%)	(%)
Male	61	85	43	57	44	50	49
Female	39	15	57	43	56	50	51
Marital status							
Married[1]	65	85	56	67	64	66	67
Single	26	10	17	17	12	14	19
Widowed, divorced, or separated	9	5	27	16	24	20	14
Age: 0–15	13	0	28	18	16	17	26
16–24	21	9	11	12	5	8	12
25–34	19	24	12	16	10	13	14
35–54	23	47	12	23	20	22	23
55–64	13	16	13	14	16	15	12
65 +	11	5	25	17	33	25	14
Socio-economic groups[2] 1	3	0	4	3	3	3	4
2	9	6	14	11	14	12	14
3	16	6	15	12	16	14	22
4	44	56	42	46	42	44	33
5	17	23	18	20	19	19	20
6	10	9	8	8	6	7	7
Total %	100	100	100	100	100	100	100
n̄	318	455	938	1711	1875	3586	33487

[1] Figures for marital status exclude persons aged under 15.

[2] This grouping excludes members of the armed forces, full-time students, and those who had never worked (which comprises Group 7 in the classification set out inTable 1.2, Note 6). The definitions of the other socio-economic groups are found in Note 6 to Table 1.2

(4) Structure of the book

The four Parts of the book deal with: I, the tort (damages) system; II, other systems of compensation and support; III, the economic

Table 1.5 *Compensation survey: prevalence of residual disability (those reporting that they were still 'affected a lot' by the illness or injury) in relation to sex, marital status, age and socio-economic grouping.*

Percentages with residual disability

	Accidents: Road	Accidents: Work	Accidents: Other	Accidents: Total	Illness	Total (all categories)
Sex	(%)	(%)	(%)	(%)	(%)	(%)
Male	34.4	45.9	31.8	38.9	55.3	44.7
Female	38.6	57.9	38.9	41.2	52.5	47.3
Marital status						
Married	33.0	47.5	32.2	38.2	47.2	42.0
Single	38.2	51.4	41.3	42.3	57.8	47.7
Widowed, divorced, or separated	56.5	45.5	44.2	46.4	73.7	62.1
Age: 0–15	17.9	—	13.2	14.3	24.3	19.0
16–24	29.2	48.4	39.3	36.8	30.2	35.4
25–34	34.5	41.0	37.7	38.4	29.3	35.7
35–54	44.9	50.3	44.4	47.9	51.8	49.4
55–64	50.0	46.9	49.2	48.5	67.8	57.6
65 +	38.7	57.9	46.7	46.5	73.0	63.6
Socio-economic groups[1] 1	25.0	0.0	14.3	17.4	27.3	22.2
2	29.2	75.0	26.0	37.2	46.5	42.0
3	34.9	38.1	36.4	36.1	44.6	40.3
4	35.4	47.9	40.4	42.5	49.5	45.1
5	22.7	47.2	31.0	36.3	57.0	44.3
6	41.7	48.4	39.3	43.4	48.8	45.2
7	54.5	33.3	37.9	41.1	67.2	55.8
Total %	36.0	47.6	35.8	39.8	53.7	45.9
n	300	399	503	1202	940	2142

[1] The definitions of the various categories are found in Note 6 to Table 1.2.

impact of ill health and compensation; and IV, conclusions and recommendations.

Part I (Chapters 2–4) discusses the findings of the survey in relation to the use of the tort system. The analysis in Chapter 2 is an attempt to discover the factors which distinguish the small minority of accident victims who make claims for damages from the vast majority who do not. The present system of awarding damages for injury is one which squarely places the initiative to claim on the injured accident victim. It is clear from our survey that most accident victims never give any thought to the possibility of making a legal claim; and of the relatively small number who do consider the possibility, even fewer actually seek legal advice and eventually obtain damages. The chapter identifies those group characteristics which are most often associated with the likelihood that a claim will be made and attempts to explain why these characteristics appear to be so important.

Chapter 3 reports the survey data on the process of making a legal claim. Various sections discuss how claimants initiate claims for damages; how they choose a lawyer; how the claims are handled by lawyers and insurance companies; and the pressures on claimants to accept offers to settle their claims out of court. Other sections report the amounts recovered as damages, victims' views on their adequacy, and their decisions on how to spend the money. A final section examines the relationship between solicitor and client, in particular, the extent of the client's dependence on legal advice, and the levels of legal expenses.

Chapter 4 analyses the ways in which accident victims in the sample attributed fault for their accidents; how this related to their views on whether they should be compensated; and how this in turn related to the decision to initiate a legal claim. Discussion of the tort system often assumes a fairly straightforward relationship between these factors. In particular, it often appears to be assumed that if an accident victim believes someone else was to blame for the accident then he or she will also believe that that person should be liable to compensate. It is also often assumed that ordinary people regard the principle of fault-based compensation as somehow morally just. Analysis of accident victims' responses to questions about fault and compensation allows these assumptions to be examined critically.

Part II of the book considers other compensation and support systems. Chapter 5, on social security, describes the benefits available to those suffering the effects of illness and injury, and the use made of them by those interviewed in the survey. In addition to reporting the current receipt of benefits, we attempt to estimate the amounts involved in future entitlements. The chapter then investigates the administration and adjudication of the social security system, and describes the extent and kind of difficulties experienced with particular benefits. Chapter 6 reports the claims for compensation made by the victims of criminal violence.

Chapter 7, on sick pay, reports the survey data on the number of employees receiving some sick pay from their employers, the periods of absence covered, and the amounts paid. An attempt is then made to explain why our data on the proportion of employees who actually receive sick pay is smaller than the proportion which, according to Government statistics, is covered by membership of a sick pay scheme. The chapter concludes with a review, in the light of our data, of Government attitudes towards proposed extensions of sick pay schemes. Chapter 8, on private insurance, examines the role of the private market in offering insurance against the consequences of illness and injury; the types of policies available; and the data from the survey on the policies actually held, on the experience of making claims under these policies, on the amounts recovered, and on problems arising under the system.

Chapter 9, on social care, examines the support offered by the Health Service and local authorities and the help offered informally by family and friends. These services are allocated according to the need of the individual: the question is raised whether the tort system is also reaching those victims of illness and injury who have special needs. By using service consumption as a proxy indicator of need, it is suggested that damages do not reach a group with particular needs. We then turn to examine patterns of service use by our population, to see which factors are associated with use of particular groups of services.

Part III deals with the impact of ill health and subsequent compensation and support on the economic well-being of the victim and his household. Attention is focused on how the allocation of time to work and other activities, and the degree of compensation and support, mitigate reduction in income following illness or injury. Chapter 10, on employment and earnings, analyses the victim's decisions about leaving and rejoining the labour force in the light of reduced income consequent upon the ill health. The determinants of sickness absence, and of unemployment following illness or injury, are considered, together with the victim's work status and earnings on recovery. Chapter 11, on household income, examines the size and direction of adjustments in the level and sources of household income consequent upon illness and injury and estimates the net financial impact of the ill health on the household. In general, Part III attempts to identify the main factors causing loss of production and of household income and to examine their implications for policy-making.

Finally, Part IV draws together the findings of the study, and proposes the broad outlines of a structure for future policy-making in the area of compensation for those suffering illness, injury, or disability.

Notes

1. Morris and Paul, 1962; Conard *et al.*, 1964; Linden, 1965; Harris and Hartz, 1968; US Department of Transportation, 1970. (Ison, 1967, Appendix C, reports a study of personal injury claims handled by solicitors.)
2. The sample design is discussed in Maclean and Genn, 1979, Chapter 6. (A major contribution to this chapter was made by Douglas Wood of Social and Community Planning Research.)
3. For full details of the sampling procedure, see Maclean and Genn, 1979, Chapter 6. Since the legal and administrative systems in Scotland differ from those in England and Wales, Scotland was not included in the survey.
4. The supplementary question which screened for accidents in the four years preceding the immediate twelve-month period (Question 4a, Appendix I) produced a total of 1,586 positive responses. However, of these, 180 were found on further questioning to fall within the twelve-month period, and were therefore included in the twelve-month sample, leaving 1,406 cases actually arising in the preceding four years. The figure of 3,630 cases in the immediate twelve-month period includes these 180 cases.
5. A comparison of the total numbers of accidents reported in the past twelve months and in the four years previous to that indicates a relatively lower incidence rate in the earlier period. It is unlikely that this difference can be explained in terms of an actual difference in accident rates, and it is likely that it results partly from less effective recall over time. The more serious events may be more likely to be reported. We were aware that this might introduce bias into our results, though we found no evidence of this. Our analyses of the combined groups therefore make the assumption that they do not differ significantly in any way which would affect our conclusions.
6. For example, about fifty cases classified as illnesses at the screening stage were reclassified as accident cases at the second stage, while about twenty-five accidents were reclassified as illnesses. Within accident categories a few further changes were made – for example, sixteen further road accidents were added to those coded 'road/work' at the screening stage.

References

Atiyah, P. S., 1980, *Accidents, Compensation and the Law* (3rd edn.), London: Weidenfeld & Nicolson.

Beveridge, Sir William, 1942, *Report on Social Insurance and Allied Services* (The Beveridge Report), London: HMSO, Cmd. 6404.

Conard, A. F., *et al.*, 1964, *Automobile Accident Costs and Payments*, Ann Arbor, Mich.: University of Michigan.

Fleming, J. G., 1977, *The Law of Torts* (5th edn.), Sydney: The Law Book Co.

General Household Survey 1976 (published by Office of Population Censuses and Surveys, 1978), London, HMSO.

George, V., 1968, *Social Security: Beveridge And After*, London: Routledge & Kegan Paul.

Harris, A. I., with Cox, E. and Smith, C. R. W., 1971–2, *Handicapped and Impaired in Great Britain* (3 vols.), London: HMSO.

Harris, D. R. and Hartz, S. J., 1968, *Report of a Pilot Survey of the Financial Consequences of Personal Injuries suffered in Road Accidents in the City of Oxford during 1965* (unpublished, but copies obtainable from D. R. Harris, Balliol College, Oxford, England). A brief report is 'A Road Accident Survey', 119 *New Law Journal* 492 (22 May 1969).

Ison, T. G., 1967, *The Forensic Lottery*, London: Staples Press.

Kish, L., 1965, *Survey Sampling*, New York: Wiley.

Linden, A. M., 1965, *Report of the Osgoode Hall Study on Compensation for Victims of Automobile Accidents*, Toronto: Osgoode Hall Law School.

Maclean, M. and Genn, H. G., 1979, *Methodological Issues in Social Surveys*, London: Macmillan.

Morris, C. and Paul, J. C. N., 1962, 'The Financial Impact of Automobile Accidents', 110 *University of Pennsylvania Law Review* 913 (reprinted by the Walter E. Meyer Research Institute of Law in *Dollars, Delay and the Automobile Victim*, 1968, Indianapolis: Bobbs-Merrill, p. 3).

Ogus, A. I. and Barendt, E. M., 1982, *The Law of Social Security* (2nd edn.), London: Butterworth.

OPCS (Office of Population Censuses and Surveys), 1970, *Classification of Occupations*, London: HMSO.

Pearson, Lord (Chairman), 1978, *Report of the Royal Commission on Civil Liability and Compensation for Personal Injury* (3 vols), London: HMSO, Cmnd. 7054.

US Department of Transportation, 1970, *Automobile Insurance and Compensation Study*, Washington, DC: US Government Printing Office.

Winfield and Jolowicz, 1979, *Winfield and Jolowicz on Tort* (11th edn. by W. V. H. Rogers), London: Sweet & Maxwell.

PART I COMPENSATION UNDER THE DAMAGES SYSTEM

2 Who Claims Compensation: Factors Associated with Claiming and Obtaining Damages

Accidental injury is a common misfortune which strikes across all social and demographic boundaries. The number of accident victims who obtain damages for their injuries through the tort system, however, is very low in comparison with the total volume of accidental injuries which occur. This situation arises, first, because the law itself draws strict limits as to when compensation for injury may be awarded by a court, and, secondly, because the vast majority of accident victims never take any steps towards bringing an action for damages, whether or not, in law, they might have a claim.

The legal rules which provide for damages to be awarded to victims of accidental injury are not framed in such a way that all those who suffer injury are entitled to be compensated. In most situations, damages are awarded only where it can be proved that the injury was caused by the negligent action of another person. It is a legal remedy which is available where the victim fulfils conditions which relate mainly to the circumstances in which the accident took place, not to the position in which the victim now finds himself. The law considers the *consequences* of injury only when assessing damages after the defendant has been found legally responsible for causing the accident. The principles upon which the tort system is founded inextricably bind together the issues of deterrence of negligence and restitution to victims: culpability must be identified before any attention is paid to the victim's need to be compensated.

A crucial factor within this system of rules is that the initiative to make a claim must come from the victim himself (or his representative), since it is he who is required to prove the fault (negligence) of the defendant. If the victim fails to claim, he will not receive damages: if he makes a claim, but cannot fulfil the relatively strict requirements for proof of negligence, the result is the same – although the latter course will naturally incur legal costs. One of the fundamental aims of the Compensation Survey was to provide quantitative evidence of the way in which the tort system is currently operating, in terms of the proportion of accident victims who bring claims for damages, the proportion who succeed, and the practical problems which they face in pressing their claims.

It can be seen from Figure 2.1 that, of the 1,711 accident victims (in the weighted sample) covered by the study, only 12 per cent succeeded in obtaining damages through the tort system; or, to put it another way, nearly 90 per cent of accident victims – all with relatively serious injuries – failed to benefit in any way from the provisions of that system. About *three-quarters* of accident victims never *considered* the question of damages at all, and of the quarter who did, only about half actually sought legal advice about claiming. Only 45 per cent of those who considered the question of claiming damages ultimately obtained any damages; and, of those who did seek legal advice, 80 per cent obtained damages (albeit generally small amounts).

These figures illustrate the problems for accident victims which are inherent in the system. First, it is clear that the legal rules for awarding damages for injury and the difficulty of *proving* that an accident was caused by the negligence of another person, ensure that even if every accident victim actually sought a solicitor's advice immediately following an accident, not all would succeed in obtaining damages. This is borne out by the fact that 20 per cent of the few victims who did actually seek the assistance of a solicitor ultimately failed to obtain any damages. The greater problem, however, indic-

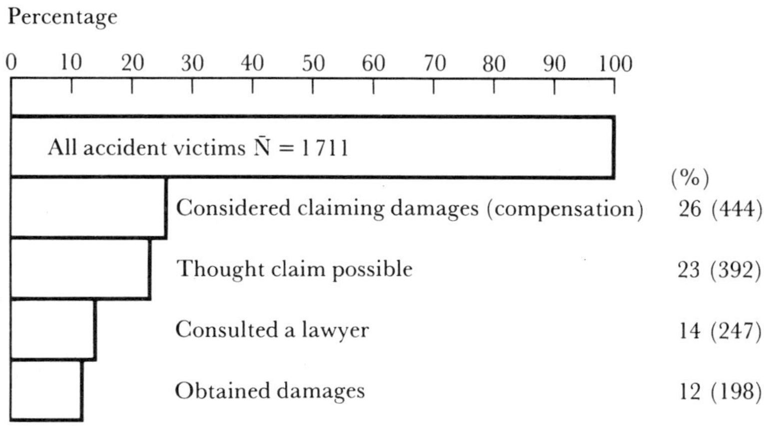

Figure 2.1 *The path to compensation (damages) of the whole accident sample (weighted)*

ated by Figure 2.1, is that the vast majority of accident victims either never considered the question of compensation, or, if they did, failed to take any positive steps to recover damages. Most potential claims are defeated at the outset: the accident victim does not realize that a legal remedy might be available or, even if he does, other constraining factors prevent him from consulting a solicitor about bringing a claim. The difficulties in providing evidence to prove negligence (even supposing that the accident had been the fault of another person) make it impossible to assess what proportion of those failing to take legal advice might have had a chance of obtaining damages. But on the other hand, we cannot assume that three-quarters of all accident victims – those without the benefit of legal advice – may have correctly decided that they had no grounds for claiming damages for their injuries. This section is concerned with the rather complex interaction of factors which appear to affect the likelihood that, following an accident, legal advice will be sought and a claim for damages made.

(1) The problem of 'unmet legal need'

The belief that people in the community with 'legal problems' should be encouraged or assisted to seek legal advice, together with the observation of variation in the actual use of available legal services between social groups, have prompted a considerable amount of socio-legal research in recent years. The result of these efforts is a body of literature from this country and abroad which reports attempts to quantify the dimensions of existing 'unmet legal needs' and to explain why such needs remain unmet. Despite a general admission of the theoretical difficulties involved in defining any or all of the concepts 'unmet', ' legal', and 'need', the approach of many empirical studies has been an attempt to document the range and prevalence of problems loosely designated as 'legal' which are said to occur in a given population, and to identify the characteristics of those groups which fail to seek legal assistance for the problems reported (e.g. Curran, 1977; Abel-Smith *et al.*, 1973; Schuyt *et al.*, 1976). These studies have developed in response to the almost untestable, and theoretically problematic proposition that many people who might benefit from the use of legal services fail to seek or obtain them, and that this failure varies systematically between different groups in society.

In the studies which have so far been published, four major

theoretical approaches to the explanation of differential use of services have been identified (see Schuyt *et al.*, 1976, for summary, and Curran, 1977, for review). The first of these suggests that the distribution of economic resources within society determines use of legal services, in that income and property are the most important requirements for access to legal services. The second explanation asserts that social-psychological resources, such as knowledge, access to social networks, and general competence determine the degree of access to legal services which individuals will enjoy. The third approach suggests that a high level of participation in economic and social life increases the likelihood of an individual being exposed to legal risks and hence increases the likelihood that legal services will be used. Finally, it is suggested that existing legal services are themselves organized in such a way that those problems which concern the wealthy are the most likely to be handled by lawyers, because solving these problems is inherently remunerative.

Despite the relative complexity of the arguments which form the basis of these explanations for differential use of legal services, it has nevertheless been further suggested that all four theoretical approaches are themselves reducible to the simple explanatory axiom that the rich use lawyers and the poor do not (Griffiths, 1977). Indeed this argument embodies apparently widely held 'commonsense' views about why people with legal problems do or do not seek legal advice: namely, that those who can afford to do so avail themselves of the services of solicitors while the less fortunate muddle through without legal assistance.

In this chapter we assume that serious accidental injury represents a potential need for legal advice, and we attempt to identify those factors associated with the likelihood that legal advice will actually be sought. Although this analysis is confined to one specific problem area, that of personal injury, it is such a pervasive phenomenon that it is possible to compare the behaviour of many different types of people in all social groups. However, we do not suggest that our conclusions would necessarily hold for other types of legal problem.

In the course of our analysis we have tried to assess the extent to which different kinds of factors operate to encourage individuals to take legal action after an accident or, conversely, constrain them from doing so. We have looked at the effect of the demographic and socio-economic characteristics of victims; the type of accidents suffered and the severity of injury and losses; and, finally, the importance of the availability of para-legal advice.

(2) The data used in analysis

Information of several types is available from the survey to describe and explain the differences between those accident victims who did make claims for damages and those who did not. During lengthy interviews, information was collected from all accident victims about the nature of their accidents; and, from those who took some steps to claim damages, we obtained information about the kinds of discussions which took place *before* the decision to consult a solicitor was made, in order to throw some light on the informal processes which lead victims towards the legal system. Those victims who considered claiming damages, but failed to take any positive action, gave brief accounts of their reasons for this failure; and for all accident victims we obtained basic social, economic, and demographic data in order to make group comparisons of the characteristics associated with claiming and with the failure to claim. In this analysis, emphasis has been placed on a comparison between the social and other group characteristics of the two groups (claimants and non-claimants), while subjective accounts of reasons for failure to take legal steps have been used as a supplementary source of data. Although the reasons given for failure to obtain damages illustrate the catalogue of difficulties perceived by individuals in attempting to obtain legal redress for injuries suffered, they nevertheless represent *post hoc* accounts given with hindsight, often at a distance of several years from the actual time of the accident. Moreover, this source of data is available only for those non-claimants who at some time actually considered the possibility of claiming damages or who at least felt themselves to have been entitled to compensation. As such, this group is conceptually distinct from those who never at any time considered the question of compensation and for whom comparable data therefore do not exist: those who said they did not consider the question of trying to obtain damages could not logically be asked *why* they did not consider it.

(3) Characteristics of claimants and non-claimants

The sample of 1,711 accidents victims included people in all age groups (but there was a higher proportion of working-age people than in the general population); more men than women (982 :729) and more people from manual workers' than non-manual workers' households (the difference here was greater than in the general population). Indeed, the families of skilled manual workers appear to suffer more accidents of all types than the families of either non-manual or unskilled manual workers, although this was most pronounced for accidents at work (Table 2.1). The most common type of accident in the sample was an accident in the home, at leisure or sport (55 per cent); just over one-quarter were accidents at work (27 per cent); and just under one-fifth were road accidents (19 per cent).

The characteristics of those people who succeeded in obtaining some damages for their injuries through the tort system, however, by no means reflect the characteristics of those suffering accidents. The single most important factor associated with a successful claim for damages was the type of accident suffered (Table 2.2). While fewer than one in three of road accident victims, and one in five of work accident victims obtained some damages, fewer than one in fifty of the victims of all other types of accident obtained any

Table 2.1 *Types of accident suffered in relation to the classification of victims by the socio-economic grouping of the head of the victim's household*

Socio-economic group[1]		Type of Accident: Road Accidents[2]	Work Accidents	Other Accidents[3]	%	All accidents ñ	(%)
1 Professional	(%)	24	3	73	100	37	2
2 Employers and Managers	(%)	17	18	65	100	149	9
3 Intermediate and Junior Non-Manual	(%)	26	14	60	100	170	10
4 Skilled manual	(%)	18	37	45	100	646	38
5 Semi-skilled manual	(%)	17	36	47	100	275	16
6 Unskilled manual	(%)	23	31	46	100	119	7
7a Unclassified	(%)	18	22	61	100	102	6
7b None	(%)	14	4	82	100	213	12
Total ñ		318	455	938		1711	100

[1] See Note 6 to Table 1.2 for definitions. See Note 1 to Table 2.5 for the division of group 7.
[2] Road accidents include 'work/road' accidents where the victim was injured in a road accident while he was engaged in his work (sixteen cases).
[3] 'Other' accidents comprise: 388 domestic accidents; 510 leisure and sport accidents; 26 criminal assaults; 12 industrial illnesses; 2 war wounds.

damages, despite the fact that this represented by far the largest category of accidents suffered. Even in road and work accidents it was only a minority of victims who actually obtained damages for their injuries; but in the case of the victims of any other type of accident, it was extremely rare for damages to be recovered. This finding is confirmed by data in each stage of the analysis, and was largely due to the fact that certain categories of people were disproportionately the victims of these 'other' accidents.

Table 2.2 *Legal outcome of accident in relation to types of accident*

Legal Outcome of Accident	Type of Accident: Work (%)	Road (%)	Other (%)	All Accidents n̄	(%)
Damages obtained	19	29	2	198[1]	12
No claim made	76	66	96	1458	85
Claim made, but later abandoned	4	3	1	42	2
Claim still unsettled, or outcome not known	2	2	—	13	1
	100	100	100		100
Total n̄	455	318	938	1711	
Percentage	27	19	55		

[1] The weighted figure of 198 cases where damages were obtained is based on 182 actual cases.

Demographic characteristics

Accident victims who obtained damages for their injuries were predominantly male: they were concentrated in the age-groups between 21 and 65, and the overwhelming number were individuals in full-time employment. These characteristics will now be examined in more detail. We found that while women represented 43 per cent of the total sample of accident victims, they comprised only 30 per cent of all successful claims for damages. A comparison within the three accident categories of sex differences in obtaining damages indicated that women who had suffered work accidents tended to claim damages less often than men who had suffered work accidents, but that the rates for the other two accident categories

Table 2.3 *Legal outcome of accidents classified by sex and accident type*

	Sex and accident type									
	Male					Female				
Outcome	Work	Road	Other	All		Work	Road	Other	All	
	(%)	(%)	(%)	(%)	n̄	(%)	(%)	(%)	(%)	n̄
Damages obtained	20	27	2	14	139	13	31	2	8	59
No claim made	74	67	97	82	808	82	65	95	89	650
Claim made but abandoned	4	4	1	2	24	4	2	2	2	18
Claim unsettled or unknown	2	1	—	1	11	—	2	—	*	2
Percentage	100	100	100	100		100	100	100	100	
Total n̄	388	195	399		982	67	123	539		729

*Less than 1 per cent

were roughly similar (Table 2.3). It appears that the low claim rate for women obtaining damages results mainly from the fact that nearly three-quarters of all accidents suffered by women occur elsewhere than on the road or at work, and that in these 'other' kinds of accidents a claim for damages is made only rarely. Table 2.3 also indicates that women are more reluctant than men to claim damages for work accidents.

In so far as the age of the victim was concerned, it appeared that victims under the age of 16 and over the age of 65 rarely made claims for damages. Despite the fact that these age-groups together represented about one-third of the total sample of accident victims, they comprised only 11 per cent of successful claimants. Again, when examining age differences in obtaining damages within accident categories, we found that people under 20 and those over 70 who suffered road accidents obtained damages less often than road accident victims in other age groups (Table 2.4). The numbers in extreme age-groups for work accidents were unfortunately too small for any firm inference to be drawn, and although the numbers obtaining damages are very small in all age-groups in the 'other' accident category our data show that those over 60 were even less likely than those in younger age-groups to obtain damages.

Comparison of success in obtaining damages between members

Table 2.4 *Proportion of accident victims obtaining damages classified by age and type of accident suffered*

Age group	Road accidents Damages obtained		n̄	Work accidents Damages obtained		n̄	Other accidents Damages obtained		n̄	All accidents Damages obtained		n̄
	n̄	(%)		n̄	(%)		n̄	(%)		n̄	(%)	
0–10	(2)	12	17	(0)	—	0	(3)	2	163	(5)	3	180
11–20	(6)	11	52	(4)	40	10	(0)	—	156	(10)	5	218
21–30	(30)	36	83	(17)	16	103	(4)	4	106	(51)	17	292
31–40	(9)	23	39	(16)	14	115	(0)	—	82	(25)	11	236
41–50	(14)	36	39	(19)	21	90	(8)	14	59	(41)	22	188
51–60	(15)	47	32	(21)	24	87	(2)	2	89	(38)	18	208
61–70	(14)	37	38	(6)	14	42	(2)	1	133	(22)	10	213
71+	(0)	—	17	(2)	67	3	(2)	1	149	(4)	2	169
Age NK	(1)		1	(1)		5	(0)		1	(2)		7
Total	(91)	19	318	(86)	29	455	(21)	2	938	(198)	12	1711

of different socio-economic groups indicated that accident victims in professional and managerial groups obtained damages proportionately *less* often than those in all other socio-economic groups (Table 2.5). The groups with the highest proportions obtaining damages were routine non-manual, unskilled manual, and semi-skilled manual workers. This finding runs directly contrary to the supposition that those with greater personal resources will be more likely to embark on a legal action. Although this result must be due in part to the activity of trade unions in the field of work accidents, it is surprising that the observed difference between socio-economic groups appears to hold across accident types (Table 2.6), which suggests that the success of manual workers is not confined to accidents at work, where trade union influence is greatest. If we were to accept those theories of differential use of legal services which suggest that wealth or high socio-economic status are the most important factors explaining the differences, we would expect to find those accident victims who succeeded in obtaining damages disproportionately concentrated in high-status groups in all categories of accident. Our data indicate, however, that the converse is true. (This point will be considered again in the section which deals with trade union activity.)

Table 2.5 *Legal outcome of accidents in relation to socio-economic group[1] of head of victim's household*

Outcome	Socio-economic group								
	Professional 1	Employers and managers 2	Intermediate and junior non-manual 3	Skilled manual 4	Semi-skilled manual 5	Unskilled manual 6	Un-classified 7a	None 7b	
	(%)	(%)	(%)	(%)	(%)	(%)	(%)	(%)	n̄
Damages obtained	3	5	18	11	16	17	—	10	198
No claim made	97	91	80	86	80	81	99	85	1458
Claim abandoned	—	3	1	2	4	1	—	4	42
Unsettled/unknown	—	1	1	*	—	2	1	*	13
Percentage	100	100	100	100	100	100	100	100	
Total n̄	37	149	170	646	275	119	102	213	1711

* Less than 1 per cent.

[1] See Note 6 to Table 1.2. In Tables 2.5 and 2.6 a distinction has been made between those who had no socio-economic group (namely, those who could not be classified under a group as a result of unclear or inadequate information (7a) and those who were economically inactive (7b). In Table 1.2 these two subgroups are combined in one category (7: 'Others').

Table 2.6 *Legal outcome of accidents in relation to socio-economic group[1] within accident categories*

Socio-economic group by number and accident type

Outcome	Road 1	Road 2	Road 3	Road 4	Road 5	Road 6	Road 7a	Road 7b		Work 1	Work 2	Work 3	Work 4	Work 5	Work 6	Work 7a	Work 7b		Other 1	Other 2	Other 3	Other 4	Other 5	Other 6	Other 7a	Other 7b	
	(%)	(%)	(%)	(%)	(%)	(%)	(%)	(%)	n̄	(%)	(%)	(%)	(%)	(%)	(%)	(%)	(%)	n̄	(%)	(%)	(%)	(%)	(%)	(%)	(%)	(%)	n̄
Damages obtained	11	20	48	19	34	30	—	57	91	—	7	25	18	26	22	—	12	86	—	—	4	2	2	7	—	2	21
No claim made	89	72	50	75	66	63	94	30	211	100	85	75	75	67	76	100	87	344	100	98	94	98	95	92	100	94	903
Abandoned/ unsettled/ unknown	—	8	2	5	—	8	6	13	16	—	8	—	7	7	3	—	—	25	—	2	2	—	3	—	—	3	14
%	100	100	100	100	100	100	100	100		100	100	100	100	100	100	100	100		100	100	100	100	100	100	100	100	
Total n̄	9	25	44	118	47	27	18	30	318	1	27	24	237	99	37	22	8	455	27	97	102	291	129	55	62	175	938

[1] For definitions and numbering of socio-economic groups, see Note 6 to Table 1.2. On the subgroups 7a and 7b see Note 1 to Table 2.5.

The economic activity of accident victims at the time of their accident was an important variable strongly related to the likelihood of damages being obtained following an accident. Although only half of all accident victims in the sample were engaged in full-time employment at the time of their accident, this group represented more than three-quarters of all successful claims for damages (78 per cent). Housewives, on the other hand, constituted 14 per cent of accident victims in the sample but only five per cent of those who obtained damages. Table 2.7 shows that for both men and women, in all accident groups, their working status at the time of the accident considerably increased the likelihood that damages would be obtained. Rather surprisingly, the receipt of sick pay from employers had no effect on the propensity of employees to claim damages. This suggests that the motivating factor for the initiation of a claim is not solely the loss or anticipated loss of income: those who did not receive sick pay were not more likely to claim damages, even though they would presumably have suffered greater financial losses.

Table 2.7 *Proportions of accident victims obtaining damages classified by sex, employment status and type of accident*

	Working men			Non-working men			Working women			Non-working women		
	Damages obtained			Damages obtained			Damages obtained			Damages obtained		
	ñ	(%)	ñ	ñ	(%)	ñ	ñ	(%)	ñ	ñ	(%)	ñ
Road Accidents	45	31	146	8	16	49	26	44	59	12	19	64
Work Accidents	77	20	386	0	—	2	9	14	66	0	—	1
Other	4	2	174	5	2	225	10	7	133	2	*	406
Total ñ	126		706	13		276	45		258	14		471

* Less than 1 per cent.

Severity of injury

While the likelihood of obtaining damages for injury was related to the demographic variables already discussed, it was difficult to find such clear associations between success in obtaining damages and various measures of severity of injury and its consequences. Admission to, and length of stay in, hospital following an accident was not related in any way to success in obtaining damages; but the existence of some residual disability and the relative length of time out of work following an accident both bore some relationship to the likelihood that damages would be recovered. While there was an increase in general in the proportions of accident victims obtaining damages associated with increased residual disability, we nevertheless found that fewer than *one-fifth* of those accident victims who were the most seriously affected in the long term by their injuries actually obtained any damages. Table 2.8 shows further that the importance of accident type in predicting the likelihood of damages being recovered is not affected by the seriousness of residual disability suffered. Road accident victims have consistently higher rates of success irrespective of their degree of residual disability and despite the fact that road accidents in general appear to result in fewer permanent injuries than either work accidents or other accidents do. (At the time of the interview, 13 per cent of road accident victims were still affected most or all of the time, as compared with 21 per cent of the victims of work accidents and 19 per cent of those

Table 2.8 *Proportion of accident victims obtaining damages classified by degree of residual disability and type of accident*

Residual disability	Road accidents: Damages obtained n̄	(%)	n̄	Work accidents: Damages obtained n̄	(%)	n̄	Other accidents: Damages obtained n̄	(%)	n̄	All accidents: Damages obtained n̄	(%)	n̄
No residual disability	40	23	175	22	11	196	4	1	559	66	7	930
Never affected a lot	10	32	31	5	12	42	2	4	49	17	14	122
Affected a lot occasionally	27	39	70	28	24	118	4	3	156	59	17	344
Affected a lot most of the time	8	32	25	18	35	52	9	9	100	35	20	177
Affected a lot all of the time	6	35	17	13	28	47	2	3	74	21	15	138
Total	91	19	318	86	29	455	21	2	938	198	12	1711

of other accidents.) In contrast with this, the proportion of work accident victims obtaining damages *does* appear to be associated with the degree of residual disability, and, although the numbers are very small, there appears to be a similar pattern among victims of 'other' types of accident. Accident victims under the age of 20 were less likely to suffer serious residual disability than other age-groups, while accident victims over the age of 60 were much more likely to suffer some permanent disability following their accident. It is clear from our interviews that for many elderly people something as simple as tripping on a paving stone or a minor road accident can signal the effective end of an independent life, as the result of the impact of the injury on brittle bones. Nevertheless, Table 2.9 shows that, for those over 60, serious residual disability *did not* increase the likelihood that damages would be obtained, although it tended to do so for other age-groups, and as Table 2.8 shows, for all victims in general.

The amount of time taken off work as a result of injuries suffered in accidents may be regarded as a proxy variable for relative seriousness of consequences, both in terms of the physical effects of accidents and, to an extent, in terms of the economic consequences or potential financial losses suffered. Table 2.10 shows that for victims employed at the time of the accident the amount of time off work was only roughly related to the likelihood that damages would be obtained, and in no absolutely consistent manner. Of those injured people who did not need to take any time off work following an accident, 14 per cent succeeded in obtaining damages, as compared with only 20 per cent of those victims who were forced to be off work for a year or more. This finding, together with the earlier observation that employers' provision of sick pay to injured employees was not related to obtaining damages, suggest that the actual, or anticipated loss of income is by no means the most important factor which forces or encourages victims to seek damages for their injuries. Further, the importance of being in employment as a predictor of obtaining damages (which was noted in the previous section) must lie not only in the risk of loss of income but also in other factors which are likely to lead to claiming, such as access to networks of advice and information.

The importance of demographic and group characteristics

We have found that certain demographic characteristics, together with the type of accident suffered, appear to be more important than various measures of severity of injury in predicting the likeli-

Table 2.9 *Proportion of accident victims obtaining damages classified by degree of residual disability and age group*

Residual disability	Age group 0–20 Damages obtained		0–20 n̄	21–40 Damages obtained		21–40 n̄	41–60 Damages obtained		41–60 n̄	61+ Damages obtained		61+ n̄	All ages n̄
	n̄	(%)		n̄	(%)		n̄	(%)		n̄	(%)		
No residual disability	6	2	293	27	10	268	26	14	186	7	4	183	930
Never affected a lot	0	—	25	4	9	44	10	32	31	3	14	22	122
Affected a lot occasionally	4	7	56	27	20	135	20	24	83	8	11	70	344
Affected a lot most of the time	3	17	18	10	21	48	16	28	58	6	11	53	177
Affected a lot all of the time	2	33	6	8	24	33	7	18	38	4	7	61	138
Total	15	4	398	76	14	528	79	20	396	28	7	389	1711

Table 2.10 *Legal outcome of accident in relation to amount of time taken off work*[1]

Outcome	Number of weeks off work None	1–3	4–7	8–25	26–51	52+	NK	
	(%)	(%)	(%)	(%)	(%)	(%)	(%)	ñ
Damages obtained	14	6	19	22	35	20	38	171
No claim made	85	92	80	73	53	65	62	753
Claim abandoned	1	2	1	3	9	8	—	28
Unsettled/ unknown	—	1	—	2	4	6	—	12
Percentages	100	100	100	100	100	100	100	
Total ñ	138	196	211	266	57	83	13	964

[1] This variable relates to the *total amount of time off work or out of work* as a direct result of the injuries suffered in the accident.

hood that damages would be obtained after an accident. Accidents which occur anywhere other than on the road or at work are highly unlikely to lead to a claim for damages. This accounts to some extent for the fact that women, the elderly and those not in full-time employment have low rates of claiming damages, since they disproportionately suffer these kinds of accidents. There is, however, some difficulty in untangling the extent to which the failure of these groups to claim damages is related to the fact that it might be harder to provide evidence of negligence for accidents in the home, or while at sport or at leisure, and to what extent the low claim rates for domestic and other accidents is due to the fact that the people who suffer these accidents, for reasons not connected with the specific accident, show a low propensity to use the legal system in general. The analysis of successful claimants within accident categories has shown that women suffering work accidents tend to claim damages less often than men suffering work accidents and that the young and elderly obtain damages less often for most types of accidents.

If we look more closely at the actual steps involved in considering the question of claiming damages, seeking the advice of a solicitor, and finally obtaining damages, we find that the importance of demographic and socio-economic characteristics tends to be confined to the 'pre-legal' stages in the process: these factors do not exert any systematic influence on success rates once legal advice *has* been obtained. In other words, being female or over 60 years of age suggests that an individual victim would be less likely to think about the question of compensation, or, having considered the possibility of claiming compensation, would be less likely to go and see a solicitor. However, if victims in these groups do actually take legal advice following an accident, the chances of finally succeeding with a claim are about as good as (and in some cases better than) those of men or younger victims of the same type of accident. Figure 2.2 shows that an important difference in claim and success rates between the three major categories of accident lies in the limited extent to which victims of 'other' types of accident *consider* the question of compensation and obtain the assistance of a solicitor. Once legal advice has been obtained the success rate of 'other' accident victims is actually higher than that of work accident victims (78 per cent of those who consulted a solicitor obtained damages as compared with 74 per cent for work accidents and 87 per cent for road accidents).[1] One problem for victims of domestic and leisure accidents is that fewer than 10 per cent ever consider the question of compensation and therefore never embark upon the legal process. In contrast, the relatively high success rate of road accident victims as compared with other victims can be partly attributed to the greater extent to which they seek legal advice and their greater ability to prove a case rather than to any greater propensity than work accident victims to consider in the first place the question of claiming. Despite the greater propensity among road accident victims to claim damages, however, the ultimate outcome is still that fewer than one in three of those suffering serious injuries in road accidents actually succeed in obtaining damages.

Figures 2.3 and 2.4 show, similarly, that while women, children, and the elderly are in general less likely to obtain damages, this failure stems primarily from a low propensity to *think* about compensation or to seek legal advice, rather than any special difficulty in proving a case once a claim has been made. In 89 per cent of cases women who had contacted a solicitor about making a claim succeeded in obtaining damages as compared with 79 per cent of men who were in contact with a solicitor. The difference in success rate over all is accounted for by the fact that women were 10 per cent less likely to consider the question of compensation than men.

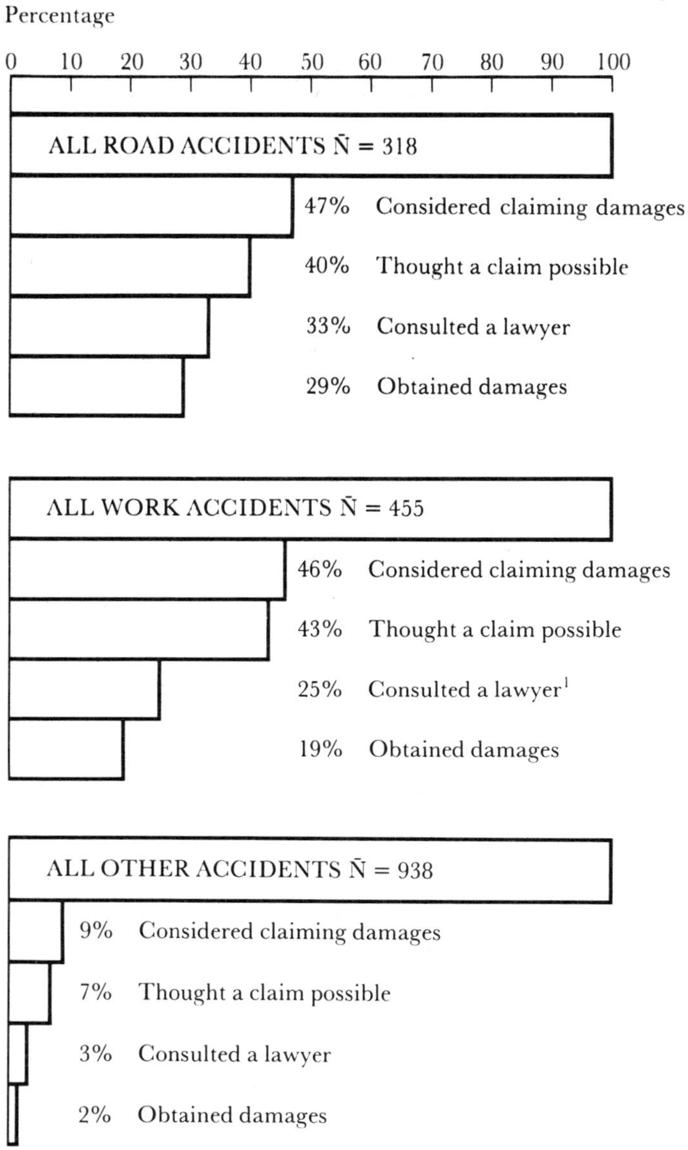

[1]This figure is not entirely reliable, since some union-assisted claimants did not know whether a lawyer had been consulted on their behalf, only that they had obtained damages.

Figure 2.2 *The path to compensation among different accident groups*

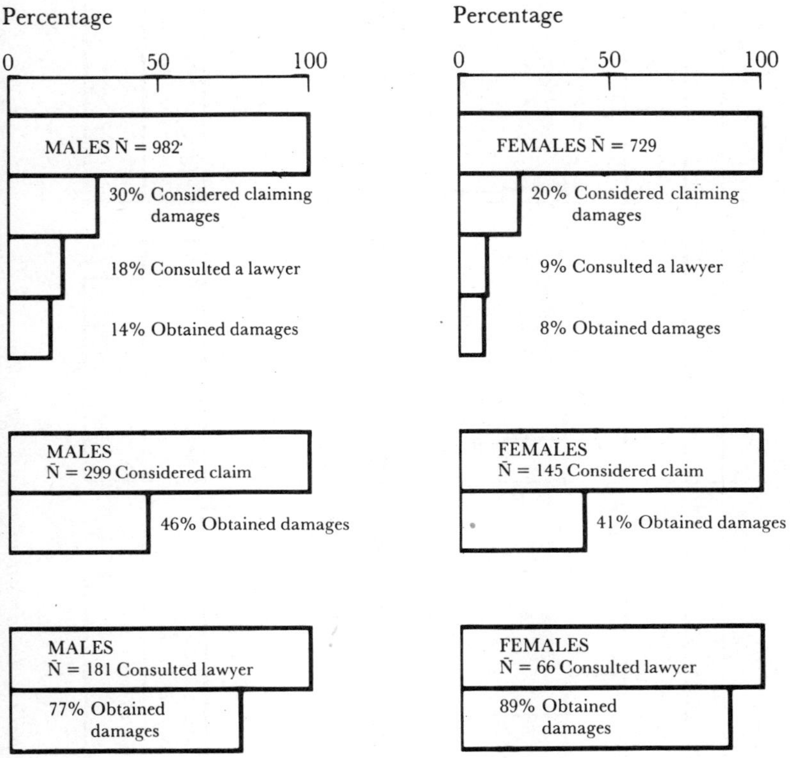

Figure 2.3 *The path to damages in relation to sex of victim*

The same sort of pattern emerges when the relationship between age and claiming is considered (Figure 2.4).

Perhaps somewhat surprisingly the same analysis of the steps involved in claiming damages indicates that the relatively low success rate amongst victims of higher socio-economic status, as compared with those of lower socio-economic status, is a result of *both* a lower propensity to think in terms of compensation and of a lower success rate once a solicitor has been consulted. This is undoubtedly the opposite of what one might expect, given the results of other studies which suggest that the middle classes are more likely to be claims-conscious or naturally litigious and to have more knowledge, or access to knowledge, about the law (Atiyah, 1980; Mayhew and Reiss, 1969).

The influence of continuing residual disability on the likelihood

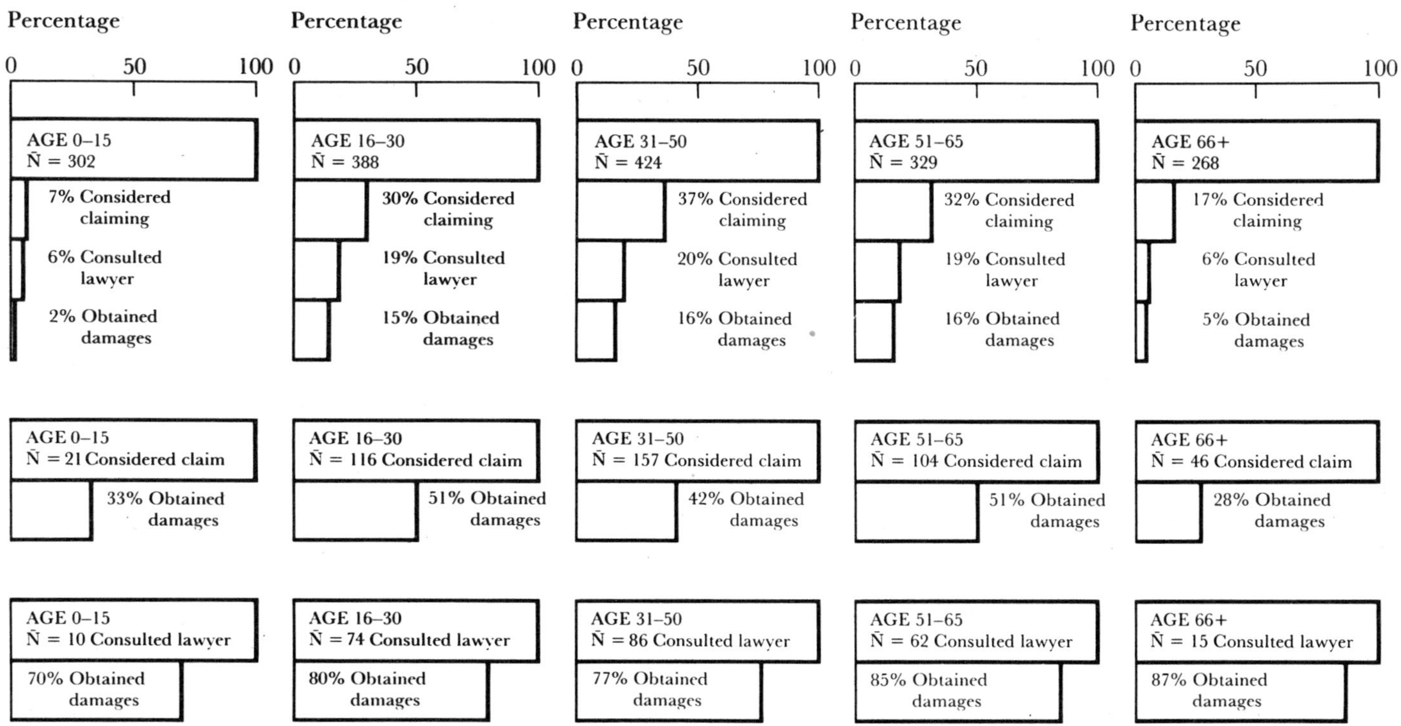

Figure 2.4 *The path to damages in relation to age groups*

that legal advice will be sought and that damages will ultimately be obtained is, on the other hand, rather less clear. Although victims are more inclined to consider the question of initiating a claim as the degree of residual disability suffered becomes more severe, those victims in the group who claimed to be affected a lot all of the time by continuing effects of injuries were considerably less likely than other groups to succeed in obtaining damages *after* a solicitor had been consulted. Only 50 per cent of this group consulting solicitors obtained damages as compared with 89 per cent of those with no residual disability and 92 per cent of those affected a lot most of the time by continuing disability. A possible reason for the high failure rate of serious claims may be that these are the cases most strongly contested by insurance companies since they could involve substantial amounts of damages.

(4) The path to legal advice

We have found that nearly 90 per cent of all the accident victims in our survey failed to obtain any damages for their injuries through the legal system, and that of this 90 per cent the vast majority never sought any legal advice. Only one in three road accident victims actually consulted a solicitor; about one in four work accident victims were in contact with a solicitor[2] but the figure for all other types of accident was just over one in fifty. This indicates clearly that for *all* categories of accident the majority of victims do not seek legal advice. What factors might be important in propelling a minority of accident victims towards the legal arena? Some evidence on this question can be found from a study of the cases where victims did make a claim for damages. Of the 247 people (weighted figure) who consulted a solicitor, about 90 per cent reported that they had previously discussed with someone else the possibility of making a claim. More significantly, of these people, about 70 per cent stated that the idea of trying to obtain damages first came from another person. More than two-thirds of all those who consulted a solicitor said that the first impetus to seek legal advice had come from another person. It seems, then, that for most people who did attempt to claim damages, the informal discussions which took place before they sought formal legal advice were extremely important in providing or reinforcing the incentive to claim.

An analysis of these pre-legal discussions indicated that many who consulted a solicitor did so on the advice of people such as trade union officials, hospital personnel, local medical practitioners, policemen, and advisers at advice bureaux, as well as relatives and friends (Table 2.11). Work accident victims who were members of a trade union naturally sought advice from their union and depended rather less than other accident groups did on the advice of people within their social and family network. Road accident victims obtained assistance from policemen and from their own insurance companies, while victims of other types of accidents depended on the advice given by doctors, relatives, and friends.

In many of these cases the suggestion about making a claim for compensation, or information about legal rights, was offered by a person who had some experience of, or knowledge about, the process of claiming damages. Most importantly, this advice was frequently offered spontaneously, without any enquiry from the

Table 2.11 *Pre-legal advice[1] in relation to victim's accident type*

Category of adviser	Work accident (%)	Road accident (%)	Other accident (%)	All accidents ñ	All accidents (%)
Trade Union	48	7	2	111	29
Medical	6	7	10	27	7
Employer[2]	10	2	2	25	6
Police	*	12	2	18	5
Potential defendant	—	7	17	16	4
AA/RAC/own insurance company	8	15	7	40	10
Workmate or fellow patient	9	5	—	25	6
Friend	5	12	20	35	9
Relative	13	34	37	88	23
Percentage	100	100	100		100
Total ñ	211	134	40	385	

[1] In this Table, each adviser is counted separately, whether he was consulted alone or as one of a number of advisers.

[2] In the case of work accidents this category may overlap with that of potential defendant.

* Less than 1 per cent.

injured person. The accident victim who suffers an injury on the road or at work is likely to have some contact immediately following the accident with someone who might tell him of the possibility of making a claim, even if the idea had not occurred to the victim himself. Hence, a possibly crucial difference between a person injured either on the road or at work and one injured at home or at leisure lies not only in the specific circumstances which surround the accident, or in the individual's experience or knowledge of the law at the time of the accident, but in the differential access to information about compensation and legal rights immediately after the accident occurs. The importance of this kind of advice goes further than its easy accessibility – it is also free.[3] Many people who may feel, perhaps intuitively, that they may or ought to be able to claim some legal redress for their injuries, are reluctant to seek advice from a solicitor, because they have a possibly exaggerated fear of the cost of legal services, or because they need reassurance that they appear to have a good case. Knowledge of the legal aid and legal advice schemes was minimal among the accident victims in our sample. Of those who actually *had* made contact with a solicitor, only one-quarter knew of the legal advice scheme, while fewer than one-half knew of the legal aid scheme. It seems reasonable to assume that the level of knowledge about these services would have been even lower amongst the very large group of victims who did not seek any legal advice after their accident.

It seems that in the first place it is not solicitors whom injured people consult about claiming damages. The 'risk' of visiting a solicitor is only taken when the injured person has been convinced, or reassured, from other sources about the strength of his claim. Although the role of pre-legal advice is undoubtedly important in propelling injured people to the door of a solicitor there are obvious dangers for potential claimants in accepting advice from unqualified persons about the possibility of claiming damages. Forty-two of our respondents who thought about the possibility of making a claim were advised at an early stage by someone other than a solicitor that they had little or no chance of success. In the event, however, six persisted in making a claim and obtained damages.

(5) Trade unions and the importance of pre-legal advice

Although the number of work accident victims who obtain damages is relatively low when compared with the success of road accident victims, trade union activity in the field of work accidents is important since it serves to overcome many of the problems faced by other victims in attempting to make, and to negotiate, a claim for damages. Unions can provide immediate advice about the possibility of claiming compensation. They can provide easy access to the legal system and insulation from the potential cost of an unsuccessful claim, which will be met by the union. Once a claim for damages has been accepted by a union (which is by no means automatic), the individual victim is entirely sheltered from many of the normal difficulties of pressing a claim. He needs no knowledge about how to proceed or how to find a solicitor, nor is he worried by legal costs. The intervention of a union on a member's behalf often occurs as a matter of course following a work accident (Latta and Lewis, 1974) and this fact is very important in providing the impetus to make a claim in the case of people who might otherwise not have considered the question at all. In addition to this, once the union has taken on the responsibility for the claim, its activity transforms the character of the negotiations between claimant and defendant from that of individual versus organization, to organization versus organization, thus possibly increasing the chances of an outcome favourable to the victim (Galanter, 1975). As far as the victim is concerned, his claim is dealt with almost entirely by proxy and he is unlikely to be told much about the progress of the claim until he is advised to accept an amount of damages offered by the defendant. This service, however, is available only to paid-up members and only in circumstances where the union thinks a claim worth pursuing.

Despite the organizational constraints on the decision of unions to press a claim for damages, union activity not only results in many successful claims for damages, but more generally appears to have raised the level of claims-consciousness amongst manual workers suffering work accidents to the extent that they appear from our data to be more inclined to press claims for damages than non-manual workers; and this feature is not confined to accidents at work (see above, Table 2.6).

Trade unions thus provide a good example of the importance of pre-legal or para-legal advice in channelling accident victims into the legal system. The transformation of a 'problem' into a matter for which legal advice should be obtained is necessarily complex (cf. Chapter 4 below), and for personal injuries, at least, it seems that the availability of the right kind of advice following an accident is related to the circumstances in which the accident took place. Road and work accident victims usually suffer injuries in a public manner: the accident scene is normally attended by police, union officials, employers' representatives, etc. who can take the names of witnesses as well as advise the victim. In addition, insurance companies should be notified of a motor accident involving personal injuries, while accidents at work are normally noted in employers' accident records even when the injuries are apparently minor. Elsewhere, there are no formal or semi-formal procedures for dealing with an accident and the very people who disproportionately suffer those accidents are often isolated from informal networks of information, i.e. women at home, the elderly, and children. If road and work accident victims, with the benefit of these referrals into the legal system, succeed in obtaining damages for their injuries in only a minority of cases, it is hardly surprising that other accident victims virtually never succeed.

Compare two cases from the survey: first, a school-kitchen attendant who was boiling washing-up cloths in a pot on the stove. She plunged her arm too far into the pot and suffered some scarring from burns. When she was asked if the accident was anyone's fault she answered firmly that it was her employer's fault for expecting her to boil cloths in such a large pot. We later discovered that her trade union had instituted a claim against her employer on her behalf and settled the claim for £400. In contrast, a housewife was mowing her lawn with a new mower purchased by her husband. A blade flew off the mower while it was in operation and badly injured the woman's legs. It was, she said, just an accident. No thought of compensation had occurred to her. The difference between the two cases is not necessarily in the degree of knowledge of the law which preceded the accidents but in the differential access of the two women to a person who could provide the relevant information and thus influence the decision to make a claim for damages.

The suggestions we have made about the importance of pre-legal contacts are supported to some extent by the characteristics of victims who never at any time considered the question of compensation. Two-thirds of these were people who had suffered accidents other than on the road or at work – the people least likely to come into contact with an informed person who could provide para-legal advice following the accident. The failure of these victims to think in terms of compensation is not, however, explained by an assumption that their accidents were in no way caused by the actions of other people and therefore not within the potential scope of the tort system. Although many victims of domestic and leisure accidents thought that their accident had been caused at least in part by another person, only 37 per cent of victims in this accident group who attributed their accident entirely to the fault of another person felt that they should have been entitled to compensation, as compared with 79 per cent of road accident victims and 88 per cent of work accident victims who blamed others entirely for their accidents. Only one-third of domestic and leisure accident victims who *entirely blamed another for their accident* thought that a claim for damages might have been possible, and in the event only 17 per cent of this group consulted a lawyer (as compared with 65 per cent of work accident victims and 58 per cent of road accident victims). (This finding must be contrasted with the fact that about six of the twenty-one 'other' accident victims in the survey who obtained damages were cases where a third party had *not* been held entirely to blame for the accident.)

We made a special analysis of those members of the sample who entirely blamed another person's fault for their accident, because we made the assumption that this might represent the group most likely to attempt to claim damages and to have some justification for doing so. This analysis suggested that the factors related to the propensity of this group to claim damages were the same as those found to be important in the sample of accident victims as a whole (see above section 3 of this chapter). Women were slightly less likely than men to consider the question of compensation (68 per cent compared with 71 per cent) but considerably less likely actually to seek legal advice (38 per cent compared with 54 per cent); but women were more likely to obtain damages once legal advice had been obtained (94 per cent compared with 88 per cent). Lower socio-economic groups showed a higher propensity to consider the question of compensation and to seek legal advice than the higher socio-economic groups. The young and the elderly rarely obtained damages, even where they had entirely blamed another person for their accidents. Thus, even among the groups of victims most likely to have a sound legal reason for attempting to claim damages, we found that the same social factors were related to the use of legal services as in the case of victims as a whole.

(6) Reasons given for failure to claim damages.

We have already identified certain group characteristics which appear to be associated with a reluctance to take positive action to recover damages following an accident. These associations can be supplemented to some extent by the actual reasons which victims gave when asked why they had not sought legal advice about the possibility of obtaining legal compensation for their losses. These questions were asked only of those people who had considered that they ought to be entitled to compensation or that it might have been possible to bring a legal claim for compensation; it was also asked in the case of those who had blamed somebody for their accident. This leaves out of consideration the very large group of victims who *never* gave any thought to the question of legal compensation and who, therefore, could not have reasons for not taking advice about it.

Table 2.12 shows the distribution of reasons for failing to claim reported by those victims who had given some thought to it. An inability or unwillingness to undergo the possible trouble or bother of making a claim, assumed difficulties in providing evidence of liability, and fear of legal costs represent the three most important groups of reasons mentioned. All of these reasons given for not claiming compensation had been formulated or arrived at *without* the benefit of legal advice. Hence, decisions not to proceed because of lack of evidence, supposed legal difficulties, or fear of the costs involved were based on possibly uninformed opinion or information. These victims had not been legally advised of potential difficulties: they had assumed them to exist.

The information from which Table 2.12 is derived indicates considerable reluctance to become involved in the strains of a legal claim. This reluctance clearly has a profound effect, since the initiative to claim is placed by the law firmly on the shoulders of the injured victim. Typical reasons in this category were: 'I just wanted to forget about it. All I wanted to do was to get better'; 'I didn't really bother – but I would if it happened again'; 'My husband said I was a fool not to [claim]. I really couldn't be bothered with it at the time. I didn't feel like it.' Three people went beyond mere inconvenience and anticipated trouble in pursuing a claim. One referred to 'the legal jargon' and continued 'I don't think you should have to go through all the rigmarole'; another (who was off work for forty-one weeks) said 'I thought it would have involved so much . . .'; (another) 'It was some time after and it was too much trouble to do anything about it.' Others said simply that 'I didn't want to claim'; 'I did not wish to mix in such things, the child is all right now.' This unwillingness to become involved in legal wrangles

Table 2.12 *Reasons for not claiming (given by those who had considered the possibility of claiming compensation (damages))*

	Male		Female		Work accidents		Road accidents		Other accidents		All accidents	
	n	(%)	n	(%)	n	(%)	n	(%)	n	(%)	n	(%)
Trouble or bother: no claims-consciousness	17	17	14	21	14	18	6	11	11	31	31	19
Problems in providing evidence	13	13	16	25	9	11	12	23	8	23	29	17
Fear of legal expenses	11	11	7	11	11	14	5	10	2	6	18	11
Accident due to own fault	13	13	4	6	7	9	8	15	2	6	17	10
Ignorance or confusion	12	12	4	6	7	9	7	13	2	6	16	10
Injuries not serious enough	9	9	4	6	5	6	5	10	3	9	13	8
Fear of affecting continuing relationship	6	6	3	5	6	8	2	4	1	3	9	5
Legal and insurance issues	2	2	7	11	3	4	2	4	4	11	9	5
No income loss	6	6	2	3	6	8	1	2	1	3	8	5
Severity of injury not realized	4	4	4	6	4	5	3	6	1	3	8	5
Satisfied with Industrial Injury Benefit	4	4	0	–	4	5	0	–	0	–	4	2
No one at fault	3	3	0	–	2	2	1	2	0	–	3	2
Totals	100	100	65	100	78	100	52	100	35	100	165	100

cannot be explained by an assumption that these were accidents with only minor consequences; for victims in employment who gave these reasons, time taken off work following the accident ranged from three to twenty-six weeks. For many people, the time following an accident is difficult enough without voluntarily adding what are seen as extra strains. 'I felt so poorly after the accident . . . that I couldn't face doing anything'; 'I felt too ill to be bothered. My mother died suddenly and with the accident and family troubles I didn't pursue the matter.'

Understandable though these sentiments may be, they are given by people who have taken no legal advice and who therefore do not know how strong a claim they might have. Moreover, we see from Table 2.12 that the frequency with which the trouble or bother of claiming is mentioned is not random. Women are more likely to give this sort of reason than men. Nearly one-quarter of all reasons mentioned by women for not claiming fell into this category, as did over one-third of reasons given by victims of 'other' accidents.

Assumed difficulties in proving negligence and fear of legal costs were also very important in deterring accident victims from claiming damages (Table 2.12). As far as evidential problems were concerned the reasons covered a broad range of difficulties. In some cases victims had initially failed to follow specific procedures for reporting the accident and later felt that this prejudiced their chance of success. Others had delayed collecting evidence, for example, 'Because I didn't get on to it straight away and I'd no proof, and by the time I thought of it, it was too late, I thought.' (This victim was still off work after six years.) Women, in particular, gave assumed lack of evidence as a reason for not claiming (Table 2.12); but the problem is a general one affecting all accident types and not just domestic and leisure accidents (where problems about evidence are commonly assumed to be the greatest).

The fact that so many people mentioned fear of the cost of consulting a solicitor and making a legal claim as a reason for not doing anything is not surprising, given the widespread ignorance of legal aid and advice which we found (see p. 67). It is none the less a disquieting finding, particularly in the light of substantial losses suffered by many of them: fear of legal expenses was given as the reason in many cases where the injury caused a long period off work, e.g. in this category, six people were off work for more than six months. Although there seems to be little difference between the sexes in concern about legal costs, victims of work accidents were more likely to give this as a reason for not claiming than road or other accident victims. This suggests that work accident victims making a claim *without* the benefit of union assistance may be particularly fearful of the cost of claiming.

Sixteen victims gave as their reason for not claiming damages that they were ignorant of, or confused about, the legal rules and the appropriate procedure for making a claim. Typical statements were: 'I didn't know how to start'; 'I didn't know who to go to, to make a claim'; 'We didn't know enough about going ahead with it.' One victim said plaintively: 'I tend to get confused about these things. I wonder whether you have any rights.' Several did not realize that the initiative in making a claim lay with them: 'The police came to see me, and I thought I should hear from the Bus Company [who were thought to be responsible], but never did'; (another) 'I thought his insurance [his boss's] would cover it without my making a claim.'

In four of the cases classified under the heading of 'Ignorance or Confusion', the injured person showed misunderstandings about the relationship between claims to social security benefits and claims to damages; for example, 'I was not informed that I could get more money' [more than Sickness Benefit]; (another) 'It was an industrial accident, and on the Sick Note, the form, it said about being entitled to compensation. You answered the questions on the form, it automatically went through.' Many of the cases under this heading were serious: the cases of employees off work for more than four weeks involved periods of absence of 8, 14, 14, 20, 24, 54, and 60 weeks respectively.

Although in each case the injury of the victim was sufficiently serious to fall within the criteria for the survey, sixteen victims gave as their reason for not claiming their opinion that their injury was not serious enough to justify a claim. In some cases, relative seriousness of the actual injury depended on the view that the accident could have caused more serious injury or even death; for example, 'Because I was too thankful to be well and alive and walking around'; (another) 'Money didn't come into it: she was alive and that was what mattered.'

Those people who were reluctant to pursue a claim for damages because of their fear of affecting a continuing relationship were most often work accident victims. The reasons given showed victims to be concerned about job security or simply unwilling to cause trouble for their employer. For instance '(I was) grateful that the firm employed me at my age of 62 and didn't want to cause them any bother'; (another) 'I got brainwashed by the firm and I was promoted to foreman. I felt under an obligation afterwards'; (another) 'At the time I didn't feel like claiming, knowing they were good enough to keep my job for me.' (This person was unable to work again.) In two cases the employee feared that if he made a claim, he might lose his job: this was seen as a risk in a small firm where there was a close working relationship between the employer and a small number of employees. Another case shows how ignorance of the legal rules causes grave misunderstandings: an injured workman thought his only claim would be against a fellow worker and said, 'How can you sue an ordinary working man who probably has a family to support?' For some people the initiation of a legal claim is seen as an essentially aggressive action. Even where the defendant is insured, and the injured person is aware of this, there is nevertheless a feeling that it is not a friendly action to bring a claim against an acquaintance, a friend, or a 'good' employer.

Ignorance of the law caused many of the assumed 'legal' or 'insurance' reasons for not making a claim. In some cases the supposed legal reasons might not, in strict law, have been grounds for invalidating a claim for damages: e.g. 'It was an accident caused by a mental patient who isn't responsible for her actions'; 'There is a clause on the booking form disclaiming responsibility for accidents' (the victim slipped on the dance floor at a holiday camp); 'I read in the paper that if one fell like that there was no redress' (tripping over an uneven pavement). In other cases the supposed legal rule which was thought to prevent recovery of damages was clearly wrong in law: such as, the victim thought that the receipt of a lump sum Disablement Benefit under the Industrial Injuries Scheme precluded him from claiming damages. In three cases the reason given was that the tortfeasor was not insured against liability or had no funds of his own to pay damages; in none of these cases was any advice obtained by the victim, who therefore did not discover that there are procedures which might have provided compensation in the two situations.

In eight cases no claim for damages was made because at the time of the accident the victim did not realize how serious the consequences of the injury would be. It is not uncommon for an apparently minor injury to develop into something more severe as, for example, with back injuries – but the victim may have failed to obtain witnesses' names or to have made a report of the accident because he did not think it was going to be serious. Although, in the eyes of the law, this failure might not preclude a claim, victims without advice could easily assume that it would.

Four work accident victims gave as their reason for not claiming damages that they were satisfied with the benefits which they were receiving under the Industrial Injuries Scheme. One, for example, said, 'I didn't want to claim damages. I thought I had got enough.' The levels of benefits under this scheme are higher than the Sickness Benefit or other social security benefits, and it is interesting that no one in receipt of other benefits gave this as a reason for not claiming damages. None of these victims receiving Industrial Injury Benefit had received advice from any source about the possibility of claiming legal damages.

(7) Conclusions

Only a small minority of accident victims initiate legal claims and obtain damages for the injuries they have suffered. Our data have shown that although the chances of obtaining damages are very good after a solicitor has been consulted about making a claim, the vast majority of accident victims do not seek legal advice: indeed, they rarely give the question any thought at all. Victims of accidents which occur other than on the road or at work only rarely think of claiming, irrespective of the extent to which they actually hold a third party to blame for their accident. Most potential claims, therefore, do not founder in the murky waters of the legal system: most victims simply never consider making a claim; of those who do, many do not actually make one.

The accident victims who do succeed in obtaining damages for their injuries are a strange group. They are not necessarily the most seriously injured, nor those who have suffered the greatest losses. They are not the people who have suffered the most prevalent types of accident, nor are they necessarily those who blamed some third party for the accident. They are not the people with most wealth and influence. But they do appear to have an important advantage in that they have access to advice about claiming and often receive this advice without soliciting it. Road and work accident victims are more likely to be involved in formal or semi-formal procedures for reporting the accidents and for dealing with the aftermath. Victims of accidents elsewhere are unlikely to become involved in any procedure which is not initiated by them.

These findings of our survey do not appear to be related to the existence of a potential defendant who is insured against his legal liability to pay damages. Although it may be more widely known that employers and users of motor-vehicles are insured, many other potential defendants are similarly covered by insurance; e.g. manufacturers of products, and occupiers of premises such as shops, restaurants, hotels, dance halls, and other places where accidents occur; many private householders are also insured. Yet very few claims are brought by those injured by defective products or on someone else's premises. It is clear that other factors have a much greater influence on the decision to claim. Perhaps in a situation where victims have only limited knowledge of their legal rights, are afraid of legal costs, and ignorant of the existence of legal aid, it is not surprising that without considerable encouragement from others, few are prepared to take the step of bringing a claim for damages.

Notes

1. It is of course possible that the success rate might not remain stable if a higher proportion of claims were made by 'other' accident victims.
2. The figures for contact with a solicitor are somewhat unreliable in the case of claims for damages made through a trade union. This is because a number of accident victims knew nothing about the details of their claim other than that the trade union handled it and that they were subsequently advised to accept an offer in settlement of the claim.
3. An experimental scheme in Manchester has shown the value of limited free legal advice in encouraging accident victims to claim damages: Genn, 1982.

References

Abel-Smith, B., Zander, M. and Brook, R., 1973, *Legal Problems and the Citizen*, London: Heinemann.

Atiyah, P. S., 1980, *Accidents, Compensation and the Law* (3rd edn.), London: Weidenfeld & Nicolson.

Curran, B., 1977, *The Legal Needs of the Public*, Chicago: American Bar Foundation.

Galanter, M., 1975, 'Why the "haves" come out ahead: Speculations on the limits of legal change', 9 *Law and Society Review* 95.

Genn, Hazel, 1982, *Meeting Legal Needs?* Oxford: Centre for Socio-Legal Studies, Wolfson College.

Griffiths, J., 1977, 'The Distribution of Legal Services in the Netherlands', Review Article, 4 *British Journal of Law and Society* 260.

Latta, G. and Lewis, R., 1974, 'Trade Union Legal Services', XII *British Journal of Industrial Relations* 63.
Mayhew, L. H. and Reiss, A. J., 1969, 'The Social Organization of Legal Contacts', 34 *American Sociological Review* 309.
Schuyt, K., Groenendijk, K. and Sloot, B., 1976, *De Weg Naar Het Recht (The Road to Justice)* Deventer: Kluwer, (Extract in *European Yearbook in Law and Sociology*, 1977.)

3 Claims for Damages: Negotiating, Settling or Abandoning

Chapter 2 has considered the ways in which a minority of accident victims come to think about making a claim for damages. This chapter analyses the data from the Compensation Survey on how that minority make and negotiate their claims: it includes all the cases where the victim follows the normal course of consulting a lawyer or trade union official and also the exceptional cases where the victim himself makes a formal claim without using a lawyer.

The chapter first considers how claimants come to select a particular lawyer and then reports the outcome of successful claims – how much money claimants actually receive in out-of-court settlements. (Very few claims reach a court hearing.) The data on the process by which lawyers and insurance companies negotiate these settlements show the many practical difficulties facing claimants, which helps to explain their willingness to compromise their claims for sums well below the amounts which the formal legal rules on assessment of damages might be expected to produce. The chapter reports the different pressures on claimants: uncertainties arising from the evidence available to prove fault or from the medical reports; the risk that a court might find that the claimant was himself partly to blame; the fear of legal expenses; delays and other difficulties arising from the law or from the practices of lawyers and insurance companies. Indeed, the difficulties faced by some claimants are so great that they are advised by their lawyers to abandon their claims.

The next section of the chapter reports the views of claimants on the adequacy of the sums received, and their decisions on how to use the money. Finally, various aspects of the relationship between solicitor and client are analysed: the extent to which clients rely on their solicitors' advice; any disagreements or complaints; and the amounts of legal expenses in relation to the size of the damages.

Data[1]

This chapter is based on two sets of data: first, the information given by those respondents who had taken some steps to make a formal claim for damages (a total of 262); secondly, information obtained from postal questionnaires completed by the solicitors handling these claims. All respondents who consulted solicitors were asked to sign consent forms authorizing their solicitor to give information about their claims. We obtained ninety-eight usable consent forms, and sixty solicitors returned completed questionnaires.[2] Fifty-one of the cases in the solicitors' survey were claims which had been settled by the time the solicitors completed the questionnaires. These fifty-one cases are not presented in this chapter as being a representative sample since they were subject to three stages of response: the willingness of the respondent to be interviewed in the first place; his willingness to sign a consent form; and finally the willingness of the solicitor to complete the questionnaire. But the information from solicitors in these fifty-one settled cases closely corroborated that given by claimants, and we have no reason to believe that the cases present an unbalanced picture of the claims process as viewed by solicitors.

(1) Initiating the claim

The selection of lawyers[3]

Just under two-thirds of the lawyers consulted by accident victims about possible claims for damages were solicitors in private practice; just over a third were 'trade union lawyers', which meant (for the survey) either lawyers employed by trade unions or solicitors in private practice who were regularly instructed by a trade union. The survey thus highlights the trade union system of referring their members to lawyers as a crucial factor in achieving the present level of recovery of damages (Latta and Lewis, 1974). Although trade union lawyers were always recommended to the victim by his union, the cases were not exclusively work accidents: one in ten were road accidents, which confirms that many unions are offering their members a legal advisory service for accidents not connected with their work. On the other hand, a quarter of the accident claims handled by solicitors in private practice were work accident cases (a number were claims by union members); of all the work accident claims in the survey, just under a third were dealt with by private practitioners, and two-thirds by trade union lawyers (fewer than 2 per cent were dealt with by Citizens' Advice Bureaux lawyers).

Where the victim had not himself chosen which lawyer to consult, he was asked who had recommended the lawyer to him. All the referrals to trade union lawyers naturally came from trade unions, but a few cases were referred by unions to ordinary private practitioners. Just over half of the victims consulting private practitioners said that the practitioner in question had been recommended to them; a little under half the recommendations came from members of the victim's family or relatives; and a quarter from friends or neighbours. The rest came from miscellaneous sources, e.g. six were recommended by medical practitioners, health visitors, or hospital almoners, six by employers, and four by Citizens' Advice Bureaux.

The fact that the accident victim consults a lawyer does not ensure success in obtaining damages: Chapter 2 has reported that just over one in four who consulted lawyers failed to obtain damages. However, our data show that both solicitors in private practice and trade union lawyers had the same success rate in obtaining damages for their clients: 72 per cent. The reasons for failure to obtain damages, despite legal advice, are reviewed later in this chapter.

Recovery of damages without using lawyers

In nearly 8 per cent of the cases where damages were recovered, the claimant had not used a lawyer. These fourteen cases were spread over all categories of accident and of victim (e.g. they divided equally between men and women).

Eight road victims settled their claims without consulting lawyers. In two, the victim was advised by his own insurance company to claim against (and later to accept the first offer made by) the other driver's insurance company; in one, the advice was that £30 was 'a fair settlement', but in the other, £940 was paid. In another case, the victim's husband wrote to the driver's insurance company, while in another, 'the trade union handled it all' for the victim. Where a bus jerked, so that a woman passenger fell and broke her leg, a friend wrote on her behalf to the bus company, whose offer of £150 was accepted; the victim trusted the 'transport people' to pay the appropriate amount. Two road victims, however, themselves went directly to the driver's insurance company (in one case on the suggestion of the driver, a friend of the victim) and accepted the first offer made to them; while a moped driver settled his claim directly with the car driver who had knocked him down, receiving £30 and 'the cost of new spectacles'.

Four people injured in work accidents also settled without using lawyers, but they were advised to claim by others, viz. a trade union official, the Medical Board dealing with a claim under the industrial injuries scheme, and the firm's safety officer (who made a claim on behalf of the injured worker against contractors working on the firm's premises: the victim of the accident was off work for six weeks, but accepted £75 after rejecting a first offer of £60). The fourth was a case of pneumoconiosis, where a mine-worker's general practitioner wrote on his behalf to his employer, making a claim: the worker accepted the employer's first offer of £2,000 ('they accepted the doctor's word').

Apart from road and work accidents, there were two cases where elderly women fell on uneven paving-stones; members of their families wrote directly to the local council, which, in both cases, 'immediately' offered to settle the claim: £200 was paid in respect of a broken arm and wrist, and three days' loss of earnings ('we got all we asked for') in the other.

Although, as shown by the amounts given above, most of these claims were settled for low amounts (i.e. from £30 to £200), several were substantial (£600, £700, and £940 in three road accidents, and £2,000 in the pneumoconiosis claim). But even these amounts appear to be well below the levels where solicitors would advise acceptance: for instance, £600 was paid to a man who 'went straight to the driver's insurance company', but he was seriously and permanently injured, spent thirty weeks off work, and had to change his type of job when he returned to work. In comparison with our data on claimants who use solicitors, this group appears to be under-compensated. They appear to assume that there are standard amounts payable, and that the insurance companies, the employers, the local authorities, or the transport undertakings, against whom they claim, can be relied upon to pay the appropriate sums. The representative character of our sample enables us to say that, over the population as a whole, several thousands of claims are settled every year without the claimant receiving legal, or even para-legal, advice. This is a disturbing finding, because the legal rules (particularly those on the assessment of damages) and the negotiation process are so complicated that no layman can safely rely on common sense to guide him. Furthermore, the categories of defendants in the fourteen cases in our sample are not publicly accountable for their conduct towards unrepresented claimants, since the settlements receive no publicity.

(2) The amounts recovered as damages

Legal rules and practice on the assessment of damages

In order to interpret the survey data on the amounts paid to the accident victims in our sample, it is necessary to know, at least in outline, the main legal rules on the assessment of damages for personal injury (see McGregor, 1980, Chapters 4–7, 33; Munkman, 1980; Kemp and Kemp, 1982; Law Commission, 1973). The professed aim of these rules is to try to restore the injured person (so far as money can) to the position he would have been in had he not been injured. The assessment is individualized to suit the actual position of the particular person and is therefore earnings related. There is no ceiling fixed by Parliament for the amount that may be awarded, which means that the judges are under no direct pressure from the taxpayer or the premium payer to keep down the levels of compensation as an economy measure. Over the years, therefore, the judges may gradually increase awards in line with general inflation (although they may not anticipate future inflation). Such changes may, of course, be implemented only with the support of the appellate judges, so that there must be some consensus among the judges for any proposed increase. Apart from damages, however, all schemes for compensation and insurance have maximum levels fixed for entitlement under the relevant statute or contract.

Pecuniary losses

Damages are usually assessed under various headings. The first is actual financial loss to date: damages should include all the out-of-pocket expenses incurred by the injured person and his net loss of salary or wages to date. (Deductions are made, however, for sick pay paid by an employer, and half of certain social security benefits received.) Secondly, damages should cover future financial losses, both expenses and loss of earnings. This heading is more speculative, because the judge must make an estimate in the light of all the known facts affecting the plaintiff's future, such as his medical prognosis (on which there can be disputes between the parties), the type of career he has chosen, and his employment prospects. Damages, being individually assessed, may be adjusted to the potential earning capacity of each person; they may take account of the future earnings of children and students, and the prospect of promotion or of increased earnings in the normal pattern of the plaintiff's career. A major advantage over the social security system, therefore, is that damages can be tailored to meet each person's future loss of earnings. For those who are permanently affected by their injuries, an award of damages should, in theory, be the best type of compensation; it can, for instance, meet the case of permanent partial disability, which causes some reduction in future earning capacity (a situation which the present social security system finds difficult to handle). In practice, however, the failure of the judges to take into account the prospects of future inflation severely undermines this advantage of flexibility, while the problems of finding sufficient evidence or of negotiating a settlement result in levels of damages well below full entitlement under the rules of assessment.

Immense practical problems are posed by the need for a once-and-for-all prediction. The law of damages requires the judge to assess all the plaintiff's losses, both past and future, at one time, and to compensate him by the award of a single lump sum: the judge has no power to order the defendant to pay periodical sums to the plaintiff, nor can he reopen the case in the light of subsequent events. If the plaintiff's injuries turn out to be more serious than his medical advisers expected at the time of the trial (or of the out-of-court settlement) he cannot bring a second action to recover more damages. This means that all future contingencies which may affect the injured person's health or employment prospects have to be taken into account at the time of the settlement or trial. Doctors are forced by this system to attempt a prognosis which is often beset with uncertainties: there may be uncertainty whether the condition of the patient may worsen in the future (e.g. that a head injury may lead to epilepsy) and even when it is virtually certain that a particular condition may develop in the future (e.g. osteo-arthritis in a joint) there may be uncertainty as to the timing and seriousness of the condition. Medical experts are asked to reduce these uncertainties to a percentage chance of a contingency occurring. Suppose a case where there is a ten per cent chance of a serious medical complication occurring in the future: if the judge notionally assesses the damages on the basis that the complication ensues, and then reduces that sum by 90 per cent, he will be able to award a definite sum now. But if the plaintiff does in fact later suffer the complication, he is seriously under-compensated, whereas if he escapes it, he may be partly over-compensated, at least in comparison with other injured people.

The lump-sum method also demands estimates of the period of the plaintiff's future working life, or his chance of future redundancy or unemployment for other reasons. If the judge makes a prophecy about these risks, and then reduces the damages on account of them, he is extremely unlikely to have hit upon the right discount to suit the future circumstances when they occur. Other difficulties arise because, although the courts refuse to take account of future wage inflation, they do make guesses about future levels of taxation: instead of leaving it exclusively to Parliament to decide whether to tax damages for lost earnings, the courts estimate those losses net of tax, using the current rates of taxation. It is notable that nearly all other types of compensation adopt the method of periodical payments to replace the loss of a regular income: social security, sick pay, and permanent sickness insurance all provide income support by periodical payments, which enables adjustments to be made in the light of medical changes and inflation (see above, Table 1.1, Column 8).

Lawyers traditionally argue that the lump sum gives freedom of choice to the injured person, who may choose to replace his loss of a regular income by using the lump sum to purchase an annuity, or by himself investing the sum to produce an income. Alternatively, he may choose to use it to buy an asset, such as a business, or transport facilities or accommodation suited to his needs (see Table 3.13 below).

Non-pecuniary losses

Damages may be awarded for both past and future 'pain and suffering', which cover all mental aspects of the victim's suffering: any neurosis caused by the injury, or mental suffering in the knowledge that his life has been shortened, that he is disabled or disfigured, or that his disability will limit his enjoyment of life.[4] Damages for 'loss of expectation of life' have been abolished as from 1983: they were intended to compensate for any shortening of the plaintiff's life, but were assessed at a conventional sum (£750 in 1973; £1,100 in 1977) whether the victim was an adult or a child.

Another heading of damages is for 'loss of amenities' (also known as 'loss of enjoyment of life'), which is designed to compensate for loss of the capacity to enjoy life: it includes impairment of the plaintiff's health or energy, inability to have children, loss of marriage prospects, disfigurement, and anything which interferes with a normal life (such as inability to play a sport or follow a leisure interest). The law treats life as worth living in every aspect, and so attempts to compensate for any *change* in 'life-style' caused by the injury, whether or not the plaintiff's life is just as 'happy' after the accident as it was before. The final heading for non-pecuniary damages is for the loss of use of part of the body, or damages for the injury itself, e.g. loss of part of the body, such as the eye, or loss of use of part of the body, such as the sense of smell. There is no market for fixing the value of any part of the body, so the judges have to fix arbitrary figures for this type of loss, using an unofficial tariff of sums to maintain comparability between people with similar injuries and to give some guidance to legal advisers. Thus, for instance, in 1975 (at the midpoint of the period covered by the settlements of damages reported in the survey) the recognized figure for loss of, or very severe injury to, an arm was between £7,000 and £10,000; for loss of the sight of an eye, between £4,000 and £5,000; and for loss of several teeth, about £500. The courts often award a single lump sum for non-pecuniary damages, and do not itemize the different components.

Compensation for non-pecuniary loss is a significant feature of the damages system, and one which is seldom found in other compensation systems. The social security system only rarely attempts to provide money for any type of non-pecuniary loss: the main aim of social security is to provide income support to replace lost income, and a subsidiary aim is to meet extra expenses arising from disability. The philosophy supporting social security therefore differs radically from that of the law on damages (see Chapter 1 above), whose flexibility can adapt to respond to psychic losses genuinely experienced by many victims; damages for these losses thus provide some compensation for injured non-earners, such as children, housewives and retired people.

The damages system in operation: the amounts actually received

The number of injured people in our survey who succeeded in obtaining damages was 182. The amounts of damages were reported in 169 cases (thirteen respondents were not willing to disclose the amount); in the fifty-one settled cases where we have completed questionnaires from solicitors, we have confirmation of the amounts reported. Table 3.1 shows the mean and median amounts recovered in the main categories of accidents, while Figure 3.1 shows the spread of amounts in all categories. The mean amount of damages was £1135, while the median was £500 (i.e. half

Table 3.1 *Amounts[1] of damages recovered*

Category of Accident	Mean[3] damages per case	Median[3] damages	Number of cases (where amounts known)
	(£s)	(£s)	
Work	850	500	73
Road	1369	412	86
Other[2]	1202	750	10
All accidents	1135	500	169[4]

[1] The amounts are rounded up to the nearest £. The spread over time of the settlements or awards of damages analysed in this and other tables or figures in this chapter is as follows: 1951–70, 5; 1971, 4; 1972, 9; 1973, 25; 1974, 33; 1975, 36; 1976, 37; 1977, 20; 1978, 8; 1979, 1. (Date unknown, 4)
[2] Sampled one in two (see Chapter 1).
[3] The mean is the average amount, while the median is the midpoint in the distribution of the amounts.
[4] The weighted number of 198 is used in Table 2.2, but the present chapter uses the actual amounts in the unweighted cases (except in Tables 3.7–9). In this chapter the two cases of damages paid for work illness are put under work accidents.

of the amounts were under £500). Nearly three-quarters of the amounts of damages recovered were under £1,000, and only one in nine was over £2,000; yet the relatively few higher amounts cause the mean to be considerably higher than the median.[5]

The relevant dates should be remembered when these figures are assessed (see Note 1 to Table 3.1): the main interviews were conducted in 1976–7, but for the fifty-seven cases where claims for damages were then unsettled, further interviews and postal surveys were conducted until mid-1979, in order to discover the outcome of the claims.[6] Although most of the settlements in Table 3.1 fall within the period 1973–7 (during which period there was some 'inflation' in judicial awards of damages) some of the earlier settlements date from a period when damages and earnings were significantly lower. Nevertheless, the general picture is unlikely to have changed. These findings show that in practice the damages system produces relatively low sums of money, which can seldom achieve the goal of the system, viz. to put the plaintiff, so far as money can do so, back into the position he would have been in had the accident not occurred. As the data given below indicate, the precision of the rules on assessing damages which aim to give the plaintiff 'full recompense' for his injuries and losses, gives way in out-of-court settlements to many practical pressures towards lower amounts.

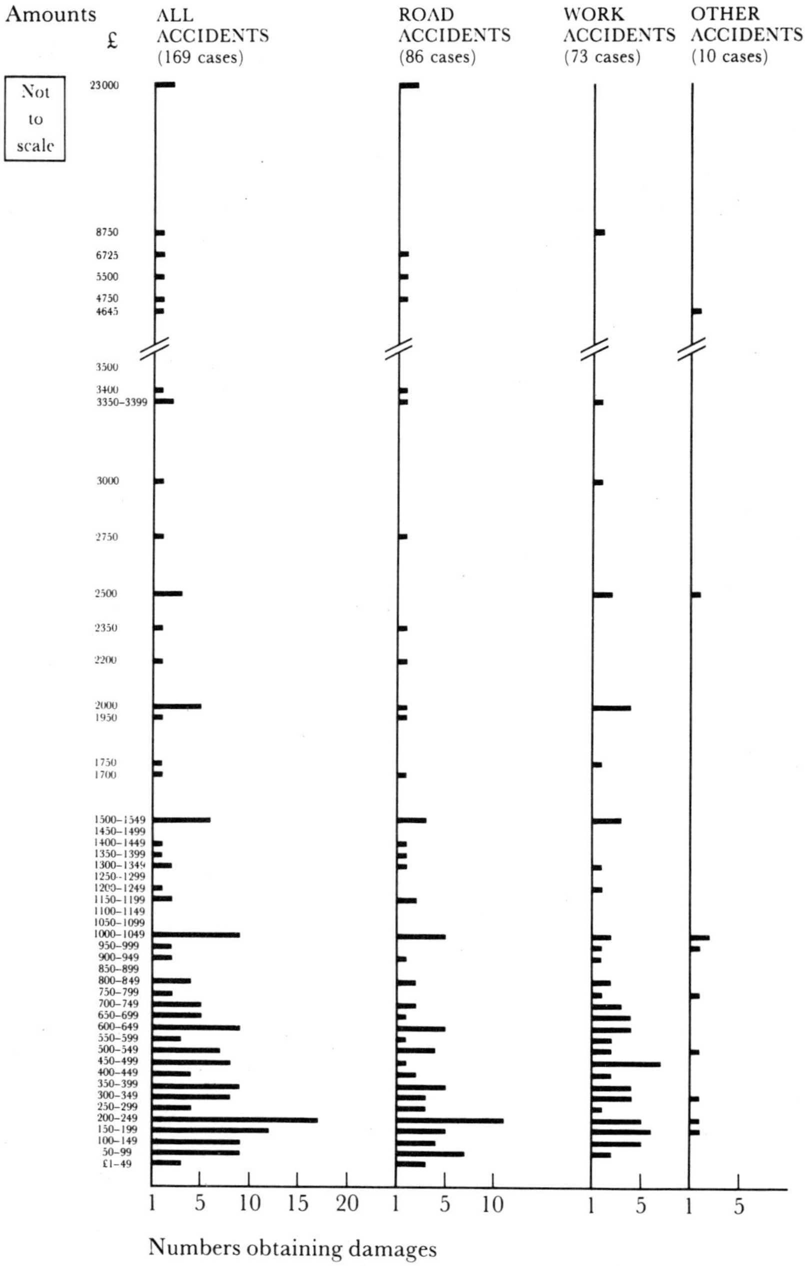

Figure 3.1 *Distribution of amounts of damages*

The full amount which a court would be likely to award, if 'full' liability were established against the defendant, is heavily discounted in an out-of-court settlement in order to take account of all the uncertainties facing the plaintiff, such as the risk that he might not be able to prove in court that it was the defendant who caused the accident, or that the defendant was at fault; the risk that he, the plaintiff, might be held partly at fault himself; or the risk of uncertainties about his medical prognosis. The prospect of further delay and further expense, if the claim is fought out in court, may induce the plaintiff to accept a lower figure offered by the defendant. It is not often worthwhile for the parties to an out-of-court settlement to use the detailed legal rules on the assessment of damages in the way in which a judge would use them *after* he had decided to hold the defendant fully liable. If the notional gross figure for damages assessed as for 'full' liability is to be discounted, say, by 20 per cent for the risk of the plaintiff not being able to prove liability, by another 30 per cent for the risk that he himself might be held contributorily negligent, and by a final 10 per cent because of the chance that the judge might hold that his medical condition may improve in the future, it is plainly not worth the parties' time and trouble to calculate the gross figure in any detail. In these circumstances, the damages are not 'tailor made' to suit the needs of the individual plaintiff, but are fixed in a rough and ready way. All the legal, evidential, and procedural difficulties facing the plaintiff may be viewed as 'bargaining chips' given to the defendant who is negotiating the settlement. The cumulative effect of all these difficulties facing the plaintiff produces a situation in which he is willing to exchange the *chance* of obtaining full damages for the *certainty* of a much smaller sum offered in settlement by the defendant.

In Figure 3.1, which shows the distribution of amounts of damages, the following features are worthy of comment.[7] First, in road and work accidents, there is bunching under £850, with many amounts under £250. Secondly, the distribution of amounts for both road and work accidents is largely similar, except that it is wider in road accidents, where there are more awards over £4,000, and more awards under £100. The fact that ten amounts agreed in road accidents were under £100 suggests either that insurance companies may be 'buying off' many smaller claims with low offers, or that claims for minor injuries are more common in road accidents than in other categories. Thirdly, the amounts reached in settlements tend to be round figures: 66 per cent were fixed at multiples of £100 or £50 ; and several figures were particularly popular: £200 (thirteen cases), £300 (seven), £450 (seven, all work accidents), £600 (eight), £700 (five), £1,000 (eight), £1,500 (six), and £2,000 (five). It appears that solicitors and insurance companies, when negotiating for a settlement, agree to think in terms of convenient multiples, which tend to increase in size as the level of damages increases.

The only detailed information on how damages were assessed came from the fifty-one solicitors who completed questionnaires in settled cases; interviews with the claimants themselves (in the main survey) showed that they were ignorant about how the total figure for damages had been reached. The mean amount of damages reported by the solicitors was £1,183, which was very close to the mean of £1,135 in all the cases reported by claimants (Table 3.1). In 69 per cent of the fifty-one cases reported by solicitors, the damages included an amount for past loss of earnings, averaging £248; in only one case was a future loss of earnings taken into account,[8] which may be explained by the fact that nearly all claimants had returned to work by the time the settlements were reached – the average delay between the accident and the settlement was over nineteen months (see Figure 3.4 and Table 3.8). In 43 per cent of the solicitors' cases, the damages included a sum for out-of-pocket expenses incurred up to the date of the settlement: the average amount for this item was £93. The mean sum for non-pecuniary losses, such as pain and suffering, was £973, which, given the unofficial tariff for such damages, is a relatively low sum,[9] especially since in just under 40 per cent of the cases the solicitors reported that the amount agreed for damages took account of some permanent disability.[10] The suggestion made above that damages in out-of-court settlements are not precisely assessed is also supported by the fact that in 14 per cent of the cases the solicitors reported that the damages were not itemized in any way.

The agreed damages were paid as a single lump sum in all but one of the 169 cases in the survey where the amounts were reported: the one exception was an uninsured defendant, who paid an instalment but was unable to raise the balance (which was never paid). Those who obtained damages were asked whether they would have preferred periodical payments linked to the cost of living rather than a lump sum (Question 127.d). Of the replies 73 per cent were negative, but the larger the damages, the more likely claimants were to favour periodical payments: where the damages were £500 and under, only about one in four preferred periodical payments; for £501–£2,000, it was one in two; while for over £2,000, it was more than one in two. It is not surprising that periodical payments did not seem worthwhile in the smaller cases, especially those under £500, but it is significant that more than half of those who received larger sums (usually those with more serious, or longer-term consequences) perceived the need for regular income support.

The effect of contributory negligence

In negotiations between solicitors and insurance companies (or solicitors acting for insurance companies) it is frequently alleged that the victim of the accident was himself wholly or partly to blame. In law, this concept of contributory negligence has the effect of reducing the 'full' damages which would have been awarded if the defendant had been solely at fault; the reduction is calculated in percentage terms to represent the victim's proportionate share of responsibility in comparison with that of the defendant. This legal doctrine places a powerful negotiating weapon in the hands of the defendant's solicitors or insurance company, which is extensively used: in the fifty-one settled cases where solicitors completed questionnaires, they reported that the settlement took account of the plaintiff's contributory negligence in a little under half the cases (45 per cent) (cf. the Pearson survey of insurance claims: Pearson Report, 1978, vol. 2, Table 117).

The role of contributory negligence is, not surprisingly, not so clearly revealed by the data provided by the victims. At the beginning of the questionnaire, before any suggestion of compensation was made, all accident victims were asked whether the accident or injury was in any way their own fault, the fault of someone else, or no one's fault. In the case of those who ultimately obtained some damages, the answer to this question is given in Table 3.2, which also shows whether some contributory negligence was reported to have been taken into account in the negotiated settlement. Only 7 per cent of the total number (177) in this Table initially acknowledged that they themselves were partly at fault in causing the accident, yet in the fifty cases where we have independent information from the solicitors, half the settlements had taken account of some contributory negligence (in the majority of these cases the accident victim had attributed blame entirely to the other person). It seems likely that many of those who receive damages were not told that their own contributory negligence was a factor in reaching

Table 3.2. *Initial attribution of blame in relation to contributory negligence*

The extent to which the settlement took account of contributory negligence	Victim's initial attribution of responsibility for the accident: Wholly the fault of another	Partly the fault of another (but not own fault)	Partly own fault (including cases where partly the fault of another)	No one's fault	Totals n
Solicitors report some[1]	15	1	5	4	25
Solicitors report none	20	1	1	3	25
Victim reports some	5	—	1	—	6
Victim reports none	5	—	1	—	6
No information on contributory negligence was provided by victim	97	5	5	8	115
Totals n	142	7	13	15	177[2]

[1] The percentages of contributory negligence reported by solicitors were as follows: unspecified, 6; 50 per cent, 4; 40–50 per cent, 3; 17–25 per cent, 7; 15 per cent and under, 5.
[2] Missing information = 5.

the agreed figure. Since, apart from contributory negligence, settlements already take account of many other uncertainties, it seems that solicitors often do not give their clients details of all the factors taken into account in a compromise: it is likely that in many of the cases where no definite information was provided by victims, contributory negligence was nevertheless a factor in the settlement. The difference between the number of cases reported by solicitors where contributory negligence reduced the damages, and the number reported by victims, may be partly explained by the latter's unwillingness to acknowledge their own fault,[11] but a more likely explanation is that solicitors see an allegation of contributory negligence merely as one of the many factors to be weighed by them, the professional negotiators, when reaching a compromise. For a solicitor to give his client full details of all the factors taken into account would be to extend his accountability to his client, and perhaps to increase the risk of disagreement between them.[12]

(3) Negotiations towards out-of-court settlements

Offers to settle

In nearly all of the 182 cases in our survey where damages were obtained the claim was settled by an agreement reached between the parties without a court hearing:[13] in only four cases were damages awarded by a court after a contested hearing (see below, section 4). Negotiations over claims are conducted between the claimant and his advisers (usually his solicitors, but sometimes trade union officials), and the defendant and his advisers (usually his insurance company, or solicitors acting for the insurance company). In nearly all cases the first formal notification of a claim for damages comes in a letter written by the claimant's solicitor to the defendant, or, if the name of the defendant's insurance company is known, to it. Formal denials or admissions of liability will also be made by letter, but negotiations aimed at achieving an out-of-court settlement of the claim may be conducted by telephone or by personal interview, as well as by correspondence. Since the negotiations are conducted by proxy through professionals, both sides know that most claims are finally settled, and the basic expectation underlying their efforts to negotiate is that a settlement out of court should and will be reached.

The normal method by which the parties move towards a compromise of a claim is for the insurance company (or its solicitors) to make an offer in cases where they think that the claimant has a reasonable chance of being able to prove some fault on the part of the defendant. An offer is a proposal to pay a definite sum of money in full and final settlement of all claims which the claimant may have against the defendant arising out of the accident. It is a concrete proposal, which, upon acceptance by the claimant, creates a binding legal agreement between the parties: the defendant is then bound to pay the agreed sum, and the claimant is precluded from pursuing his claim to a court hearing. If the offer is definitely rejected, it ceases to be available for acceptance thereafter, even if the claimant later changes his mind and is willing to accept it. Unless a higher offer is made, or the offer is renewed at the same amount, the claimant's only remedy is to take his claim to a formal court hearing, where he must prove his case without reference to the offer: offers to compromise or settle a claim are in law always understood to be 'without prejudice' to any litigation which may follow failure to agree on the proposed compromise, which means that the willingness of the defendant to pay something may not be given in evidence to the court. The claimant who rejects an offer therefore faces not only the risks of further delay and expense in going to court but also the risk that he may fail to prove his case in court and so recover no damages at all.

The outcome of the negotiations depends on the relative bargaining strength of the parties, and the tactics which they adopt (Ross, 1980; Phillips and Hawkins, 1976): each side is estimating the relative strength of its own case in relation to its guesses about that of the other side, and making estimates of the effects of the different types of uncertainty which may affect the case: uncertainty as to whether the evidence would support a finding that the accident was due to the defendant's fault; uncertainty as to the medical prognosis about the plaintiff's condition; uncertainty as to whether a court would find contributory negligence against the plaintiff; and uncertainty as to how much a court would award for the plaintiff's injuries. This section will first examine the data about the number of offers made, and then discuss whether inferences may be drawn from the data about the negotiating tactics adopted by insurance companies.

The data on offers come from that reported by claimants and that reported by their solicitors in the fifty-one cases where solicitors completed questionnaires (in case of conflict, the solicitors' data were used). Although there is an obligation on a solicitor to report to his client any offer received from the other side, we assume that not all offers actually made may have been reported to claimants, or by them to our interviewers. Since solicitors needed to consult their files when completing our questionnaires, the information supplied by them is likely to be more reliable; in fact, however, data from solicitors usually confirmed the information given by claimants. Thus, although we accept that our data on offers are probably incomplete, we believe that our data are sufficiently reliable to give a realistic general picture of the practice on offers (Table 3.3).

In nearly two cases out of three (63 per cent) where an out-of-court settlement was reached, the claimant accepted the first offer made by the defendant or his insurance company; in nearly all cases, the offer was accepted on the basis of legal (or trade union) advice. This finding is corroborated by the data from solicitors when they are analysed separately from the data from claimants: in just over half of the fifty-one settlements reported by solicitors they had advised acceptance of the first offer.[14] In these cases there may have been previous discussions between the solicitors and the

Table 3.3 *Numbers of out-of-court settlements in relation to which successive offer was accepted*

	Number	Number accepting	Percentage accepting in each category
1st offer made	166[1]	104	63
2nd offer made	62[1]	32	52
3rd offer made	29	23	79
4th offer made	6	4	67
5th offer made	2	2	100
		165	
Court awards of damages in contested cases		4	
Total number of cases where amounts of damages were reported		169	

[1]Includes one case where two offers were refused before it went to court and an award of damages was made by a judge.

defendants' insurance companies about an appropriate figure, but the first definite figure offered by the insurance company was accepted.

A possible explanation for the successive offers in our data might be that more offers are rejected in the more serious cases. We tested this in several ways. On the assumption that the relative size of the final settlement may be one indication of the relative seriousness of the case (whether judged by the severity of the injuries or by the severity of the consequences), Table 3.4 categorizes the data on the number of offers according to the size of the settlement. Some differences emerge, in that a higher proportion of offers are rejected in cases involving sums over £500, than in those of £500 and below, but there is no corresponding increase in cases involving sums over £1,000. One or more previous offers had been rejected in 30 per cent of the cases where the final settlement did not exceed £500, in 45 per cent of those between £501 and £1,000, but in only 43 per cent of those over £1,000. The data do not permit the explanation that first offers tend to be accepted only in the less serious cases.

Another possible indication of relative seriousness is the degree of residual disability reported by the victim: Table 3.5 gives the number of offers in relation to this factor. Although there is a slight

Table 3.4. *Number of offers in relation to the size of the final settlement*

	Size of final settlement		
Number of offers to reach settlement	£1–500	£501–1000	Over £1000
One (i.e. the first offer was accepted)	61	23	21
Two offers	16	9	7
Three offers	7	8	8
Four and five offers	3	2	1
Mean number of offers in each category	1.45	1.79	1.70
Percentage of cases where more than one offer was made	30%	45%	43%

Table 3.5. *Number of offers in relation to the degree of residual disability*

	Residual disability reported by accident victims				
No. of offers to reach settlement	None	'Never affected a lot'	'Affected a lot – just occasionally'	'Affected a lot – most of the time'	'Affected a lot – all of the time'
One (i.e. the first offer was accepted)	40	9	31	14	11
Two	10	5	8	8	1
Three	5	1	11	4	1
Four and five	1	1	1	2	1
Mean number of offers in each category	1.41	1.62	1.66	1.82	1.42

increase in the mean number of offers as the degree of residual disability increases (which may be due to increased medical problems), the increase is not maintained in the most serious category of residual disability (where the mean number of offers reverts to the same figure as for cases where no residual disability at all was reported). Further analysis of the data by the main categories of accident (road, work, or other) showed no different patterns in the numbers of offers. The conclusions which we draw from these data are: first, that the number of successive offers made and rejected is only to a small extent explained by the relative seriousness of the case; and, secondly, to the extent that the number of offers indicates the amount of negotiating between the parties, there is no evidence that more negotiations take place in the more serious cases.

Negotiating strategies: the pressures to settle

Table 3.6 analyses the data on previous offers where the first offer was rejected. Each offer is taken as a percentage of the amount of damages finally agreed between the parties, and the Table presents the mean percentages of the successive offers in each category. Following the rejection of a first offer, the second offer is, on average, between a third and a half higher than the amount of the first offer. (Column 2 of Table 3.6 shows an average increase from 73 to 100 per cent, Column 3 from 52 to 77 per cent.) When a third offer is made following the rejection of a second offer, the amount of the third offer is a little under a third higher than the second (from 77 to 100 per cent: Column 3). Figure 3.2 shows the spread of offers in each category, expressed as percentages of the previous offer.

These percentages might appear to suggest that the strategy of rejecting early offers would produce a higher final settlement. But the data on offers do not disclose the element of risk for the claimant who rejects an offer: a higher offer may not be made, and the same offer may not be renewed. (This happened in one case in our survey where the claim was later abandoned). In the light of all the difficulties and uncertainties faced by claimants and reported by them in our survey, it is not surprising that many prefer to accept the first offer rather than continue to face them. When an offer is made, the claimant must take a difficult decision which depends on the careful weighing of many separate factors. (In practice, of course, it is the claimant's adviser who takes the effective decision, since the claimant is seldom in a position to challenge that advice.) The claimant faces, first, the uncertainty about the strength of the evidence available to him: is the evidence which his witnesses can give sufficiently strong to establish in court (should the case go to court) that the accident was caused by negligence on the part of the defendant? In weighing this evidence, the claimant can often only guess what evidence to contradict it might be available to the defendant. Secondly, even if he is confident that he can prove negligence, he may be uncertain whether he can prove the causal link between the negligence and his injuries and losses, or whether he can prove the full extent of those injuries and losses. Another frequent problem for the claimant is uncertainty about the medical prognosis: a conflict of medical opinions on his future prospects regularly produces serious uncertainty about how the judge might assess his chances of either recovery or further deterioration. And even in the absence of these problems of prognosis, the assessment of damages for intangible losses like pain and suffering, or the loss of the ability to lead a normal life, depends on the subjective impressions formed by the judge on all the evidence, and despite the unofficial 'tariff' system, cannot be predicted with accuracy. Thirdly, the claimant may face uncertainty as to whether the defence evidence might establish some fault on his part (contributory negligence), and to what extent this might reduce his damages. Finally, rejection of an offer will always cause some further delay, which not only prolongs the claimant's emotional stress owing to uncertainty about the outcome of the claim but also increases the legal costs which he may incur should the claim ultimately fail. The cumulative effect of all these uncertainties is that if the claimant is under financial pressure (as many are), he will naturally be more willing to accept a lower sum which is immediately available to meet his urgent needs or debts than he will be to suffer continuing pressure in the hope that a greater (unknown) sum may be offered at some (unknown) time in the future.

Yet further explanations for claimants' willingness to accept the first offer may be found in the reasons given by them for accepting an offer which was lower than the amount which they originally had hoped to get (see below, section 5 of this chapter). A further possible explanation concerns legal fees.[15] An offer by an insurance company of a sum of money as damages also incorporates the company's willingness to pay in addition the reasonable costs of the claimants' solicitors. Few solicitors in personal injury claims appear to advise their clients to apply for legal aid (see below, Section 6) and the majority appear to rely on the expectation that in nearly all cases they will be able to negotiate an offer from the defendant's insurance company and so obtain payment of their fees. An offer from an insurance company may therefore create a conflict of interest for the claimant's solicitor in cases not covered by legal aid, nor supported by a trade union: if he advises acceptance, his reasonable fees will be assured, whereas if he advises rejection, in the hope that a larger sum will be offered or awarded by a court, he runs some risk that the claim might ultimately fail, with the result that he would be left to look to his (uncompensated) client to pay the fees out of his own pocket. Although solicitors are entitled to charge for work actually done, it is also possible that some may feel that the extra fees to be earned by negotiating for a higher offer are not worth the extra effort involved, or not justified in the light of the further delay and inconvenience which would be imposed on their client.

Our survey was designed to collect data on the experience of victims, and therefore has no direct data about the strategies adopted by insurance companies in negotiating the settlement of claims. From the data on offers, however, some tentative inferences may be drawn. For instance, to us it is intuitively likely that the strategy adopted by insurance officers will depend largely on their assessment of the same factors which a claimant must weigh. Thus, when deciding whether to make an offer, and how much to offer, they will make a judgement about the strengths and weaknesses of the particular claim, in the light of all the factors, such as: their guess about the strength of the claimant's evidence in the light of their knowledge of the strength of the defence evidence, and their estimates of the likelihood that they could establish some contributory negligence, of the percentage which might be fixed for the claimant's fault, of what the damages might be for 'full' liability, and of what view a judge might take of the medical prognosis.

There are, however, some additional factors which will not enter the claimant's own assessment. The insurance company is in the business of handling claims, and making profits; it will be concerned to minimize its total costs, viz. the total of the damages and costs paid to claimants and its own costs in defending claims. Although it has the resources to fight many cases to the stage of a full hearing in court, the company must estimate in each case whether it will be cheaper to settle out of court, perhaps for a slightly higher figure than a court might award, than both to pay a court award and also to incur further expense on its own side in preparation for, and during the court hearing. It is often claimed that small but probably unfounded claims have a 'nuisance value' to the insurance company, since it will often be cheaper to settle them by making some offer than to incur the expense of fighting them for as long as the claimant persists (Ross, 1980, pp. 204–11). As with other organizations, insurance companies like to manage their activities as smoothly and efficiently as possible. An American study of insurance practice, for example, reported that insurance adjusters are very conscious of pressure from their superiors within the company to settle claims in order to close their claims files 'as expeditiously as possible' (Ross, 1980, pp. 59, 127).

But there is an asymmetry between the parties. What is routine for an insurance company is unique for a claimant. Companies handle many claims for damages and can thus spread or 'average' their risks over all their cases. But there is no mechanism available to the claimant to enable him to spread his risks: for him (although not necessarily for his advisers), the claim is an exceptional experience which is unlikely to be repeated in his lifetime. The claimant is therefore much more concerned than the insurance company about the risks and uncertainties of the case, and delay in reaching a settlement (Ross, 1980, pp. 224 ff.). Nor is there a continuing personal relationship between the parties (as in industrial relations) which might restrain the company from exploiting to the full all of its negotiating advantages; the company may assess how the claimant will be affected by the financial and emotional pressure caused by further delay and uncertainty, and then adopt a strategy based on its belief that he has no 'stomach for a fight'.

The insurance company is also likely to form some opinion about the degree of specialization and the negotiating skills of the claimant's solicitor (which may well depend not only on the solicitor's experience but also on his willingness to fight). If the insurance company is dealing with a solicitor known to specialize in personal injury claims, with extensive experience in conducting litigation, his threat to take a case to court must be more credible than one from a non-specialist with little experience of litigation. Although there may be a few small firms of specialists, we assumed that, normally, the larger the solicitor's firm, the more likely he is to specialize; we then examined the data on offers in the solicitors' survey in relation to the size of the firms. The data showed that, in firms with four or fewer solicitors, first offers were accepted in over half of the cases (thirteen out of twenty-four), while for those of five or more solicitors, first offers were accepted in only a third of the cases (nine out of twenty-seven). This result may be related to relevant experience in negotiating with insurance companies. But, in contrast with negotiating skills, the quality of the advice on the law available to the claimant need not depend on the size of the firm of solicitors. Since a solicitor may consult any barrister specializing in any area of legal practice, even a solicitor practising on his own has access to specialist advice. Data from the solicitors' questionnaires show that in just over half of the settlements, a barrister was consulted by the claimant's solicitor, and that the rate of consultation was not related to the size of the solicitor's firm.

Negotiations involve a progressive and strategic release of information from one side to the other. An offer gives some clue to the claimant's advisers about the insurance company's view of the ultimate settlement 'range' and the rejection of an offer conveys some information to the company about the claimant's expectations and intentions. If some reasons are given for the rejection (for example, references to medical reports), they are likely to be indications of the strength of the claimant's case and the company can estimate even more accurately what is the range of the claimant's expectations about an appropriate figure. The company may attempt to reduce the claimant's expectations by giving some indication that it is aware of weaknesses in his case: any doubts may be used as negotiating weapons. It is therefore to be expected that successive offers should be successively more finely tuned. Table 3.6

Table 3.6 *Offers*[1] *expressed as percentages of the settlement finally agreed.*
(In this Table, the final settlement represents 100 per cent and previous offers are shown as percentages.)

	Column 1	Column 2		Column 3	
Category of accident	Number of cases where *first* offer was accepted	Number of cases where *second* offer was accepted	Offers as mean percentages of settlement (%)	Number of cases where *third* offer was accepted	Offers as mean percentages of settlement (%)
Work	42	13	69; 100	11	45; 76; 100
Road	59	13	77; 100	11	58; 77; 100
Other	3	6	70; 100	1	60; 80; 100
All accidents	104	32	73; 100	23	52; 77; 100

[1] In four cases in the survey there were four offers: three were work accidents (the offers being, respectively, 2, 10, 60, 100 per cent; 33, 44, 88, 100 per cent; and 46, 61, 67, 100 per cent); one was a road accident (67, 78, 93, 100 per cent). Only two cases gave data of five offers: one was a work accident (the offers being 70, 72, 85, 97, 100 per cent) and the other road (29, 49, 61, 79, 100 per cent).

and Figure 3.2 show that the amounts of second offers are, on average, between one-third and one-half more than first offers; whereas the amounts of third offers are, on average, a little under

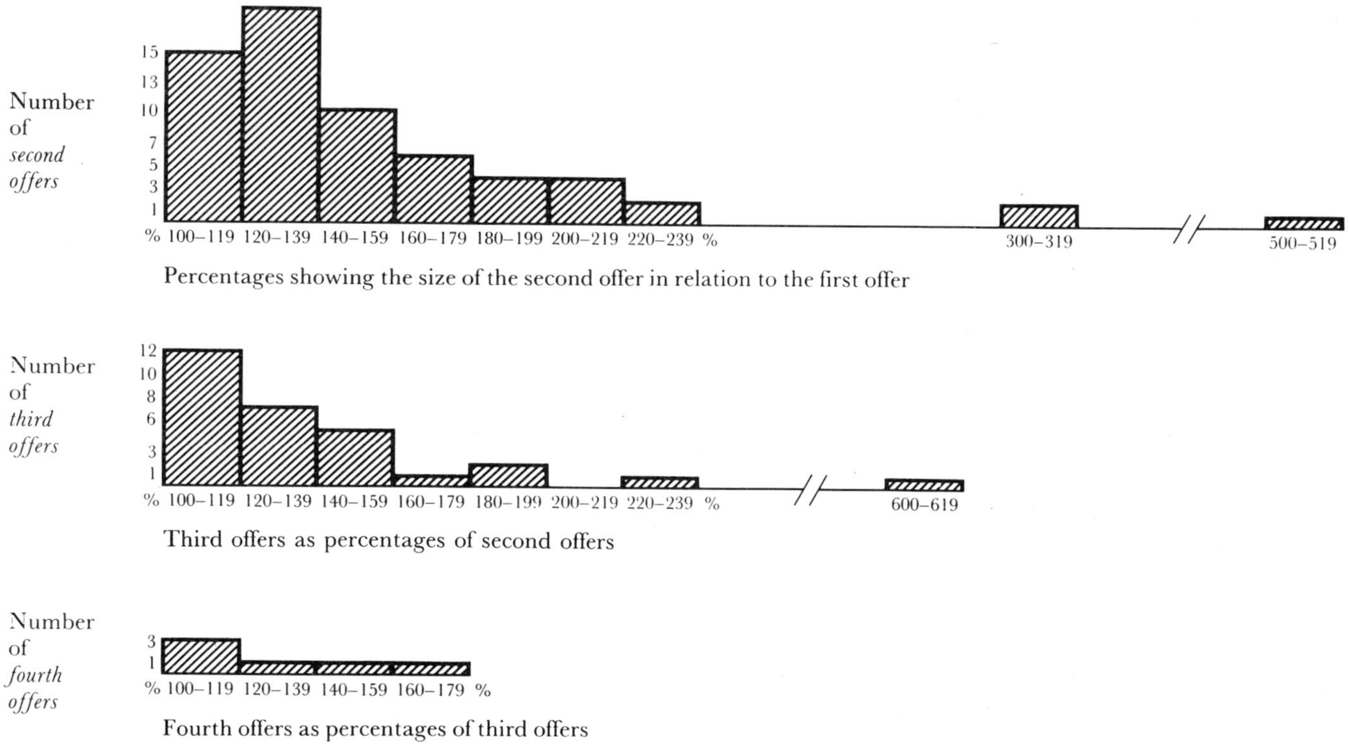

Figure 3.2 *The spread of offers in each category expressed as percentages of the previous offer*

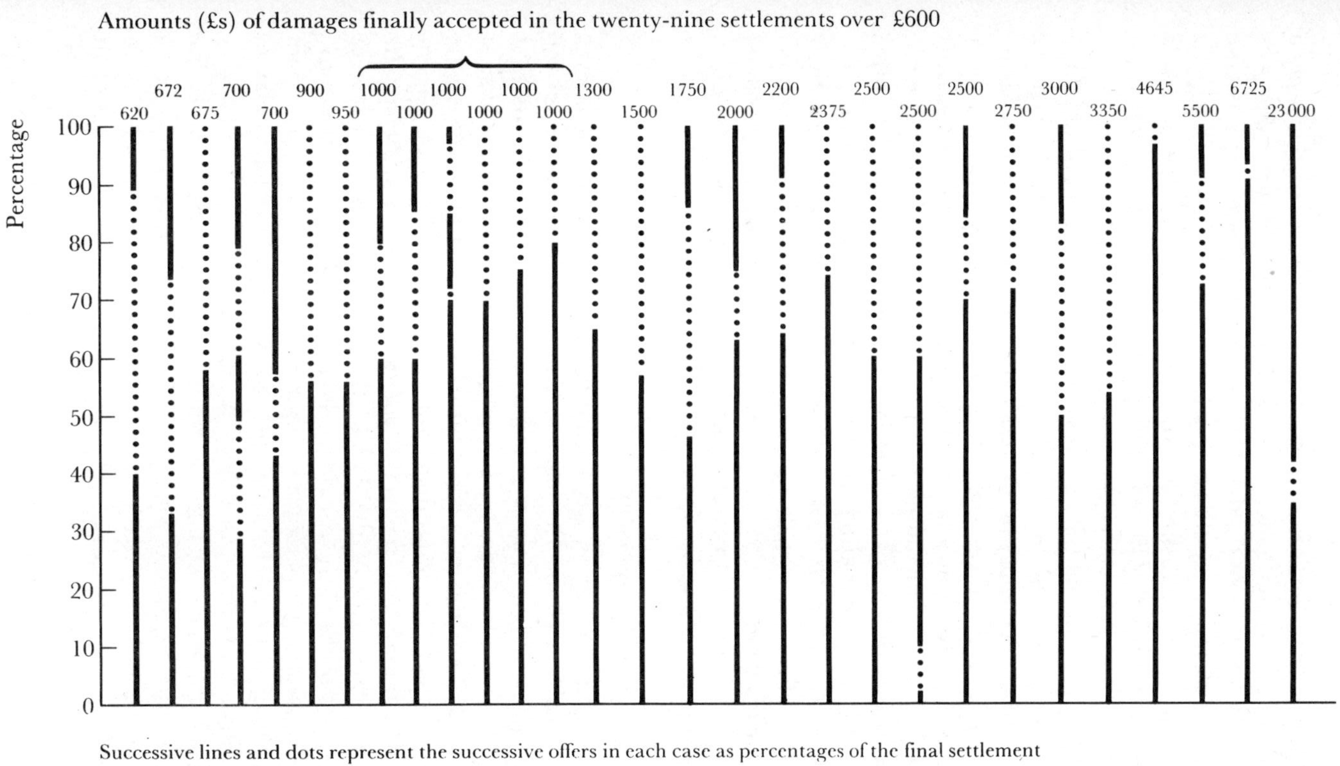

Figure 3.3 *Successive offers shown as percentages of the amounts of damages finally accepted in all cases of settlements over £600 where the first offer was rejected*

one-third more than second offers. Figure 3.3, however, shows each individual case of settlements over £600 where the first offer was rejected: the successive offers are shown as percentages of the amounts of damages finally accepted. It can easily be seen from this Figure that there is substantial variation from the averages in Table 3.6 and Figure 3.2. The percentage sizes of successive offers in individual cases follow no apparent pattern, but tend to confirm the hypothesis that, at the time of each offer, and in the light of all the information then available, a highly individualized decision is made on the cumulative effect of all the factors outlined above. Separate examination of the successive offers in the larger settlements (over £1,000) shows the same wide variations as in the smaller settlements (£1,000 and below, including those of £600 or below, which are not shown in Figure 3.3). It is therefore difficult to detect any simple pattern for the negotiating practices of insurance companies. We suggest that the practice of insurance companies is to pitch their successive offers at levels designed to secure, on average, an acceptance rate of 50 per cent or over for each successive category of offers: on our data, about 60 per cent of claimants accept the first offer, about 50 per cent the second and 80 per cent the third.

Delay in consulting lawyers

There is often delay before an injured person consults a lawyer about making a claim: the legal system puts the initiative on the injured person, but it is a reasonable supposition that his first concern is, understandably, his medical treatment and physical recovery. But the longer a claimant delays consulting a lawyer, the worse his chance of obtaining damages (Table 3.7). The percentages of claimants who recover damages remain fairly stable for the first three categories in the Table (those who consulted a lawyer within six months of the accident). But for those who delayed more than six months, the chance of obtaining damages dropped from over 70 to 45 per cent. It is possible that some cases of long delay in consulting a lawyer may be due to the fear of the victim (or of his lay advisers) that little evidence is available to support his claim. In the solicitors' survey, about 25 per cent of the solicitors who achieved a settlement reported that they had experienced difficulties in handling the claim as a result of delay between the time of the accident and the time they were consulted.[16] They reported, as expected, that the delay caused difficulties in collecting evidence.

Two features of delay in consulting lawyers deserve notice. First,

Table 3.7 *Delay in consulting a lawyer, by outcome of claim*

Delay after the accident before consulting lawyer	Outcome of Claim: Damages obtained	No claim made	Claim abandoned	Unsettled (or result unknown.[1])	Number of cases in each category
	(%)	(%)	(%)	(%)	(%)
Under one week	77	7	12	4	26 (100)
From one week to under one month	81	9	8	3	80 (100)
From one month to under six months	71	10	11	9	82 (100)
Six months or longer	45	21	24	10	29 (100)
Total ñ					217

[1] 'Result unknown' covers a few 'unsettled' claims where, at the final stage of the follow-up survey (July 1979), the claimant could no longer be traced.

nearly 70 per cent of those who consulted lawyers within one week of the accident were road accident victims (whose belief that such accidents must be reported to the police and to their insurance companies may have led them also to consider consulting a lawyer). On the other hand, 83 per cent of those who delayed six months or longer before doing so were work accident victims.[17] The role of trade unions probably accounts for the difference. Our data show that nearly half of the work accident victims who later consulted a lawyer had first gone to a trade union for advice about making a claim (Table 2.11), which would explain why few cases are referred to lawyers within the first week. Secondly, many unions handle the early stages of work-related claims (attempting to collect evidence, etc.) with the result that some claims are not referred to trade union lawyers until after six months from the accident.

Delay in negotiating a settlement

The complexities of negotiating the settlement of a personal injury claim or of preparing a claim for a court hearing inevitably lead to delays. For all cases in the survey, including court awards, the mean delay between the date of the accident and the date when damages were received was a little over nineteen months and the median was sixteen months (calculated in whole months for each case); for the fifty-one cases in the solicitors' questionnaire, the mean was twenty-two and a half months and the median was nineteen months. Delay of this length means that the tort system can seldom meet the victim's need for income maintenance *during* his absence from work: this type of support is in practice left to sick pay and social security.

The distribution of delay is shown in Figure 3.4 which gives the numbers of cases settled in each period of two months from the date of the accident (cf. the Pearson insurance survey, 1978, Vol. 2, Tables 17 and 113–16): there is some bunching around the first, second, and third anniversaries of accidents, which may suggest that an effort is made to settle claims as they come up to their anniversaries. Three-quarters of the settlements are made within two years of the accident, and 90 per cent within three years. We analysed the data to see, first, whether the longer delays occurred in the more serious cases. Table 3.8 indicates some relationship between the length of time off work and the length of delay in settling claims: the trend is that the longer a victim is off work, the longer the delay. The Table shows that most victims are back at

Table 3.8 *Delay between the date of the accident and the date of settlement in relation to time off work as a result of the accident*

	Months off work[1]						
Delay in months between accident and settlement	No time off work	Under 1 month	Over 1 month but under 2 months	Between 2 and 6 months	Over 6 but under 12 months	12 months and over	Numbers in each category
months	(%)	(%)	(%)	(%)	(%)	(%)	
1–6	42	20	23	7	10	12	27
7–12	21	30	33	25	10	6	37
13–24	37	50	20	41	35	37	56
25–36	—	—	15	14	35	31	26
37–48	—	—	5	7	5	6	8
Over 49	—	—	2	3	5	6	5
	100	100	100	100	100	100	
Numbers in each category (ñ)	19	10	39	55	20	16	159

[1] This Table includes only those who were at work immediately before the accident.

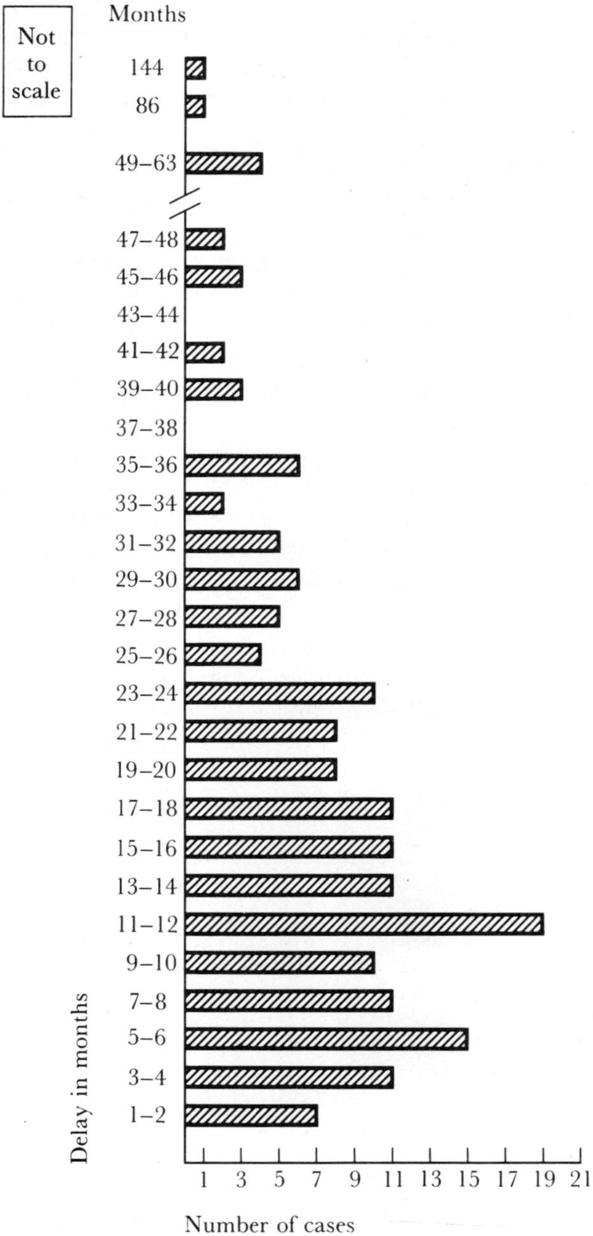

Figure 3.4 *Delay between the date of the accident and receipt of damages*

work before their claims for damages are settled (a finding confirmed in the solicitors' questionnaires), but that a small number who were off work for more than six and twelve months respectively settled before they returned to work. Secondly, we analysed the relationship between the degree of residual disability reported by victims and the delay between the accident and the settlement (Table 3.9): the trend is that the greater the residual disability, the longer the delay. Such delay is often due to problems of medical prognosis, which are likely to be greater in the more serious cases of residual disability; yet Table 3.9 also shows that some of the cases within the higher categories of residual disability were settled within six months of the accident, which would seem to imply that in these cases an early medical prognosis was accepted as reliable by claimants and their advisers. The earlier the settlement in cases of residual disability, however, the greater the chance that later developments in the claimant's condition might disprove the prognosis: the legal rule is that, once a settlement has been agreed, it cannot be reopened in the light of any later information. Finally, we considered the data on delay in the light of the relative size of the damages agreed upon, but no clear pattern emerged (cf. Pearson, 1978, Vol. 2, Table 115). Although there was some tendency for larger settlements to be associated with longer delays, there were also many smaller claims which were delayed for two or more years.

Table 3.9 *Delay between the accident and the settlement in relation to the degree of residual disability*

	Residual disability reported by accident victims				
Delay	None	'Never affected a lot'	'Affected a lot – just occasionally'	'Affected a lot – most of the time'	'Affected a lot – all of the time'
months	(%)	(%)	(%)	(%)	(%)
1–6	30	12	11	18	11
7–12	40	18	19	9	5
13–24	25	47	42	29	32
25–36	3	18	19	29	37
37–48	2	—	7	12	5
Over 49	—	6	2	3	11
	100	100	100	100	100
Numbers in each category (ñ)	63	17	57	34	19

This was not unexpected, because the problems which cause delay in the tort system are not confined to the larger claims; furthermore, claimants with less serious injuries whose living expenses are met from other sources, may believe that there is little risk in holding out for a higher offer.

Reasons given for delay

All victims whose lawyers had taken some action towards claiming damages were asked about delay. Two-thirds of the 182 who answered the question reported that there had been 'delays or waiting periods' in the handling of their claims. A quarter of the reasons for delay given by them concerned medical questions: one in six reported a delay while a course of medical treatments was completed, or until his physical condition had stabilized sufficiently to enable the medical advisers to come to a reasonably clear view about the prognosis (two-thirds of these were road accident victims); while one in ten said there was a delay while medical reports were obtained. Solicitors in their replies confirmed these reports: just under 40 per cent of the solicitors said that they had advised their client to delay pursuing his claim. The reason invariably given was the uncertainty about the medical prognosis: they had advised delay until the claimant's medical treatment was complete or his condition had stabilized sufficiently for medical reports on his prognosis to be made with some confidence.

A wide variety of additional explanations was given by claimants to account for the delays (cf. Pearson, 1978, Vol. 2, Table 116). Each of the following accounted for about one in ten of the reported delays: difficulties in collecting evidence; disputes over whether the evidence could prove the defendant's or the claimant's fault; delays or mistakes by the claimant's solicitors; delays by the defendant's insurance company or his solicitors (e.g. they 'are just stalling in the hope that I will lose heart and give up'); and disputes over the amount of damages to be paid. Relatively infrequent explanations (those given by fewer than one in twenty) were: the defendant's failure to answer letters or to report the accident to his insurance company; the defendant's not being insured, or not being adequately insured; delay until the defendant was prosecuted, or while an application for legal aid was being made; disputes between the defendant and a third party; delays because the claimant's trade union handled dealings with the solicitors; the death or illness of the claimant's solicitor, or his moving from the locality; and, in one case, the illness of a judge.

Claimants' views about delay received substantial support from the fifty-one solicitors who returned questionnaires. They were asked a slightly different question – whether there had been 'undue delay (on either side) in settling' the claim. Eleven reported that there had been 'undue delay'. Delays were said to have been caused by the defendant's insurance company (e.g. failure to answer correspondence; delay while two insurance companies fought over which was liable (motor insurers versus employers' liability insurers)); while medical reports were obtained; by one claimant in applying to his trade union for support; by a union in handling the claim; by a dispute between the defendant and a third party; by the process server in serving a writ; and by difficulties in reaching agreement on quantum.

The conclusion we draw from the data in the survey is that a considerable amount of delay is unavoidable, given the requirements of the present rules on proof of fault, the adversary system, and the present methods of assessing damages.

Difficulties in negotiating: issues in dispute

Only 13 per cent of the 182 who obtained damages reported that they had had difficulties in trying to reach agreements to settle their claims. This may reflect their interpretation of the word 'difficulties', or it may indicate their ignorance about the details of the claims process. (Several explained their 'Don't know' answers by adding: 'The lawyer saw to it all' ; 'The lawyer sorted it all out'; 'The union did it all.') As delay had been the subject of an earlier question, it is unlikely that respondents would have repeated what they had already reported about problems of delay. They were asked whether the other side at any time 'argued about' one or more of the issues set out in Table 3.10.

Solicitors have a different view about the difficulties of negotiating. Two-thirds of those reporting on settlements said they had had difficulties in negotiating with the defendant's insurance company or solicitors; Table 3.11 shows the issues in dispute as reported by the solicitors (with most cases having more than one issue in dispute).

Two problems dominate the difficulties faced by solicitors: establishing liability (proving the defendant's negligence), and negotiating the amount to be paid as damages (cf. the Pearson

Table 3.10 *Issues in dispute reported by those obtaining damages (Total: 182)*

Issue disputed[1]	Number of cases where the issue was disputed	Percentage of total (182)
		(%)
Which witnesses should be believed	10	5
Which medical evidence should be accepted	18	10
Whether, on the facts of the case, they were at fault ('Liability')[2]	29	16
How much they should pay you in compensation ('Quantum')	50	27
None of these, or no information provided	93	51

[1] Positive replies from eighty-nine respondents reported 107 disputed issues.
[2] Although the question did not specifically raise the issue of contributory negligence, in six cases it was mentioned as a disputed issue.

Table 3.11 *Difficulties in negotiating reported by solicitors (in thirty-three cases out of a total of fifty-one)*

Issues in dispute causing difficulties	Number of cases where the issue was disputed	Percentage of all cases (51)
		(%)
Lack of evidence	6	12
The medical prognosis	11	22
The question of liability	25	49
Contributory negligence	12	24
The quantum of damages	27	53
No difficulty reported	18	35

insurance survey, 1978, Vol. 2, Table 112). Lack of evidence, according to the solicitors, was not a frequent problem, which may be due to the decision of potential claimants not to consult solicitors where they suspect that there is insufficient evidence. The absence of direct witnesses to the accident was the main difficulty where lack of evidence was a problem, but there was one complaint that witnesses were reluctant to become involved in the case. All the difficulties reported in the course of negotiations are also familiar as reasons given for not making a claim in the first place (Table 2.12) or for abandoning a claim (Table 3.12).[18]

(4) When negotiations fail

If the parties are unable to reach an out-of-court settlement, there are only two alternatives available to the claimant: he must either take his claim to a court hearing, or abandon it. This section considers in turn the data from the survey on these alternatives.

Court proceedings following the breakdown of negotiations

The ultimate stage of a disputed claim for damages is a full hearing by a judge of the evidence on both sides. This rarely takes place. Although the solicitors' survey disclosed that formal proceedings (viz. the issue of a writ) had been commenced in just under 40 per cent of the cases where an out-of-court settlement was finally reached, few cases reach the stage of an actual hearing. Of the 1177 accident cases (unweighted number) in the survey, only five (0.4 per cent) led to a contested hearing (cf. the Pearson Report, 1978, Vol. 2, para. 516, Tables 12 and 104). In one, a work accident was held by a High Court judge to have been caused by the plaintiff's own negligence, with the result that no damages were awarded. (The plaintiff's costs were met by his trade union.) In the other four (two work accident cases supported by trade unions and two road accident claims brought without legal aid) damages were awarded after full hearings (one in the High Court and three in the County Court). The defendants in each case were ordered to pay all the plaintiff's legal costs. In two of these contested cases we have information on the issues in dispute at the hearing: they were both 'liability' and 'quantum'. Two of the successful plaintiffs said they were 'satisfied' with the award, but a third said he was 'very dissatisfied' because his solicitor had advised him to expect twice as much as he was awarded by the judge. No appeal, however, was brought in any of the five contested cases.

In addition to these contested hearings, the court was asked to give judgment by consent in two cases, i.e. without a real contest between the parties in court. The two judgments arose in different circumstances. In the first, the case was settled on the very morning that it was due to be heard in the High Court. The plaintiff's QC advised him to settle before the full hearing because (he said) 'it could happen that if you go into court you don't get as much'; the solicitor in the same case reported that the injuries merited a higher figure for damages but it was substantially reduced because of the likelihood that the judge would find up to 50 per cent contributory negligence on the part of the plaintiff. In the second case, the consent judgment in favour of the plaintiff was given within fifteen minutes of the start of the hearing, and the real fight then began between the defendant and the third party whom the defendant alleged was also partly responsible for causing the accident: the judge apportioned liability between them at 60:40.

Court proceedings were also necessary in three other cases, because a judge must give his approval to a settlement involving a person under age. In each of these cases, the court gave its approval, after a short hearing, to the amount of the damages agreed to by the defendant's insurance company and the solicitors for the infant victim.

The survey data thus show that the role of the judges in actually deciding personal injury claims is very limited in relation to the total number of accidents, and to the total number of claims made. The legal costs and delay involved in pursuing a claim to the final stage in court are strong incentives to claimants to settle at the highest figure which can be negotiated out of court. But the possibility that the claimant could press his claim to a full hearing obviously provides the background to these negotiations, and is the only pressure on insurance companies to make offers to settle before a hearing. The judges still play an important role in establishing, developing, and clarifying the legal standards for liability and quantum.

The decision to abandon a claim

Some claimants in the survey made a claim against a potential defendant, but later decided to abandon it; others decided, after consulting a solicitor or trade union official, not to pursue a claim. These together totalled eighty cases in the survey, and this section examines the reasons they gave for their decisions.[19] These reasons are subjectively reported, being their own explanations for their actions, and must be treated as incomplete, as there could well be other explanations. But other evidence, wherever available to us (e.g. from solicitors), corroborated claimants' own accounts, and their reasons are likely to be reliable to the extent that they are based on reported facts (e.g. based on a solicitor's advice that there was insufficient evidence to support the claim). Furthermore, we believe that the policy-maker should not ignore the genuine belief of claimants that these are the reasons for their failure to obtain damages. We proceed to examine the main reasons given for abandoning claims; several infrequent reasons are given in Table 3.12 without being discussed in the text.

Table 3.12 *Reasons given for abandoning claims*[1]

	Number of cases in which the reason was given[2]	Percentage of the total number of cases (80)
		(%)
Problems over obtaining evidence (including two cases where witnesses were unwilling to give evidence)	36	45
Victim's own fault caused the accident	14	18
Fear of legal expenses	13	16
Denial of liability by the potential defendant	12	15
Problems over trade unions' handling of claims	12	15
Problems over solicitors' handling of claims	6	8
Delay in the claims process	5	6
The bother or trouble involved in claiming	5	6
Fear of affecting a continuing relationship	5	6
Legal or insurance problems	4	5
Injuries not serious enough (3); or the severity of the injury not realized at the time (1)	4	5
No one at fault	3	4
No loss of income	2	3
Satisfied with industrial injury benefits	2	3

[1] This Table includes all the cases where a claim was made against a potential defendant, but later abandoned; and all cases where, after a solicitor or trade union official was consulted, a claim was not pursued.
[2] More than one reason was given in about half the cases, yielding a total of 123 reasons given in the eighty cases.

Avoiding trouble.

Chapter 2, above, reported the reasons for not making a claim which were given by those who did consider making one (Table 2.12), and many of the same reasons are found in cases of abandonment. For instance, although unwillingness to undergo the 'bother' or 'trouble' of making a claim is a regular reason for not doing so in the first place, five claims actually made (including two handled by solicitors) were later abandoned on similar grounds. The claimants explained their decisions to abandon in terms such as: 'it was not worth all the bother'; 'I didn't want a lot of fuss about it'; and 'when I had to keep going to court over the accident [as a witness for a prosecution] it all took so long I lost interest . . . I just wasn't interested to start another lot . . . I said not to bother.'

Preserving relationships.

As explained in the earlier section on reasons for not claiming, some accident victims are unwilling to claim for fear of upsetting a continuing relationship with the potential defendant. Three claims handled by solicitors were later abandoned on the same ground. One was a work accident case, where the injured employee trusted his employer, who offered him a future advantage if he dropped his claim. Another claim was thought to risk affecting a tenant's relationship with his landlord: the victim, injured in an accident at the entrance door to a block of Council flats, abandoned a claim for damages because he was frightened that the Council, against whom the claim was made, 'might put pressure on his family to get them out of the flat'. The desire to avoid unpleasantness between neighbours was the reason given in the third case: a potential claim against a near neighbour was not pursued because 'I didn't want to make any unpleasantness: the village is small and I have to live nearby. It just wasn't worth it.'

Two claims where trade union advice was taken were dropped by injured workers: one said he did not claim 'because [the person blamed] was only the mechanic and he's a friend of ours'; the other said, 'I got brainwashed by the firm and was promoted to foreman; I felt under obligation afterwards.'

Fear of legal expense.

Where fear of legal expense was mentioned, it was normally given as a reason for not making any claim at all (Table 2.12). But our data produced thirteen cases where claims were abandoned because the claimants feared that they would be unable to pay the legal expenses which they might incur (e.g. 'I was told not to bother to claim, it would cost me too much'). Seven of the claims were handled by solicitors, who presumably considered that their clients were neither eligible for legal aid (there are capital and income limits on eligibility) nor yet able to bear the cost themselves.

Although the majority of claimants' solicitors usually rely on the defendant's insurance company to meet their fees and expenses (a result which regularly follows from either an out-of-court settlement or a court award of damages), it may be that solicitors are less likely to do so in the more uncertain claims.

Problems of evidence.

In thirty-six cases (twenty-nine on legal advice), lack of evidence was the reason given for abandoning a claim. The main problem reported was insufficient evidence to prove that the accident was caused by fault on the part of the other person involved (thirty-two cases). In all but six of these cases, the decision to drop the claim was made on the advice of solicitors, which shows that the failure of accident victims to obtain damages is not simply a problem of access to legal services, but of the legal rules themselves, particularly that which places the onus of proof on the accident victim. Several victims blamed themselves for some months' delay before they consulted solicitors, which led to their failure to obtain sufficient evidence. Although it is possible that some solicitors may use alleged problems over evidence to cover their unwillingness on other grounds to take on a claim, we believe that the great majority of explanations given to us should be accepted at their face value: solicitors themselves, in their questionnaires, confirmed that they sometimes had to advise that a claim should be abandoned because of lack of evidence to support it.[20]

Three claims were abandoned on the advice of solicitors about other problems of evidence: in one, the evidence could not identify the owner of the dog which caused a road accident; and in two work accident cases, the potential witnesses were workmates of the injured person and were unwilling to act as witnesses in claims against their employer: they were 'afraid of losing their jobs' in one case, and 'were threatened with sacking if they went to court to testify for me' in the other. These instances support the view that the tort action, with its adversarial context, is ill-suited to work accidents where the parties and witnesses are normally in a continuing relationship.

Fault of the claimant, or no one at fault.

Fourteen injured people were advised by their solicitors that they should abandon their claims because the accident was caused by their own fault: normally the advice was that the victim was wholly to blame but, in two cases, solicitors advised that there was a serious risk that contributory negligence would substantially reduce the damages. In two other cases solicitors advised that claims should be abandoned because the evidence showed that there had been no fault on the part of the potential defendant.

Other legal obstacles.

Four cases were dropped on special legal grounds. For instance, there is a 'limitation period' of three years from the date of the accident within which formal legal proceedings must be commenced for a claim for damages: one intending claimant delayed more than this time before consulting a solicitor, who (on advice from counsel) said a claim would fail for this reason. In another case, the potential defendant was a foreign tourist driving a car registered abroad: a solicitor, according to the victim, advised her that she could not claim. In a third case, a claimant, without taking legal advice, decided not to challenge the defendant's denial of liability made on legal grounds: following a pavement accident, the defendant local authority said that the statute only allowed compensation where the pavement was 'missing' and not where it was 'only cracked or broken'.

Denial of liability by the potential defendant.

A firm denial of liability by the potential defendant can deter the making of a claim for damages or may encourage the abandonment of a claim. This was the reason given by twelve accident victims in our sample, some of whom were off work for long periods of time. Six of the potential defendants were employers of the accident victim: the parties were thus in a continuing relationship which the employee might not wish to disturb by pursuing a claim for damages. A typical explanation was: 'They denied liability but the managing director sent for me after I went back to work and told me that, if I dropped the claim, the insurance company would deal more leniently with me, and I would get more compensation. So I dropped the claim and they would not pay me anything.' There were five cases where the potential defendant was a public body (four were local authorities and one a transport undertaking), whose denial of liability might be seen as an 'official' decision. Both employers and public bodies may also be seen by victims as having the financial and institutional resources to support a denial of liability by employing lawyers to defend any legal action brought against them. Most lawyers would probably treat the denials of these potential defendants merely as an attempt at bluffing, and it is significant that only one of the twelve accident victims in this group consulted a solicitor: in only two cases was any independent advice received even from a friend or relative. The others discussed their claims only with the potential defendants or their officials or agents, whose firm denial was sufficient to deter them from pursuing their claims further or from seeking independent or professional advice.

Solicitors' alleged incompetence, delay, or failure to make progress.

Six claimants said they abandoned their claims because of their solicitors' alleged incompetence, delay, or failure to make progress. According to one, his solicitor 'said he would contact me, but he never did, so I thought I didn't have a case . . .' Another said 'I thought my solicitor could have answered the letter. I left it to him . . . I just gave up because I waited twelve months and nothing came of it. You can't keep on fighting for nothing.' A third complained of 'long delaying tactics' in the way the case was handled by lawyers: 'I got bored to tears . . . It's nearly three years ago . . . I've just given up hope.' A fourth (a road traffic victim who saw her solicitor on six occasions) said 'My lawyer was totally incompetent; showed very little interest; was too easily persuaded by the other side. I consulted another solicitor, who said: "Due to the way your case has been handled, you have lost any chance of getting compensation."'

A fifth said that the first solicitor he consulted 'was quite certain I had a good case, and he worked on it. But then he was moved up to the North . . . by his firm and another lawyer took over the case. He started right back at the beginning . . . There were no witnesses except the police and fire brigade who were later on the scene and could have verified [a fact disputed by the defendant's insurers] but they weren't asked for statements . . . and after three and a half years it was too late to go back and get them.' In the sixth case, the victim of a road accident reported that his claim for damages had not been settled after fourteen years, despite the fact that the car driver involved had been convicted of dangerous driving; there was a dispute over medical evidence, and the 'present position' was a 'stalemate'.

Trade unions' alleged incompetence, delay, or failure to make progress. Twelve accident victims[21] explained their failure to obtain damages by reference to their trade unions' role in advising on or handling claims to damages (in five of the cases, solicitors had also been involved). Four complained of the union's failure to pursue the claim. One victim reported that his union was 'just not interested'; in two cases, the union would not act for the victim because he had not been a member of the union for the required period. In another, the victim changed his job and 'had to change unions. My former shop steward said I would have to keep up my payments [i.e. regular dues to the first union] to continue with the claim. Well, I haven't and I haven't heard anything, so have given up.'

In five cases the accident victim's reason was, in effect, that he relied completely on his union to claim for him anything to which he was entitled (saying, for example, 'I couldn't afford to fight the company on my own without the union's backing'): the victim either accepted the union's advice, or accepted the inactivity of the union as meaning that he was not entitled to anything. In one case where the union obtained a disablement benefit lump sum for the injured man, he explained the position about a claim for compensation: 'All negotiations were placed in the hands of the union . . . [I] knew very little of any of the legal negotiations . . . They just saw to it all.' In the second case, the victim thought about making a claim, consulted his union, but did not contact a lawyer 'because the . . . union are for that purpose: they should do it.' In the third case, the victim relied on the union representative 'automatically' to put in a claim and when this was not done 'didn't bother to take it further'. In the fourth case, the victim abandoned his claim because 'the trade union lawyer said he couldn't get any money'. In the fifth case, the employee broke her foot when she tripped on an uneven pavement on the way to the bank on her employer's business: she made no claim for damages because her trade union official said she was not eligible to do so because she was injured away from the employer's premises; he said she was 'not at work actually in my place of work'.

Another union member complained of delay: 'I was not happy about the way the union and its lawyer handled the case, and was going to contact another lawyer but I had a letter from the union saying it was three weeks too late to consult another lawyer . . . It was the union's fault that it was too late.' Another victim, who was off work for sixty-eight weeks, 'thought the trade union was too lax, it did not take it [the claim] up in time.' He 'lost faith in the union' on account of the delay before the union lawyer was consulted: the lawyer's advice was to drop the idea of making a claim because 'nothing could be proved as the time lag was too great.' Finally, a victim who was off work for fifty-six weeks, explained that he had abandoned his claim because the union and their lawyer were 'no good towards my claim'; he had tried to get another lawyer to take up his claim, but he could not afford to pay the costs involved.

We conclude from these accounts of union members who entrust their claims to unions that they feel as dependent on the advice and competence of the union officials as do clients in relation to their solicitors. This dependence usually gives the union officials the effective control over the claim, and enables them to provide an important, individual service to their members.

When the reasons given by accident victims for not making a claim for damages (Table 2.12) are combined with those given in the above Table for abandoning claims, a few key issues emerge (cf. the Pearson Report, 1978, Vol. 2, Table 84). Problems in obtaining sufficient evidence were given as reasons in nearly one in three of the total number of cases (211); the bother or trouble involved in claiming, or ignorance or confusion about claiming, were explanations in one case in four; and the fear of legal expenses, and the fact that the victim was himself at fault, each accounted for one case in seven. All other reasons were far less frequently given.

(5) Damages: their use and adequacy

The use of damages

Accident victims who received damages were asked about the use of the damages and about the advice which they received on their use. Table 3.13 summarizes the information obtained on these issues (cf. the Pearson Survey, 1978, Vol. 2, para. 404 and Table 89).

Investment and expenditure.

Recipients of damages giving details of how they spent the money numbered 152: as many put the money to several uses, the percentages in the Table add up to more than 100. Since nearly 70 per cent of settlements reported in the solicitors' survey included an amount calculated to replace lost earnings, it might have been expected that one of the main uses of damages would be to cover ordinary living

Table 3.13 *Use of damages*

Amount of Damages (£)	1–500	501–1000	1001–2000	2001–10,000	over 10,000	Totals	Percentages of Total
Total Number of Recipients	85	32	21	12	2	152[1]	
							(%)
Used as ordinary living expenses[2]	16	4	3	3	1	27	18
Repaid loans (used for expenses while ill)	7	4	1	2	—	14	9
Paid off debt	1	1	—	—	—	2	1
Paid for holiday	5	3	1	1	1	11	7
Bought clothing	6	1	1	1	—	9	6
Bought furniture, carpets, household items, or appliances	14	8	3	3	—	28	18
Bought house (or paid deposit on house or repaid mortgage)	2	2	5	3	—	12	8
Improvements or repairs to house	7	7	2	1	1	18	12
Bought (or repaired) car or motorcycle	8	3	6	3	—	20	13
Presents or loans to relatives	7	4	1	2	1	15	10
Banked (still in bank at time of interview)	31	10	4	3	1	49	32
Deposited with Building Society	2	3	2	3	—	10	7
Invested in shares, etc.	2	—	1	3	2	8	5
Invested by the Court	1	1	—	—	—	2	1

[1] This total is of the cases where both the amount of the damages and their use were known.
[2] This column includes answers such as 'spent it', making up for 'lost wages', and 'bought small items'.

expenses. But the delay in receiving damages (the average for our sample was nineteen months: see Figure 3.4) meant that most accident victims had returned to work by the time they received them; indeed, only 18 per cent said that they had used all or some of the damages as ordinary living expenses. Another 9 per cent used damages to repay loans made to them to cover expenses while they were ill; (1 per cent paid off other debts). Thus, only about a quarter of those receiving damages used any part to meet regular living expenses in the absence of earnings. Essential living expenses are normally met from other sources, particularly sick pay and social security benefits, while other, less essential expenditure (which would normally have been met from earnings) is forgone or postponed until damages are received.

The majority used some or all of the money in a way which sought to preserve the benefit for a considerable period. About 45 per cent saved some or all for the future: 32 per cent said they had banked some, 7 per cent deposited some in a building society, but only 5 per cent put money in other forms of investment, such as ordinary shares. A large number used the damages to pay for a special, tangible item of a 'durable' type: 18 per cent bought furniture, carpets, and other household items and appliances (such as refrigerators, cookers, freezers, washing machines, television and video equipment); 13 per cent, motor-cars and motor-cycles; and 6 per cent, clothing. Others used the damages to 'invest' in houses: 8 per cent used the money to pay a deposit on a house or to repay a mortgage, and 12 per cent to repair or to make improvements to their houses (often installing central heating).

Another group of expenditures was aimed at providing an enjoyable but transitory experience: 7 per cent used some of the money to pay for a holiday, and 10 per cent to pay for presents to relatives, or to make loans to them. ('Presents to relatives' often referred to gifts to those who had nursed the accident victim during his recovery; but in four of these fifteen cases, the money was used to pay for a wedding.) We may speculate whether expenditure of this type provides a pleasurable experience to balance the memory of pain and suffering caused by the accident.

Many of the uses of damages reported in Table 3.13 seem far removed from the judicial assumptions behind the rules for the assessment of damages. The money is often used in the same ways as might be expected in the case of any unexpected lump-sum windfall, such as a win on the pools. We believe that the future of the damages system should be assessed in the light of how people actually use money received as damages, and in comparison with alternative ways in which society might use the money now supporting the damages system, e.g. by improvements in social security benefits for the permanently disabled.

Advice.

As many amounts of damages are relatively low (the median of all settlements in the survey was £500) it is not surprising that few recipients seek advice on what to do with the money. Of those giving information on this matter, 95 per cent (97 respondents) reported that they had received no advice from anyone (Question 153). Few of those receiving damages, however, are likely to have had any previous experience in handling a large sum of money. But even for the larger sums in the survey – damages of over £1,000 – only four out of eighteen received any advice; of two who had obtained sums of £23,000 as damages, only one said he had received advice (from his employer, and a stockbroker). We infer from this that most solicitors do not see such advice as part of the service which they should give to clients.

Views on the adequacy of damages received

Ninety per cent of the fifty-one solicitors who completed questionnaires in settled cases reported that in their opinion the settlement eventually received was 'adequate in the circumstances', but they often qualified their answers, making clear that they were commenting on their own performance, given the constraints of the present system: their concept of 'adequacy' was dependent on the prevailing scale of awards for similar cases. For instance, one solicitor commented: 'Adequate in view of the law, but the plaintiff is never properly compensated'. In replying to this question on 'adequacy', a number of solicitors explicitly relied on the advice of barristers that the figure was adequate, and many mentioned the risk that contributory negligence might be found by a court, or fixed at a higher percentage than that taken into account in the negotiations for the settlement. Two typical comments were that there was 'always a risk that the Court would find 25–33 per cent of contributory negligence', and that the damages were 'adequate, when account is taken of contributory negligence'. Other solicitors referred to the costs and other risks involved in further negotiations or a court hearing: 'Bearing in mind the hazards of litigation, it was a reasonable settlement'; 'Time and expense made it not worthwhile seeking a higher settlement'; 'The claim was discounted due to evidential difficulties.' Only three of the solicitors said that the settlement was definitely not adequate: in one, the payment into court[22] put pressure on the victim to accept the offer; in another, the allegation of contributory negligence led to an inadequate settlement; in the third, the client would have sued had he received legal aid: his financial position was poor, and he was anxious for any sort of settlement. Two solicitors gave other qualified answers: 'Adequate, but our client was reluctant to press court proceedings because of difficulties in paying his legal aid contribution'; (another) was a 'difficult case – a high element of contributory negligence was alleged . . . The plaintiff was in financial difficulty and therefore could not hold out for more.'

Accident victims were also asked how much they had originally hoped to get, and who had first thought of this sum (Question 126). The replies showed that they were almost invariably ignorant of what sums the legal system of damages might produce, and that their expectations came (in all but a few cases) from advice given by their lawyers. Half the replies were that they did not know what to expect: the most common answer was 'I had no idea', and other typical answers were: 'I never thought of a particular sum'; 'Very hard to say: I didn't know the value they'd put on it'; or 'What price do you put on a child's eye?' A further quarter of the replies gave a definite figure which had been suggested to them by their lawyers; most of the remaining quarter mentioned a figure which they claimed they had thought of themselves, but their answers, when considered in the light of the whole interview, showed that many were using their later knowledge of the sum they actually obtained and relating it back to what they thought they had previously hoped to get.[23]

Almost everyone who accepted an out-of-court settlement said that they had done so on the advice of their lawyers; a handful said it was on trade union advice. Those who had previously expected a higher amount were asked specifically why they accepted it 'rather than trying to get more' (Question 126.c.) Almost half of the seventy-one replies were to the effect that the claimant had relied entirely on his lawyer's advice that the offer of the lower amount should be accepted: no other reason was given. This emphasizes the complete reliance placed on the lawyers. Typical answers were: 'The lawyer said it was no good trying to get more'; 'My solicitor said if I refused the offer I may lose the lot'; 'My solicitor said I was lucky to get anything at all'; 'At one time, my barrister advised me to claim £22,000; by waiting, I improved so much it reduced to £2,750.'

Over a third of the replies gave reasons for accepting a sum lower than that hoped for; the reasons fell into three categories: unwillingness to tolerate further delay or trouble over the claim (14 per cent); urgent financial need (10 per cent); and fear of being involved in, or of losing a court case (14 per cent). Typical reasons about delay and trouble were 'The waiting was that long I got fed up with it'; 'I did not think it was worth all the messing'; 'I couldn't be bothered'; 'I was fed up with the whole thing'; 'I didn't want to wait any longer'. Reasons of financial need were illustrated by these comments: 'I was fed up with waiting, and needed the money'; 'My solicitor said if I fought for more it would take three or four years and I wanted the money to pay off my debts'; 'I was so much financially in debt at the time that I had to settle out of court'; 'Due to financial embarrassment at the moment I must accept it.' The fear of being a party to a court hearing or of an adverse outcome in court is shown by the following replies: 'I was scared stiff of going to court; my solicitor thought I could get more but I didn't want to go to court'; 'My solicitor . . . wanted me to take it to court but I refused as it was a very emotional time for me, having lost a son a few months previous to the accident'; 'The union were not willing to fight it out in court . . . I might have come out with less money even if I had won . . .'; 'My solicitor strongly advised acceptance – it would cost a packet to go to court, and there was a risk of getting less'; 'I was advised [if there was a fight in court] there was a risk of getting only half . . . and of long delay'; 'I was frightened I would lose the lot against a barrister'; 'My solicitor said it was better to take the offer than fight and lose.' These comments reflect many of the issues which arise in negotiations for a settlement, and which have already been discussed in this chapter. The problems and uncertainties which confront the claimant and his advisers not only make it difficult to achieve any settlement at all, but also have the effect of reducing the amount of damages in the settlement.

(6) The solicitor-and-client relationship

Throughout this chapter, our data on the handling of claims for damages show that the main feature of the relationship between solicitor and client is the client's almost complete dependence on his solicitor's knowledge and advice, and on his combativeness (for a New York study, see Rosenthal, 1974). The average client has only the vaguest knowledge of the legal rules on liability, and virtually no knowledge of how a claim is made and negotiated, nor how to bring a case to court.

On the question of the amount of damages, the dependence of claimants on their solicitors was almost complete. As this chapter has reported, claimants frequently said that they had 'no idea' how much money their claim was worth, and that they had to rely on their solicitors' knowledge of the current scale of court awards. Although some claimants may have had some previous experience of claiming against their own insurance company (e.g. a 'loss' claim under a householder's policy), they seldom have had any experience of negotiating a 'liability' claim with a third person's insurance company; they must therefore accept their solicitor's advice on the best strategy to adopt. Our data showed that the decision whether to accept or reject an offer was almost invariably based on the solicitor's advice: clients have no alternative to accepting such advice on the amount a court is likely to award, and on the further delay, trouble, and expense which would follow the rejection of an offer. The client can exercise his own judgment on only a few relevant issues, such as the urgency of his own financial needs, his willingness to tolerate further delay and uncertainty, or his emotional capacity to face a court hearing. On all other matters, the solicitor must know that his client is entirely dependent on his advice: this dependence gives the solicitor in most cases the effective control over the decision to settle a claim out of court. As an earlier section has shown, claimants also rely heavily on their solicitors for advice about abandoning a claim. The advice to drop a claim is not welcome to the client, but our data show that it is extremely rare for the client to reject it.

The only matter on which claimants do not regularly receive legal advice is the decision how to use or invest the money received as damages. Very few reported that their solicitors had offered advice on what they could do with the money. Solicitors may perhaps feel that their role is complete on the recovery of the money, that they cannot offer any special expertise on investment which is not available from bank managers or others, or that the decision is a personal matter for their clients.

Problems, disagreements, and complaints

When handling personal injury claims, the solicitor must often bring bad news to his client; for example, the insurance company may delay, refuse to pay anything at all, or may refuse to increase an offer. This situation might be expected to lead to general dissatisfaction with the work of solicitors, but in practice, they are largely protected from criticism by being able to point to the many uncertainties created by the legal rules and procedures. However, the fact that the client feels so dependent on his solicitor does not necessarily lead to a satisfactory relationship: indeed the client's knowledge of the extent of his dependence may exacerbate a problem. All those who had consulted solicitors in our survey were asked whether they had ever had any 'complaints, disagreements or problems of any sort about the way [their] case was handled by lawyers': 17 per cent gave an affirmative answer. The chief complaint (ten cases) was that the solicitor showed a lack of interest in the case: for example 'They did not seem to be interested in it'; 'They would never put you in the picture about what was going on'; and 'I felt he was taking his time, not bothering about it.' Two victims whose claims were handled by 'trade union lawyers' (private practitioners retained by a trade union) complained that the solicitors did not see them: 'I haven't seen the solicitor at any point and have no idea how the case is going'; and 'I would never go to a T.U. lawyer anymore . . . They would not agree to meet you, were "not available" for you to see them.' A further group of five complained that their solicitors did not keep them informed about the progress of their claims; e.g. 'our solicitor wouldn't tell us what was going on – my husband always had to phone or go to see him to ask'; [the claim has] 'taken too long', [and there has been] 'a lack of correspondence – only two or three letters in one and a half years, and whenever we turned up we were palmed off on his assistant. He was always in court.' These complaints indicate that, despite complete reliance on the solicitor's legal expertise, many clients still have expectations that they will receive a personal service through reports and interviews.

Nine clients made a general complaint about the delay involved in claiming (e.g. 'I got sick of waiting so long'), while one said that he was 'confused by all the details involved'. (As a previous question had asked about delay in handling the claim, most claimants did not again report delay in answer to this question.) Other miscellaneous complaints were: difficulties caused by changes in the member of the solicitors' staff handling the claim (two cases), and by the wrong filing of papers; the solicitor's ignorance of relevant legislation; and the solicitor's being too closely connected with the defendant local authority.

'Disagreements' with lawyers were reported by eight claimants. In every case the issue was the amount of damages: the claimants felt that the solicitors and barristers advising them had been willing to settle for amounts which they considered too low, e.g. 'I was talked out of going through with the case and into settling out of court'; (another) 'He said that if I claimed [more] I would be up against a barrister and might lose the lot, so I dare not.' Although uncertainty may arise over many aspects of a claim, uncertainty over the amount to be paid was the only one where clients perceived 'disagreement' between themselves and their lawyers. It seems that the realization of their dependence on their lawyers' advice may here lead to frustration.

Legal expenses

The fees charged by lawyers for their work in handling claims for damages relate to work actually done; they therefore vary considerably from case to case and bear no particular relationship to the amount of damages recovered (cf. the data in Ison, 1967, Tables 15–28). In the USA lawyers nearly always charge a 'contingency fee' for work done on personal injury claims, often taking one-third or more of the amount recovered, but nothing if no damages are obtained (MacKinnon, 1964; O'Connell, 1971, Chapter V; Zander, 1978, pp. 219–20). Solicitors in England and Wales, however, are not permitted to charge a percentage of the amount recovered, even if it is agreed beforehand with the client. Thus, the data from the survey show no consistency in legal expenses as a percentage of damages recovered (see Figure 3.5).

The usual rule in English courts is that a plaintiff who is awarded damages against a defendant should, in addition, be awarded his reasonable legal expenses; a similar practice is followed in out-of-court settlements. Our data show that the plaintiff's legal expenses in personal injury claims are almost always paid by the insurance company which pays the damages on behalf of the defendant; from the fifty-one settled cases for which we have solicitors' questionnaires, it emerged that the total legal expenses of the plaintiff's solicitors were paid by the defendant's insurance company in all but three cases.[24] In the three exceptional cases, the bulk of the expenses were paid by the defendant's insurance company (94, 68, and 86 per cent respectively), while the balances were met, respectively, by the Legal Aid Fund (6 per cent), by the plaintiff's trade union (32 per cent), and by the plaintiff himself (14 per cent).[25] In our sample, few

A. *Individual settlements up to £1000 damages*. (Damages shown in unbroken lines, and plaintiff's legal expenses in broken lines.)

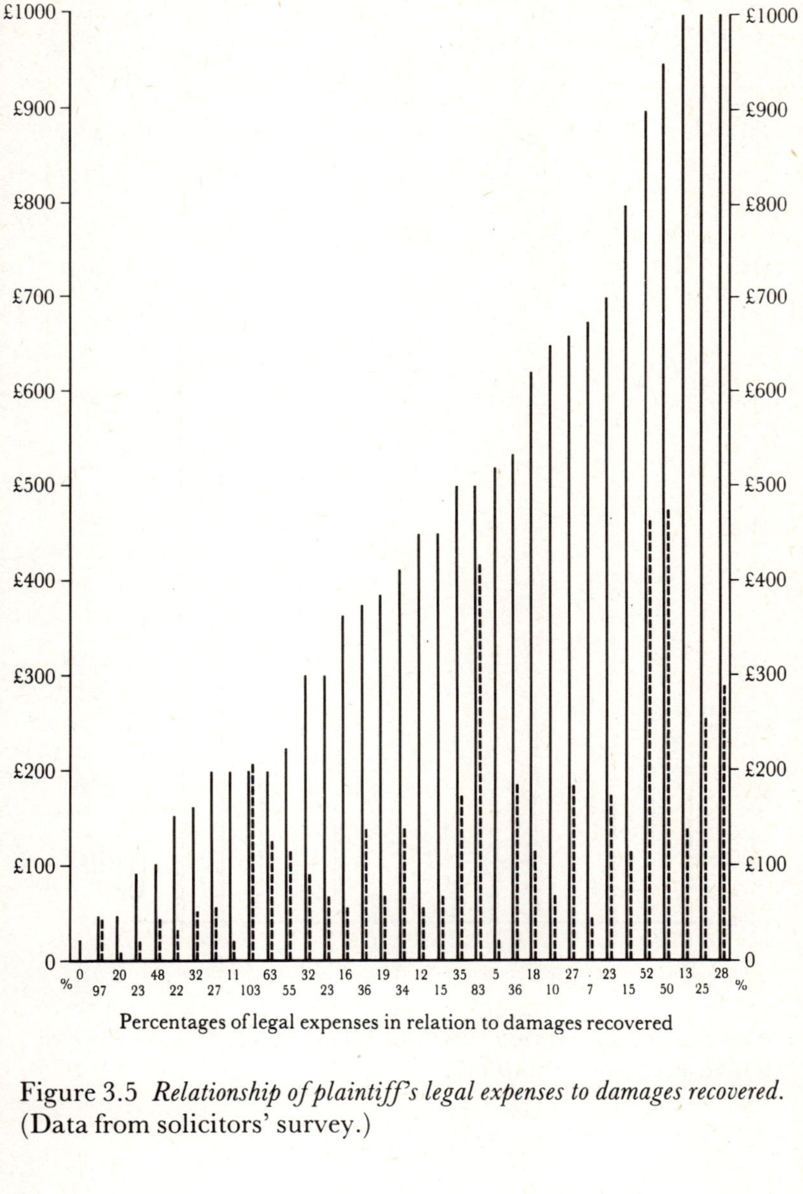

Figure 3.5 *Relationship of plaintiff's legal expenses to damages recovered.* (Data from solicitors' survey.)

B. *Individual settlements over £1000 damages.* (Damages shown in unbroken lines, and plaintiff's legal expenses in broken lines.)

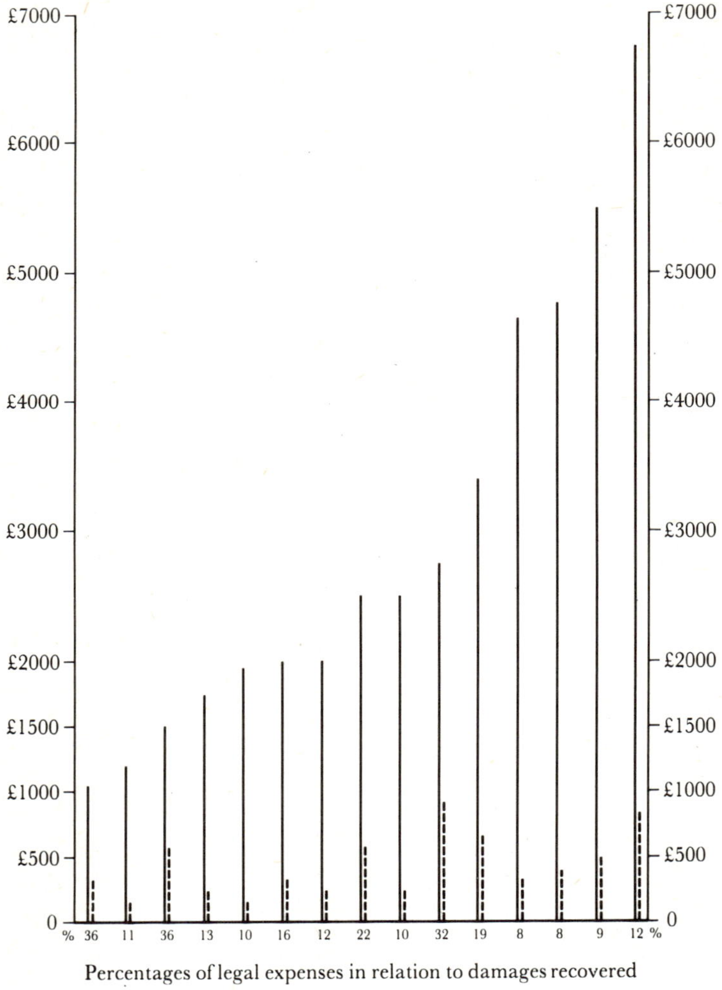

Figure 3.5 *Relationship of plaintiff's legal expenses to damages recovered.* (Data from solicitors' survey.)

applications for legal aid were made: the fifty-one solicitors reported that applications were made in only eight cases, of which six were successful. (In their interviews, most victims were unclear whether such an application had been made in their case.[26]) We infer from our data that the major explanation for the paucity of applications for legal aid is that plaintiffs' solicitors confidently expect that some settlement will be reached in the vast majority[27] of claims, and that, as part of the settlement, the insurance company will pay their expenses. Solicitors may also be deterred from using the legal aid scheme by the form filling which is required, by the delay caused (the average delay between the application and the decision of the Legal Aid Committee in the eight cases in our sample was just under seven weeks), and by the lower fees which are payable under the scheme.

In fifty cases in the solicitors' survey, details were supplied about the plaintiff's legal expenses (no survey was conducted of defendants' insurance companies' legal or other expenses). The mean (average) total legal expenses on the plaintiff's side were £220, which is 18 per cent of the mean amount received as damages in those cases.[28] There is, however, an important contrast between the smaller and larger cases: where the damages did not exceed £1,000 (Figure 3.5A), the plaintiff's legal expenses averaged just under 29 per cent of the damages; whereas for cases of damages over £1,000 (Figure 3.5B), the expenses averaged only 15 per cent of the damages. There is a significant reduction in the larger cases: although the average expenses for damages of £1,000 or over was 15 per cent, for half of those cases the percentage of expenses was between 8 per cent and 12 per cent, which became the regular range for expenses at the top of the damages range (cases over £4,500). These findings confirm that solicitors are charging for work done, and are not charging a regular percentage of the amount recovered. Thus, for the larger claims settled out of court, the legal expenses of the claimant in England, viewed as a percentage of damages recovered, are only about one-third of what they would be under the American contingency fee system, but for the smaller (and commoner) cases, the claimants' legal expenses in England average out not far below the typical American percentage.

In Figure 3.5A and B, the total legal expenses on the plaintiff's side are shown in comparison with the amount of damages recovered in the fifty cases where details of legal expenses were given. The wide variation in expenses is probably explained largely by the different amounts of work involved: each case is unique, with its own problems of evidence, of conflicting medical reports, and so forth. In a quarter of the cases in Figure 3.5A where the damages were under £1,000, the plaintiff's legal expenses were 48 per cent or more of the damages; but in only one small case did they actually exceed the amount of damages (£200). If the reasonable assumption is made that the amount of work on the defendant's side (including the work done by the staff of insurance companies) is approximately the same as that on the plaintiff's side, and that the cost is similar, the total 'legal' expenses on both sides are likely to be approximately twice the percentages shown in this Figure. On the basis of 1972 data, the Pearson Royal Commission estimated that the total cost of operating the tort system, including insurers' own costs, was 87 per cent of the total damages paid out as compensation under the system (Pearson, 1978, Table 158). The policy-maker must decide whether the alleged advantages of the present tort system justify the cost of operating it, especially in the smaller cases.

In just over half the cases where details were given of legal expenses, a fee paid to counsel (viz. a barrister consulted by the solicitor for specialist advice about the case) was an item. The average fee paid to counsel, however, was only £42, compared with the average solicitor's fee (as distinct from other expenses) of £163. It is clear from this, and other data in the survey, that the bulk of the legal work in advising claimants and negotiating out-of-court settlements is done by solicitors.

A final point concerns the information given to the client. Our survey produced only four cases where the successful claimant said that he knew the total *amount* of legal expenses charged by his solicitors: claims for legal expenses were normally made direct to the defendant's insurance company and settled without reference to the client. It is not a professional obligation of a solicitor to disclose to his client the amount of his fees or of the total legal expenses in cases where they are met by a third party (Law Society, 1974; Lund, 1960).

(7) Conclusions

The overall picture provided by the survey data, and especially by the explanations for their actions given by accident victims and their advisers, may be likened to a compulsory, long-distance obstacle race. The victims, without their consent, are placed at the starting line, and told that if they complete the whole course, the umpire at the finishing line will compel the race-promoters to give them a prize; the amount of the prize, however, must remain uncertain until the last moment because the umpire has discretion to fix it individually for each finisher. None of the runners is told the distance he must cover to complete the course, nor the time it is likely to take. Some of the obstacles in the race are fixed hurdles (rules of law), while others can, without warning, be thrown into the path of a runner by the race-promoters, who obviously have every incentive to restrict the number of runners who can complete the course. As the runners' physical fitness, and their psychological preparedness for the race, varies greatly, the relative difficulty of the obstacles also varies from runner to runner. In view of all the uncertainties, and particularly the difficulties which could be presented by the unknown, future obstacles, many runners drop out of the race at each obstacle; others press on, but are progressively weakened by their exertions. At any stage of the race, the promoters alongside the race-track are permitted to induce a runner to retire from the race in return for an immediate payment, which they fix at a figure less than the prize which they expect to be awarded by the umpire upon completion of the course. After waiting to see how many runners drop out at the early obstacles without any inducement, the promoters begin to tempt the remaining runners with offers of money to retire; the amounts of the offers tend to increase the longer the runner stays in the race. In view of the uncertainties about the remaining obstacles, their ability to finish the course, and the time it might take, most runners accept an offer and retire. The few hardy ones who actually finish may still be disappointed with the prize-money.

Our data show how rarely accident claims reach a full hearing before a judge. Yet the rules of law and procedure seem to have been designed to produce optimal solutions in that rare situation, rather than in the normal situation of out-of-court negotiations. A rule which may be ideal for achieving justice in an individualized decision by a judge is not likely to be ideal for achieving justice in direct negotiations between the parties. The best strategy for the law-maker to meet the former situation may well be to create rules conferring wide discretion on the judge – discretion in assessing the evidence, in deciding what standards of conduct are reasonable, in deciding whether the accident victim was partly at fault (and, if so, in assessing the relative percentage of that fault), in choosing between conflicting medical reports or prognoses, and in quantifying the victim's actual and potential losses on an individual basis. But our data show that these discretionary rules operate harshly upon claimants who negotiate settlements out of court: each discretionary rule produces uncertainty, which, given the unequal bargaining strength of the parties, may in turn lead to a discount in the size of the settlement. Furthermore, the cumulative effect of these uncertainties and discounts is to undermine the apparent objectives of the law, whether compensation for victims, deterrence of potential carelessness, or the conduct of inquests into accidents to encourage preventive measures. If the damages system is to survive, and if nearly all claims are to continue to be settled, we believe that the rules of law and procedure should be re-examined to assess their effect on the relative negotiating strength of the parties. The law-maker may be able to assume that the impartiality of the judge will prevent any inequality between the parties in court, but that protection is lacking when they must normally 'negotiate in the shadow of the law'.[29] Perhaps the law-maker should focus his attention on the 'shadow' cast by the rules, rather than on their judicial application.

Notes

1. The main empirical surveys previously conducted into the process of claiming damages for personal injuries are listed in Note 1 to Chapter 1 above. Except for references to the surveys conducted for the Pearson Report, 1978 (the survey is reported in Vol. 2), space in the notes to this chapter does not permit comparisons to be drawn between the data of the Compensation Survey and the data in those surveys. When comparison is made to the Pearson surveys, however, it should be remembered that:
   (i) the Pearson Personal Injury survey was of a different population: it covered injured people who had been *treated in hospital or by a doctor*, and whose injury had led to at least *four days' incapacity* for work or for other normal activities, such as housework (Vol. 2, paras. 467 *et seq.*: compare the population described in Chapter 1, section 3 of the present volume); (ii) just over one-third of the claims for damages in the Pearson Personal Injury survey were unsettled at the time of their interviews (Vol. 2, para. 393, and Table 86; estimates were made of the expected outcomes: see Note 1 to Table 87). In the survey reported in the present volume, unsettled cases were followed-up for over two years following the original interview: see Note 6 below; and (iii) a survey of solicitors was an important part of the Compensation Survey.
2. Another nine solicitors reported that the relevant file had been destroyed and five that no trace of the client could be found; sixteen requests led to no response, but only three firms of solicitors (covering eight cases) refused to take part in the survey, giving lack of time as their reason.

3. There is an extensive literature on the provision of legal services for dispute resolution: see the bibliography by Wilkinson, 1980, section B of which is on legal services. Studies in the UK include Abel-Smith *et al.*, 1973; Zander, 1978; and those conducted for the Royal Commission on Legal Services, 1980.
4. An empirical study of this category of damages has been conducted in the USA: O'Connell and Simon, 1972. Cf. Pearson Report, Vol. 1, paras. 359–98, 448–64.
5. The Pearson survey found that the average amount for damages paid (at Jan. 1977 prices) was nearly £900 for work injuries, £1080 for motor vehicle injuries, less than £500 for injuries caused by defective products or services, but £2,000 for industrial diseases: Vol. 2, paras. 72, 169, 180, 231, and Table 43. (The insurance claims survey showed an average payment in Nov. 1973 of £566: Vol. 2, Table 102.)
6. Following the further interviews and postal surveys, the final outcome of these fifty-seven claims (at July 1979) was: claims settled, thirty; abandoned, thirteen; still unsettled, five; result unknown (claimants could not be traced, or refused further information) eight; court judgment in defendant's favour, one. (Cf. the estimates of the outcome of unsettled claims made in the Pearson Commission's survey: Vol. 2, Table 87, Note 1.)
7. For the distribution of the amounts of damages paid in the Pearson surveys, see Vol. 2, Tables 13, 108, and 109; and para. 522.
8. The Pearson Commission's survey of insurance claims found that 8.3 per cent of the total amount of damages paid was in respect of future earnings loss: Vol. 2, Table 107 (cf. paras. 43, 44).
9. The Pearson Report (Vol. 2, paras. 69, 519–21, and Tables 107 and 108) found that more than half of the amount paid in tort compensation was for non-pecuniary loss.
10. The percentage (40 per cent) contrasts strongly with the fact (see the text above at Note 8) that in only one of the fifty-one cases was it reported that a future loss of earnings was taken into account: perhaps the effect of reduced earning capacity is underestimated by plaintiffs' solicitors.
11. See Tables 2.12 and 3.12 on the reasons given for not making a claim for damages, or for abandoning a claim: the victim's own fault accounted for one case in seven, taking the data from both Tables together.
12. Confirmation of this interpretation is found in the reasons given by claimants for accepting offers: see section 5 of this chapter (views on the adequacy of damages received), and section 6 (problems etc. between solicitors and clients).
13. Negotiations are conducted against the background of the formal procedure for bringing a claim for damages to court, on which see: Pritchard, 1978; Winn Committee Report, 1968; Cantley Committee Report, 1979; JUSTICE Report, 1966. For a socio-legal bibliography on dispute resolution, see Wilkinson, 1980.
14. In the fifty-eight settled cases where trade unions had been consulted about claiming, the first offer was accepted in 59 per cent of the cases. Cf. the Pearson survey, Vol. 2, paras. 401–2.
15. Another pressure on claimants arises from a rule of procedure which applies when an offer is made by paying the sum offered into court: Zander, 1975b; Phillips and Hawkins, 1976, pp. 506–7.
16. In one case, the solicitor was consulted only ten days before the three year limitation period expired; in another, the delay was due to the solicitor being

consulted only after the claimant's trade union had failed to negotiate a settlement.

17. For the other periods, the distribution between accident categories was fairly equal.
18. The survey data permitted a comparison in some cases between the clients' and the solicitors' accounts of difficulties in negotiations, which, together with the contrast between Tables 3.10 and 3.11, suggested either that the difficulties of negotiating a claim for damages are not fully reported by solicitors to their clients, or, if they are reported, that they are not properly understood or not remembered by clients.
19. Cf. the comments of unsuccessful claimants in the Pearson survey, 1978, Vol. 2, paras. 406–11 (see also Table 90).
20. In six cases, solicitors reported the following reasons for their advice to their clients to abandon claims for damages: lack or conflict of evidence, five (including, in one case, the risk of serious contributory negligence); and delay in consulting the solicitor so that the claim was out of time, one.
21. In a further case, the victim's reason for not claiming was that he was not a member of a union at the time of the accident: 'If I had been in a union, they would have done something for me. That is where I slipped up.'
22. For an explanation of this practice, see the references in Note 15 above.
23. Very few mentioned amounts which had been suggested to them by relatives, friends, or trade union officials.
24. Cf. Pearson Report, 1978, Vol. 2, Table 110 (showing that, according to reports from insurance companies for November 1973, claimants' fees were paid in 76 per cent of cases where damages were paid).
25. Fifteen of those obtaining damages reported that they had paid their solicitors *some* fees out of the damages. (These were *not* cases of legal aid contributions.)
26. In the survey of accident victims, twenty-seven of those who consulted solicitors about making a claim (a total of 247) reported that they had applied for legal aid. Only one application was refused, but three offers of legal aid were not accepted because the applicants thought that the contributions fixed were too high. In eleven cases, those who obtained damages reported that the defendant (or his insurance company) later paid all, or nearly all their legal expenses, so that any legal aid contribution paid by them had been repaid; although other claimants may not have realized the position, it is likely that this result followed in all the successful claims.
27. Where, after obtaining legal advice, victims made no claim or abandoned their claims, most reported that they had themselves paid their solicitors' legal expenses; in two cases it was reported that the victim's trade union had paid them. In several 'no-claim' cases, however, it was reported that solicitors had made no charge for their advice, and in others that they had charged low fees (e.g. £10–20). But in some cases where claims were made and later abandoned, claimants had paid substantial amounts for legal expenses: viz. £100, £150 (two cases), and £331.
28. A survey of insurance companies found that in November 1973 legal and other fees paid to claimants averaged £89, which was 16 per cent of the average amount paid as damages in those cases (£572): Pearson Report, 1978, Vol. 2, Tables 105 and 111. An unpublished survey of four firms of solicitors found that

the average for legal costs in personal injury cases settled in 1975 was £196: Pearson Report, Vol. 2, paras. 91–3 (cf. Zander, 1975a).

29. A phrase coined by Mnookin and Kornhauser (1979).

References

Abel-Smith, B., Zander, M., and Brooke, R., 1973, *Legal Problems and the Citizen*, London: Heinemann.

Cantley Committee, 1979, *Report of the Personal Injuries Litigation Procedure Working Party*, London: HMSO, (Cmnd. 7476).

Ison, T. G., 1967, *The Forensic Lottery*, London: Staples Press.

JUSTICE Committee Report, 1966, *Trial of Motor Accident Cases*, London: Stevens & Sons.

Kemp, D. A. M. and Kemp, M. S., 1982, *The Quantum of Damages* (rev. edn. 2 vols.), London: Sweet & Maxwell.

Latta, G., and Lewis, R., 1974, 'Trade Union Legal Services', XII *British Journal of Industrial Relations* 63.

Law Commission, 1973, *Report on Personal Injury Litigation – Assessment of Damages*, London: HMSO, Law Com. No. 56.

Law Society, 1974, *A Guide to the Professional Conduct of Solicitors*, London: the Law Society.

Lund, Thomas, 1960, *The Professional Conduct and Etiquette of Solicitors*, London: the Law Society.

McGregor, 1980, *Damages* (14th edn.), London: Sweet & Maxwell.

MacKinnon, F. B., 1964, *Contingent Fees for Legal Services*, Chicago: Aldine Publishing Co.

Mnookin, R. H., and Kornhauser, L., 1979, 'Bargaining in the Shadow of the Law', 88 *Yale Law Journal* 950.

Munkman, J. H., 1980, *Damages for Personal Injuries and Death* (6th ed.), London: Butterworths.

O'Connell, Jeffrey, 1971, *The Injury Industry: And the Remedy of No-fault Insurance*, Chicago: Commerce Clearing House.

—— and Simon, Rita James, 1972, *Payment for Pain and Suffering: Who Wants What, When and Why?* Urbana, Ill.: University of Illinois Press.

Pearson, Lord (Chairman), 1978, *Report of the Royal Commission on Civil Liability and Compensation for Personal Injury* (3 vols.), London: HMSO, (Cmnd. 7054).

Phillips, J., and Hawkins, K., 1976, 'Some Economic Aspects of the Settlement Process: A Study of Personal Injury Claims', 39 *Modern Law Review* 497.

Pritchard, J., 1978, *Personal Injuries Litigation* (2nd edn.), London: Oyez Publishing Co.

Rosenthal, D., 1974, *Lawyer and Client: Who's in Charge?* New York: Russell Sage Foundation.

Ross, H. Laurence, 1980, *Settled Out of Court: The Social Process of Insurance Claims Adjustment* (2nd edn.), Chicago: Aldine Publishing Co.

Royal Commission on Legal Services, 1980, London: HMSO, Cmnd. 7648.

Wilkinson, P. J., 1980, *The Social Organisation of Disputes and Dispute Processing and Methods for the Investigation of their Social, Legal and Interactive Properties* (Bibliography in Socio-Legal Studies, No. 1), Oxford: Centre for Socio-Legal Studies, Wolfson College.

Winn Committee, 1968, *Report of the Committee on Personal Injuries Litigation*, London: HMSO, Cmnd. 3691.

Zander, Michael, 1975a, 'Costs of Litigation – a Study in the Queen's Bench Division', *Guardian Gazette*, 25 June, p. 680.

—— 1975b, 'Payment into Court', 125 *New Law Journal* 638 (3 July).

—— 1978, *Legal Services for the Community*, London: Temple Smith.

4 Fault and Liability for Accidents: the Accident Victim's Perspective[1]

Underlying the tort system is the idea, embodied in the fault principle, that it is somehow accepted as a matter of common justice that fault provides grounds for the payment of compensation.[2] This chapter examines this idea in practice by looking at how accident victims attribute fault for their accidents; why they say they did or did not feel that they were entitled to compensation; and how these views relate to their decision to embark on a legal claim for damages. The chapter will show that, contrary to what one might expect, the victim's attribution of fault for the accident does not predict whether he or she takes steps towards claiming damages under the tort system, nor against whom an attempt to claim will be made. This negative conclusion is important not only because it rules out a certain type of explanation of the injured person's 'pre-legal' behaviour, but also because it shows that discussion of the tort system is often predicated on an unrealistic model. The system is frequently discussed in the legal literature and elsewhere as one which shifts the costs of an accident from the victim to the person at fault in accordance with common-sense moral principles. This model of adjusting the relationship between victim and negligent harmdoer is acknowledged to be a fiction in practice, but none the less it underlies many statements and assumptions made in the legal literature and elsewhere about the rationale, functions and impact of the tort system. It underlies, for example, the idea that pursuing a legal claim provides an outlet for the victim's presumed feelings of hostility towards the person to blame for the accident; that a fault system upholds desirable standards of individual behaviour; and that it acts as a deterrent to negligent or dangerous behaviour. If a model of this kind is to provide either a useful understanding of the workings and impact of the tort system, or a useful framework for discussion of the justice of the system in principle, then it must bear some relationship to the operation of the system in practice. It will be argued in this chapter that such a model is too far removed from the complexities and realities of actual cases to serve either of these purposes.

The aim of the chapter is to relate empirical data to certain aspects of legal discussion of the tort system – in particular discussion in terms of common sense morality and the relationship between victim and negligent harmdoer. Before reporting the survey results it is therefore necessary to clarify how the empirical data are relevant to the issues raised in these discussions. The first section of the chapter therefore sets out more specifically how ideas of this sort underlie much discussion of the system, and how they can be set in terms of psychological research and theory. The chapter then presents and discusses data on these questions from the Compensation Survey.

(1) The legal and psychological background

Common sense morality as a base for the tort system

There is no definitive statement of the intended functions and rationale for the tort system of compensation against which the operation and impact of that system in practice can be assessed. It is, however, possible to identify in legal writing, court judgments, and so on, recurrent lines of argument and beliefs of the kind mentioned above. Thus, for example, Williams and Hepple (1976) write: 'At best, English law regards compensation as the expression of a moral principle' (p. 72) and 'Common sense morality suggests that a man who has been negligent ought to pay compensation to those whom he injures' (p. 116). Atiyah (1980) writes: 'If the fault principle has any justification at all, it must be that it rests on some ultimate moral judgments which would be generally acceptable in society today' (p. 475); and Linden's account of tort law as educator includes frequent reference to such ideas as 'common moral values' and 'the traditional moral principles of Anglo-American society' (1977, pp. 12 f.). Judges have frequently claimed that the common law use of concepts of responsibility has its roots in common sense, (see Hart and Honoré, 1961, p. 326; *Barty-King* v. *Ministry of Defence* [1979] 2 All ER 88). The members of the Pearson Commission also imply that the fault principle may be justified by recourse to accepted concepts of justice or common sense morality when they write that 'There is elementary justice in the principle of the tort action that he who has by his fault injured his neighbour should make reparation. The concept of individual responsibility still has value.' (Pearson Report, 1978, p. 65.)

If such statements are to be more than statements of opinion, or restatements of the values embodied in the fault principle and legal definitions of fault, they must imply that abandoning fault as grounds for compensation would in fact run counter to common sense morality or important values held by members of our society. As explanations or justifications of law and legal decisions, they involve empirical claims about the psychological reactions of ordinary people to accidents of the kind covered by the tort system.

Psychological reactions to harmdoing

The idea that the tort system reflects common sense moral principles has in fact been looked at in more psychological terms by lawyers. For example, Williams and Hepple (1976) suggest that, although unprovable as an ethical proposition, the fault principle

> may be attributed not to an eternal principle of justice, but to a psychological reaction of a distinctly human kind. A person who has been wronged feels resentment, and society sympathetically identifies itself with the victim. The resentment of the victim and of society can be appeased by punishment (the criminal sanction) or satisfied by reparation (the civil sanction). (p. 116)

Williams and Hepple thus link the common-sense morality idea with the idea that a system such as the tort system provides an outlet for feelings of hostility generated by the victim's outraged sense of justice at having been wronged. Their suggestion resembles the theoretical framework provided by equity theory in social psychology, which has drawn together much of the empirical research on reactions to wrongdoing and harmdoing. As a testable psychological theory, equity theory leaves much to be desired. None the less formulations of the theory, and work it has generated, provide some important insights of relevance here. Full formulations of the theory are provided by Walster *et al.* (1973) and Austin *et al.* (1976) and aspects of its relevance to law are examined by Macaulay and Walster (1971) and Austin *et al.* (1976).

Equity theory is concerned with the adjustments which are made to restore equity to relationships between people. One such adjustment may be the payment of compensation on grounds of negligence, and the theory is close to the implicit – sometimes explicit – theory of human relationships underlying the tort system and much that is claimed for it. Explanations are offered of the reactions of victims, harmdoers, and outsiders to a perceived inequity in terms of their desire to reduce the distress this induces, by restoring the balance or justifying the imbalance in the relationship between victim and harmdoer. Negligence might be seen as a negative input, entitling the victim to an equivalent increase in positive outcomes in the form of compensation. Methods of restoring equity include punishment and retaliation as well as compensation.

However, in equity theory the norms or values governing what constitutes inequity are seen not as a matter of natural justice, but as a matter of history, custom, and acceptance of the status quo. In common with much psychological theory in the area of morality and justice, equity theory applies a kind of utility maximization analysis to social relationships, and starts from the proposition that individuals seek to maximize their outcomes from relationships, where outcomes are rewards minus costs. Rewards and costs here may be psychological as well as material or social. It may, for instance, be psychologically costly to act in a way which conflicts with one's own sense of justice. Norms of fair behaviour evolve and are enforced in a community because this can maximize overall outcomes, and they come to feel right through various processes of socialization so that their violation is in some way distressing. Most explanations of 'morality' in research on reactions to wrongdoing and harmdoing, whether or not carried out within equity theory, similarly involve some form of social learning theory, so that 'morality' is explained in terms of conformity to cultural norms learned by social reinforcement, modelling, and other socialization processes (e.g. Berkowitz, 1972; Walster *et al.*, 1973). Lerner (1977) provides a critical review of the major models and theories. Conformity to internalized norms can seem morally right, with implications for the individual's self-esteem and sense of moral goodness.

It seems rather doubtful whether a feeling of moral rightness acquired in this way could provide much justification for a system of compensation. A number of writers on equity theory have warned against equating what is 'accepted' with what is in some sense 'natural', and have shown how vigorously-defended norms can be dysfunctional, exploitative, and discriminatory, and how they vary substantially from one culture to another, and from one context to another within the same society (Sampson, 1975; Deutsch, 1975; Walster and Walster, 1975). It is worth noting that one factor influencing what will be seen as fair in a particular context is the cost of applying strictly equitable norms. Such norms are frequently abandoned in everyday life in favour of norms simpler and less costly to apply, and such solutions are accepted as perfectly just. Abandoning the tort system on grounds of cost may have a greater claim to accord with 'common sense morality' than does retaining it.

There is, admittedly, something unsatisfactory about reducing just or moral behaviour to the outcome of weighing costs and benefits, and reducing moral principles to norms to which certain kinds of costs and rewards have come to be attached through socialization. Socialization must, however, remain an important element in alternative theories, to account for the fact that what is defined as just and deserved in one culture can be seen as cruelly unjust in another. The exact source of motivation to act according to cultural norms, feelings of guilt, and so on, is of less importance here than the fact that what specifically constitutes justice and elicits such feelings is both learned and variable.

To draw on common sense morality thus seems potentially to be at best a weak justification of the tort system as reinforcing or perpetuating norms on the grounds that they have come to be accepted and perhaps that a change would not be well received. Questions about the origins and effects in practice of such norms would appear to be more relevant than whether or not they are currently accepted.

Before even this weak justification can have any substance one needs to know whether the equity norms embodied in the system are in fact widely held. Almost any system could be justified on the very general grounds that norms of equity are often applied in our society. Whether or not the fault principle reflects psychological reaction to inequity is almost wholly irrelevant if law and the ordinary citizen define inequity differently, or if meeting needs irrespective of fault is seen as the proper primary aim of any accident compensation system. In other words, are the kinds of accident cases covered by tort in fact instances of the kind of relationship which elicits these reactions?

Some attempts have been made to explore this empirically in relation to compensation through surveys (see, e.g., O'Connell and Wilson, 1970). There seems to be rather little evidence that, when asked, people actually do express consensus support for a fault-based compensation system. It seems to depend rather on who is asked and how the question is put. Differences in replies to survey questionnaires have been found to relate to whether or not the respondent has been injured, and how seriously (Linden, 1965; US

Dept. of Transportation, 1970); how great his economic losses have been (Linden, 1965); and whether or not he has recovered under tort (US Dept. of Transportation, 1970). Different replies have also been elicited when the question is put as a choice between fault and no-fault rather than for or against fault, and when the possibility that a no-fault system would be cheaper is presented (US Dept. of Transportation, 1970). These results relate to the USA and Canada. Atiyah (1980, p. 476) quotes evidence that in England the ordinary man, particularly the victim, does not easily accept that damages are dependent on fault. As well as lack of consensus, which makes generalizations about popular views difficult, many methodological problems are involved, and it is not always clear how replies are to be interpreted. Can they be said to be a measure of people's moral principles? The kinds of study described above probably tell us something about people's willingness to accept the status quo and the effect of experience on this, and the ease with which different replies are elicited according to the way alternatives are presented. They may provide encouragement to believe that the public could be won over, at least eventually, to a no-fault system. But overall Atiyah's conclusion seems justified, that the results of such surveys have not been particularly helpful in deciding what popular justice demands.

It is in any case not enough simply to ask people whether they agree in principle with basing compensation on fault. Their replies may give little indication of how they would react to a specific case. Moreover, there will be a number of different perspectives on the same accident. The victim, others involved in the accident, and outsiders, may define the situation differently, making different norms relevant, and may disagree about the justice of a particular outcome. Indeed, equity theory emphasizes that individuals' distress at inequity is a reaction of their *subjective* evaluation, not some objective definition of a relationship; and that conflicting definitions are to be expected. Furthermore, reactions to an actual accident in which they were themselves involved may differ from what people say they would regard as fair in a specific, but hypothetical, case.

This potential for conflicting definitions of an event, and consequent disagreement over what is a just outcome, arises from the fact that the same set of circumstances can provide grounds for a range of interpretations and attributions of causes, fault, and liability, depending on the individual's motives and the context. What constitutes an acceptable and adequate explanation of an event, or attribution of cause, responsibility, or liability, is a function of the social context in which the question arises. Furthermore, in any given context there may still be some leeway for an individual to adopt a particular point of view which is more advantageous – materially or otherwise. Context is usually given little, if any, consideration in legal discussion of the concepts of cause and responsibility, and motives even less, although Collingwood gives the individual's point of view central importance when he writes that 'for any given person the cause of a given thing is that one of its conditions which he is able to produce or prevent' (1961, p. 303). In his example, we can expect different causes for an accident to be assigned by the driver (his driving), the county surveyor (the road) and the vehicle manufacturer (the car design). When each is threatened with sanctions, however, one might expect a shift in orientation to a defensive one, and a consequent shift in perceived responsibility, while the injured victim interested in compensation might interpret events in such a way as to attribute responsibility to the most likely source.

Much of the psychological literature on the attribution of responsibility for harmful events has focused on 'motivational biases' of various kinds, frequently emphasizing that the definition of an event is influenced by what the individual sees as the implications for himself of one definition rather than another. In equity theory, for example, an important element is the idea of 'psychological equity', where people justify inequity or deny that it exists, thus neutralizing the need for any actual adjustment. By convincing themselves as well as others, they avoid feeling distress arising from guilt or conditioned fear. The counterpart to this is making a favourable adjustment appropriate. This need not involve distortion, as is implied in the idea of psychological equity, but may be achieved by defining what has happened in a way which makes relevant the preferred norms. This does not have to be seen as a conscious process, and can be very rapid.

The possibility that there may be several alternative ways of explaining an event and of attributing fault has important implications for the notion that the tort system might serve a deterrent function, and that by leading us to enquire into the causes of accidents, it furthers the goal of accident prevention. A system such as the tort system focuses attention narrowly on a certain cause or causes out of the many causes and conditions which contribute to the event, and concentrates there all the weight of its deterrent function. (It is another question whether nominal liability such as we now have, in practice, where insurance companies are the real defendants, actually amounts to a significant deterrent.) However, it is apparent that the explanation generated by such a system, while it may be appropriate in the context of that system, is not an all-purpose explanation which can serve as the basis for effective accident prevention. It is not even clear that it would be particularly useful or desirable to deter the person found legally liable from acting in the way that made him or her liable. There may be far more effective and less costly ways of minimizing loss from accidents. In structuring people's perceptions of the causes, the tort system may well detract from a broader and more useful understanding of how and why accidents happen and hence how they may be minimized or prevented.

This is not a new observation. The point is made, for instance, by Atiyah (1980), citing research on road accidents. The surface of the road may be a major contributing factor in skidding accidents: laying a special non-skid surface has indeed been shown in accident research to lead to dramatic reductions in the accident rate on a particular stretch of road. But the law diverts attention from such possibilities, by leading us to look for the *person* to blame for each accident, and obscuring the need for measures not directed at the motorist (Atiyah, 1980, p. 459).

While this general point has been made for some years, it seems not to have figured at all prominently in discussions which assume a deterrent function of legal liability to compensate, based on fault. Even Atiyah (who is sceptical about such a function) raises the point in his discussion of the fault principle, and of legal definitions of fault, rather than in his section on the supposed deterrent function of the tort system.

(2) Research questions

The various legal viewpoints discussed above raise a wide range of questions of empirical fact about how people react to accidents. To explore these fully one would need a correspondingly wide range of different sorts of information and could not expect a clear-cut answer. Accident victims' answers to questions about whether they thought anyone should pay them compensation, and on what grounds, are only a part of this, but an important part. It is the victim's resentment with which, according to Williams and Hepple

(1976), society sympathizes, and it is the victim to whom the tort system is supposedly available as a means of redress.

If the possibilities of alternative legitimate attributions of fault, and alternative definitions of relationships, are taken into account, the model of social relationships underlying the tort system becomes much more complex than is usually allowed for by lawyers (or, for that matter, economists). Many factors other than the causes of the accident will govern not only the victim's actions in claiming or not claiming, but also his perceptions of, and feelings about the accident. Such factors may include the prospect of compensation, other aspects of the relationships involved, and the anticipated costs and benefits of various courses of action. Moreover, the victim's motives in claiming cannot be deduced directly from the replies he gives to questions about why he did or did not claim, blame anyone, feel he should be compensated, and so on. This is partly because the answers which can be expected to such questions are governed by a range of social rules and understandings about what would constitute an acceptable response. One would not expect a victim asked, for example, why he blamed someone, to reply that it was because there was a good prospect of compensation – the question would be taken as a question about the *grounds* for attributing blame, and this does not constitute an acceptable ground. Yet this factor needs to be considered as a possible source of *motivation* to blame. As well as this, the answers which will be elicited by such questions are limited to those factors which constitute the victim's present conscious understanding of events. This understanding may have crystallized over time, and been influenced by many factors both before and after the accident, which may not be directly mentioned by the victim, but which must instead be inferred from the pattern of responses across different types of victim and accident. The point is not that the victim is in any way concealing his 'true' reasons, consciously offering rationalizations and justifications for actions which he 'really' preferred for other reasons, but rather that the accident victims' replies cannot be taken as straightforward or full explanations of their feelings and actions.

Bearing these complexities in mind, the analyses presented in the next section will examine the following questions:

1. To what extent does the initiative to explore a potential legal claim arise from the accident victim's sense of justice? In particular, how does the victim's action relate to his or her attributions

of fault and liability, and what factors, in turn, govern these attributions?

2. How far does the victim think of making a claim for damages in terms of adjustments to the relationship between himself/herself and a negligent other party?
3. To what extent is fault perceived as grounds for payment of compensation?
4. On what grounds is fault attributed:
 (i) how does the accident victim's attribution of fault relate to legal definitions of fault? and
 (ii) how does the victim's attribution of fault relate to his or her possible motives in the context?
5. More peripherally, what evidence is there that the present system dispels feelings of hostility and/or serves a deterrent function?

(3) The data used in the analysis

The series of questions asked about fault and the perceived possibility of a claim reflected a possible sequence of reasoning and action which the law implies will be followed by the accident victim. Consideration of the causes of his accident may lead him to an attribution of fault, which implies that the person at fault should compensate him. This in turn leads him to pursue a claim to damages, and an award or settlement may be made.

Since one of the main interests was in the connection or absence of a connection in the mind of the victim between fault and liability to compensate, questions were divided between two different sections of the questionnaire to avoid suggesting a connection, and the legal system was not mentioned until after these 'pre-legal' questions were completed. The interview began with questions about how and where the accident happened, whether it was anyone's fault, and if so in what way (Questions 2–5). A final section of the questionnaire administered perhaps half an hour later was concerned with who the victim thought should compensate him and why (Questions 99–100) and with any legal sequel. Accident victims could drop out of this sequence at a number of points. For example, they might attribute fault but not liability, or they might feel that they should be compensated but not pursue a legal claim. Further questions were asked about reasons for each step, as appropriate.

(4) Results and discussion

The tables in this chapter exclude the minority of cases where the respondent was not the accident victim, but a proxy. This has the effect of excluding accidents to children. Since the conclusions drawn do not relate to rates in the population as a whole, the numbers are unweighted. The tables are thus based on an unweighted total of 1,014 accidents.

Fault as a justification for compensation

Legal discussion generally assumes that, in ordinary thinking, fault implies liability to compensate. This does not, of course, rule out the possibility that there may be other grounds for demanding compensation, though Atiyah's statement of the fault principle includes the statement that someone who is not at fault should not be required to compensate (1980, p. 470). Whatever definition of the fault principle one adopts, it is obviously of relevance to the above arguments both if victims attribute fault without liability, and if victims frequently attribute liability without fault. Table 4.1 shows the relationship between saying that someone was wholly or partly at fault, and saying that someone should pay compensation.

Table 4.1 *Whether anyone else at fault by whether anyone should pay compensation*[1]

Someone else at fault		Someone should compensate Yes n	(%)	No n	(%)	Totals n	(%)
Yes	same person/organisation	201	51	106	17	393	39
	different person/organisation	86	22				
No		105	27	516	83	621	61
Totals		392	100	622	100	1014	100

[1] All percentages are column percentages.

A straightforward cross-tabulation of these would conceal the fact that the person said to be at fault and the person it was said should compensate were by no means always the same. The table therefore further subdivides the category of the person/organization who should pay. It is then clear that of the 392 victims who said that someone should pay them compensation, only 201 had said that the accident was that person's fault. The remainder either blamed no one else (105) or some different person or organization (86). And of the 393 who blamed someone, 192 (106 plus 86) said they did not now or at any time think that person should pay them compensation.

These discrepancies are quite startling. The relationship between 'at fault' and 'should pay' is far from one of equivalence. Nor does the victim's attribution of fault go far towards accounting for whether or not a legal claim is considered and/or initiated (see Table 4.2). Table 4.2 shows the interrelationships amongst attributing fault, attributing liability, and taking steps towards a legal claim. Clearly these variables are significantly related, but in complex ways. The results do not support the simple model whereby fault entails liability, and this leads to steps towards a claim being made. Only 52 per cent of those who took even preliminary steps towards a legal claim said they thought the accident was someone else's fault and that that person should compensate them (Table 4.2).

Table 4.2 *Whether someone else at fault by whether any steps taken towards claiming damages*[1]

	Steps taken[2]				
	Yes		No		Totals
	n	(%)	n	(%)	
Someone else at fault and same person should compensate	151	52	50	7	201
Someone else at fault but not mentioned as person who should compensate	80	27	112	15	192
No one else at fault	61	21	560	78	621
Totals	292	100	722	100	1014

[1] All percentages are column percentages.
[2] i.e. at least one of the following: contacted a lawyer; discussed the possibility of a claim or sought advice from someone else; or someone else did something on victim's behalf before a lawyer was contacted.

Furthermore, as discussed above, it is not possible to assume that where these variables do correspond, it is the fault which always comes first, and the liability, and hence further steps, which follow. Rather,the victim may have the idea, possibly from his awareness of the law, that compensation must be justified by fault, and attribute fault in order to get compensation or to justify having got it. In other words, *the attribution of fault is a justification rather than a motive for seeking damages*. It is, of course, very difficult to prove, but there are clear indications in the pattern of responses from victims that this is what is happening. Where there is a prospect of compensation, the victim attributes fault in a way which justifies his claim. Fault is attributed most often in those accidents where the possibility is likely to occur to the victim, and is attributed to the person most likely to be able to pay – that is, the employer in work accidents and the other driver in road accidents (see Tables 4.3 and 4.4).

Table 4.3 *Type of accident by whether anyone else at fault, and whether anyone should pay compensation*[1]

Type of accident	Someone at fault		Someone should pay		Total number of accidents
	n	%	n	%	
Road	165	67	132	54	246
Work (including road/ industrial combined)	155	38	217	53	409
Other (leisure/sport)	44	24	35	19	184
Domestic	7	4	0	0	142
Assault	19	90	13	62	21
Industrial illness	3	25	5	42	12
Totals	393	39	402	40	1014

[1] All percentages are row percentages.

Table 4.4 *Breakdown of who was said to be at fault*

	n
Other driver	145
Other road user	3
Employer	85
Workmate/colleague/immediate superior at work	40
Child	2
Other individual or group of individuals	74
Organisation/system/corporate body	34
Don't know, not stated	10
Total where someone at fault	393

Particularly in the many cases where an employer is blamed for an accident, the employee seems to be thinking in terms of liability to compensate. Both drivers and employers are covered by compulsory liability insurance, and work and road accidents account for the vast majority of legal claims to damages. Table 4.3 shows that fault is attributed most often in work and road accidents. It is rare for anyone to be blamed for domestic accidents, and comparatively rare in leisure and sport accidents, the other main category. This difference between types of accident becomes even more marked when one looks at the data concerning the victim's opinion as to whether anyone should pay compensation, and is carried through in the data on cases where claims were actually made (see Chapter 2).

As well as who is held to be at fault and for what type of accident, there are striking differences between work and road accidents in the *way* in which someone is said to be at fault. Responses were not always easily classified in detail, but there was no difficulty in placing them in the two general categories of interest here: cases where fault is in terms of the immediate causes of the accident (e.g. 'he dropped a hammer on my foot'; 'he pulled out in front of me without looking') and those where fault is in terms of more remote or background factors (e.g. 'they sent two men to do a three-man job'; 'the handrail had not been fixed'; 'the building was in poor repair'). Table 4.5 shows that in road accidents, fault is almost always attributed with reference to immediate causes, whereas in work accidents it is the second, less proximate, more background type of cause which predominates.

To some extent this may simply reflect the way in which accidents happen. Road accidents can be caused by someone doing something careless at the time. Work accidents are often caused by poor management and safety standards, and home and leisure

Table 4.5 *Type of fault by type of accident (work and road only)*

Type of fault	Road accidents		Work accidents	
	n	%	n	%
Careless/negligent act at the time	149	90	31	20
Negligence at another time or place: background conditions	12	7	122	79
Not stated/not codable	4	—	2	—
Total where someone at fault	165		155	

accidents sometimes are 'just accidents'. But this is an inadequate explanation. As already suggested in the first section of this chapter, it seems to be a question of which, if any, out of a range of possible causes and conditions, gets the label 'fault' attached. Again, this appears to be influenced by the prospect of damages. The insured other driver's causal contribution is likely to be an immediate one, while the insured employer's is likely to be more remote.

The impact of legal norms

Another, related factor accounting for these differences in the grounds on which fault is attributed may be the victim's previous or subsequent contact with rules and norms which make a particular interpretation not only potentially more profitable or less costly, but also more available and acceptable to others. Especially where there is some ambiguity or uncertainty, what are seen as the rights and wrongs of a situation are likely to be influenced by the acceptability to others of a particular interpretation (see, e.g., Walster *et al.*, 1973).

The norms available to accident victims, particularly in the case of road and work accidents, and to victims of assaults, are very likely to be legal norms of some kind. Thus, driving is governed by all kinds of legal rules about speed, right of way, and so on, which provide guidelines for establishing who was in the wrong. The police are likely to be called where injury is suffered in a road accident and the account they are looking for will be in terms of who, if anyone, has broken the criminal law, which is likely to be determined by the person's actions at the time of the accident. Thinking someone else was legally in the wrong not only protects the victim against prosecution or damages claims (it is unusual for victims to distinguish between the civil and criminal law), but can also have the added advantage of feeling morally right because these are the rules the victim is used to and which are acceptable to those with whom he has contact.

At work, on the other hand, there is a variety of rule systems with a long historical tradition putting responsibility on the employer for ensuring safety and compensating the injured, moving the emphasis away from 'fault' in the more immediate sense. There are statutory duties, strict and vicarious liability, and other compensation systems, such as industrial injuries compensation, where fault is irrelevant anyway. In 80 per cent of work accidents where someone was said to be at fault, it was in terms of responsibility for safety, good management, and other remote causes and conditions. Moreover, a whole new category of simply being liable *per se* for compensating appears. In forty-seven of the 217 work accidents where the victim said someone should compensate, it was said that the employer should pay simply because the accident happened on his premises or in the course of employment. Even if the victim had not previously thought about the employer's responsibilities in this way, contacts with his fellow employees and trade union after the accident would probably suggest it to him.

As well as this influence of legal rules on when and how fault is attributed, there is some general mixing and confusion of rule systems. Losses arising from accidents may be covered by a variety of systems, such as social security benefits, sick pay schemes, and industrial injuries benefits – besides any tort claim. The criteria for eligibility under these systems are often mixed. Thus one victim of a work accident thought he should get compensation because he had paid his stamp; another because he had been off work six months and therefore qualified (he was in fact claiming under tort). It is hard to argue, therefore, that fault is seen as the proper base for a compensation system. Victims talk about what they feel should happen very much in terms of existing systems, whether or not these are fault based.

The explanations suggested so far of differences in the attribution of fault in different types of accident have concentrated on factors applying to work and road accidents. A rather different type of explanation, which applies more to home and leisure accidents, is the relationship already existing between victim and harmdoer before the accident happened. This returns us to the underlying rationale of the tort system – the adjustment of the relationship between victim and harmdoer.

The relationship between victim and harmdoer

It was suggested in the first section of this chapter that many factors other than the causes of the accident will govern the accident victim's assessment of the 'equity' of a relationship with the person who might, potentially, be sued for damages. The survey data clearly confirm that this is so. The impact of such factors as detrimental effects on existing relationships and other anticipated social or material costs of blaming and claiming is evident throughout the victims' replies.

Attributing fault brings with it potential conflict which people may prefer to avoid altogether rather than resolve. Blaming, holding people liable, and pursuing a legal claim will obviously have different sorts of impact on relationships between friends, family members, employer and employee, fellow employees, and those who were strangers until the accident. Where the costs of blaming (including costs usually ignored by economists) are high and the prospects of benefit in the form of compensation remote, accidents tend to be seen as 'just accidents'. Burman *et al.* (1977) show that victims of domestic accidents very rarely sue the person they blame. The data presented here suggest that most potential legal cases arising from such accidents are filtered out at an earlier stage, since the victim does not attribute fault in the first place. Even accidents at work are seen far more often as the fault of the employer than of a fellow employee, although either could provide grounds for a claim against the insured employer.

Accident victims themselves mention these kinds of considerations when they give reasons for saying that someone at fault should not pay them compensation and for not pursuing what they thought might be a legal claim (see Chapter 2 for further analysis of these replies). The victim may appreciate that the person at fault could be thought liable, but prefers not to take this view because he or she is a friend, neighbour, or family member. Taking legal action is seen as a rather nasty, vindictive thing to do. As one victim put it, 'I didn't want blood money'. Another said she would not 'do something like that – though an American probably would'. A number were worried about causing trouble with their employers. In fact, there were cases where employers were obstructive and even threatened to sack or blacklist employees who claimed, or gave evidence against them. It has been suggested (e.g. by Ehrenzweig, 1953; and Linden, 1977) that vindicating the angry victim can be one function of the tort system. The idea that pursuing a legal claim has some kind of cathartic effect appears anyway to be rather doubtful, in the light of research on aggression. The results here suggest that taking legal action is indeed a way of getting back at the person at fault but that this prevents the system from working rather than gives it added advantages. Vindication and/or punishment as well as compensation is overdoing it and creates a new inequity in the opposite direction.

There are two further points to be made on the basis of the data, concerning the simple model of adjustment to the 'negligence –

harm' relationship between victim and harmdoer. First, it is evident that fault, even where attributed, does not necessarily create a relationship where the payment of compensation is an appropriate consequence. Second, it is evident that the victim not only does not decide to claim on this basis: he does not even see what he is doing in claiming, primarily in terms of this kind of adjustment.

Reasons given for not thinking that the person said to be at fault should compensate provide examples of the first point. Fault and liability simply do not coincide. Sometimes payment of money is inappropriate because there was no financial loss. Or the other person may have already 'paid' in some other way: he may have been very upset, prosecuted, or trying to help. Punishing the person or making sure it does not happen again may be seen as more appropriate than compensation. Sometimes the type of fault is not of the appropriate kind – e.g., 'He couldn't really help it', 'You couldn't blame him,' 'He didn't mean to do it', or even 'It was just an accident.' This apparent ambivalence over fault and blame need not mean that the respondents, or the principles they are applying, are confused, but rather that these principles are complex and flexible, depending on the context and anticipated consequences. These respondents may be acknowledging that fault can provide grounds for compensation, but not in their particular case.

This has implications for comparisons between legal and non-legal or everyday concepts of fault and liability. Atiyah (1980) regards it as relevant to compare the circumstances in which someone could be legally liable to compensate with a whole range of ways in which someone might be morally blamed. This follows from his conclusion that justifying the fault principle as a moral principle means restating it in terms of moral guilt or innocence, the morally guilty party paying for any loss or damage for which he is responsible. However, there may be several different reasons for making judgments of moral guilt, not all of which necessarily provide grounds for requiring compensation to be paid. Furthermore, as Atiyah goes on to mention, there may be circumstances when justice requires the payment of compensation without moral fault or blameworthiness. As already mentioned, the results here show that fault is not seen as a necessary basis for compensation. Table 4.6 shows further that 'fault' by no means always implies 'moral blame'. Of the 393 who said someone else was at fault, eighty-seven said that person was not morally to blame. Of the 306 who did say that person was morally to blame, sixty-four said they felt some

Table 4.6 *Whether person at fault was morally to blame by whether compensation should be paid*[1]

Person at fault morally to blame		Compensation should be paid: Yes n	(%)	No n	(%)	Totals
Yes	same person	180	59	62	20	306
	different person	64	21			
No		43	49	44	51	87
Total where someone else said to be at fault		287		106		393

[1] All percentages are row percentages.

other person or organization should pay compensation. There may be a danger, therefore, of mixing closely related, perhaps overlapping, but different purposes. If the fault principle is to be justified by comparison with common sense morality it must be compared with what people feel is the just thing to do about *compensation*. To compare the law with everyday attributions of fault or moral blame ignores the fact that such judgments are not all-purpose, but are geared to the social context in which they are made.

The second point is concerned more with the impact of legal structures and procedures on the relationship the tort system is supposedly adjusting. Victims' replies quoted above have already illustrated how the ideas of vindication and punishment as supplementary functions of the system seem to be misconceived. In addition, the accident victim's conceptualization of his decision whether to pursue a legal case seems to be based not so much on what he sees as the justice of the situation as on the balance between the anticipated expense, trouble, upset, and uncertainties of claiming on the one hand, and the prospect of compensation on the other. Some of the costs of claiming are, as already mentioned, its damaging effects on the victim's relationships with the other party, but most costs (financial and otherwise) mentioned by victims who got as far as considering a claim, arise out of the legal process itself. Moreover, it is not always clear with whom the victim sees a relationship when he starts to think about claiming for damages. Thus it may be the insurance company that he thinks of as liable; the law, or, as one put it, 'the legal swindle' as the source of difficulties and expense; and the person at fault as the target of vindictiveness.

In practice, of course, the notion of the law as impartial outsider intervening to restore or adjust the relationship between victim and harmdoer breaks down. The main relationship becomes one of explicit bargaining between insurance companies, lawyers, and other representatives of the parties, according to their own rules (see, for example, Phillips and Hawkins, 1976; Ross, 1980).

The accident victim's 'initiative'

Although the initiative in making a legal claim usually must come from the accident victim, there is little evidence that he takes this initiative or pursues it on the basis of what common sense morality tells him are his rights. The victim often appears not to have his own independent, strong feelings about what should happen – he simply does not really know. In particular, he has no idea how much money he should get. Questions asked of victims who did pursue a legal claim confirm that the idea of making a claim often comes from someone else, and that the amount of damages they hope to receive is determined by others (see Chapters 2 and 3).

It is not just that the victim does not know his legal rights or how much he *could* receive. In a situation which is unfamiliar, he lacks specific norms of his own and does not feel competent to generate them for himself from more general principles, because there is a range of possibilities. What he *feels* is, therefore, often largely the result of what his lawyer, trade union, the police, friends, and others have suggested to him since his accident. Having arrived at an account he may then vigorously defend it. It was suggested above that the norms available to the victim at the time of the accident are likely to be legal norms of one sort or another in any case. A more direct impact of the law is seen in cases where the idea that the victim might get compensation is suggested to him by someone else and he relies on experts to interpret and define what has happened to him and what he is entitled to receive.

(5) Conclusions

In this chapter data from the survey have been used to try to assess

(a) how far accident victims' attributions of fault and ideas of justice explain whether a legal claim to damages is initiated, and (b) how far victims' reactions to their accidents support the idea that the tort system, either in principle or in practice, is based on common sense morality. Both these questions are predicated on an idealized model of the tort system as shifting the burden of the costs of an accident from the accident victim to the negligent harmdoer. For such a model to fit the reality, the victim's reasoning and action must follow a sequence in which he or she considers the causes and circumstances of the accident and on this basis attributes fault; fault in turn implies liability to compensate; and hence the victim is motivated to initiate a legal claim. The data described suggest that these stages do not occur in this sequence, and that many other factors enter – indeed predominate – in the victim's perspective and decision to make a legal claim. It seems that the interpretation accident victims put on their accidents is not so much an *explanation* of their subsequent actions, as itself the *outcome* of a rather complex process. The present data obviously cannot provide the basis for a definitive account of this process, but, taken together with related research and theory in psychology, they suggest a general pattern which can be summarized as follows.

In attributing fault and applying norms of responsibility to compensate, the victim is influenced by the anticipated consequences for himself of one interpretation rather than another—the actual or psychological costs or benefits. Social norms delimit the range of definitions acceptable to the victim and his social group, and indicate the socially mediated consequences which may follow. Both the social norms available to the victim of an accident and the social outcomes which affect him are likely to have their origins in the law or legal procedures. The influence of moral costs and rewards seems to be minimal compared with the more practical costs and benefits of obtaining compensation or avoiding conflict in relationships, and takes the form of justification of definitions preferred for other reasons.

The evidence suggests that the norms embodied in law do indeed correspond to those often applied by ordinary people. But it seems also that the way in which accident victims attribute fault for their accidents and responsibility for compensating them is a reflection of, rather than reflected in, the law. Comparing legal and everyday concepts of fault and liability thus seems to amount largely to comparing the law with its own somewhat confused reflection, and it is difficult to find anything one would want to call common sense morality which the law could embody. Furthermore, there are several important ways in which responses of victims are in conflict with the general rationale of the tort system. There are clear indications that fault, including moral fault, does not necessarily imply liability and that, where it does, it is probably a justification rather than a reason for claiming damages. The way in which fault is attributed and the decision to make a claim appear to be explained by such factors as, who has contact with the victim after his accident, how realistic is the prospect of damages, and what will be the financial and other costs of pursuing a claim, rather than how the accident was caused (see Chapters 2 and 3).

Since the notion that the tort system adjusts the relationship between victim and harmdoer is a fiction, it is not surprising to discover that the system in practice does not operate as if it were true. The data show that the victim's decision to claim is not related in a simple, direct way to his attributions of fault and liability based on the causes and circumstances of the accident. The relationships created by the accident and its legal and other sequelae are far more complex than this, and victims' actions and reactions need to be understood in a wider and more realistic context. Far from feeling that the law is backing him in what he sees as his moral rights, the accident victim involved in a legal claim seems frequently to feel confused, anxious, and buffeted by the system.

The results have implications for wider questions than those usually included in discussion of the moral base of the system. Looking at the system in terms of a psychological theory, such as equity theory, shows that questions about the justice of the system in principle are not altogether separable from matters of more clearly empirical fact about the cost, functions, and impact of the system, and the mechanism of change. Thus, for example, the data confirm that vindication and punishment are alternative ways of restoring equity, and may be a drawback rather than an incidental bonus to the present system. And a simpler, cheaper system may be more readily accepted as just than a complex, costly but more strictly equitable one. Added to this, the system encourages and, once invoked, perpetuates and quite probably deepens a conflict. Legal procedures tend to encourage the harmdoer to minimize, and the victim to maximize, the extent of inequity in their relationship. The system cannot even be claimed to uphold the standards of behaviour embodied in the fault principle. As Macaulay and

Walster (1971) point out, the defendant is in practice encouraged not to accept responsibility and pay compensation, but rather to deny responsibility and refuse to pay anything at all. It is widely recognized that the process of pursuing a legal claim can be extremely distressing for the victim and that physical recovery can be delayed while litigation continues (see, e.g. O'Connell, 1975, pp. 114–15). However, the evidence that the present system is divisive, and creates more hostility than it dispels, does not seem to have been given serious enough consideration. The above results may also be of relevance to the supposed deterrent function of tort, which seems plausible, since fault is concerned with the causes of accidents. The results show that attributions of fault are very much geared to the context, so that attributing fault for the purposes of compensation and examining causes for the purpose of accident prevention are indeed, as suggested earlier, likely to be quite different matters (cf. Atiyah, 1980, pp. 494 f.).

A costly, inefficient system based on dysfunctional norms can justifiably be changed. Such a change might meet with some resistance, partly because the status quo, by virtue of being the status quo, seems right, and partly because some people benefit from it. Resistance from trade unions, insurance companies, and sections of the legal profession can be seen to reflect various vested interests rather than an outraged sense of justice. However, looking at the responses of accident victims, it is by no means clear that the kinds of principles threatened here would be what one would want to call moral principles of any special status. The data suggest that victims' reactions would soon reflect a new system. It would be interesting to see what happens to attributions of fault in such circumstances.

Notes

1. Some of the data and discussions in this chapter were presented in an earlier publication, Lloyd-Bostock, 1979. The numbers reported in the analyses presented here differ slightly from those in the earlier publication. This is partly because the data have been re-analysed to exclude proxy respondents, and partly because finer categorizations have been employed since the initial analyses. The differences in no way affect the conclusions drawn.
2. The main alternative might be a version of the theory of market deterrence, which sees the aim of the law as to provide an incentive to keep activities safe by

placing the costs of accidents on the people and activities which cause them. However, this kind of economic analysis of the law does not exclude there being other important goals in accident compensation including 'justice' (see e.g., Calabresi, 1970; Shavell, 1980).

References

Atiyah, P. S., 1980, *Accidents, Compensation and the Law* (3rd edn.), London: Weidenfeld & Nicolson.

Austin, W., Walster, E. and Utne, M., 1976, 'Equity and the Law: the Effect of a Harmdoer's "Suffering in the Act" on Liking and Assigned Punishment', in Berkowitz, L. and Walster, E., eds, *Advances in Experimental Social Psychology* Vol. 9, p. 163, New York: Academic Press.

Berkowitz, L., 1972, 'Social Norms, Feelings and other Factors affecting Helping and Altruism', in Berkowitz, L., ed, *Advances in Experimental Social Psychology*, Vol. 6, New York: Academic Press.

Burman, S. B., Genn, H. G., and Lyons, J., 1977, 'Pilot Study of the Use of Legal Services by Victims of Accidents in the Home', 40 *Modern Law Review*, 47.

Calabresi, G., 1970, *The Costs of Accidents: A Legal and Economic Analysis*, New Haven, Connecticut: Yale University Press.

Collingwood, R. G., 1938, 'On the So-called Idea of Causation', reprinted in Morris, H., ed., *Freedom and Responsibility* (1961), p. 303, Stanford: Stanford University Press.

Deutsch, M., 1975, 'Equity, Equality and Need: What Determines Which Value will be used as the Basis of Distributive Justice?', 26 *Journal of Social Issues*, 137.

Ehrenzweig, A., 1953, 'A Psychoanalysis of Negligence', 40 *Northwestern University Law Review*, 855.

Hart, H. L. A., and Honoré, A. M., 1961, 'Causation in the Law' reprinted in Morris, H., ed., *Freedom and Responsibility*, p. 325, Stanford: Stanford University Press.

Lerner, M. J., 1977, 'The Justice Motive: Some Hypotheses as to its Origins and Forms', 45 *Journal of Personality*, 1.

Linden, A. M., 1965, *Report of the Osgoode Hall Study on Compensation for Victims of Automobile Accidents*, Toronto: Osgoode Hall Law School.

——, 1977, *Canadian Negligence Law* (2nd edn.), Toronto: Butterworth.

Lloyd-Bostock, S., 1979, 'Commonsense Morality and Accident Compensation', in Farrington, D. P., Hawkins, K., and Lloyd-Bostock, S., eds., *Psychology, Law and Legal Processes*, London: Macmillan.

Macaulay, S., and Walster, E., 1971, 'Legal Structures and Restoring Equity', 27 *Journal of Social Issues*, 173.

O'Connell, J., 1975, *Ending Insult to Injury*, Urbana, Ill.: University of Illinois Press.

——, and Wilson, W., 1970, 'Public Opinion on No-fault Auto-Insurance: A Survey of the Surveys', 8 *Illinois Law Forum*, 307.

Pearson, Lord (Chairman), 1978, *Report of the Royal Commission on Civil Liability and Compensation for Personal Injury* (3 vols.) London: HMSO (Cmnd. 7054).

Phillips, J., and Hawkins, K., 1976, 'Some Economic Aspects of the Settlement Process: A Study of Personal Injury Claims', 39 *Modern Law Review*, 497.

Ross, H. Laurence, 1980, *Settled Out of Court: The Social Process of Insurance Claims Adjustment*, Chicago: Aldine.

Sampson, E. E., 1975, 'On Justice as Equality', 31 *Journal of Social Issues* 45.

Shavell, S., 1980, 'Analysis of Causation and the Scope of Liability in the Law of Torts', 9 *Journal of Legal Studies* 463.

US Department of Transportation, 1970, 'The Economic Consequences of Automobile Accident Injuries: Public Attitudes Supplement', in the *Automobile Insurance and Compensation Study*, Washington, DC: US Government Printing Office.

Walster, E., Berscheid, E., and Walster, G. W., 1973, 'New Directions in Equity Research', 25 *Journal of Personality and Social Psychology* 151.

Walster, E., and Walster, G. W., 1975, 'Equity and Social Justice', 31 *Journal of Social Issues*, 21.

Williams G., and Hepple, B. A., 1976, *Foundations of the Law of Tort*, London: Butterworths.

PART II OTHER SYSTEMS OF COMPENSATION AND SUPPORT

5 Social Security

(1) Benefits available[1]

The cash benefits payable by the Department of Health and Social Security to those suffering from a disability, as defined for the purposes of the Compensation Survey, have been developed at different times and for different purposes. Reference has already been made to the objectives of the various benefits (see above, Chapter 1, p. 21). In this section we look in more detail at their impact on compensation for illness and injury and at their administration. One group of benefits is payable under the *contributory* social security scheme (formerly known as National Insurance) which was first established in 1911. A second group is available under the *industrial injuries scheme* (which replaced Workmen's Compensation in 1948) for those whose injury or sickness resulted from their employment. A third group comprises those *non-contributory* benefits introduced between 1970 and 1977 for disabled persons with special needs. There are, finally, the *means-tested* benefits for those whose resources are below a specified level.

(a) Contributory benefits.

These benefits have in common the feature that they are intended to provide some compensation for the loss or interruption of earnings (claimants must thus establish that they are 'incapable of work') and that entitlement is dependent on the fulfilment of contribution conditions. Contrary to some popular misconceptions, this does not mean incapable of performing the claimant's regular work: he must be incapable of 'work which [he] can reasonably be expected to do' (Social Security Act 1975, s. 17(1)(a)). In practice, for the first six months of disability the Department generally demands no more than incapacity to follow his normal occupation. After that period has elapsed he will be expected to undertake other kinds of work for which he is capable. (See Report of the Committee on Abuse of Social Security Benefits, 1973, Cmnd. 5228, Appendix 7, paras. 6–7.) Until 1975 contributions were predominantly on a flat-rate basis. Since that date they have been earnings related: at the time of writing employees contribute 9 per cent of their earnings up to a ceiling, and employers pay an equivalent 11.45 per cent. However, the employers' figure includes a 1% surcharge which is simply a payroll tax. Both employers' and employees' contributions are reduced if the employment is contracted out of the new pensions scheme. The Exchequer contributes about 13 per cent of the fund. *Sickness benefit* is payable for the first six months of incapacity (though not for the first three days): this contains a basic flat-rate weekly payment, plus additions for dependants, and, until 1982, an earnings-related supplement payable after two weeks. After six months of receipt of sickness benefit, a claimant still incapable of work becomes entitled to *invalidity benefit*. No further contribution conditions are imposed as entitlement is based on the fulfilment of the sickness benefit contribution conditions, and the benefit is payable for incapacity lasting until retirement age (60 for women, 65 for men, though in both cases retirement may be deferred for five years). The amounts payable differ significantly from the short-term benefit. The benefit comprises a weekly flat-rate pension and allowances for dependants, both of which are more generous than their sickness benefit counterparts. At the time of the survey no earnings-related supplement was available, but since April 1979 there has been payable under the new state pension scheme an additional component related to pre-disability earnings. Independently of the pension, there is payable an allowance which is a weekly addition, variable according to the age at which the beneficiary became incapable. The younger the claimant at this date, the higher the rate of the allowance. At the time of the survey the relevant age groups were: higher rate, those under 35 when first incapable; middle rate, those between 35 and 45 on that date; lower rate, those over 45 on that date. From April 1979 the age limits for the higher and middle rates were changed to 40 and 50 respectively. The assumption is that a person suffering from the incapacity at an earlier age will have greater financial (e.g. family) needs and will not have had an opportunity himself to accrue savings for retirement or disability. Mention should also be made of the contributory *unemployment benefit*. Though this is intended primarily to deal with loss of earnings which does not result from physical incapacity, nevertheless it might become payable to those who suffered illness or injury within the terms of the survey. This will occur when the illness or injury caused a person to lose his employment but did not render him incapable of work. The contribution conditions and amounts payable are the same as for sickness benefit, but entitlement is limited to a year's interruption of employment. A claimant must also be fit and available for work to qualify. Self-employed persons may be entitled to sickness and invalidity benefits but not to unemployment benefit.

(b) Industrial injury benefits.

The structure of the industrial injury scheme is much more complicated. There are no contribution conditions to be satisfied, though the claimant must have been an 'employed earner' at the time of the accident or disease. Benefits are financed by the National Insurance Fund. The present system replaces one in which there was a separate Industrial Injuries Fund to which employers and employees contributed on a flat-rate basis (see Ogus and Barendt, 1982, p. 261). Under both old and new arrangements there has thus been no attempt to relate contributions to the safety record of enterprises or industries, notwithstanding arguments by Beveridge, (1942, p. 88) and others (Calabresi, 1970; Phillips, 1976) that such premium-rating was desirable on the grounds of incentives and to avoid price distortion. The Royal Commission on Civil Liability rejected differentiation on the grounds of administrative cost (Pearson Report, 1978, para. 802). The claimant's incapacity or loss of faculty must have resulted from an accident 'arising out of and in the course of employment' or from a disease[2] which was prescribed in relation to that employment. Until it was abolished in 1983, the short-term *injury benefit* was payable for the first six months of incapacity for work and was analogous to sickness benefit (which, from 1983, will replace it; previously, however, those suffering from pneumoconiosis or byssinosis were only entitled to industrial disablement benefit). It comprised a flat-rate weekly benefit, slightly higher than that payable for sickness, plus dependency allowances. Strictly speaking no earnings-related supplement was payable, but a beneficiary qualified for the supplement to a sickness benefit if he satisfied the contribution conditions for that benefit. The long-term *disablement benefit* involves a very different principle. It is payable for loss of faculty resulting from an industrial accident or disease and need not be accompanied by any loss of earnings. (Payment could not, however, be combined with injury benefit so that, in the ordinary case, entitlement to disablement benefit accrued only when the six-month period of injury benefit had elapsed or the claimant had returned to work, albeit with a continuing loss of faculty; from 1983, entitlement arises after thirteen weeks). The degree of disablement resulting from the loss of faculty is determined by a medical board with the aid of a statutory tariff which prescribes percentages (up to 100 per cent) for different conditions objectively determined but on a somewhat arbitrary basis. Disablement benefit comprises a lump sum gratuity for assessments of 19 per cent or less, or a weekly pension on a sliding scale from 20 to 100 per cent. The disablement benefit can be accumulated with sickness, invalidity, or unemployment benefit. In addition there are a number of allowances which may be paid with disablement benefit. A special hardship allowance is payable to those who have returned to work but at lower earnings than previously. The allowance comprises a weekly sum representing this loss to a statutory maximum. It is, currently, the only benefit payable under our social security system for partial loss of earnings. An unemployability supplement is payable to those rendered permanently incapable of work: it is equivalent to the invalidity benefit intended for those who do not qualify for that benefit and involves a weekly flat-rate sum, a dependency benefit, and an allowance payable on the same basis as the invalidity allowance. The remaining increases are payable to those severely disabled to provide assistance for their assumed additional needs: the constant attendance allowance for those with a disablement of 100 per cent and who need constant care and attendance, is paid at two fixed rates depending on the severity of the case; the exceptionally severe disablement allowance to those in receipt of the constant attendance allowance and where the need for the attendance is likely to be permanent; and the hospital treatment allowance for those receiving treatment for the injury or disease in a hospital, which regards the claimant as if he were suffering from a 100 per cent disablement for the period of inpatient treatment.

(c) Non-contributory benefits.

During the period 1970–7 successive governments introduced new non-contributory benefits financed from general taxation to assist those who either did not qualify under the above schemes or whose needs were particularly acute. The *non-contributory invalidity pension* is payable to persons incapable of work for a minimum of six months and who do not qualify for the contributory invalidity pension. The flat-rate pension and dependency additions are payable at two-thirds of the rate of the contributory pension; there is no entitlement to the invalidity allowance, and benefits under the new pension scheme will not be payable. From November 1977 a new form of this pension was introduced for housewives incapable of performing normal household duties: the benefit was not available at the time of the Compensation Survey. The *attendance allowance* is payable on terms similar to but not identical with those giving rise to entitlement to the equivalent benefit under the industrial scheme. For the higher of the two rates payable the claimant must be in need of continual or repeated attention during both the day and the night. The statutory criteria are complex and have led to problems of interpretation (see Carson, 1975). The *mobility allowance* was introduced shortly before the Survey and at that time covered persons aged 15 to 50. It is a flat-rate weekly sum paid to those unable or virtually unable to walk.

(d) Means-tested benefits.

The remaining two benefits are part of the general social security provisions for those with inadequate resources and, like those in the previous category, are financed by the Exchequer. *Supplementary benefit* is paid to those not in full-time employment. With certain exceptions (e.g. where there are domestic responsibilities), the claimant must either register as being available for full-time employment or else satisfy the authorities that he is incapable of work. The administrative controls on entitlement therefore closely mirror those for unemployment and sickness benefits. *Family income supplement* is paid to a person in full-time work who is head of a family with at least one child. In both cases, the amount payable is assessed on the difference between 'requirements', a notional figure prescribed for families of different sizes and ages, and the actual resources of the claimant. These resources include the benefits described above (except mobility allowance and a part of industrial disablement benefit), so that, in most cases, supplementary benefit is used to 'top up' such other provisions.

(e) Taxation.

The interrelation of tax and social security is important but complex, not least because of the failure of successive governments to rationalize its implications or to deal consistently with policy objectives (Atkinson, 1975). Two different issues call for discussion here: the tax system itself as a welfare instrument; and the liability to pay tax on the receipt of social security benefits.

The tax system itself may constitute a means of welfare to the extent that it allows individuals some relief or allowance to be set off against their tax liabilities. However, it is not consistent with generally accepted distributional objectives since it is regressive in its effect. Only those benefit who are liable to tax and the value of the relief increases as the rate of tax increases. Not surprisingly, therefore, it plays a minor role in the income support of victims of illness and injury. A blind person is entitled to a deduction from taxable income (currently of £360 per annum) though the figure is reduced by any tax-free disability payments (see Income and Corporation Taxes Act 1970, ss. 16–18). A taxpayer with a dependent relative who is infirm may claim a deduction of £100. Conversely, and somewhat anachronistically, a taxpayer who is himself infirm and who is thereby compelled to depend on the services of a daughter resident with him may deduct £55.

There are two main arguments for taxing the receipt of social security benefits, or at least some of them. First, like tax reliefs, the value of social security benefits which are not taxable increases progressively with the income of tax-paying beneficiaries, thus giving rise to regressive distribution. Secondly, where the social security payment constitutes a replacement for earnings which are taxable, there is the risk that if benefits are not taxable their recipients may be better off out of work than when employed, thus giving rise to the problem of work incentives and the 'poverty trap' (see Tiley, 1978; Houghton, 1967; Ogus and Barendt, 1982). These arguments are difficult to repudiate but there are political obstacles to their implementation. No government likes to be seen to be 'taxing the sick' (Houghton, 1967, p. 18) and there is no necessary expectation that the funds derived from such a tax will be used to ameliorate the position of the disadvantaged; for example, by raising the general level of benefits.

The history of government attempts to grapple with this problem has produced haphazard and inconsistent results. After the Second World War it was decided that national insurance benefits, including sickness benefit (but anomalously not industrial injury benefit) should be taxed (Finance Act 1946, s. 27(2)). As regards the short-term benefit, this decision was reversed in the 1949 Finance Act mainly because of high administrative costs. Beneficiaries could not be incorporated into the PAYE scheme and thus these often small amounts of tax had to be collected individually and retrospectively. Despite forceful criticism, this position has remained substantially unchanged until recently. Retirement and widows' pensions, however, remained taxable. The new disability benefits introduced by the Social Security Pensions Act 1975 (mobility allowance and the earnings-related component in invalidity pension) were to attract tax liability in the second Finance Act of 1979. Given the aim of integrating occupational coverage (which is taxable) with the state scheme, one can understand the motives behind the inclusion of pensions, but until 1982 there was the anomaly that mobility allowance was taxable but not attendance allowance. As part of its radical reappraisal of the social security system, the present Conservative administration has indicated an intention to tax social security benefits generally but, at the time of writing, such proposals are still at the discussion stage (see DHSS, 1980, para. 5).

(f) Overlap of benefits.

Within social security, the principle of avoiding overlapping is clear, though the rules are sometimes complex. Benefits may be accumulated only to the extent that they serve different purposes. Thus, one basic subsistence benefit (sickness, unemployment, invalidity, or industrial injury benefit) cannot be aggregated with another of the same type but may be augmented by a benefit directed towards a specific need (e.g. attendance or mobility allowance) or one designed to compensate for non-pecuniary losses (industrial disablement benefit). As regards the means-tested benefits directed towards poverty as such, as has been seen, the general rule is that all disability benefits are regarded as resources and therefore effectively deducted from the amount payable, but industrial disablement benefit is only partially taken into account and there is a curious anomaly whereby mobility allowance, but not attendance allowance, is totally ignored.

Social security, apart from the means-tested benefits, gives rise to entitlements independent of other resources. No account is therefore taken of an individual's right to compensation from other sources, whether from private or group insurance, or to damages under a tort claim. Major exceptions exist in relation to unemployment benefit, where account is taken of certain severance and guarantee payments (Ogus and Barendt, 1982, p. 100) but, for no obvious reason, the principle was not extended to sick pay until 1982 (see Chapter 12 below; Reid and Robertson, 1965). Nor, in this latter case, has the National Insurance Fund a subrogated right to recover an idemnity from the defendant. This is in marked contrast to the practice in several European jurisdictions. The British reluctance to admit the principle has typically rested on the administrative cost involved (see Committee on Alternative Remedies, 1946, para. 41; and Pearson Report, 1978, paras. 214, 296–7). It is therefore left to the alternative source to make what adjustment is deemed appropriate in the light of social security entitlement. There is a serious lack of consistency among the various compensation schemes. Private insurance invariably ignores social security entitlement; occupational sick pay and disability schemes often make a deduction but there is no uniformity of approach; criminal injuries compensation deducts in full. The relevant rules for the assessment of damages are complex, inconsistent, and in places obscure. There is a deduction of one half of the value of rights to sickness, invalidity, and the industrial injuries benefits accruing for a maximum of five years; unemployment and supplementary benefit is deducted in full; but the position as regards attendance and mobility allowance remains uncertain.

(2) Benefits obtained

(a) Amounts.

The social security system proved to be the most important source of monetary compensation for the victims of illness or injury interviewed in the Compensation Survey. Some 37.5 per cent of respondents claimed to have received one or more of the social security benefits available to the ill or injured. The mean amount received up to the time of the interview was £731 but the amounts received varied from a few pounds to almost £10,000; the duration of receipts varied from a few weeks to several years. Table 5.1 presents a summary of this variation.

The estimated total amount of social security benefit paid to recipients was £984,244. A breakdown of this amount by the type of benefit (Table 5.2) reveals an important feature of the social security arrangements for victims of illness and injury. An estimated 31 per cent of all receipts are accounted for by means-tested supplementary benefit; this fact indicates the failure of other benefits (which, with the exception of family income supplement and unemployment benefit, were specifically intended for the victims of illness and injury) to maintain incomes at or above the minimum requirements established by the Supplementary Benefits Commission. Relatively insignificant contributions to total receipts were made by attendance allowance, mobility allowance and non-contributory

Table 5.1. *The distribution of total amounts received in social security benefits*

Total amount received up to the time of interview	Number of beneficiaries
(£s)	
Up to 50	179
51–200	255
201–500	133
501–1000	81
1001–1500	41
1501–2000	28
2001–2500	24
2501–10,000	49
Amount unknown	557
Total N̄	1347

invalidity pension; together they account for only 4.2 per cent of total social security receipts by people in the survey.

A substantial majority (62 per cent) of the ill or injured in the Survey did not report the receipt of a social security benefit. The questionnaires of a random subsample of these non-recipients were carefully examined in an attempt to detect biases caused by failure to report benefits which had in fact been received. In three of the thirty-eight cases in the subsample there was prima facie evidence of an entitlement to a relevant benefit. One victim incapable of work during a paid holiday had made no claim, wrongly assuming that he had no entitlement. In two others it was not possible to distinguish failure to claim from failure to report a benefit, if indeed there was a genuine entitlement. In thirty-five cases non-entitlement could be accounted for by factors such as age, employment status, contribution record, incapacity not resulting in time off work, or other readily identifiable factors. For attendance allowance, mobility allowance, supplementary benefit, and industrial disablement benefit the entitlement criteria were applied with a lesser degree of certainty, but we found no evidence of an apparently unsatisfied entitlement or unreported receipt. The biases found in the subsample were judged insufficient to justify a more extensive examination of the questionnaires of respondents reporting no social security receipts. However, the social security estimates of those obtaining benefits must be interpreted with some caution. Given the inherently complex nature of the subject there would certainly be

Table 5.2 *Social security recipients and the mean and total amounts received by the type of benefit*

	Number of recipients*	Mean amount received**	Mean duration of benefit in weeks	Total amount of benefit	Money received for each category as percentage of total social security benefits
		(£s)		(£s)	(%)
Industrial Injury Benefit	237 (92)	192.8	12	45,683	4.6
Disablement Pension	30 (15)	1365.5	408	40,966	4.2
Disablement Lump Sum	76 (7)	199.4	—	15,154	1.5
Sickness Benefit	991 (367)	188.5	13	186,760	19.0
Invalidity Benefit	219 (75)	1441.4	128	315,657	32.1
Unemployment Benefit	81 (16)	416.4	40	33,727	3.4
Supplementary Benefit	192 (76)	1590.0	181	305,272	31.0
Attendance Allowance	46 (8)	551.7	117	25,380	2.6
Mobility Allowance	16 (3)	183.8	37	2,942	0.3
Non-contributory Invalidity Pension	23 (10)	552.3	57	12,703	1.3
				984,244	

* In brackets the number of cases in which the amount of benefit could not be calculated. These cases are included in the number of recipients. The figures for total amount of benefit also include them on the assumption that they obtained the mean amount of the benefit in question.

** Rounded to one decimal point.

mistakes made by respondents. Furthermore, there is a large number of cases in which no calculation of total benefits could be made and these are concentrated among long-term recipients, thus weakening an assumption common in survey research that over a large sample, unknown cases are broadly similar to known cases. Amounts received by those long-term recipients for whom recoveries were computed are in fact underestimates as the method of calculation used could not take proper account of regular increases in benefit levels.

(b) Future entitlements.

The social security benefits reported by respondents were received between the date of the accident or illness and the date of their interview. In comparing social security receipts with other sources of compensation – in particular, damages – it is necessary to allow for the fact that damages paid in a capital sum might include an element of compensation for losses beyond the date of the interview; indeed damages purport to provide compensation for the remainder of the estimated life expectancy of the long-term victim. It was decided to make estimates of the social security benefits which would be received for a corresponding future period by those respondents who were still receiving benefits when they were interviewed at the second stage of the survey.

The questionnaires of those victims who were still in receipt of a social security benefit at the time of the second interview were identified and a subsample (stratified by benefit) was taken. For each selected questionnaire an assessment was made of the period for which the benefit would continue. In many cases this called for a medical prognosis and an estimate of life expectancy; medical advice was obtained on these issues. Future receipts were calculated by multiplying the November 1976 weekly benefit by the number of weeks for which benefit was expected to continue. The result is an estimate of future social security recoveries in November 1976 terms, which ignores future inflation. However, there was one special case – the 1976 rate for mobility allowance was not a good base for the calculation as the benefit was doubled in July 1978; we therefore considered that the 1978 amount deflated to 1976 terms provided a better basis. Those current recipients of benefits for whom an estimate of future benefits was not made were assigned a value equal to the mean of the cases in which an estimate was obtained.

In assessing life expectancy, cases were assigned to one of three categories: normal, normal less 30 per cent, or normal less 60 per cent. The assessments were made on epidemiological criteria and were based on the Registrar General's mortality tables. It was necessary to assess the probability of rehabilitation and recovery and the consequent loss of entitlement to social security benefits. In most cases the probability was very low and was assumed to be zero. For the remainder a probability was assigned which was then multiplied by the estimated lifetime entitlement. No account was taken of labour market conditions in assessing the probability of rehabilitation. Social security benefits are usually discontinued or reduced if a recipient goes into hospital. In some cases an estimate was made of the number of benefit years lost for this reason, taking account of social factors such as the availability of home care in addition to the victim's medical condition. Damages may in theory take account of the risk of a future deterioration in health, but no attempt was made to estimate any future entitlements to social security benefits which might arise from such a deterioration. The estimate does not include any amount for benefits not taken up which might be taken up at some time in the future, benefits to which an entitlement might arise in the future, such as invalid care allowance, non-contributory invalidity pension, attendance allowance, widows' benefits payable should the victim die as a result of his illness or injury, or mobility allowance which might accrue to a child when he is old enough to qualify. Furthermore, it must be stressed that the figures take no account of the increased amounts which will accrue to recipients if benefits are allowed to increase in real value or if they are allowed to maintain their purchasing power in times of inflation.

The results of this exercise are given in Table 5.3. Future entitlements in these cases are shown to be worth many thousands of pounds, which is to be compared with the relatively low average amount of damages received by those in the survey who succeeded in a legal claim (Table 3.1). It need hardly be said that the figures can provide only a rough approximation. Nevertheless, an attempt to minimize the limitations of 'point-in-time' estimates improves the comparison of the relative importance of social security recoveries and damages. Given the assumptions used in calculating future benefits, the estimates err in the direction of understating total future social security recoveries. The estimates for attendance allowance, mobility allowance, and industrial disablement benefit

Table 5.3 *Estimates of future entitlement to some social security benefits for those victims in the Compensation Survey who were in receipt of the benefit when interviewed*

	Number of recipients at the time of the interview*	Mean of the estimated future entitlements	Mean duration of benefit (in years)	Total future entitlements**
		(£s)		(£s)
Industrial Disablement Benefit	10	13,500	20	135,000 (10)
Attendance Allowance	42	5,000	12	210,000 (23)
Non-contributory Invalidity Pension	6	6,500	8	39,000 (6)
Invalidity Benefit	125	3,300	4	412,500 (10)
Mobility Allowance	13	7,800	15	101,400 (10)
				897,900

* Some victims were in receipt of more than one benefit at the time of the interview.
** In brackets is given the number of cases (weighted) on which the estimate was based.

are likely to be somewhat better than those for invalidity benefit, non-contributory invalidity pension and unemployment benefit. The latter are more dependent on judgments about difficult questions, in particular, the date when a beneficiary will return to work. Those benefits in the former group, once awarded, are assumed to be payable for life in the case of attendance allowance and industrial disablement benefit, and until age 70 in the case of mobility allowance. The figures are in November 1976 terms. As all interviews were conducted at least six months after the accident or the beginning of the illness no one was in receipt of industrial injury benefit or sickness benefit. Estimates of future entitlement to supplementary benefit and family income supplement were considered impracticable, as they depend upon too many unpredictable changes in financial circumstances in addition to the medical prognosis.

(c) Demographic characteristics.

It was to be expected that men would be more likely than women to obtain social security benefits following illness or injury. Women are less often entitled to the contributory benefits since if married they could – until 1975 – opt to pay no contributions and they are less likely to be in contributory employment. Furthermore, women are not normally entitled to means-tested benefits if their husbands are in full-time work. The combined effect of these and perhaps other factors is to limit very significantly the role of social security benefits in providing compensation to women who are ill or injured. In the Compensation Survey 56 per cent of men, but only 19 per cent of women obtained at least one social security benefit. However, among recipients of social security benefits there was no evidence that women received less (or more) than men. It should be remembered, however, that the very marked differences in receipt of benefit by sex are in part explained by the emphasis in the social security system on providing benefits to those in employment, an emphasis only marginally affected by the introduction of the housewives non-contributory invalidity pension.

Table 5.4 shows receipt of benefits by employment status at the time the illness started or the injury was suffered. Full-time workers are much more likely to be compensated than all other groups.

Table 5.4 *The receipt of social security benefits in relation to employment status at the time of the illness or injury*

Work status of victim	Total number of victims in each category	Percentage of victims in each category receiving benefit
	n̄	(%)
Full-time work	1486	73
Part-time work	251	18
Full-time education	543	5
Not working/retired	389	17
Full-time housewife	651	11
Other	266	17
Total (N̄)	3586	37

(d) Spending from savings and borrowing.

The above analysis of social security receipts reveals some of the strengths and weaknesses of the social security system but says little about its effectiveness in directing compensation to victims who suffer serious losses in preference to those who suffer little or no loss. An attempt was made to look at one possible indicator of effectiveness by asking victims about the impact of their illness or injury on household saving and borrowing. The data were derived from two questions, one about borrowing and debts, and a second about spending from saving, or stopping saving. Of victims who had received social security benefits, 32 per cent had used savings. Among non-recipients, the corresponding figure was 11 per cent. This difference is presumably less than it would have been had recipients not received the income from the benefit itself. An identical analysis was carried out for recipients and non-recipients of occupational sick pay but no significant difference was observed. It is unlikely that the observed differences in the use of savings can be explained by variability in the availability of savings. Such indications as are available from the survey suggest that those who obtained no benefits are likely to have more rather than less available savings than benefit recipients, in that non-recipients were in higher-income households than recipients and the propensity to save was found to be similar for all income groups.

Among recipients of social security benefit the likelihood of savings being used increased as the amount of social security they had received increased (Table 5.5). This relationship held for all levels of receipt of benefit except the very highest. Victims were much more likely to use savings than to borrow money and incur debts following their illness or injury; 11 per cent of benefit recipients but only 3 per cent of non-recipients incurred debts (5 per cent of the whole sample). There was a small increase in the likelihood of

Table 5.5 *Proportion of victims using savings in relation to the amount of social security benefit obtained*

Amount of social security benefit received (£s)	Total number of victims in each category	Percentage using savings
	n̄	(%)
No benefit	2239	11
Up to 50	179	27
51 – 200	255	30
201 – 500	133	49
501 – 1000	81	53
1001 – 1500	41	44
1501 – 2000	28	61
2001 – 2500	24	62
2501 – 10,000	49	26
Amount unknown	557	25
Total	3586	19

borrowing as the amount of social security benefit increased but the amounts involved were small; only six respondents reported debts of over £500 and over 50 per cent reported amounts of £100 or less.

The savings and debts data are consistent in suggesting that the social security system succeeds to some extent in distinguishing victims with greater financial losses from those with lesser losses. The savings data in particular (Table 5.5) are suggestive of a pattern of expenditure in which benefits pay for regular weekly expenses, but not the less regular expenses, until the point is reached when savings are exhausted.

(e) Conclusions.

The social security system was shown by the Compensation Survey to be an important – indeed the single most important – system of financial support for the victims of illness and injury. In spite of this, its coverage was shown to be far from comprehensive: only 37.5 per cent of those in our sample actually obtained any benefits at all; over half the men, but fewer than a fifth of the women received some benefit. A large number of the ill and injured were forced to rely on non-contributory means-tested supplementary benefit.

The information on the scope and importance of social security benefits necessarily relies on reports of benefit receipts up to the date of the interview. In comparing this with the amounts received as damages for personal injury, some account must be taken of the fact that the latter are once and for all payments, whereas social security entitlements will continue to provide weekly payments, in some cases for many years beyond the date of interview in the survey. We chose to attempt an approximation of the value of such future entitlements. After this adjustment, our estimate of the overall contribution of social security benefits to those in our sample rose from £984,244 to £1,882,144, which shows the relative importance of the long-term benefits. Although there are some anomalies and gaps in the present social security coverage for the ill and the injured, it is clear that it must continue to be the main source of their financial support. The ways in which we would like to see the role of social security develop for these groups are discussed in Chapter 12 (see p. 334).

(3) Administration and adjudication

In comparison with the tort system, social security is said to be 'quick, certain, and inexpensive to administer'. These may certainly be regarded as the objectives of the system and may be seen to lie behind the methods of administering and adjudicating upon claims. The comparison with the tort system is striking. The Royal Commission on Civil Liability (Pearson, 1978, paras. 83 and 12) estimated that administrative costs constituted 85 per cent of damages payments and only 11 per cent of social security benefits.

While in its details the social security system is clearly complicated and gives rise to many legal difficulties, the assumption is that its basic structure of rights can be understood by potential claimants without resource to expert advice. To this end, the Department of Health and Social Security publishes a series of leaflets explaining entitlement to benefits, and these are freely available at local offices, post offices, and elsewhere. In recent years there have been efforts to improve the comprehensibility of these leaflets, particularly in the area of means-tested benefits.

Claims must be submitted in writing and although the expectation is that these will be on the forms provided by the Department, this is not strictly necessary. In general, for most of the disability benefits, they must be made within twenty-one days of the earliest day for which benefit is claimed; there are special rules for the admission of late claims. The claim must be accompanied by evidence of the disability which forms the basis of the entitlement. For the purposes of sickness, invalidity, and industrial injury benefits this was normally accomplished through a medical certificate, now termed a statement of incapacity (see Ogus and Barendt, 1982, p. 150) which is obtained from the claimant's general practitioner. The opinion of the doctor is not conclusive: the insurance officer who is initially responsible for making a decision on entitlement may seek an alternative opinion from a Regional Medical Officer. If that differs from the opinion of the claimant's doctor, he must adjudicate between them. To that very limited extent, the system of adversarial assessment present in a tort claim exists also in relation to social security benefits. For the more refined disability criteria of other benefits, a correspondingly more sophisticated assessment is required, and this is typically performed by a body established for the purpose, whose approach is predominantly inquisitorial in character. A claim based on a prescribed disease under the industrial injuries scheme is normally accompanied by evidence from a doctor specialized in the particular disease. (There are special bodies established to diagnose pneumoconiosis and byssinosis.) Entitlement to mobility allowance normally depends on an examination by a doctor nominated by the Department. For the complex attendance allowance requirements there is the specially constituted Attendance Allowance Board (which frequently delegates to a nominated medical practitioner); and the extent of disablement for the purposes of an industrial disablement benefit is determined by a Medical Board.

As has been seen, the private law character of a tort claim for damages manifested itself particularly in the way in which rights were compromised through the settlement process, with legal proceedings constituting a constraint in the light of which the parties would negotiate. Under the social security system, while uncertain claims might be settled informally in the sense that an aggrieved claimant might persuade an insurance officer to reverse the decision without recourse to the appeal process, the element of compromise is absent: the claimant will receive either the whole of his statutory entitlement or none at all. Further, litigation in private law constitutes a very real cost to both parties – even the winner will not recover a full indemnity from the loser. The social security appeal system is intended to be costless to the claimant. Expenses and compensation for loss of earnings are paid to claimants and the travelling expenses of non-professional representatives are normally reimbursed. Appeals against decisions on entitlement or amount are for most purposes made to the national insurance Local Appeal Tribunals, with a further right of appeal to the Social Security Commissioners, and a final appeal on questions of law to the Court of Appeal. On medical issues arising under the industrial injuries scheme (e.g. diagnosis of a prescribed disease or assessment of disablement) an appeal lies from the Medical Board to a Medical Appeal Tribunal, with a further right of appeal on questions of law only to the Commissioners. Similarly, on entitlement to attendance allowance there is a right of appeal on a question of law from the Attendance Allowance Board to the Commissioners. As regards the means-tested benefits, from November 1980 appeals related to supplementary benefit decisions are to be made to the Social Security Commissioners. At the time of the survey a decision of a Supplementary Benefit Appeal Tribunal was conclusive, though theoretically a claimant might seek an administrative law remedy from the Divisional Court.

If, in general, the relative speed, cheapness, and informality of appeals proceedings under the social security system confer advantages on claimants compared with the tort claim for damages, nevertheless serious criticisms have been directed towards them. First, there is the controversial issue of representation (see Fulbrook, 1978, p. 276). Legal aid, as at presently constituted, does not extend to advocacy at tribunal hearings,[3] presumably to the disadvantage of claimants who cannot avail themselves of facilities provided by trade unions or voluntary agencies. Second, at least in the area of supplementary benefits, there have been substantial allegations, supported by empirical findings, that the quality of tribunal adjudication does not attain a satisfactory standard. The criticisms have been directed particularly at Supplementary Benefit Appeal Tribunals (see Bell, 1975; Adler and Bradley, 1975). Under legislation passed in 1983, these will be amalgamated with national insurance Local Appeal Tribunals and both the composition and the style of decision-making of the new body will follow the model established by the latter.

(4) Difficulties with claims

A social security claimant, like a claimant for damages, must overcome a number of legal and administrative obstacles if he is to succeed in obtaining compensation for an illness or injury. In the case of damages these obstacles can be dauntingly numerous and complex, and one of the main objectives of the Compensation Survey was to describe them and examine their practical importance. A parallel examination of social security administration was well beyond the scope of the Survey, but it was possible to explore some aspects of user satisfaction with the handling of claims. (For further discussion see Bell, 1975; Bell *et al.*, 1975; Blaxter, 1978; Briar, 1966; Harris *et al.*, 1972; Sainsbury, 1970; Adler and Bradley, 1975). Respondents to the survey were shown lists of the main social security benefits available to the ill, injured, or handicapped (industrial injury and disablement benefit, sickness, invalidity, and unemployment benefit, non-contributory and invalidity pension, attendance and mobility allowance, supplementary benefit, and family income supplement); and were asked whether they had made an application. Those who had were asked 'Did you ever have any difficulties of any sort with your application for any of these benefits?' and 'Did you ever have to use the appeals procedure in connection with your application for any of these benefits?' These simple questions produced an informative data set which allows tentative generalizations about the nature and frequency of the difficulties experienced by social security claimants. It must be stressed that the conclusions relate only to claims made as a direct result of illness or injury.

Following an assessment of each 'difficulty' for plausibility and consistency with other information contained in the questionnaire, two distinct approaches were taken in the analysis of the replies to these 'open-ended' questions. The first was to comment on those aspects of social security law and administration which were raised by respondents. The commentary looks at problems of legal interpretation, demarcation and administration (paras. (a), (b), and (c) below).

In the second type of analysis we boldly treated respondents' accounts of difficulty as those of a disinterested observer rather than of an interested participant and used them to evaluate the administrative standards experienced by ill and injured social security claimants (para. (d) below).

The data common to both types of analysis consisted of 138 reports of difficulty from a total of 1262 claims for benefit. Fourteen

Table 5.6 *Number of applications for the various social security benefits in relation to the number of reported difficulties**

Category of benefit	Number of Applications	Number of Difficulties	Number of difficulties as percentage of applications
			(%)
Mobility Allowance	11	4	36.4
Attendance Allowance	33	9	27.3
Supplementary Benefit	127	34	26.8
Industrial Disablement Benefit	68	15	22.1
Industrial Injury Benefit	236	24	10.2
Family Income Supplement	11	1	9.1
Invalidity Benefit	91	6	6.6
Sickness Benefit	634	39	6.2
Unemployment Benefit	43	2	4.7
Non-contributory Invalidity Pension	8	0	0.0
Not allocated to a particular benefit	—	4	—
Total	1262	138	10.9

* The numbers listed in this table are not weighted.

claimants were deemed to have encountered two difficulties (there were 124 claimants in the study.) These numbers are unweighted as our analysis was essentially of individual replies to open-ended questions and involved the use of very small subgroups of our sample. The ratio of difficulties to claims varied in marked and interesting ways for each of the benefits (Table 5.6). Industrial disablement benefit, attendance allowance, mobility allowance and supplementary benefit produced one report of difficulty for three to five applications. For the remaining benefits, difficulties were reported at the rate of one for ten to twenty applications.

(a) Problems of legal interpretation

In seventy-four of the 138 cases of reported difficulty particular emphasis was given to the 'legal' character of the difficulty which had been experienced. It arose from the application or interpretation of the legal criteria governing entitlement. Table 5.7 categorizes these legal issues.

Of the nine cases in which entitlement to, or amount of industrial disablement benefit created difficulties, four seem to have been decided in the last resort by a Medical Appeal Tribunal. In five, the claimant was dissatisfied with the degree of disablement assessed by the Medical Board; in two of the latter group it was decided that, contrary to his expectations, he had no permanent disability (or one which was assessed at less than 1 per cent with legally the same result) (Ogus and Barendt, 1982, p. 300); in one case, the question was whether the disablement resulting from the industrial accident should have taken account of an existing impairment to a 'paired organ' resulting from an extraneous cause (Ogus and Barendt, 1982, pp. 304–5); in another case, an injured police officer succeeded in persuading a Medical Appeal Tribunal to substitute a provisional for a final award of a disablement gratuity, thus enabling him to maintain the possibility of receiving a disablement pension on a subsequent reassessment. The pension is payable only for degrees of disablement of 20 per cent or more (see Ogus and Barendt, 1982, p. 308).

The most frequently encountered medico-legal criterion of entitlement to social security benefits payable to the ill or injured is incapacity for work (sickness, invalidity, and industrial injury benefits). In the light of the number of decisions which have to be made on this question, it is perhaps surprising that there were only seven cases in which the fulfilment of this condition was reported as

Table 5.7 *Issues of a 'legal' character in the difficulties reported by social security claimants**

Assessment of physical condition		22
whether incapable of work (sickness, invalidity and injury benefits)	7	
degree of disablement (disablement benefit)	9	
unable to walk (mobility allowance)	1	
requiring attendance (attendance allowance)	5	
Incapable of work but not within scope of industrial injury scheme		13
whether 'employed earner'	1	
whether 'by accident'	2	
whether 'arising out of and in course of employment'	4	
whether incapacity results from industrial accident	2	
whether disease prescribed in relation to him	4	
Fulfilment of contribution conditions		5
Age requirement (mobility allowance)		3
Period of entitlement		2
Disqualification from benefit		2
Late claim		2
Calculation of requirements and resources (means-tested benefits)		14
Exercise of discretion with reference to entitlement to, or amount of, supplementary benefit		7
Calculation of benefit (excluding calculation of degree of disability, calculation of requirements and resources for and the exercise of discretion with reference to supplementary benefit)		4
Total number of 'legal' difficulties		74
Total number of reported difficulties		138
Total number of social security claims		1262

* The numbers in this table are not weighted.

having caused difficulties. As a result of such difficulties, three of these respondents were, for a short period of time, subjected to the rules of unemployment benefit, including the requirement to register for work at the Employment Exchange. In two cases, it was alleged that the doctor responsible for the medical certificate had made a mistake: one in not recognizing the incapacitating nature of the claimant's ailment and the other in not extending the period of certification for the (then) maximum of thirteen weeks.

Mobility allowance was introduced for the age group 15–50

shortly before the Compensation Survey and only one respondent reported difficulties in satisfying the test of 'unable to walk or virtually unable to do so' (Social Security Act 1975, s. 37 A(1)). On the other hand, as might have been anticipated from literature on the subject (Carson, 1975; Micklethwait, 1976), assessment of the complex criteria (see Social Security Act 1975, s. 35(1)) for the attendance allowance gave rise to difficulties and dissatisfaction.

The assessment of financial resources for a means-tested benefit produced fourteen reports of 'difficulty'. In most cases the claims had failed because the claimant's income was too high. In seven more cases, it was a question of the Supplementary Benefit Commission exercising discretion conferred by the legislation. The statutory regulations which came into effect in November 1980, however, greatly reduced the extent of this discretion. In some cases extra money was sought (in the form either of regular discretionary additions to the weekly benefit or of exceptional needs lump-sum payments) for such items as clothing, bedding, furniture, heating, laundry, and diet (see also Stowell, 1980). One claimant sought and was refused help with paternity payments which had fallen into arrears (a summons had been lodged against him). The Commission had discretion to make such payments, but would normally have expected the mother to make the claim in her own right. In two interesting cases, a husband gave up work to look after a sick wife. This confirms Blaxter's reporting of serious difficulties in every case in which a husband gave up work to look after a sick wife (1978, p. 104). In neither case was he paid supplementary benefit at the standard rates, because the Commission was not prepared to exercise its discretionary power to waive the normal requirement that he should register as available for full-time employment.

(b) Demarcation problems

In a sense, any difficulties encountered in satisfying legal criteria for entitlement to a benefit can be regarded as a 'demarcation' problem, but it seemed important to distinguish instances in which a disabled person is admittedly entitled to one or more different benefits and yet uncertainty or difficulty has been caused by the process of placing him in one category rather than another. A common criticism of social security provision for disabled persons is that it is far too complex, and that as a result administrative costs are too high (Atiyah, 1980, p. 395; Pearson Commission, 1978, Vol.

1, para. 266). From our sample, thirty-eight out of the 138 reported difficulties may be characterized as arising, at least in part, from a demarcation problem.

The industrial injury/sickness borderline was an important demarcation for disabled persons. The distinction between the industrial and non-industrial schemes depends on a number of difficult and often legally complex criteria. Difficulties arising from this complexity were to be found in our sample. In thirteen cases, the respondent was clearly incapable of work but had difficulties in establishing that he could recover under the industrial injuries scheme. In two cases, the question was whether the claimant's incapacity resulted from an accident at work or rather was the consequence of an extraneous cause. In another two, benefit was denied on the grounds that though the incapacity was caused by the conditions of work, it resulted from a continuous process rather than an event or series of events, and therefore did not satisfy the statutory criterion of arising 'by accident' (see Ogus and Barendt, 1982, p. 269; and Social Security Act 1975, s. 50 (1)). In four other such cases, the claimant failed to establish that the illness in question was covered by the prescribed diseases provisions, either because he was not working in an occupation for which the relevant disease was prescribed or (in two cases) apparently because the authorities found evidence on which the statutory presumption of a causal connection between the work and the disease could be rebutted.[4] The need to prove that an accident arose 'out of and in the course of . . . employment' (Social Security Act 1975, s. 50 (1)) created difficulties in four cases. Two of these were typical borderline areas, where the law is notoriously uncertain (Ogus and Barendt, 1982, p. 287; Ogus, 1976): in one case a home help, and in another a television aerial erector being injured on the way back from an assignment. One respondent was denied benefit on the ground that he was not an 'employed earner'. It seems likely from other answers given to the questionnaire that he was, at the time, working under a 'lump' arrangement with his 'employer'.[5]

The relationship between the industrial (injury benefit) and non-industrial (sickness benefit) schemes gave rise to practical as well as legal difficulties. Even claims which fall clearly within the industrial scheme may create confusion in the mind of the claimant because, typically, sickness benefit was paid immediately on proof of incapacity, pending investigation of the circumstances of the accident; and earnings-related supplement, which was paid with injury benefit, was formally classified as sickness benefit; to be entitled the claimant must satisfy the contribution conditions for that benefit. Many respondents were clearly confused as between sickness and injury benefit and it is likely that much of this confusion resulted from the complicated relationship between the two (Social Security Act 1975, s. 14(7)). The DHSS leaflet on Injury Benefit (N15) did little to reduce the confusion. It indicated that generally the supplement is paid 'if you would have been entitled to sickness benefit but for the fact you were receiving injury benefit'. Quite independently of this, seven complained of the delay in receiving the industrial benefit and it is likely that the majority were referring to the 'transfer' arrangements. The difficulties reported by six respondents drew attention to another demarcation issue, the arrangements for transfer between the unemployment and the incapacity benefits.

(c) Administrative difficulties

It is difficult to draw the line clearly between 'legal' and 'administrative' problems, but the latter are assumed to arise generally when there is no dispute as to entitlement. Thirty-five of the 138 'difficulties' reported in our survey were characterized as predominantly administrative. A perhaps surprising number of problems – seven – related to the employer's obligations under the social security legislation, the majority arising under the industrial injury scheme where the employer is bound to enter a record of all accidents. There was no evidence that respondents considered the medical certification procedure by general practitioners to be irksome. This is in marked contrast with the dissatisfaction which the medical profession has expressed on this subject in recent years.[6] In eleven cases the claimant had experienced difficulties which were attributed to the claims-processing or record-keeping mechanisms of the Department. In a further six cases, the difficulty was characterized as delay without reference to the legal issue or administrative malfunction believed to be its cause.

Almost all respondents gave an account of their difficulty which made reference to some substantive, and plausible, legal or administrative problem. Indeed, in a number of cases respondents gave remarkably accurate accounts of the complexities of social security law and practice. However, mention must be made of explanations of difficulties which relied wholly or partly on the proposition that those who were administering the social security system were biased against the claimant. A claimant who had proved that a suspicion of abuse had been unfounded commented that 'they were not very kind about it' – she had received no apology. One single parent complained that she had always had difficulty dealing with 'the social security'; another respondent who had apparently applied for a wide variety of benefits, observed with regard to each 'they don't want to know you'; a respondent who had made a number of unsuccessful applications for attendance allowance said, 'they don't seem to want to give it to me'; and a similar remark was made with respect to a visiting officer of the Supplementary Benefits Commission. Four respondents suggested bias in formal hearings: one thought that he had lost the appeal because 'by that time . . . they owed me too much'; another whose disablement came up for assessment before a Medical Board thought that he had been penalized for his honesty in reporting that his condition had improved over the last six months; and there were two respondents who felt that their case had not been treated with sufficiently serious consideration – in one, the hearing had lasted only eight minutes.

(d) An assessment of administrative standards

In this section an attempt is made to classify the accounts of 'difficulties' reported by claimants so as to assess the administrative system in its own terms. This involves making a distinction between those problems which should not have arisen if the system was functioning as intended and those which arose from a clear application of known legal rules or normal administrative standards. Our concept was based on 'normal' not 'average' standards. The test we applied was to assess whether the central authorities would have considered such standards to be acceptable in a properly staffed local office. The distinction was relatively easy when the claimant referred to a legal rule, but more difficult when it was necessary to make judgments about normal administrative standards. The intention was to identify breaches of procedure or of administrative standards which have some legal foundation, such as the requirements to notify claimants of decisions (Supplementary Benefits (Gen.) Regulations SI 1977, No. 1141) or to give reasons for decisions (Social Security (Determination of Claims and Questions) Regulations SI 1975, No. 559). Thus in one case the difficulty arose from a claimant's attempt to obtain supplementary benefit during absences from work to care for his sick wife. The authorities offered a repayable advance and appeared to misrepresent the extent of the discretionary powers available to them in such circumstances. There are, however, procedural and administrative standards which might be considered desirable by the central authorities but without any legal basis. An example illustrates a breach of these hypothetical standards. An appellant whose claim was rejected for a second time focused his dissatisfaction on a complaint that the hearing had lasted just eight minutes. Bell has drawn attention to the fact that National Insurance tribunals can and often do satisfy appellants that they have had a fair hearing even when they are not successful (1975, p. 18), which is surely a necessary feature of any system of adjudication. Altogether we judged fifty-four cases out of the total 138 reported difficulties to be examples of unsatisfactory administrative standards on the part of the social security authorities (see Table 5.8). They were of four types:

(i) Minor difficulties in obtaining benefits

Twenty-two of our cases were categorized as examples of minor difficulty; claimants obtained a benefit only after some inconvenience, delay or extra effort on their part. Difficulties arising from delay accounted for over half the cases included in this category.

(ii) More serious difficulties in obtaining benefits

Twenty-three difficulties were distinguished from the above as the claimants had been successful only after considerable inconvenience or determined effort on their part, or after a long delay.

(iii) No benefit obtained when there was an apparent entitlement

Five claimants reported difficulties which arose from an application being turned down when there was an apparent entitlement. This does not include victims of injury or illness who would have succeeded had they applied for a benefit. Among the five cases in this category were two applicants for injury benefit who obtained sickness benefit. In only one of the remaining cases was there any likelihood that the entitlement, and hence the non-payment, would last more than a few weeks.

(iv) No benefit was obtained and difficulties arose from the authorities' failure to maintain appropriate standards of administrative behaviour

Four cases were put into this category. It has been seen that forty-five difficulties arose in circumstances where the claimant

Table 5.8 *An assessment of the standards of social security administration by the benefit for which an application was made (expressed as a percentage of the unweighted number of applications for that benefit)* *

	Industrial injury benefit	Disablement benefit	Sickness benefit	Invalidity benefit	Unemployment benefit	Non-contributory invalidity pension	Attendance allowance	Mobility allowance	Family income supplement	Supplementary benefit	Percentages of total applications (n. 1262)
	(%)	(%)	(%)	(%)	(%)	(%)	(%)	(%)	(%)	(%)	n
Total reports of difficulties	10	22	6	7	5	0	27	36	9	27	138 (11%)
Administration Judged Unsatisfactory	6	7	3	4	0	0	9	0	0	5	54 (4%)
Administration Judged Satisfactory	3	3	2	0	2	0	3	27	9	14	42 (3%)
Unable to make an assessment	2	12	1	2	2	0	15	9	0	8	42 (3%)
Number of cases	24	15	39	6	2	0	9	4	1	34	138 (11%)

* Four cases of difficulty were not allocated to a particular benefit.

obtained a benefit (paras. (i) and (ii) above). There is no obvious reason why success or failure should affect the incidence of administrative difficulties to such a marked degree; it is more likely that it affected the way in which they were reported. An unsuccessful claimant might be dissatisfied with both the administrative procedure and its results, but the result and the legal reason for it are likely to be uppermost in his mind. In contrast, a successful claimant will be more likely to comment on procedural and administrative difficulties.

In forty-two cases we concluded that the authorities had maintained satisfactory administrative standards. These cases were of two kinds:

(i) Benefit obtained, but normal administrative practice perceived by the respondent as causing difficulty. There were seven cases of reported difficulty in which the claimant seemed to be dissatisfied with what we considered to be a normal administrative practice. It is perhaps not without significance that the majority of these cases involved official checks on a claimant's medical condition.

(ii) No benefit obtained and a reasonable application of the rules perceived by the respondent as causing difficulty. In thirty-five cases the claimant referred to a difficulty but gave enough information to permit a reasonable inference that the application had been treated in accordance with social security law and practice at the time of the claim as we understood it to be. This is not to say that they should be ignored as unjustifiable complaints; they might draw attention to rules and practices which create particular problems. No fewer than seventeen cases in this category arose from supplementary benefit assessments which resulted in no entitlement.

In forty-two cases it was not possible to make an assessment of the administrative standards experienced by claimants. Difficulties which arose from the exercise of judgment or discretion could not be properly evaluated, given the limitations of the data. Where entitlement was determined by a discretionary decision at the local level it was not possible to distinguish between an 'unsatisfied entitlement' and a 'reasonable application of the rules'. There were seventeen cases of this kind in which no benefit was obtained and four cases in which the claim was successful. Among those who failed to obtain benefit were four applicants who were refused regular discretionary additions or special needs lump-sum payments under the supplementary benefit scheme, six who wanted some, or some more industrial disablement benefit, and three who failed to satisfy the medical conditions for mobility or attendance allowances.

Of the remaining twenty-one cases, five were respondents who had taken some action in applying for a benefit but had subsequently failed to continue their claim for some reason other than their belief that they were not entitled. In two further cases claimants reported that they had been unaware of their entitlement for some considerable time and in fourteen cases the respondent or the interviewer had failed to elaborate on an affirmative reply to the question about difficulties or had produced reports which were too confusing to be of any use. In Table 5.8 we summarize the results of our assessment of the standard of social security administration and analyse them by type of benefit.

(e) Conclusions

The findings reported in this section are not easy to evaluate: we are not aware of studies with which they can usefully be compared but we are aware of the methodological difficulties of obtaining this kind of information. However, our analysis permits a number of tentative observations. The most important arises from the clear distinction between those benefits which produce one report of 'difficulty' for every three to five applications and those which produce one 'difficulty' for every ten to twenty applications. The former group consists of supplementary benefit, attendance allowance, mobility allowance, and industrial disablement benefit. In relation to attendance allowance and disablement benefit, difficulties seem to arise from a combination of two factors: firstly, it is necessary for all claimants to be medically examined by the authorities, and secondly, the criteria for the award of benefit – and indeed for the level of benefit – are complex. Most of the difficulties which supplementary benefit claimants reported arose from their wrong assumptions about the level of income necessary to qualify. Claimants expected to be entitled to benefit but found they were not, generally because they failed to allow for the fact that one of their sources of income (e.g. a pension, income from wife's earnings, or income from capital) would be taken into account in assessing supplementary benefit entitlement.

It is worth observing that the medical certification of incapacity for work did not appear to create difficulties for claimants. A number of problems indicated that claimants are confused by the distinctions necessary to the preferential treatment for work accident victims and for those who suffer from one of the 'prescribed' industrial diseases. As regards the former, our study also suggests that the system of reporting accidents is working far from perfectly. Finally, it is noteworthy that our study produced little evidence to suggest that claimants feel themselves 'stigmatized' by making an application for social security benefits following an illness or injury (Briggs and Rees, 1980).

Notes

1. This summary is necessarily simplified. For details, see Ogus and Barendt, 1982; Calvert, 1978. Because they were not covered by the survey, war pensions are omitted: for a description, see Ogus and Barendt, 1982, Chapter 9.
2. The current list of prescribed diseases is to be found in SI 1983, No. 1094, Sch. 1, Part I. From time to time new diseases are added, the principle being that the relevant employment creates a vulnerability to the disease greater than that of the general public.
3. Under the 'Green Form' scheme, free legal advice is available on a tribunal matter. Following a dictum in *McKenzie v. McKenzie* [1970] 3 All ER 1034, it is clear that such advice may extend to sitting in at the tribunal hearings and making suggestions to the appellant. The Lord Chancellor's Advisory Committee on Legal Aid (24th Report, 1973–4 HC 20) has recommended that legal aid be extended to cover tribunal hearings, but at the time of writing this has not been implemented.
4. See the Social Security (Industrial Injuries) (Prescribed Diseases) Regulations 1980, SI 1980/377, Reg. 4(1). The Royal Commission on Civil Liability and Compensation for Personal Injury has made recommendations which, if implemented, would considerably ease the burden on claimants in such cases: Pearson Report, 1978, Vol. 1, paras. 869, 887.
5. *Cf. Ferguson* v. *John Dawson* [1976] 3 All ER 817, and for discussions of the problem, see Standing Committee E Debates on the Social Security Bill 1973, cols. 83–122.
6. See especially report of the Committee on Abuse of Social Security Benefits (Fisher Committee), Cmnd. 5228, para. 187; and the Report of the National Insurance Advisory Committee on the Draft Medical Certification Regulations, 1975–6 HC 349. From April 1983, for the small number of employees not covered by the new statutory sick pay scheme (Chapter 12, p. 343 below), a system of self-certification has been introduced for spells of incapacity lasting seven days or less, or for the first seven days of a longer spell.

References

Adler, M., and Bradley, A., eds., 1975, *Justice, Discretion and Poverty*, Lon-

don: Professional Books.
Atiyah, P. S., 1980, *Accidents, Compensation and the Law* (3rd edn.), London: Weidenfeld & Nicolson.
Atkinson, A. B., 1975, *The Economics of Inequality*, Oxford: Oxford University Press.
Bell, K., 1975, *Research on Supplementary Benefit Appeal Tribunals: Review of Main Findings*, London: Routledge & Kegan Paul.
——, Collison, P., Turner, S., and Webber, S., 1974, 'National Insurance Local Tribunals', Part I, 3 *Journal of Social Policy* 289.
——, 1975, 'National Insurance Local Tribunals', Part II, 4 *Journal of Social Policy* 1.
Beveridge Report, 1942, *Report of the Inter-Departmental Committee on Social Insurance and Allied Services*, London: HMSO, Cmd. 6404.
Blaxter, M., 1978, *The Meaning of Disability*, London: Routledge & Kegan Paul.
Briar, S., 1966, 'Welfare from Below', 54 *California Law Review* 370.
Briggs, E., and Rees, T., 1980, 'Lost in the Puzzle of Social Security', *New Society* (10 Jan.) 60.
Calabresi, G., 1970, *The Costs of Accidents: A Legal and Economic Analysis*, New Haven, Connecticut: Yale University Press.
Calvert, H., 1978, *Social Security Law* (2nd edn.), London: Sweet & Maxwell.
Carson, D., 1975, 'The Attendance Allowance', 26 *Northern Ireland Law Quarterly*, 291.
Committee on Alternative Remedies, 1946, *Final Report*, London: HMSO, Cmd. 6800.
DHSS (Department of Health and Social Security), 1977, *Supplementary Benefit Appeal Tribunals, A Guide to Procedure*, London: HMSO.
——, 1980, *Income During Initial Sickness*, London: HMSO, Cmnd. 7864.
Fulbrook, J., 1978, *Administrative Justice and the Unemployed*, London: Mansell.
Harris, A. I., Smith, C. R. W., and Head, E., 1972, *Income and Entitlement to Supplementary Benefit of Impaired People in Great Britain*, London: HMSO.
Houghton, D., 1967, *Paying for the Social Services*, London: Institute of Economic Affairs.
Micklethwait, R., 1976, *The National Insurance Commissioners*, London: Stevens.
Ogus, A., 1976, 'Recent Decisions on Industrial Injury Benefit', 5 *Industrial Law Journal* 188.
——, and Barendt, E. M., 1982, *The Law of Social Security* (2nd edn.), London: Butterworth.
Pearson, Lord (Chairman), 1978, *Report of the Royal Commission on Civil Liability and Compensation for Personal Injury* (3 vols.), London: HMSO, Cmnd. 7054.

Phillips, J., 1976, 'Economic Deterrence and the Prevention of Industrial Accidents', 5 *Industrial Law Journal* 148.
Reid, G. L., and Robertson, D. J., 1965, *Fringe Benefits, Labour Costs and Social Security*, London: Allen & Unwin.
Sainsbury, S., 1970, *Registered as Disabled*, London: Bell.
Stowell, R., 1980, *The Discretionary Element in Supplementary Benefit for Disabled People*, London: Disablement Income Group.
Tiley, J., 1978, *Revenue Law* (2nd edn.), London: Butterworth.

6 Criminal Injuries Compensation

(1) The scheme and its rationale

Victims of deliberate attack and those injured as a result of criminal activity constitute a further subcategory of injured people which has been singled out for special arrangements for compensation. The social and political pressures which culminated in the establishment of the Criminal Injuries Compensation Scheme (CICS) in 1964 have been well analysed elsewhere (Miers, 1978), and it is sufficient to state here that the expressed justification for a tailor-made compensation scheme for victims of criminal injury hinged on the peculiarly unpleasant way in which such injuries were suffered, together with the lack of alternative compensation. Although it was, and is, technically possible to pursue a claim for damages under the tort system against the perpetrator of a criminal attack, in the vast majority of cases this is either impossible (because no offender has been apprehended) or impractical (since most offenders are impecunious). In addition, many victims of criminal injury, such as the elderly, women at home, and children usually are not eligible for social security benefits.

A White Paper in 1964 introduced the Government's proposals for compensating victims of crime. While this paper emphasized that 'the Government do not accept that the State is liable for injuries caused to people by the acts of others', it nevertheless provided a justification for the scheme on the ground that 'the public does, however, feel a sense of responsibility for and sympathy with the innocent victim, and it is right that this feeling should find practical expression in the provision of compensation on behalf of the community.' It has been argued that this justification for singling out yet another subgroup of the injured population for special consideration only served to exacerbate the anomalies which already existed in a complex array of compensatory provision (Atiyah, 1980; and see also Chapter 1 above). The fundamental humanitarian appeal of compensation for innocent victims of crime, it was also argued, rested on a stereotype of violent crime which is not always easy to support and which has posed difficulties for the operation of the scheme (Miers, 1978). Violent attack is by no means always unexpected and unprovoked nor is it always perpetrated by an unknown stranger.

The scheme as it now operates is designed to make *ex gratia* payments of compensation to applicants who have sustained personal injury (including shock) directly attributable to a crime of violence or to assisting in an arrest or preventing a crime from taking place. The most important conditions for eligibility are first that compensation is payable only if the award would be more than £400; secondly that the offence has been the subject of criminal proceedings or that the police were informed of the offence without delay. Until October 1979, applications were not accepted under the scheme where the victim and offender were living together as members of the same family. This particular restriction was the subject of much criticism and was amended following a review of the scheme in 1978.[1] Compensation may now be awarded where victim and offender were living together at the time of the offence if the person responsible has been prosecuted; and if the amount of compensation paid would not be less than £500 (as compared with £400 for other applications). Where the claimant and offender are both adults the Board must be satisfied that they had stopped living in the same household before the application for compensation was made and that they seem unlikely to live together again. Where the claimant is a minor still living in the same household as the offender, an award can be made if the Board considers that it would not be against the interests of the minor. The purpose of these detailed restrictions on compensation for domestic violence is to protect the scheme against abuses where the offender might actually benefit financially from awards made to victims.

The procedure for awarding compensation

The scheme is something of a hybrid in that the procedure for making applications is like that for the social security system (i.e. by written application), while on the other hand compensation is assessed on the same basis as common law damages. The standard of proof applied by the Board to decide whether a crime has in fact been committed is based on a balance of probabilities, rather than proof beyond a reasonable doubt. Initial decisions on the amount of compensation to be awarded are made by one member of the Board. If the applicant is not satisfied with this decision, he may appeal at a hearing before three members of the Board. The Board will not pay for legal representation at hearings, although it may pay witnesses' expenses.

In principle, compensation is assessed in the same way as common law damages, and it is paid as a lump sum; but there is provision for interim payments which are made quite often. An upper limit of twice the average industrial earnings is imposed on the calculation of loss of earnings; this differs from the common law assessment of damages, where no limit is imposed. The justification for the limit in the scheme is 'the protection of the public purse' and the assumption that high earners are best placed to make private provision for loss (Home Office, 1978).

The desire to protect the public purse causes another departure from common law assessment of damages in that the scheme does not permit any 'double recovery' from public funds. Whereas common law damages are reduced by half the entitlement to certain social security benefits, the scheme reduces compensation by the full amount to which the victim is entitled.

Compensation for non-pecuniary loss may be awarded, and for cases of rape and sexual assault the Board will consider applications for compensation in respect of pain, suffering, and shock, and the expenses of childbirth (see the Board's Eleventh Report, 1975). Awards for pain and suffering will not be paid, however, to the dependants of a deceased victim in respect of the sorrow caused by the bereavement.

Awards under the scheme may be reduced or applications may be rejected if it is considered that the conduct or lifestyle of the victim – both before and after the incident – made it 'inappropriate' that he or she should be granted a full award or any award at all. This rule is not really analogous to the principle of contributory negligence at common law since its application under the scheme is not confined to the circumstances in which injury occurred. While a victim who is said to have provoked or contributed to his or her injuries may find the award reduced or refused, it is also possible for the general character and way of life of the victim to be assessed beyond the details of the incident under consideration. These rather broad limitations on awards stem from the justification for the scheme which requires an 'innocent victim' for whom sympathy in the form of compensation is being expressed. It is therefore not in keeping with the spirit of the scheme to provide compensation for those who are deemed undeserving. The Board is required to make such subjective assessments of character, and, since the inception of the scheme, about one-quarter of the cases where applications were disallowed failed on this criterion.

The Report of the Board for the year 1978–9 (Fifteenth Report) shows that of the 19,107 applications resolved, 3 per cent were withdrawn or abandoned, 84 per cent received full awards, 2 per cent obtained reduced awards, 2 per cent were not awarded compensation due to the low value of the claim, and 10 per cent were not awarded compensation for other reasons. The total amount of compensation awarded in that year was £13,045,641, with 87 per cent of awards being for sums of less than £1,000.

(2) The survey data

The analysis of criminal injuries is based on data collected in the Compensation Survey from twenty-one victims of violent crime.[2] The size of the sample is a reflection of the relatively rare occurrence of serious criminal injury in the general population, combined with the difficulty, without a specially designed survey instrument, of screening out of the general population victims of personal attack. Victim research abroad and in this country has suggested that victims of assault are often reluctant to report such incidents to survey interviewers (Biderman *et al.*, 1967; Sparks *et al.*, 1977); this is especially so for domestic violence and for assaults where the offender is a friend or acquaintance of the victim. This general reluctance to report criminal assaults is compounded when using proxy respondents who may not be aware that injuries suffered by household members were in fact caused by assault rather than by accident (Reiss 1967; Sparks *et al.*, 1977). Since the questionnaire used in the screening survey was designed to identify from the general population cases of serious injury and illness, irrespective of specific cause, it was not possible to devote extra interviewing time to discovering criminal injuries. As a result, only twenty-three cases of criminal injury were reported in the screening survey and two of these cases could not be interviewed in the recall survey.

A related response problem is that of concealed criminal injury. It is likely that some injuries reported as domestic or other accidents in the screening survey were in fact criminal assaults. We have definite evidence of this in one case (case 20 below). In the screening survey a woman reported that she slipped outside the house and broke her arm. This was coded as a domestic accident and she was sampled for a recall interview on this basis. In the recall interview she first stated that someone caught her arm and it broke. When pressed for more details she finally said that the real facts were that she caught her husband with another woman and tried to attack the other woman, but her husband broke her arm trying to restrain her. This one case illustrates the difficulty of obtaining accurate information about assaults: it is impossible to assess how many other cases in the general sample of accident victims were actually concealed criminal injuries. The cases reported in this section are not, therefore, presented as being a representative national sample of serious criminal injury, but rather as a case-study exercise.

(3) Characteristics of criminal victims

Of the twenty-one victims interviewed in the Compensation Survey fourteen were men and seven were women. Half of these people were under the age of 30 at the time of their injuries, although a surprisingly high number (seven) were over 60. On the whole, the events reported appeared quite serious, as would be expected, given the survey threshold of an injury which caused two weeks' or more interruption in normal activities. Seven of the attacks involved the use of weapons (four of these were knives) and a very high proportion of the attacks were reported as having been committed by strangers (thirteen of the twenty-one reported incidents). This last finding is likely to be a reflection of greater willingness to report attacks by strangers, both to the police and to survey interviewers. Four of the incidents reported in our survey had not been reported to the police, but two of these were attacks on wives by husbands. The other two which were not reported to the police were injuries which occurred during fights between acquaintances or people known to each other by sight. All attacks by strangers were reported to the police.

Ten of these victims of criminal injury reported some continuing residual disability at the time of the interview, although two of these were as a result of scars and two were continuing serious nervousness. Only two people claimed still to be affected a lot, all of the time, as a result of their injury.

Thirteen of the victims were working at the time of their injury. They all took time off work and one man was forced into premature retirement. Not counting this case, the average number of weeks taken off work as a result of criminal injury was 10.54 weeks.

(4) Claims for compensation

Of the twenty victims of criminal injury who were asked about

Table 6.1. *Cases where compensation was obtained, either under the Criminal Injuries Compensation Scheme or from the offender*

	Nature of Attack	Time off work (weeks)	Residual disability	Amount[2] of Award (£s)	Year	Representation in making the claim
Case 1.	Policeman (35) deliberately knocked down by stolen car driven by juveniles	13	mild	402	1974	Police Federation made claim to CICB
Case 2.	Elderly man (76) mugged in Underground	8	none	354	1975	Solicitor made claim to CICB
Case 3.	Woman (24) raped by taxi driver and injured	8	severe nervousness	460	1975	Solicitor made claim to CICB
Case 4.	Man (27) stabbed in chest while in bed with assailant's wife	9	scar only	207	1973	Solicitor made claim to CICB
Case 5.	Girl (18) stabbed following brief fight	unemployed at the time	slight	95[1]	1975	Father applied directly to CICB
Case 6.	Man (23) had face cut with knife while fighting in pub	5	scars	67	1973	Applied directly to CICB
Case 7.	Man (46) had hand cut with knife in street fight	28	none	Not known	Not known	CAB official applied to CICB
Case 8.	Woman (79) pushed off bus by conductress	Housewife	none	130	1972	Solicitor obtained settlement from Bus Company

[1] Award reduced because of the claimant's own conduct.
[2] At the time of the survey the minimum award was £150.

Table 6.2 *Cases where compensation was not obtained*

	Nature of attack	Reported to police	Time off work (weeks)	Residual disability	Comments and reasons for not claiming compensation
Case 9.	Man (62) kicked and punched by youths when he told them to stop scratching cars	Yes	9	severe	Friend wrote to CICB. Offenders were never found. 'I couldn't prove who it was so was unable to apply for compensation.' Case went before a QC but he said it was not criminal so could not give any compensation. 'I could have appealed but didn't think it worthwhile. The CICB said a mugging didn't come under criminal offences.'
Case 10.	Elderly man (69) assaulted at work by customer who was unhappy with car he had bought	Yes	Retired early	severe	Saw lawyer and was advised to claim but to wait for outcome of prosecution of offender. Case dropped later on advice of solicitor because 'courts went against me'.
Case 11.	Man (62) punched at work during an argument; vision temporarily impaired	Yes	12	none	'Police said leave it to us and nothing came of it. I did nothing about it and never knew what happened. He pleaded guilty.'
Case 12.	Man (27) assaulted while in night club; broken nose	Yes	3	none	'Because the police couldn't prove anything against him because of lack of witnesses.'
Case 13.	Man (21) beaten about the head during argument	No	2	mild	Attacker should pay because he caused pain and loss of earnings. 'When I called at the solicitor's office it was closed. Also there were no witnesses to support the claim.'

Case 14.	Man (29) attacked in street by youths and stabbed with bottle	Yes	24	mild	'They ran off. . . I don't know who they were. I don't know why they did it. I didn't know them, but London is a funny place. I had no money to make claims and the police never got in touch about it.'
Case 15.	Elderly woman (68) attacked just inside her front door by man who followed her off bus; bag stolen	Yes	Housewife	none	'It was no use feeling he should pay if you didn't know who it was. I'd have been satisfied if I'd got my goods back and he had been caught and imprisoned.'
Case 16.	Man (26) walking home at night, hit on head with piece of wood by unknown assailant	Yes	6	none	'If you don't know who it is, it's a bit difficult to claim.' (no other reason given)
Case 17.	Young man (17) attacked on way to station by gang in street. Thrown through window of a department store	Yes	In full-time education	none	'Because we never found the boys who attacked me.'
Case 18.	Young man (19) injured kneecap in fight	No	10	none	'Partly my fault. It was just one of those things.'
Case 19.	Battered wife (27): continual attacks; one caused miscarriage	No	Housewife	none	'It was not the type of thing I would expect compensation for. Not relevant in cases of violent husbands and battered wives.'
Case 20.	Woman (31) caught husband with other woman; when she attempted to hit the woman her husband restrained her and broke her arm	No	Housewife	severe	'Didn't know what to do.'
Case 21.	Elderly woman (83) attacked by burglars in her home	Yes	Housewife	severe nervousness	Reason not given.

compensation, eight had obtained compensation from some source. Seven respondents had made successful claims to the Criminal Injuries Compensation Board and one respondent had obtained some money from a bus company. The awards were all made during the period 1972–5 and the average amount received was £245 (median £207). Details of these eight cases are presented in Table 6.1.

Although the proportion of criminally injured victims obtaining compensation is higher than the proportion of accident victims who obtained common law damages, it is perhaps surprising that not more than 40 per cent of a group with substantial injuries were able to benefit from the provisions of the Scheme. It is also interesting to consider that three of the seven people who did obtain compensation under the scheme were actually fighting when they sustained their injuries and that a fourth was engaged in what could be described as a 'provocative' activity (case 4 in Table 6.1). The policeman (Case 1) was injured in the course of his duties trying to prevent a crime. Indeed, only two of the seven successful claims to the Board actually conform to the classic stereotype of the innocent victim subjected to an unexpected and unprovoked attack (Cases 2 and 3), while, on the information given to our interviewers, five of those who *did not* make a claim to the Board appear to come into this category (Cases 14, 15, 16, 17, and 21).

(5) Non-claimants

There were twelve victims of criminal injury who did not obtain any compensation from either the scheme or from the offender. Details of these cases are presented in Table 6.2. Of these twelve victims only two actually took any steps at all to recover compensation (cases 9 and 10 of Table 6.2). Case 9 is difficult to assess. This man of 62 suffered severe injuries when he was kicked and punched by some young men who had been scratching cars. The police were called and, although on the face of it one would have thought him entitled to compensation, his account of his application to the Board and their apparent rejection of it is so confused that it defies analysis. Case 10 seems to suggest that the alleged offender was apprehended, brought to trial, and then acquitted. The solicitor acting for the victim apparently advised against proceeding with an application to the Board, although the injuries he sustained were substantial. The information obtained from the victim in the interview did not contain sufficient detail to make a firm assessment of the case.

The remaining cases, where no steps were taken to recover compensation, consist of those victims who did not quite know what to do in the circumstances and expected the police to help them in some way; those who completely misunderstood the operation of the scheme in assuming that the offender had to be apprehended in order for a claim to be allowed (Cases 14, 15, 16, and 17); and two people who did not think that compensation would be available or appropriate (Cases 18 and 19). In eight of the cases where no claim was made, the event had been reported to the police and it might have been expected that some information or guidance about claiming compensation would have been offered by the police. However, our interviews provided no evidence that such information was given.

Although the number of cases of criminal injury in our sample was small, two points arise from our analysis of the information obtained. The first is that many of these victims of relatively serious criminal injury failed to obtain compensation, notwithstanding the existence of the Criminal Injuries Compensation Scheme. This failure was often the result of ignorance of the existence of the Scheme, or of confusion about the grounds upon which a claim might be made or about the procedure for making an application. Secondly, the information or guidance which might have avoided these difficulties was not apparently available to these victims of crime.

Notes

1. Home Office, 1978
2. This does not include four schoolchildren who suffered injuries at school and who might have been eligible to claim compensation under the Scheme.

References

Atiyah, P. S., 1980, *Accidents, Compensation and the Law* (3rd. edn.), London: Weidenfeld & Nicolson.

Biderman, A. D., Johnson, L., McIntyre, J., and Weir, A., 1967, *Report on a Pilot Study in the District of Columbia on Victimization and Attitudes to Law Enforcement*, President's Commission on Law Enforcement and Administration of Justice, Field Surveys I, Washington, DC: US Government Printing Office.

Home Office, 1978, *Review of the Criminal Injuries Compensation Scheme: Report of an Interdepartmental Working Party*, London: HMSO.

Miers, D., 1978, *Responses to Victimisation*, London: Professional Books.

Reiss, A. J., 1967, *Studies in Crime and Law Enforcement in Major Metropolitan Areas*, President's Commission, Field Surveys III, Washington DC: US Government Printing Office.

Sparks, R. F., Genn, H. G., and Dodd, D. J., 1977, *Surveying Victims*, Chichester: Wiley.

7 Sick Pay

(1) Receipts of sick pay

Occupational sick pay can be regarded as a form of private group insurance attached to a particular employment. However, it is unlike private insurance in so far as individual employees, once they have chosen a particular employment, cannot usually decide whether they would prefer to forgo membership of a scheme and perhaps instead to receive higher wages. Furthermore, the scope of cover customarily available is limited by the presumed reluctance of employers to include a number of significant risks in the schemes, notably long-term interruption in earnings.

Many sick pay schemes developed from customary and entirely discretionary payments made to employees in times of financial hardship arising from illness or injury. In recent years, schemes have become more formalized and less discretionary and they are more often the subject of free collective bargaining, a development probably related to the fact that the legal and voluntary wage restraints of recent years were sometimes not extended to occupational sick pay (Incomes Data Services, 1979, p. 3).

Table 7.1 *The distribution of occupational sick pay by total amount received*

Total amount of occupational sick pay received	Number of recipients $\bar{n}$
(£s)	
1 – 50	178
51 – 250	273
251 – 500	98
501 – 1000	41
1001 – 1500	13
1501 – 2000	2
2001 – 2500	4
2501 – 5000	6
Amount not known	260
Total $\bar{N}$	875

Schemes vary considerably in their qualifying conditions, benefit formulas, and exclusions (Incomes Data Services, 1979, pp. 39–71). It is usual to require employees to complete a period of service before granting them membership of a scheme. In the Compensation Survey, of those who had held their employment for less than six months, only 25 per cent obtained some sick pay; for those with six months but less than two years' service, 49 per cent obtained some sick pay; for those with two years but less than five years' service, 58 per cent obtained some sick pay; and for those with more than five years' service, 62.5 per cent obtained some sick pay. The maximum *duration* of sick pay also often varies with length of service. The amount of benefit is most often related to basic wages (not actual earnings), although a declining number of manual workers' schemes pay flat-rate benefits (see Table 7.1 for total amounts).

Exclusions in sick pay schemes are many and varied, but little is known about their actual impact on day-to-day administration. Exclusions often deny benefit if the illness or injury results from criminal acts, drug or alcohol abuse, attempted suicide, self-injury, insanity, wilful misconduct, or negligence. Sporting injuries are a significant cause of time off work and such absences are sometimes excluded from the scope of sick pay cover. Some schemes specify dangerous sports for which claims will not be paid. Almost all schemes terminate benefits to claimants who are shown to be not incapable of work, the test and proof of incapacity usually being borrowed from the National Insurance system. Another common exclusion relates to claims arising from a second, spare-time employment.

In the Compensation Survey, the mean of total receipts of sick pay among recipients was £248 (Table 7.2) and the mean duration of absence for the same group was 29.8 weeks, giving a mean weekly benefit of little more than £8. A number of victims reporting long absences from work but receiving sick pay for only a part of the absence reduces the mean value to this low level (Table 7.2). A more typical recipient of sick pay is someone absent for up to twenty-six weeks being paid £20 to £30 per week. When added to social security benefits, these amounts can provide total compensation equal to full pay: indeed, 78 per cent of sick pay recipients reported 'full pay' or 'made up pay' for the whole or a part of their period of absence. In the survey, as many as 76 per cent of all those who obtained sick pay received it for the whole of the period they were off work (Table 7.2). The proportion was higher for victims

Table 7.2 *Receipt of occupational sick pay for all or part of absence and mean amount received by length of absence from work*

Length of absence from work (weeks)	Occupational sick pay for whole of absence[1]		Occupational sick pay for part of absence		Mean amount of occupational sick pay
	(%)	n̄	(%)	n̄	(£s)
0 – 2	94.4	119	5.6	7	44
3 – 4	89.9	124	10.1	14	98
5 – 8	88.6	164	11.4	21	143
9 – 13	77.0	94	23.0	28	244
14 – 26	80.2	85	19.8	21	366
27–52	50.7	37	49.3	36	590
53 – 104	38.9	14	61.1	22	372
More than 104[2]	45.9	28	54.1	33	576
All sick pay recipients[3]	76.0	665	20.8	182	248

[1] Includes cases where sick pay was not received for the first three days of a period of absence.
[2] Figures for longer absence are biased downwards as a result of the difficulty in taking account of inflationary increases in sick pay received in different years.
[3] Total number who received occupational sick pay is 875. However, in twenty-eight cases (3.2 per cent) there was no information about duration of absence or duration of sick pay.

with shorter absences. Well over 80 per cent of all recipients with absences of up to twenty-six weeks obtained sick pay for the whole of their absence. For those absent from work for more than twenty-six weeks, the corresponding figure was no more than 40 per cent.

(2) Factors influencing receipt of sick pay

In 1974 an estimated 79.5 per cent of full-time workers were members of sick pay schemes (DHSS Report, 1977). Consequently, it was surprising to discover that, of the full-time workers in the Compensation Survey who were off work as a result of their illness or injury, only 56.2 per cent reported that they had actually obtained sick pay from their employer.[1] Part of the difference can be accounted for by workers who are deemed to be members of schemes but who have not satisfied a qualification period or who have exhausted their entitlement and must complete a further qualification period. Allowing for this factor reduces the 1974 membership estimate from 79.5 to 70.5 per cent. On the reasonable assumption that the remaining difference between 70.5 and 56.2 per cent is not a result of survey biases, we should consider its likely causes. It is possible that employers are less inclined to establish sick pay schemes in those industries and in those occupations where there is an above-average risk of incapacity. The Compensation Survey provided information about sick pay receipts by occupational group. There were marked differences in the sick pay entitlements found among the various occupational groups but there was no evidence that above-average risks of incapacity were to be found in the seven occupational groups where fewer than 40 per cent of employees obtained sick pay. However, the evidence is not conclusive as the analysis was based on small numbers and the indicator of occupational risk was not completely suitable.[2] Mention has already been made of the exclusions and limitations frequently contained in occupational sick pay agreements and it is quite possible that their use could explain part of the difference between membership and benefit statistics. Many sick pay agreements leave some decisions to employers' discretion, indeed, an estimated 15.2 per cent of full-time workers are in schemes which give the employer almost complete discretion to decide the amount of benefit (DHSS, 1977). Furthermore, scheme membership might be denied to some employees on medical grounds analogous to those used in the private insurance sector if it were thought that they were particularly likely to suffer long periods of incapacity.

The relative importance of these factors in explaining the difference between the proportion of sick pay scheme members and actual beneficiaries is unknown. However, the data serve to underline the necessity to interpret sick pay scheme membership statistics with some caution. It would clearly be optimistic to assume that the 80 per cent of full-time employees covered can expect to receive sick pay in the event of incapacity for work. Small employers might be expected to be somewhat less likely to provide sick pay schemes than large employers. The latter will benefit from economies of scale in administration; furthermore, the small employer can less easily carry the risk of large claims and will more often resort to the private insurance market to dispose of these risks. The Compensation Survey found that 50 per cent of victims employed in establishments with fewer than twenty-five employees obtained sick pay, whereas the figure was 60 per cent for those in establishments with more than twenty-five employees.

Men in employment are not more likely to receive occupational sick pay than women. This was a finding to be expected from surveys of sick pay scheme membership (DHSS, 1977; Dept. of Employment, *Gazette*, 1971, pp. 690–710). But this apparent equality of treatment has concealed substantial sex differences in the benefits obtained. In the Compensation Survey the mean amount of total sick pay paid to men was £300.50 but that paid to women was £133.50. As women generally had longer periods of absence from work than men (see Table 10.5), a comparison based on mean weekly benefit would reveal even greater differences. This large discrepancy is mainly a consequence of sex differences in income levels but might also reflect a tendency to pay women sick pay based on a lower proportion of weekly earnings or for a shorter proportion of the absence from work.

(3) Sick pay and the development of government policy

The first part of this section has drawn on the Compensation Survey findings to outline the scope and importance of occupational sick pay. This exercise is relevant to policy discussion about the relative roles of National Insurance and private provision for income support during absence from work. Until recently, National Insurance policy-making had taken insufficient account of the occupational sick pay sector and little thought had been given to an integration of the two systems, let alone to the principles which might shape such an integration. The publication of a Green Paper in 1980, on this issue (and its partial enactment in the Social Security and Housing Benefits Act 1982 – see Chapter 12, below) has gone some way towards remedying this neglect, although the recommendations in the paper will require further discussion in the light of our data.

One consequence of the recent expansion in occupational sick pay has been a change in the allocation of the costs of incapacity for work. In the absence of compensation, clearly the costs fall on the ill or injured person himself, or his family. To the extent that National Insurance provides compensation, victims are relieved of at least a part of the burden. To say where it actually falls requires a more complex analysis than can be attempted here, but it has the same impact as a payroll tax. Two companies of the same size producing the same product with the same wage levels and other costs of production will make exactly equal contributions to the National Insurance fund. These contributions would not be affected by one company relying on processes or management methods which result in a higher level of sickness absence than that experienced by its competitor. However, in so far as sick pay schemes replace wages during periods of incapacity, they will be counted as one of the costs of producing the goods or services and will affect the competitiveness of the firms. The result is to provide employers with a cost incentive to reduce potential sources of accidental injury or illness.

If changes in policy (see Green Paper, 1980) were to require employers to pay a greater part of the wage costs of sickness absence than they do at present, it would be sensible to encourage the expansion of occupational sick pay. A similar effect would be obtained by the technically more complex, though politically probably less acceptable, policy of isolating that part of the National Insurance contribution which pays for sickness benefit and making it risk-related. The present use of flat-rate contributions to the National Insurance fund carries the implication that illness or injury causing absence from work strikes at random, all employers running the roughly equal risk of losing man-hours from this cause. This is somewhat unrealistic, though it would be equally unrealistic to go to the opposite extreme and argue that variability in the conditions of employment can account for the whole of the variability in absence rates. The Compensation Survey provides a basis on which to compare the relative importance of National Insurance benefits and employers' sick pay in maintaining income during periods of incapacity. The appropriateness of this division of function depends upon – among other things – some assessment of the importance of employment conditions as factors which can explain the variability in absence rates. In the case of work accidents, we can assume that incapacity arising from the accidents is one of the costs of producing the goods or services. Incapacity for work arising from illness is more problematic but attention can be drawn to three factors which point to the importance of employment conditions. First, there are the more or less established connections between particular illnesses and particular occupations such as pneumoconiosis in the coal industry or silicosis among foundry workers. There can be little doubt that illness caused by work conditions is much more extensive than that which is specially compensated under the extensions to the Industrial Injuries scheme.[3] Secondly, there is some evidence that low job satisfaction is associated with high levels of absence (Taylor, 1967; *General Household Survey 1972*, p. 207). An employer might or might not be able to improve the job satisfaction of his employees but the extra costs of sickness absence attributable to low job satisfaction can properly be regarded as a cost of production. Thirdly, it is necessary to consider how the interaction between the effects of an illness and the specific physical and mental demands of a particular job determine the point at which illness creates incapacity for work. When a job is such that trivial illnesses create incapacity, the extra costs can be regarded as consequent upon a particular method of providing the goods or services. The collective impact of these three factors is hard to assess but they all add to the argument for extending the scope of occupational sick pay schemes.

The combined effects of sick pay and National Insurance benefits occasionally provide a beneficiary with more income when ill than when working. This occurs for two reasons. First, National Insurance sickness benefit is not at present taxable, although there are recent proposals to bring it into the tax net. Occupational sick pay, on the other hand, is taxed as ordinary income.[4] Sick pay schemes which make up the difference between the state benefit and normal earnings do not take into account the tax saving on the state benefit. Secondly, some schemes make no deductions for National Insurance benefits and allow a beneficiary to collect both in full. The level of income replacement may therefore lead to disincentives to early return to work; this is examined in Chapter 10. Previous published evidence is not conclusive but contains few examples of increases in sickness absence attributed to the introduction of a sick pay scheme (Moonman, 1973; Ministry of Labour, 1964). Furthermore, the rules for the payment of the earnings-related supplement to National Insurance benefit (payable until 1982) limited the total benefit to 85 per cent of earnings. One justification for this rule was presumably to maintain some incentive for a beneficiary to return to work; another was to take account, in a rough way, of the saving of the cost of travel to work and the saving in tax on the state benefit. But the 85 per cent rule had no effect when sick pay was received in addition to the state benefit. A necessary condition for the payment of National Insurance sickness benefit is incapacity for work, but no attention is paid to the receipt or non-receipt of sick pay.[5] However, the rules of sick pay schemes usually do take some account of entitlement to National Insurance benefit. Methods vary a great deal but an estimated 40 per cent of sick pay scheme members can expect to have the full value of

National Insurance benefits deducted from their entitlement. The remaining 60 per cent of scheme members can expect one of three other solutions: a partial deduction of National Insurance benefits, no deduction at all, or deduction of an amount which is at the discretion of the employer (DHSS, 1977). The net effect of occupational sick pay schemes will be in many instances to counteract the redistributive effects of National Insurance. A simple example illustrates this point: in a scheme where the full value of National Insurance benefits is deducted, a single man earning £100 per week would obtain, let us say, £30 per week in National Insurance benefits and £70 per week in sick pay; but a married man with the same earnings would receive perhaps £50 per week in National Insurance benefits and £50 in sick pay. The extra £20 award for his dependants is lost in the 'topping-up' process. This neutralization of the dependency benefits payable with National Insurance sickness benefit robs them of their function, with the result that the National Insurance dependency benefits often act as a subsidy to firms with a high proportion of married men among their employees. The effect of sick pay on work incentives might be to encourage unwarranted absence but also to free the genuinely ill from the financial necessity to present themselves as fit for work.

The Compensation Survey data relating to sick pay permit us to conclude that occupational sick pay schemes make an important contribution to the replacement of earnings which are lost as a result of illness or injury. The benefits are, of course, confined to those in employment when illness or injury strikes and, furthermore, the benefits tend to be provided in the early weeks of a spell of absence: the amount of sick pay paid in respect of absences beyond six months is relatively small.

A further important conclusion from the survey data concerns the actual proportion of employees who are, in a real sense, covered by the provisions of an occupational sick pay scheme. It has been shown that membership statistics cannot be taken as a reliable guide and resort must be made to surveys of actual recipients. This finding has an important bearing on the feasibility of proposed reductions in the role of National Insurance benefits. These proposals rely on the assumption that National Insurance benefits can be replaced by relatively minor and inexpensive extensions of already existing occupational sick pay schemes (Green Paper, 1980; and the Social Security and Housing Benefits Act 1982, which is discussed below in Chapter 12).

Notes

1. Martin and Morgan (1976, Table 5.1, p. 49) estimate that 45 per cent of people claiming National Insurance sickness benefit for periods of one month or more received sick pay from their employer for at least a part of their period of absence.
2. The sick pay data were categorized by occupational orders and unit groups; the risk data taken from DHSS *Social Security Statistics* are presented in the not totally comparable Standard Industrial Classification; furthermore, DHSS published statistics refer to occupational risk of accident or industrial disease and do not include non-industrial sickness.
3. Particular diseases are listed in relation to specific occupations. Diseases are only included in the list after exhaustive investigations to establish: (i) that they are risks of a particular occupation and not risks common to all persons; and (ii) that the attribution of particular cases to the nature of the employment can be established or presumed with reasonable certainty (see Industrial Injuries Advisory Council, 1981).
4. Employee contributions towards the cost of a sick pay scheme receive no tax relief, but employer contributions are (like wages) treated as a business expense and can be offset against liability to corporation tax: for this reason, most sick pay schemes are financed entirely by the latter method.
5. When employers are required to pay statutory sick pay during the first eight weeks of any sickness absence, this problem is unlikely to arise during that period: see the Social Security and Housing Benefits Act 1982 (discussed in Chapter 12 below).

References

Department of Employment *Gazette*, 1971, London: Department of Employment, August.

DHSS (Department of Health and Social Security), 1977, *Report on a Survey of Occupational Sick Pay Schemes*, London: HMSO.

General Household Survey 1972, (published by the Office of Population Censuses and Surveys, 1975), London: HMSO.

Green Paper, 1980, *Income During Initial Sickness: A New Strategy*, London: HMSO, Cmnd. 7864.

Incomes Data Services, 1979, *Guide to Sick Pay and Absence*, London: Incomes Data Services.

Industrial Injuries Advisory Council, 1981, *Report on Industrial Diseases*, London: HMSO, Cmnd. 8393.

Martin, J., and Morgan, M., 1976, *Prolonged Sickness and the Return to Work*, London: HMSO.

Ministry of Labour, 1964, *Sick Pay Schemes: A Report*, London: HMSO.

Moonman, J., 1973, *The Effectiveness of Fringe Benefits in Industry*, London: Gower Press.

Taylor, P. J., 1967, 'Personal Factors Associated with Sickness Absence', 24 *British Journal of Industrial Medicine* 93.

8 Private Insurance

The purchase of a private insurance policy can be characterized as one of the possible responses to risk, real or imagined. Other responses include a reduction or elimination of the risk by safety measures, abstention from the activity which gives rise to it, or acceptance of the risk. In the context of risks of loss following illness and injury, such choices are complicated by the existence of other mechanisms which remove some of the risks. In the United Kingdom these mechanisms are numerous and include national insurance, supplementary benefits, the National Health Service, legal aid, the common law damages system, and rights to occupational sick pay. Nevertheless, substantial risks of loss through illness or injury are untouched by these mechanisms, leaving some scope for a private insurance market.

The social usefulness of markets to transfer risk is seen by Arrow (1971, pp. 134–43) as simple to justify. If insurers and insured enter freely into contracts of insurance, then both must be better off, and if both are better off then so is society, unless other individuals are injured in some way. He argues that the possibility of shifting risks permits individuals to engage in risky activities beneficial to society which they would not otherwise undertake. He states that in ideal arrangements for shifting risks, 'we would want to find a market where we could insure freely against any economically relevant event' (Arrow, 1971, p. 135).

This is a principled, rather than a pragmatic, justification for the existence of private insurance. However, it provides a perspective from which the role of private insurance in compensating for the consequences of illness or injury can be assessed and a basis for reconsidering whether government policy in relation to this sector should be to encourage, discourage, ignore, or prohibit private insurance contracts. This section looks first at the types of cover available in the United Kingdom, then at empirical evidence of its actual contribution to compensation, and finally at some of the imperfections and unsatisfactory features of this small part of the United Kingdom insurance market. Both the discussion and the survey data refer to policies which can be purchased by individuals.

Group contracts are not included, except in the case of medical expenses insurance where they account for an estimated 77 per cent of subscription income to the provident societies (DHSS, 1977). Group loss of income and personal accident insurances are in effect a form of occupational sick pay when they are provided through an employer's scheme (see Chapter 7 above).

(1) Types of insurance available

Life insurance contracts have many functions, only one of which, minimizing the financial risk of premature death, is relevant to this discussion. The market is large and complex with a wide choice of supplier and type of contract; benefits are usually paid as a capital sum, but periodic payments are also available; contracts can be written for a specified time period or for the whole life of the insured. Claims present few potential sources of disagreement between insurer and beneficiary. It is not necessary to prove the amount of a loss, and the occurrence of the insured event is unambiguous; limitations and exclusions in life policies are in practice kept to a minimum. Claims data were not sought in the Compensation Survey because of the particular difficulties of interviewing members of families who have recently suffered a bereavement. Victims of illness or injury were, however, asked whether they had experienced difficulties in obtaining life cover since their illness or injury (see Question 83a, Appendix II).

The life insurance sector in the United Kingdom has an important advantage over all other types of accident and illness insurance. For many years it has enjoyed what amounts to a subsidy from the Exchequer equivalent to more than 15 per cent of premiums collected. To our knowledge, there is no published account of the supposed objectives of this very costly support, nor any critical examination of its effects. We draw attention to this implicit Government preference for encouraging the purchase of life insurance, but recognize that the subsidy is particularly relevant to the use of life insurance as a long-term savings medium.

Personal accident insurance is written as an annual contract, with no obligation on insurer or insured to renew the policy. Benefits are provided in the form of lump sums and/or periodic payments. The lump sum, or a proportion of it, is payable for death or scheduled impairments such as loss of a limb, loss of an eye, loss of a hand or foot. The periodic payments can be claimed when the insured is incapable of work or satisfies the particular definition of total or partial incapacity; periodic payments sometimes extend to incapacity caused by illness. The relative sums insured for the various losses appear to be arbitrarily chosen, but the overall level of benefits is in principle selected by the purchaser on his own valuation of his own 'life and limb'. Personal accident cover, without provision for periodic payments, is frequently provided in a comprehensive motor insurance for the policyholder and his or her spouse; it is also included in the multi-risk contracts specially designed for holiday travel.

Loss of income insurance is usually referred to by insurance companies as permanent health insurance, although contracts with a similar function are written by Friendly Societies under different names. It is permanent in the sense that once an insurer has accepted a proposal, the terms of the policy are that renewal cannot be refused until some prearranged expiry date, usually the retirement of the insured. Benefits are in the form of periodic payments and can be payable until the prearranged expiry date. There is often a waiting period after the onset of incapacity before benefit becomes payable, usually of six or twelve months. The first months of income loss due to prolonged illness are usually met by National Insurance benefits, an employer's sick pay scheme, or the victim's own resources. Only one or two companies offer contracts with very short waiting periods. It is not clear whether this is due to lack of demand or the reluctance of suppliers. In general, insurers appear to be very cautious and conservative in their approach to the marketing of permanent health contracts, and the choice available to the consumer is poor in comparison with that available in the life insurance market.[1]

One of the functions of legal expenses insurance is to meet the often considerable costs of pursuing a claim for common law damages (see Figure 3.5). Cover of this kind has been available in England and Wales since 1974 (Pfennigstorf, 1975, p. 27). English law has shown a persistent objection to the promotion of litigation by persons without an interest in the action but the Criminal Law Act 1967, ss. 13(1), 14(1), abolished the offence and the tort of 'maintenance'; case law[2] also has dispelled some of the doubts about the legality of legal expenses insurance. However, legal expenses contracts which financed legal actions in return for a share in the proceeds might still be treated by the courts as contrary to public policy. This question was not clarified by the 1967 Act.

Another little-used private insurance mechanism for remedying the defects of the common law damages system is reverse liability cover. Personal liability cover is extended to pay the amount of an unsatisfied judgment in circumstances which, had the positions of the insured and the person responsible for the loss been reversed, then the insured would have been entitled to an indemnity under the personal liability cover.

Private health care policies provide cover under a number of headings. More than half the total benefits paid are for hospital accommodation (DHSS, 1977, p. 7, Table 8). Most of the remainder pays for consultants' fees, but it is possible to include physiotherapy, home nursing, and even general practitioner services. Under most contracts the insurer cannot refuse to renew a policy in the event of a deterioration in the health of the insured. The amount of a 'loss' is relatively easy to determine, with little scope for an insured person to exaggerate the expenses he has incurred. Hospital cash policies do not even require the insured to incur expenses: they usually provide a benefit for each day spent in hospital, whether or not the insured opts for private accommodation or treatment.

(2) The private insurance policies held by victims

All victims in the Compensation Survey were asked whether at the time of their illness or injury they had one or more of a number of types of private insurance coverage (not including life insurance) (see Question 81a, Appendix II). Some 14 per cent reported relevant policies (Table 8.1). Personal accident was the most common type of insurance held. Apart from the special case of personal accident cover under a motor policy,[3] the types of insurance held by victims in the survey were given the same order of importance as that derived from published premium income statistics. The total UK premium income under personal accident, medical fees, hospital costs, and loss of income insurance was probably less than £130 million in 1975 (the year in which a majority of our respondents made their claims). It was distributed broadly as follows: personal accident, £50–70 million (Insurance Year Book, 1977); medical fees/hospital costs, £54 million (DHSS, 1977); loss of income (permanent health insurance only), £15 million (Life Insurance Association, 1977). Other insurances include holiday policies and insurance to continue hire purchase payments during illness as well as those which were inadequately described.

Table 8.1 *Number of victims who held private insurance at the time of their illness or injury by type of policy*

Type of policy	Number reporting insurance cover[1] n̄	Percentage of total sample (%)	
Personal accident	222	6.2	14[2]
Personal accident section of a motor policy	177	5.0	
Medical fees/hospital costs	86	2.4	
Loss of income when ill or injured	38	1.0	
Other/type of policy not known	77	2.1	
No relevant insurance	3049	85.0	
Don't know/no reply	42	1.2	
Total N̄	3586		

[1] Some people reported more than one type of cover, consequently the columns do not sum to the sample size.
[2] A total of 14 per cent had one or more policies within these categories.

A comparison of the above figures with premium income and policy statistics for life insurance reveals a marked consumer preference for the latter. The Family Expenditure Survey for 1976 found 78.9 per cent of households with some life cover. The total life insurance expenditure for 1976 was, according to the same source, more than £1,200 million.[4] At most ages the risk of premature death is small by comparison with the risks of illness or injury, but insurance against the former hazard is far more common than insurance against the latter. The explanation is perhaps to be sought in some peculiarity in attitudes to risk or more probably in imperfections in the private market for personal insurances against illness, injury, and death.

(3) Claims under the policies

Of those victims who reported a policy covering illness or injury, (n̄ = 495) 41 per cent (n̄ = 205) obtained some insurance payment. No attempt was made to discover why 59 per cent of policy-holders obtained no payment under their policies. In many cases the explanation would be quite simply that their policy did not purport to provide for their particular misfortune. If we consider private insurance beneficiaries as a proportion of the whole sample and not just of policy-holders, the contribution made by this sector is put into perspective. Only 205 individuals, i.e. 5.7 per cent of those interviewed in the survey, actually obtained a benefit. Thus, private insurance provides benefits for only a small proportion of the victims of illness and injury. Furthermore, even for this small minority, it can make only a trivial contribution to the costs of illness or injury (Table 8.2). This conclusion is confirmed by the results of a survey prepared for the Royal Commission which found that 7 per cent of accident victims obtained payments under private insurance; the mean amount received was £70 (in 1977 terms) (Pearson Report, 1978, para. 154). In the Compensation Survey, the mean amount obtained was somewhat higher at £81 and furthermore referred to receipts in 1975 and earlier years. Medical fees/hospital costs policies provided the highest mean amounts of benefits and were also responsible for almost half the total compensation attributable to the private insurance sector. The number of claims paid under the personal accident section of a motor policy suggests that, with the possible exception of payments for accidental death, such cover is of little value to road accident victims.

The expectations of policy-holders

Policy-holders were questioned about the correspondence between their expectations of entitlement and the payments received under private insurance policies as a result of illness or injury. Only ten policy-holders reported that they had not received expected benefits. Those who actually obtained benefits were asked if they had received about the expected amount; 75 per cent replied 'yes' and the remainder were evenly split between those who had obtained more and those who had obtained less than expected. Respondents whose expectations had not been met were asked to comment on the reasons. No clear pattern could be discerned in their replies, nor was it possible to make judgments about the reasonableness of their expectations. Some comments are reproduced for illustrative purposes.

(Case 1) A road accident victim who held a medical expenses insurance had National Health Service treatment. He then wrote to his insurer pointing out that they had been saved a considerable amount of money. The insurer agreed to pay for a home help for a

Table 8.2 *Numbers of claimants and the mean and total amounts received in claims under private insurance policies in relation to type of policy*

Type of Policy	Number of claims paid	Claims paid as a percentage of policies reported	Amounts received in claims £1 – 50	51 – 200	201 – 1000	not known	Mean amount received per claim[1]	Total receipts[2] for all cases in the survey
		(%)	(£s)	(£s)	(£s)	(£s)	(£s)	(£s)
Personal accident	110	50	89	12	2	7	47	5,110
Personal accident section of a motor policy	3	2	1	0	1	1	135	405
Medical fees/hospital costs	47	55	16	8	11	12	167	7,842
Loss of income when ill or injured	27	71	22	5	0	0	30	803
Other/type of policy not known	19	25	11	4	4	0	178	3,385
All policies	206[3]	34	139	29	18	20	81	17,545

[1] Rounded to nearest pound.
[2] Total receipts have been adjusted to include cases where the amount of the claim was not reported or not known.
It was assumed that they obtained the mean amount for the relevant type of policy.
[3] One victim obtained payment of a claim under each of two policies.

year. The victim thought they might have done more than that.
(Case 2) An industrial accident victim with a personal accident policy, '. . . paid £5 a year and when it came time to claim they only gave me half of what I should have had because they said it was not an accident, it was just a recurrence of an old one, so when it came time for renewal I told them to get lost.'
(Case 3) An industrial accident victim with a personal accident policy commented: 'by the time all the certificates were available it was too late to make a claim. A claim should be made within seven days. These seven days were too hectic to give any claim any thought.'
(Case 4) A personal accident policy-holder fractured his hand at a dance. It was not broken above the wrist so he did not get the higher benefit he expected.

(4) Problems associated with the private insurance system

One of the objections raised by critics of a system of social welfare based more or less on the operation of the market derives from the supposition that insurance companies in pursuing their commercial interests will classify some risks as uninsurable (Titmuss, 1968). This is a problem which has arisen in relation to compulsory insurance, particularly in the USA where special pooling arrangements have been made for motorists considered to be poor risks (USA Dept. of Transportation, 1970a). In the UK it has not been necessary to make such arrangements for compulsory insurance, probably because insurers have found various methods of sharing out the poor risks among themselves.[5] Certainly in relation to motor insurance they appear to have avoided a potential source of criticism quite successfully, unlike their US counterparts (US Dept. of Transportation, 1970b). The problem of the uninsurable risk is highlighted by legislation which makes insurance compulsory, but it should not be forgotten that the total refusal of insurance can have serious consequences for a family even where the purchase of cover is not compulsory.

Data from the Compensation Survey permit a tentative estimate that about 64,000 people in the household population of England and Wales have effectively been denied insurance because an insurance company has decided that they are too likely to die or to suffer illness or injury. The figure, which is most probably an underestimate (as the survey did not include the institutional population in

England and Wales, and it is probable that others not screened in to the sample would nevertheless have experienced a refusal of insurance), was derived from affirmative replies to a question about the difficulties experienced in obtaining accident, illness, or life insurance at any time in the respondent's life. In thirty-six cases the respondent reported a refusal of cover. The assumption was then made that a proportion of 'refusals' similar to that found among the 3,586 respondents would have been found among non-respondents and among those illness victims not approached for an interview. As the survey was addressed to a known proportion of the household population of England and Wales (see Maclean and Genn, 1979, Chapter 6), a national estimate could be made.

It is important to remember that the figure of 64,000 refers to people who have actively sought insurance and have been denied it; it does not include those who have not considered the possibility of insurance or have themselves decided that they would not qualify, nor those who have obtained a policy which specifically excludes the misfortune they are most likely to suffer. Many of the people in the sample were suffering from illnesses which began or were diagnosed some years ago and it is evident that the refusals of insurance cover had occurred over a period of years. It is probable that, had some of these people tried to obtain insurance on a second occasion, they would have been successful. Only two respondents actually mentioned that they had been told to try again, in one case after two years, and in the other, after five years. They are not included in the above estimate.

Once someone has been refused insurance it might have the effect of making them unwilling to risk a further refusal. It is likely that the refusal of insurance on medical grounds will add something to an individual's perception of his prognosis. It is even possible that such information might affect their attitude to rehabilitation. The insurance industry does not seem to have considered these questions. In discussing permanent health insurance, one commentator from the industry states, 'some few diseases rule out any form of health insurance, but outside staffs are trained to avoid such cases and the proportion of health declinatures is only about 4%' (Biggs, 1968). The implication is that the problem is solved, as far as is possible, by diplomacy on the part of the salesman to ensure that proposers who are likely to be refused insurance do not get as far as completing a proposal form. In making the above comment, the writer was chiefly concerned to correct the widespread impression among insurance management that the required medical standard for permanent health insurance is so high that a company which began to offer it might prejudice its reputation by declining to insure a large number of its clients.

In the Compensation Survey some respondents who reported difficulty in obtaining cover provided the following explanations: 'Won't give it to me – too big a risk'; 'My wife took out insurance on my life and she paid for it but a few weeks later an insurance man called and said my claim was rejected because of my illnesses'; 'We tried and they said we couldn't as I was under the doctor'; 'As soon as I mentioned heart and chest that was it, they would not consider it'; 'I have tried to get a mortgage protection for this house, I can't get one because I have cancer. I told them the truth and of course they said they couldn't insure me. I am not bitter about it – I am only trying to protect my wife and children'. Only one respondent actually mentioned having tried several companies before giving up hope of obtaining insurance cover. It is not known how many of those refused insurance would find cover if they were not discouraged. The chief underwriter of a large life company commented:

> In the last ten to twenty years there has been a marked advancement in the treatment of many of our common medical conditions and this has been reflecting itself in the better underwriting terms and the acceptance of a wider market for impaired lives. Take the person who has had a coronary thrombosis. Twenty years ago he had little chance of being accepted. Today the better cases can get quite moderate terms, particularly if a few years have elapsed since the episode. (Reynolds, 1976).

The same writer stated that the life insurance industry in the British Isles accepts 93 per cent of proposers at 'standard or tabular rates'. The remaining 7 per cent are uprated in one of three ways: by a premium loading, by a reduction of the sum insured in the event of early death, or by rating the proposer at an age above his actual age. The most interesting implication of these comments is that refusals do not exist. One can only assume that the sales staff have 'skills' which ensure that proposals which would be refused do not reach the underwriter.

(5) The amounts of benefit

The amounts of benefit reported in the Compensation survey were trivial in all but a small number of instances (see Table 8.2). Within limits, it is the insured who decides on the sum insured, and certainly sums insured much higher than those found in the Compensation Survey are available in the insurance market. However, the data do serve to underline an acknowledged weakness of the private insurance mechanism, its response to inflation. There is no automatic procedure to increase the sum insured to maintain its real value. Furthermore, beneficiaries who receive periodic payments often have no protection against a decline in the real value of their benefits.

(6) Competition

There are a number of indications that the market for illness and injury insurance is uncompetitive. Clayton, using price surveys prepared by the Consumers' Association and *The Economist*, argued that the market for life assurance was very imperfect, suggesting that the reasons were to be derived from the demand side and from the structure of the intermediary market (Clayton, 1971, Chapter 13). Wide variations in price continue to be a feature of the life market,[6] but this must be interpreted cautiously when there is no information as to the amount of business transacted at various prices. Price comparisons must take into account variations in the scope of cover provided. This is a task of considerable complexity, as standard policy wordings have not been adopted in this sector of the market. In the life market comparisons of the cover are less important than comparisons of the conditions under which the sum insured may be increased or the policy type changed in the event of a deterioration in health. In personal accident and permanent health contracts, definitions of 'accident' or 'disability' vary significantly, as do the excluded risks.

A second kind of imperfection derives from the apparent reluctance of insurers to supply some types of illness and injury insurance. From an insurer's point of view, certain types of risk are more attractive than others. The characteristics which make a risk suitable to be handled by private insurers have been summarised as follows:

(i) The market must be constituted by a large number of similar risks.

(ii) The causes of loss within a class of risks must be independent of one another.

(iii) The overall level of losses must be predictable and the insurers

must be satisfied that they can estimate the probability of loss for particular subcategories of risk.
(iv) There must be a degree of uncertainty about whether a particular insured will sustain a loss, or, in the case of life or annuity business, when the loss will occur. (Carter, 1973, p. 1; Hauser and Burrows, 1969, p. 28).

There are many types of insurance available which do not satisfy these conditions, but illness and injury policies come near to meeting them. Condition (iii) is well satisfied in relation to life coverage, as mortality statistics have been collected for many years in England and Wales. Statistics from which to estimate the probability of accident or illness have not received anything like the attention which has been given to mortality data. An actuary writing in 1970 commented:

> We have long studied the variations in mortality in relation to geographical, social and environmental factors. In the past similar studies were made of the sickness experience of Friendly Societies. Now with the decline of Friendly Societies, actuaries are again becoming interested in sickness in the form of permanent sickness insurance (Daw, 1970).

No doubt data would have been collected had there been a substantial demand for accident and illness cover, but it is probable that insurers prefer not to sell such cover as aggressively as they sell life insurance. Quite apart from the absence of sound rating statistics, there is the fear of exaggerated claims – a problem which hardly arises under a life policy. This reluctance does not extend to one type of accident and illness insurance usually described as a 'hospital cash plan'. It provides a few pounds for every day spent in hospital. Rating statistics are easily available and there is little scope for exaggerating claims as an insured has almost no control over admission to hospital and length of stay. However, from the point of view of the insured the function of such an insurance is not at all apparent. It is difficult to imagine the circumstances in which an individual would be well advised to buy hospital cash insurance, with or without a medical expenses policy and a permanent health policy. Hospital cash insurances do not represent a very large part of the total market for accident and illness covers, but they illustrate an attitude which might be of importance in understanding the supply side of that market.

Brokers play an important role in the market for private insurance against the risks of accident and illness. They are remunerated by commission from the insurance company, which is usually based on the premium collected, or less often the sum insured. Commissions vary from company to company and by type of contract. The intermediary thus has a financial disincentive to recommend that a client purchase a policy with a low premium or a low rate of commission, irrespective of the merits of the policy. This system of remuneration does not encourage brokers to give their clients independent advice and is clearly a potential, if not a proven, cause of uncompetitiveness in all branches of private insurance. The Consumers' Association (1977, pp. 680–2) attempted to assess the quality of advice provided by insurance brokers. They anonymously asked 163 brokers to advise on the life insurance requirements of a particular family. Only 15 per cent of the brokers recommended the type of contract thought most suitable by the Consumers' Association and their advisers. Many brokers advised the family to spend more than was necessary to obtain the recommended amount of cover. However, the Consumers' Association survey provided no clear evidence that rates of commission are the main cause of the poor advice. Professional incompetence seemed to be a factor of some importance.

(7) Conclusions

The Beveridge Report (1942) made proposals for social security reform which were consistent with, and indeed envisaged, the development of private provision to supplement the basic benefits provided by national insurance. In two areas, retirement pensions and life insurance, the private sector has grown considerably since 1942, even if partnership between state provision and private provision has not developed quite as Beveridge expected. But, as has been seen, the private sector remains insignificant in providing compensation for the risks of illness and injury.

The Royal Commission on Personal Injury briefly discussed the role of private first party insurance in the present mixed system of compensation for personal injury (Pearson, 1978, paras. 149–54). Some members of the Commission felt that, 'greater facilities . . . by way of tax concessions or otherwise, might be offered for additional cover by first party insurance' (para. 1715). However, this view did not have the force of a recommendation, and we are left with the impression that the Commission were content to allow the private insurance market to continue to provide a modest contribution to injury compensation. It is submitted that the policy alternatives considered in the Royal Commission report allowed room for a more careful evaluation of the role played by the private insurance sector than was attempted by the Commission.

Attention has been drawn in this chapter to a number of weaknesses in the insurance mechanism; other relevant issues are the high ratio of administrative costs to benefits paid, and the unequal relationship of insurer and insured when disputes arise under a contract. But it does not necessarily follow that the private insurance contribution to illness and injury compensation should be discouraged. If private arrangements are to be left to perform a supplementary social policy function it is important to understand their limitations and to identify those areas where legislation or insurance industry wide co-operation could mitigate the effects of some of their weaknesses. Although it is difficult to give direct encouragement to competition and innovation, some of the weaknesses can be tackled. For instance, schemes could be devised for the pooling of poor risks, or for the remuneration of intermediaries in a form which would encourage them to give independent advice. Similarly, industry wide mechanisms for handling disputes between insurers and their policy-holders could be introduced, perhaps based on and parallel to the appeals procedures now available to dissatisfied social security claimants.

In conclusion, it is worth drawing attention to the emphasis in this discussion on explaining the insignificant contribution of the private insurance sector by reference to factors which are internal to that sector. This is in marked contrast to an approach which asserts that the effective demand for private insurance has been seriously undermined by the risk-bearing mechanisms of the Welfare State.

Notes

1. The range available can be seen in the annual Permanent Health Insurance Supplement to the *Policy Holder Insurance Journal*.
2. *Hill* v. *Archbold* [1968] 1QB 686.
3. It was to be expected that a much greater proportion than 5 per cent of the total sample would be covered by the personal accident extension of a comprehensive motor insurance policy. See also Sentry Insurance, *Motor Insurance Survey*, by Louis Harris International and the City University Business School, for survey data on motorists' knowledge of the scope of their insurance coverage.
4. Information supplied by the Department of Employment from *Family Expenditure Survey* data and published in: British Insurance Association, *Insurance Facts and*

Figures, 1979 edn.

5. The methods are believed to be of an informal kind. Insurers rarely cancel or refuse to renew the motor policy of a customer who has proved to be a very poor risk.
6. See, e.g., the comparisons of life assurance returns published periodically in *The Economist*.

References

Arrow, K. J., 1971, 'Insurance Risk and Resource Allocation', in *Essays in the Theory of Risk-Bearing*, Chicago: Markham.

Beveridge Report, 1942, *Social Insurance and Allied Services*, London: HMSO, Cmd. 6404.

Biggs, D. B., 1968, 'Permanent Health Insurance', 65 *Journal of the Chartered Insurance Institute* 111.

Carter. R. L., ed., 1973, *Handbook of Insurance*, Kluwer-Harrap Handbooks.

Clayton, G., 1971, *British Insurance*, London: Elek Books.

Consumers' Association, 1977, *Money Which,* Dec., 680.

Daw, R. H., 1970, 'A Comparison of Mortality and Sickness in relation to Geographical and Socio-economic Factors', 97 *Journal of the Institute of Actuaries* 17.

DHSS (Department of Health and Social Security), 1977, *UK Private Medical Care: Provident Scheme Statistics 1976* (commissioned report), London: Lee Donaldson Associates.

Hauser, M., and Burrows, P., 1969, *The Economics of Unemployment Insurance*, London: Allen & Unwin.

The Insurance Year Book, 1977, London: Policyholder Insurance Press.

Life Assurance Association, 1977, *Life Insurance in the United Kingdom 1972–1976*, London.

Maclean, M., and Genn, H., 1979, *Methodological Issues in Social Surveys,* London: Macmillan.

Pearson, Lord (Chairman), 1978, *Report of the Royal Commission on Civil Liability and Personal Injury* (3 vols), London: HMSO, Cmnd. 7054.

Pfennigstorf, W., 1975, *Legal Expense Insurance: The European Experience in Financing Legal Services*, Chicago: American Bar Foundation.

Reynolds, M., 1976, 'Dr. Mary Reynolds on Life Underwriting Today', *Policy Holder Insurance Journal*, 17 Dec., p. 2278.

Titmuss, R. M., 1968, 'Models of Redistribution in Social Security and Private Insurance', in *Commitment to Welfare*, London: Allen & Unwin.

USA Department of Transportation, 1970a, *Motor Vehicle Assigned Risks Plans* in the *Automobile Insurance and Compensation Study*, Washington DC: US Government Printing Office.

——, 1970b, *Insurance Accessibility for the Hard-to-Place Driver*, in the *Automobile Insurance and Compensation Study*, Washington DC: US Government Printing Office.

9 Social Care

This chapter describes briefly the kinds of social care available to victims of illness and injury, all of which are allocated primarily on the basis of the individual's need. The question is then raised whether meeting need is a possible concern of the tort system – and if so, given that damages payments reach only a subgroup of those affected by illness or injury, do they reach a group with special needs? In the absence of any indication of a relationship between the likelihood of receiving damages and the presence of special needs as indicated by high use of health and welfare support, this chapter closes with a description of the patterns of service consumption observed in our population of those affected by illness and injury.

The social care available to victims of illness and injury includes, first, the National Health Service; both hospital in-patient and out-patient facilities, the general practitioner services, and local community health services, particularly home nursing. The service offered is free at the point of consumption (except for prescription charges) and no distinction is made by cause of the difficulty, except in a very limited way for road accident victims where some charges may be made against insurance companies. Secondly, it includes the welfare support offered by local authorities. Under the National Assistance Act 1948 local authorities were given discretionary powers to provide various forms of assistance to groups, such as the disabled, whose needs were not being met. Under the Chronically Sick and Disabled Persons Act 1970, the local authority is given discretion to decide what are the needs of a disabled person for the types of assistance specified in the Act. This discretion in assessing needs, and the lack of additional funding, has led to disappointingly little development of provision under this Act. Nevertheless, local authorities now have a duty to seek out and register the chronically sick and disabled in their areas. They provide for a small proportion of these various services in the home – particularly, home helps to assist with the shopping and housework, meals on wheels, laundry, a telephone, and social work advice and support. Outside the home many authorities run day centres offering social activities and light employment, help with transport, other recreational facilities, and sometimes short-term institutional care. The local housing department will co-operate with the social services department in offering special housing, or adaptations of existing housing. The local offices of the Department of Employment are also involved in offering registration and special help to the disabled in finding employment. In this study we have also looked at a third source of social care, which we have called informal support. Under this heading we include the kinds of help received from friends and relatives by those suffering the effects of illness and injury. This support may be long term, regular, and even paid, but is provided directly within the community without the intervention of any agency.

The common law claim for damages has in the past paid very little attention to such support in kind. However, in a case in 1973, the Court of Appeal[1] in assessing damages for personal injuries 'took into account' (in an unspecified way) the prospect that the claimant might receive help from his local authority under the Chronically Sick and Disabled Persons Act 1970. But the same court said later[2] that it would not be right to regard the services as free, as the local authority is empowered to recover such charges as it determines. If the tort system is retained in some form, there is a need for much greater understanding of this kind of support so that it can be intelligently taken into account when assessing damages.

The Compensation project as a whole set out to examine the present operation of the tort system for compensating victims of personal injury in the context of other systems of support used by this population, and by those suffering similar levels of functional incapacity caused by illness. (For a full discussion of the screening process, described briefly in the Introduction, see Maclean and Genn, 1979). However, 'information and data can never be understood in isolation from the context of ideas which give them meaning. Problem setting is as important as problem solving because the frames which organize thoughts shape the conclusions we reach' (Rein, 1976). If one accepts the value critical approach to the relationship between social research and policy questions described above, it is important to make explicit the basic assumptions underlying the material presented here. The stimulus for embarking on the Compensation project was a concern about the present operation of compensation for personal injury through the tort system. Although resources are generously allocated to effecting a finely assessed individual decision, the process becomes less finely tuned when the actual settlement is reached; for example, when contributory negligence and uncertainties lead to discounts from the 'full' amount of damages (see Chapter 3). The present chapter is concerned with the effects of the allocation criteria involved. If the tort system is regarded as one of many agencies concerned with redistributing resources it appears to do so expensively, using criteria with unexpected results as seen in Chapters 2 and 3. Perhaps both these factors are the price to be paid for decisions within a legal context based on close examination of the individual case, using a limited selection of facts, as compared with political or administrative decisions which are preceded by more awareness of pressures resulting from a series of events, and which may therefore be more aware of the relative demands of various groups, and may also be more flexible. (These issues are discussed at length in Horowitz, 1979.)

If the tort system is seen as a means of allocating resources, rather than as an act of justice or retribution, this may be undertaken to achieve a variety of goals. The expressed goal of the tort system is to restore the victim of another's negligence to his position before that act, when the defendant has the resources to make the payment as an individual, or acting through the intermediary of insurance. While these criteria restrict the allocation of tort payments to a subgroup of the total population affected by the consequences of illness or injury, there are further rationing devices in operation, related to the claimant's ability to formulate and carry through a claim, which affect the allocation of these payments in a disturbing way. These have been discussed in Chapter 2. Perhaps the most valuable aspect of tort settlements in personal injury cases is their potential capacity for dealing with 'diswelfares' (see Titmuss, 1974) or general losses of well-being, legally summarized as non-pecuniary losses. This individual approach should enable the tort system, for the cases which it covers, to fill some of the gaps left by other institutions covering specific requirements such as medical care or income maintenance. But although a previous study has estimated that more than half the money awarded falls under the head of non-pecuniary loss (Pearson Report, 1978), it was found through the small-scale postal inquiry to solicitors following the Compensation Survey that over two-thirds of itemized awards included an income maintenance element (see Chapter 3, p. 90). This would imply that where a non-pecuniary award is made it is usually in addition to a payment in respect of lost income (see

Chapter 3, p. 90). The pain and suffering experienced by an elderly person as a result of an accident in the home – even where a defective product may be involved or a negligent landlord has caused an accident by failure to maintain a property – is extremely unlikely to result in a settled claim under the tort system as administered at present (see Table 2.2). Should a system which is, at least theoretically, able to make such an award be valued for the sake of that possibility, or at a time of reduced public expenditure is it necessary to concentrate on provision concerned with meeting need?

The tort system did not develop with the intention of meeting need: historically it was associated with attempts to minimize conflict, to deter negligence, and to provide justice. However, as the relationship between law and society becomes a concern of both lawyers and social scientists, discussion of the role of tort in relation to other supporting agencies is becoming more widespread and more sophisticated, and the policy implications and outcomes as well as the formal aims of the system are being scrutinized (Carrier and Kendall, 1979; Walker and Townsend, 1980.) The term 'need' has now appeared in recent judgments, and in the recommendations of the recent Royal Commission dealing with the tort system. For example, in 1974 in the Court of Appeal the judgment said that the plaintiff's 'loss is the existence of the need for [X] the value of which for the purposes of damages . . . is the . . . cost of supplying those needs'.[3] Although the most obvious head of damage following injury is pecuniary loss, which should be made good, assessment of damages also includes non-pecuniary loss such as the loss of services and society, where damages should be recoverable for an injured person's need to have services rendered and expenses incurred by others for his benefit. This kind of approach must inevitably involve lawyers in the business of attempting to define individual needs, and of considering the various sources from which they might be met. Perhaps we may draw a parallel with the way lawyers have become involved in the field of social security provisions as described by Sir Leslie Scarman in the Hamlyn lectures (Scarman, 1974). In his introduction to the 1976 Symposium on these lectures Sir Leslie speaks of regarding the law as 'one of the social sciences . . . in practice of great assistance . . . offering a low key review of ordinary problems', and hence developing into an 'effective weapon of social policy'. There is evidence of movement in this direction also from the discussion in the report of the Royal Commission on Civil

Liability of the growing interrelationship between law in the social security field, and the law of tort in relation to personal injury. It is clearly stated in the report (Pearson, 1978, Chapter 2, p. 8,) that the 'need' for cash compensation is diminished by provision through the National Health Service and social security. This implies moving away from aiming at retributive justice for the individual to a broader consideration of the needs of accident victims as a whole, and an awareness of the variety of sources from which they are being met.

If this is the case, discussion is necessary of the kinds of needs which the tort system may be attempting to meet. Is a professionally defined standard of living to be laid down, against which deficiency indicates a normative need? (See Bradshaw, 1972.) Is the need expressed by an individual to be accepted at its face value? Or should comparative measures of need for various goods and services be used? The latter approach has been used to compare welfare provision in different geographical areas in the hope of stimulating levelling up of standards of provision by local authorities (Davies, 1978). Alternatively one might use a philosophically based construction (see Barry, 1965), which perceives the statement '*A* needs *X*' as incomplete. To complete the construct, one requires the addition: '*A* needs *X* in order to do *Y*'. In the case of compensation for personal injury, *A* has suffered the effects of *I* – which may include pain and suffering as well as monetary loss. *A* therefore needs *X* (a monetary award) to alleviate the effects of *I*, to put him back, so far as money can do it, in the situation he enjoyed before experiencing injury. In this formulation the provision of *X*, a compensation award, meets *A*'s need to alleviate the effects of *I*. Alternatively, *A* also deserves *X*. In the interest of justice he must be returned as far as possible to his pre-*I* situation, at the expense of the defendant. These alternatives are not mutually exclusive. But the emphasis placed on each affects the approach to evaluating the present system.

If the tort system is approached as a resource distributing agency with a concern to meet 'needs' as one of its allocation criteria, it becomes relevant to ask whether it does so equitably and efficiently. This chapter focuses on the provision of social care to those victims of illness and injury who may benefit through a tort action, and on others with similar functional difficulties. The question at issue in the following section is whether those likely to obtain damages display any special needs which are being met by the tort system, rather than by any other support system. As it becomes clear that the groups of accident victims most likely to benefit under the tort system do not show particularly high levels of use of health and welfare services, the final section of this chapter will examine more closely how services are used, singly and in combination, by our respondents, according to their demographic characteristics.

(1) Use of health and welfare services

In order to find an objective way of assessing the needs of illness and accident victims for various forms of support, we concentrated on non-cash forms of support; then in order to see whether the 'needs' of these groups differed, we examined the services and support actually used by these groups, looking for evidence of different patterns of consumption. We made no attempt to establish normative need, or expressed need, but looked directly at service use achieved. The likelihood of receiving damages is closely related to the type of accident suffered. As Chapter 2 has reported one in three of road accident victims and one in five of work accident victims compared with one in fifty of other accident victims obtained damages through a tort claim. We therefore grouped users of services by the cause of the illness or injury, bearing in mind that road and work accident victims are those likely to benefit through the tort system. We examined use of the National Health Service, local authority services, and the informal support given by family and friends to road and work accident victims, to see whether the pattern of use differed from that of other accident victims and of those suffering a similar level of functional incapacity caused by illness.

The first need to be met, or service to be consumed, by the victim is the need for medical attention. Tables 9.1 and following describe use of medical care by the various groups of victims, defined by the cause of their incapacity. Forty per cent of respondents spent at least one night in hospital, over half of them staying for two weeks or more. Amongst the subgroups, the cases of illness were less likely to be admitted for one night stays (which are largely used for observation after injury), and more likely to stay for two weeks or more. One in three of those who were ill stayed in for two weeks or more, compared with one in four of road accident victims, one in ten of work accident, and one in eight of other accident victims. Road accident victims spent more time in hospital than other accident

Table 9.1 *Use of medical care in relation to cause of incapacity*

Hospital in-patient nights[1]	Cause of Incapacity Road accident	Work accident	Other accident	Illness	Total
	(%)	(%)	(%)	(%)	(%)
None	52	76	78	49	60
1	5	4	2	1	2
2 – 6	10	5	7	8	7
7 – 13	7	4	2	10	8
2 weeks or more	25	10	12	32	23
	100	100	100	100	100
Total ñ	318	455	938	1875	3586

[1] The average length of a stay in hospital is reported as eleven days in the *General Household Survey 1976*, Table 8.24, p. 238, where 20.3 per 1,000 of the sample were in-patients during a three-month period.

victims, but were less likely to stay more than one week than the cases of illness. If length of hospitalization is used as an indication of medical seriousness, this finding supports the assumption sometimes made that, because road accidents have higher mortality rates than other accidents, they also involve more serious medical problems. The cases of illness, however, appear far more serious in terms of requiring hospitalization than even road accidents.

If medical seriousness is measured according to an alternative subjective assessment by the respondent of the amount of residual incapacity experienced at the time of interview (i.e. at least six months after onset), illness continues to appear to be causing the most serious conditions (Table 9.2).

Table 9.2 *Residual disability[1] experienced in relation to cause of incapacity*

Health status at time of interview	Road accident	Work accident	Other accident	Illness	Total
	(%)	(%)	(%)	(%)	(%)
Affected a lot, all or most of the time	13	22	18	39	29
Occasionally	22	26	17	15	17
Never affected	64	52	65	46	53
Total	100	100	100	100	100
Total ñ	318	455	938	1875	3586

[1] See Introduction, p. 36, for discussion of the measure of residual disability used.

A far lower proportion (one in seven) of road and other accident victims than of the other groups were at the time of the interview affected 'a lot' 'all or most of the time' by their condition. It seems that although accidents, particularly road accidents, are severe in the sense of requiring hospitalization, even quite lengthy hospitalization, nevertheless the effects of road accidents are less likely to persist than those of work accidents; the most serious residual effects are more likely to be suffered by the victims of illness, amongst whom nearly 40 per cent reported serious and continuous difficulties at least six months after the onset of their condition. Clearly, residual disability is likely to be affected by the victim's age, as well as by the cause of his condition, though age and cause are also related to each other (see Table 1.5).

Overall, victims of illness were most likely to suffer some residual incapacity (53.7 per cent), followed by work accident victims (47.6 per cent) (though this distribution is affected by the lack of an under-16 age group in this category – the age group most likely to recover fully from any illness or accident – and by under-representation of the group over retirement age). With this exception, the likelihood of experiencing lasting incapacity increased gradually with age for accident victims up to retirement age, but for illness victims the tendency was far more pronounced, and three quarters of those who were ill and over 65 reported lasting effects (Table 1.5).

When we look at use of out-patient departments and general practitioner services, again victims of illness emerge as those most likely to make use of the service (see Table 9.3). Out-patient care was used by almost a third of all victims. Within that population, road accident victims were more likely to use such care than work and other accident victims, but accident victims as a whole were less likely to use it than the victims of illness. Four out of five of our sample saw their general practitioner in connection with their accident or illness, but again almost all the people who were ill were in touch with their general practitioner, compared with about two-thirds of road and other accident victims, and four-fifths of work accident victims. A higher proportion of work than road accident victims consulted their general practitioner, perhaps because of certification requirements for securing sick pay and social security benefits, but again their use of the service appears slightly less frequent than that of those who were ill.

To summarize, those who were ill were more likely than accident victims to use all of the medical services discussed, and more likely

Table 9.3 *Use of out-patient and general practitioner services in relation to cause of incapacity*[1]

Cause of incapacity	Percentage using outpatient services	Percentage using general practitioner services	Total ñ	Percentage
	%	%		
Road accident	36	67	318	9
Work accident	21	84	455	13
Other accident	20	58	938	26
Illness	36	93	1875	52
Total	30	81	3586	100

[1] The only possible comparison for these data is contained in General Household Survey 1976, p. 237. Out-patient attendance in a three-month period was 92 per 1,000 of the general population (England and Wales); GP consultations in a two-week period were 106 per 1,000 of the general population. (N.B. Our data are based on a different time period.)

to experience residual disability. There were, however, marked differences between the accident subgroups, with road accident victims resembling the ill in the propensity to stay in hospital, and work accident victims resembling the ill in the likelihood of consulting their general practitioner.

(2) Use of local authority and community health services

Use of welfare support offered by local authorities was then examined: this includes social work support; domiciliary help with housework, i.e. home helps and meals on wheels; and the local community medical services, including home nurses and other para-medical care such as physiotherapy. When our respondents were asked about this kind of support, including that coming from voluntary organisations, 18 per cent reported some contact. Accident victims were again less likely to use this kind of support than the ill; the difference between road, work and other accident victims was less marked than in the use of medical care. Accident victims are therefore represented as one group in Table 9.4, which describes use of local authority and community health services in relation to cause of incapacity.

For every local authority or community health service used,

Table 9.4 *Use of local authority and community health services*[1]

	Social worker (%)	Home nurse (%)	Health visitor (%)	Home help (%)	Meals on wheels (%)	Bath attendant (%)	Physio-therapist (%)	Total ñ	Percentages in contact with any of these services (%)
All accident victims in contact with	3.6	3.4	2.6	2.3	0.6	0.2	0.2	1711	8
Illness victims in contact with	9.2	9.0	7.5	10.3	3.3	1.2	0.6	1875	26
Total sample in contact with	6.5	6.3	5.2	6.5	2.0	0.8	0.4	3586	18
Total ñ	236	229	187	234	73	29	16		

[1] Each victim may have used more than one service.

illness victims as a group made nearly three times as much use of these services as did accident victims. This is not surprising in view of the relationship between age and illness (see Table 1.4). We therefore still have no evidence for assuming special needs in this area amongst accident victims.

(3) Informal support

In addition to health care and local authority support we looked at a third aspect of social care, the support provided informally in the community by neighbours and kin. If one is concerned to make effective use of local authority social services budgets, and to take into account changes in the labour market, the 'pool' of informal care available in the neighbourhood is a topic of increased concern (see Elston, 1979; Abrams, 1978). This kind of support, though acknowledged to some extent in damages by the judiciary (see Clarke and Ogus, 1978), remains an unknown quantity. The most remarkable documented instance in the literature is perhaps the Japanese *tsukiai* (Dore, 1959, p. 255) where effective care is provided in a socially open setting (i.e. not through an agency or institution), but on a comprehensive and continuous basis. Family network and neighbouring studies here and in the United States have revealed similar instances, from the classic Bethnal Green studies (Wilmott and Young, 1957) to the more specialized analysis of latent (Mann, 1954) and manifest (McGahan, 1972) neighbouring. There are also studies of reciprocating care (Mauss, 1969; Titmuss, 1971; Hadley, *et al.*, 1975), showing that caring for others can be an important means of obtaining care for oneself in certain groups, particularly in the case of middle-aged women, and, increasingly, men who retire early. In pilot work, reported in *Accidents in the Home* (Burman and Genn, 1978, Chapter 6) we were surprised by the numbers of activities with which care was offered for considerable lengths of time in support of the functionally impaired respondents. In the Compensation interview we asked about tasks carried out by helpers for victims, the relationships of the carer to the recipient and how long they had known each other, whether a cash payment was involved, and what other responsibilities the carer had in his or her own home.

Table 9.5 *Use of informal support*

Cause of incapacity	Receiving informal support	Total n̄
	(%)	
Road accident	55	318
Work accident	53	455
Other accident	65	938
Illness	54	1875
Total	57	3586

Table 9.5 indicates the proportions of each group of victims receiving informal support as a result of their incapacity. Use of informal support remained at a more consistent level than any other kind of support reported, regardless of the cause of the individual victim's problem. This kind of support, the only one operating outside any officially organized institution, appears to function at a consistently high level, irrespective of the age of the recipient or the cause of his incapacity. This might be interpreted as the most reliable measure of need – and certainly offers no indication of any particular need amongst work or road accident victims. Perhaps if one takes into account the willingness of helpers to undertake a commitment of this kind, one might expect a higher level of response to the dramatic event of an accident rather than in the long process of supporting a chronically sick individual. Nevertheless, at least one in two of all our victims were supported informally in this way.

We were interested to see whether this kind of support acted as a substitute for local health and welfare services, or in conjunction with them. From pilot work (Burman and Genn, 1978), it appeared to function with, rather than instead of local authority services. In the main study this finding was confirmed (Table 9.6).

Eighteen per cent of the population received a local authority service (Table 9.4) while over 56 per cent received informal support. Of those receiving informal support 21 per cent also received local authority support, i.e. use of informal support was associated with a slightly higher level of local authority support. There was no evidence of substitutability between these two forms of care.

Of the 3,074 helpers involved, two-thirds were described by our respondents as their main helper, 23 per cent were described as the

Table 9.6 *Use of local authority services in relation to informal support*

	Local authority service used		Local authority service not used		Total
	(%)		(%)		n̄
Informal support used	21	420	79	1617	2037
Not used	14	213	86	1336	1549
	18	633	82	2953	3586

Table 9.7 *Duration and frequency of help with specific tasks by primary helpers*

Duration of help	Self-care	Leisure	Mobility inside the home	Mobility outside the home	House-work	Child care
	(%)	(%)	(%)	(%)	(%)	(%)
Under 1 week	14	11	11	7	5	0
1 week – 1 month	34	34	27	20	21	19
1 – 6 months	28	31	32	22	32	52
over 6 months	24	25	31	51	40	25
Frequency: help given every day	84	81	85	73	93	95
n̄	2021	1113	662	305	94	21

second source of help and the remaining 8 per cent as third helpers. All of these individuals had helped with self-care, one in two with leisure activities, one in four with mobility in the home, 13 per cent with mobility outside, 5 per cent with housework, and 1 per cent with child care.

Fewer than one in ten of these specific tasks was supported for less than a week, and between 25 and 50 per cent were supported for more than six months. Most tasks, with the exception of helping the victim to get about outside the house, were performed every day. It appears that the affected individual can recover sufficiently to cope with self-care and mobility within the home (i.e. with those problems related to his own actions) before he or she recovers sufficiently to cope with running a home and caring for children. Over half of those helping with child care did so for one to six months and with housework for over six months (Table 9.7).

Table 9.8 shows the relationship of helpers to victims. The family clearly emerges as the primary source of informal care: 87 per cent of main helpers, 78 per cent of second helpers, and 74 per cent of third helpers were members of the victim's family. Friends and neighbours, including non-family household members, were very seldom the main source of support, though they did provide one in six of secondary helpers and one in four of third helpers. Payment for informal help was very rare, occurring in fewer than 5 per cent of cases, although gifts to helpful friends and relatives are reported in accounts of use made of damages received (Table 3.13). Over all,

Table 9.8 *Relationship of helpers to victims*

	Main helper (%)	Second helper (%)	Third helper (%)
Family			
Spouse	45	5	9
Parent/parent in law	25	32	9
Child/child in law	14	29	25
Other relatives	3	12	31
Non-family			
Others in household	1	3	4
Friends/neighbours	6	14	21
Other	6	5	1
n̄	2021	714	240

the picture which emerges is of an extensive caring network, persisting over time, and offering support particularly with self-care, mobility, and housework. The support comes predominantly from family members, and can be offered over long periods of time, particularly to those suffering chronic illness and to the victims of domestic accidents.

From this description of the use of health and welfare support by the sample in relation to the cause of their accident, it is clear that although the variation between accident categories in levels of consumption is considerable, over all the victims of illness in our population were clearly the group most likely to make use of all the services and support described above. This indicates that whatever else it may achieve, the tort system is not compensating a group who may be considered to have special needs on the basis of their use of other supporting services. In the following section, therefore, we go on to examine how use of the tort system (viz. recovery of damages) is related to use of other supporting systems. That is, in what combinations of services used together by groups of individuals does the tort claim appear? Does it appear in the more commonly used combinations of supporting services? What are the demographic characteristics of the groups of respondents using particular combinations of services?

(4) Patterns of service use

The data collected on use of health and welfare services were explored to see whether groups of services were used by consumers with similar demographic characteristics.

Table 9.9 shows services used, in relation to cause of incapacity, age group, presence of residual disability, and recovery of damages. For this section we selected a battery of supporting services provided by central and local government, informal sources, and private agencies i.e. insurance companies. As the Table indicates, use of general practitioner services increased with age and residual disability, and was more likely to be made by victims of illness than of accident. But amongst accident victims, those injured at work were more likely to consult general practitioners than those injured on the road or at home. The use of informal support was not differentiated by age, cause, recovery of damages, or even the presence of residual disability. Social security support was most likely to have been used by adults of working age, and particularly by those injured at work, and those receiving tort damages. One in three of the victim population received a social security benefit, while 70 per cent of those obtaining damages also received a social security benefit.

On looking at the group using social security with general practitioner support (Table 9.9 (ii)), we find that work accident victims and middle-aged adults were over represented, together with those who had received damages. The same Table shows that amongst those using the general practitioner with informal support and

Table 9.9 *Percentage of victim population by cause of incapacity, residual disability, age, and recovery of damages in relation to the use of services (i) individually, and (ii) and (iii) in combination*[1]

(i) *Services used individually*

	Using GP	Using informal support	Using social security	Using local authority	Using private insurance	Total population	Total population
	(%)	(%)	(%)	(%)	(%)	ñ	(%)
Accident victims							
work	84	53	83	5	15	455	13
road	67	53	42	7	11	318	9
other	58	65	18	11	7	935	26
Illness victims	93	54	35	26	4	1875	52
Residual disability: victims still affected 'a lot' at time of interview	90	50	46	26	7	1665	46
Age groups							
0 – 15	65	55	2	8	1	636	18
16 – 30	76	54	57	8	10	548	15
31 – 64	87	58	55	14	9	1558	43
65+	84	59	18	39	4	841	23
Victims who had obtained damages at time of interview[2]	76	53	71	7	17	167	5
All cases (%)	81	57	37	18	7		100
Total ñ	2899	2037	1337	633	237	3586	

[1] Only combinations used by a weighted sample of at least seventy-five cases are reported.

[2] This column excludes cases not settled at time of interview. (The figures used in chapters 2 and 3, however, include the final outcome of nearly all the unsettled cases.)

Table 9.9 (ii) *Percentage of victims using general practitioner in combination with other forms of support*

	Informal support	Social security	Informal support and social security	Local authority services	Private insurance	Local authority and private insurance	Informal support and private insurance	Social security and private insurance
	(%)	(%)	(%)	(%)	(%)	(%)	(%)	(%)
Accident victims								
work	46	73	39	5	15	5	8	13
road	37	34	17	7	8	3	6	5
other	37	15	9	7	6	2	4	0
Illness victims	51	34	18	24	3	9	2	2
People still affected 'a lot' at time of interview	54	43	26	24	7	10	5	4
Age groups								
0 – 15	32	2	1	7	1	1	0	0
16 – 30	43	5	25	7	8	3	5	6
31 – 64	50	51	27	13	8	9	5	6
65+	50	16	10	33	3	7	2	0
Victims who had obtained damages at time of interview	43	57	32	7	13	5	13	10
All cases	46	34	18	16	6	6	6	3
Total n̄	1634	1214	658	559	207	218	204	124

Table 9.9 *(iii) Percentage of victims using informal support in combination with other forms of support*

	Social security	Local authority services	Private insurance	Local authority and social security	Social security and private insurance
	(%)	(%)	(%)	(%)	(%)
Accident victims					
work	44	4	9	4	8
road	23	5	8	3	4
other	11	8	5	2	1
Illness victims	19	17	2	7	1
People still affected 'a lot' at time of interview	28	18	5	8	3
Age groups					
0 – 15	0	4	1	1	0
16 – 30	30	6	6	3	3
31 – 64	30	10	6	6	0
65+	11	22	0	6	0
Victims who had obtained damages at time of interview	38	3	13	3	10
All cases	20	12	4	5	2
Total n̄	724	423	153	164	78

social security, work accident victims were over-represented, as were those who had received damages. When local authority services are used with general practitioner support, again the elderly, the sick, and the disabled predominate (Table 9.9 (ii)). When private insurance is added to general practitioner support, a particularly high percentage of work accident victims appears – two and a half times the percentage in the population as a whole using that combination of services. This characteristic remains when social security is added to private insurance with the general practitioner support (Table 9.9 (ii)). Propensity to consult a general practitioner and to be helped informally did not appear to be affected particularly by age, cause of incapacity, persistence of disability, or receipt of damages.

Table 9.9 as a whole indicates that social security and private insurance were more likely to be used by work accident victims and by those who received damages. (It should be noted, however, that retirement pensions were not included.) Local authority welfare services, as expected, were used primarily by the sick, the disabled, and the elderly. When use of services in combination was examined, first, the general practitioner in combination with other services, this pattern was confirmed – where general practitioner care was combined with informal support, the age, cause of incapacity, and extent of disability did not affect the level of use (Table 9.9 (ii)). Some services – particularly the general practitioner and informal support – were used by the population evenly; others were clearly used by particular subgroups, e.g. local authority welfare support by the elderly, the sick, and the disabled. The aim of Table 9.9 as a whole was to establish the role of tort damages in this network. The receipt of damages emerged clearly as being associated with the receipt of other income support, notably social security and private insurance.

(5) Conclusions

Two questions have been examined. As a way of investigating whether or not 'tort users' (those obtaining damages) have special needs, we looked for evidence that the groups most likely to benefit through damages (i.e. work and road accident victims) contain a higher proportion of users of health and welfare support systems (in-patient and out-patient care, the general practitioner, local authority, and informal support) than illness and accident victims as a whole. In fact they do not. A lower proportion of road and work accident victims use the support agencies likely to cater for severe social or medical problems. The work and road accident cases using the medical services may be severe in that they use hospital in-patient care, but are less likely to experience lasting effects from their condition. It is not the case that we have a population of those likely to obtain damages who, as a whole, have higher overall need for medical care, or general welfare support either from the local authority or from their family and friends.

The factor which emerges most clearly from the final cross-tabulations (Table 9.9) is the association between obtaining damages and receipt of the other income maintenance services, particularly the short-term wage-related benefits. If we look at the total population with similar needs – using the definition from the screening survey (see Appendix I) of all those suffering interruption of everyday functioning for two weeks or more in the study period – and examine the services used by this population, then of those obtaining damages, a high proportion are also using social security and private insurance. The only services used less often by those obtaining damages are the local authority welfare services, i.e. the welfare services of last resort. If this is the case – that the tort system is used mainly by those in the labour market who have suffered an income loss (see Chapter 2) including a range of cases in terms of medical severity – then, if the tort system is to be retained, it should perhaps be regarded not as an agent of general compensation, but as an additional income maintenance system with an earnings-related supplement for those fortunate enough to be able to relate their income loss to the negligence of a well-insured and clearly identifiable individual.

Notes

1. *Cunningham* v. *Harrison* [1973] QB 942, at pp. 952, 954, 957.
2. *Taylor* v. *Bristol Omnibus Co. Ltd.* [1975] 1 WLR 1054, 1058, 1063.
3. *Donnelly* v. *Joyce* [1974] QB 454, 462.

References

Abrams, P., 1978, 'Community Care: Some Research Problems and Priorities', in *Social Care Research*, London: Policy Studies Institute, Bedford Square Press.

Barry, Brian, 1965, *Political Argument*, London: Routledge & Kegan Paul.

Bradshaw, Jonathan, 1972, 'The Taxonomy of Social Need', in G. McLaclan, ed., *Problems and Progress in Medical Care*, Oxford: Oxford University Press.

Burman, Sandra, and Genn, Hazel, eds., 1978, *Accidents in the Home*, London: Croom Helm.

Carrier, J., and Kendall, I., 1979, 'The Law, Social Policy, and Medical Negligence', paper presented to Social Administration Association, July.

Clarke, Karen, and Ogus, Anthony, 1978, 'The Price of a Wife', 5 *British Journal of Law and Society* 1.

Davies, Bleddyn, 1978, *Local Needs and Social Resources*, London: Michael Joseph.

Dore, R., 1959, *City Life in Japan*, London: Routledge & Kegan Paul.

Elston, May Ann, 1979, 'Women's Role in Unpaid Health Care', Paper presented to the British Sociological Association Conference, April.

General Household Survey 1976 (published by Office of Population Censuses and Surveys, 1978), London: HMSO.

Hadley, R., Webb, A., and Farrell, C., 1975, *Across the Generations*, London: Allen & Unwin.

Horowitz, Donald, 1979, *The Courts and Social Policy*, Washington DC: Brookings Institution.

McGahan, M., 'The Neighbour Role and Neighbours', 13 *Sociological Quarterly* 397.

Maclean, M., and Genn, H., 1979, *Methodological Issues in Social Surveys*, London: Macmillan.

Mann, P. H., 1954, 'The Concept of Neighborliness', 60 *American Journal of Sociology* 163.

Mauss, Marcel, 1969, *The Gift*, London: Cohen and West.

Pearson, Lord (Chairman), 1978, *Report of the Royal Commission on Civil Liability and Compensation for Personal Injury* (3 vols.), London: HMSO, Cmnd. 7054.

Rein, Martin, 1976, *Social Science and Public Policy*, London: Penguin.

Scarman, Sir Leslie, 1974, *English Law: The New Dimension*, London: Stevens.

——, 1976, *English Law and Social Policy* (a symposium based on Scarman, 1974), London: Centre for Studies in Social Policy.

Titmuss, Richard, 1971, *The Gift Relationship*, London: Allen & Unwin.

——, 1974, *Social Policy*, London: Allen & Unwin.

Walker, A., and Townsend, P., 1979, 'Compensation for Disability: the Wrong Course', in M. Brown and S. Baldwin, eds., *The Yearbook of Social Policy*, London: Routledge & Kegan Paul.

Wilmott, Peter, and Young, Michael, 1957, *Family and Kinship in East London*, London: Routledge & Kegan Paul.

Part III EMPLOYMENT AND HOUSEHOLD INCOME UNDER PRESENT SYSTEMS OF COMPENSATION

10 Employment and Earnings

Illness and injury are defined in the Compensation Survey in terms of interruption to normal activities. Such interruptions, as well as being distressing to the victims, are of wider concern to the community through their impact on production. Indeed it has recently been pointed out (Doherty, 1979) that the loss in working days due to sickness in Great Britain is at least as great as the loss due to unemployment. In less developed economies, the burden of this lost product is generally allowed to lie where it falls – that is, with the victim or his family. Most modern economies, however, have evolved institutional arrangements for insurance and compensation, so that the losses from illness or injury are, to an extent, spread through the community. Compensation through tort law damages, with its aim of full restitution, attempts to take account of the victim's full loss, actual and anticipated, following injury: there are heads of damages to cover earnings loss to date, future earnings loss, and 'unemployability' (Chapters 2 and 3). In addition, the social security system in the UK provides a basic minimum cover for victims of both injury and illness, as well as any subsequent unemployment (Chapter 5). For those employees who are covered by occupational sick pay schemes or private insurance policies, full or partial recoveries are obtained for limited periods (Chapters 7 and 8).

The major concern of this Chapter is to examine the way in which different individuals are affected in the labour market by illness or injury, and the extent to which their recovery and subsequent productivity is influenced by arrangements for compensation. Victims are seen in part as passively experiencing the physical consequences of illness or injury, but also partly as responsible for determining their own pattern of recovery and subsequent employment. Public policy towards the sick and the disabled has to consider both medical and non-medical parameters of individual behaviour.

(1) Compensation and the economic theory of the labour market

It is usual for economists to consider problems of this nature in terms of constraints to choices.[1] In the first instance, illness and injury are expected to restrict the victim's freedom to work effectively for as many hours as he wishes in a given period. He will therefore suffer a financial loss equivalent to the earnings he would otherwise have received. This may be mitigated by compensation from various sources, or by extra earnings from other household members (see Chapter 11). Over a period of time, however, we would expect the physical effects of the illness or injury to become less restricting, and a return to gainful employment will become feasible. The victim must then choose at what stage in his recovery he will actually return to work. Of course, eligibility for social security benefits and employers' sick pay is normally subject to continuing medical certification, so that, in theory, such compensation would be discontinued at the point at which the victim became 'fit for work'. However, the notion that this can be objectively determined has drawn considerable criticism, not least from the medical profession itself. The victim's incentive to return to work early will therefore depend partly on the extent to which he is losing income by being off work, and partly on his financial commitments and family responsibilities. These will presumably be balanced against the value of additional recuperation time, both in terms of extra leisure and a speedier recovery to full fitness.

Some injuries and illnesses will, of course, leave the victim with residual impairment of a more permanent nature. In its most extreme, this impairment may prevent the victim from ever working again. In less severe cases, there may be no effective limitation on the amount or type of work performed, so that the victim will normally return after his absence to his previous employment. Between these two extremes, there is a wide range of impairments which in some way restrict the affected person in the labour market. He may be forced to work fewer hours on a less arduous job, at a lower rate of pay, with his previous employer, or he may have to search for alternative employment elsewhere, in which case his opportunities will vary with the state of demand in the local labour market for employees of his experience and qualifications. The impact of illness or injury on employment and earnings may consequently be felt over the rest of the victim's entire lifetime.

Analysis of the Compensation Survey should enable us to examine the effects of illness and injury over long periods against a background of changing circumstances. The minimum lapse of time between the onset of the relevant illness or injury and the final interview was some six months, and the maximum could be a considerable number of years, given that the criteria for selection involved the *effects* of any given illness or injury. Consequently, many victims during this period changed their status in the labour market. Table 10.1 shows labour market status immediately before the onset of illness or injury, and at the time of the interview, for all who were initially in full- or part-time work.

Table 10.1 *Labour market status of all victims in full- or part-time work at onset of illness or injury*

	Work status at onset			
Work status at time of interview	Full time (over 30 hours)	Part time (11–30 hours)	(6–10 hours)	n
Full-time (Over 30 hours)	711	14	0	725
Part-time (11–30 hours)	22	60	5	87
Part-time (6–10 hours)	4	2	17	23
Retired	158	22	12	192
Unemployed	39	2	1	42
Other	60	8	2	70
NK	19	0	0	19
n	1013	108	37	1158

From Table 10.1 we note that some 1,158 individuals were employed at the time of the illness or injury, predominantly in full-time work. Of these, 835 were still working when interviewed, 192 had retired permanently from the labour force, 42 were unemployed, and 70 ('other') were presumably still absent from work due to sickness. Some of these transitions would, of course, have taken place without the intervening illness or injury. Some of the older victims would have retired from the labour force, some victims would have changed jobs and some would have become unemployed. Status in the labour market depends, as we have seen, on the interaction between the victim's preferences and the physical and financial constraints with which he is faced. This chapter attempts to separate the independent effect of the individual's illness or injury on his labour market experience. The first section looks at the factors which might be expected to affect the length of time over which the victim is out of employment owing to injury or illness. The second section examines the extent to which injury or illness results in permanent changes in employment or earnings, and the final section considers the implications of our findings for compensation for the sick and disabled.

(2) Time off work

The distribution of reported duration of absence from work (including any subsequent unemployment) is markedly skewed towards zero in our sample. That is, there is a large number of very short absences, with far fewer lengthy absences. This is illustrated in Figure 10.1, which shows the distribution of time off work for the weighted sample of employees ($\bar{N}$=1515, equivalent to the unweighted total of 1158).

One consequence of the skewed nature of this distribution is that the variance (or 'spread') of any given subsample will be in direct proportion to the mean (or 'average'), and this is clearly demonstrated in subsequent tables, where the means will appear to be high relative to 'usual' periods of absence. For instance, whereas the mean of the distribution in Figure 10.1 is 42.3 weeks, the *median*,

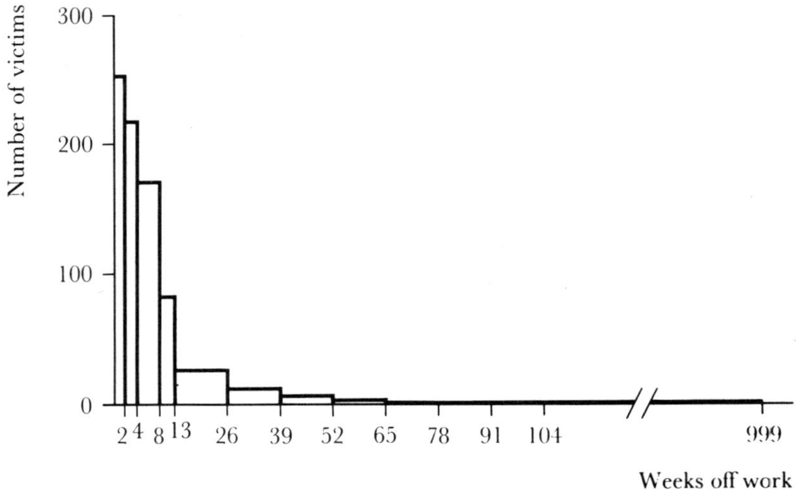

Figure 10.1 *Distribution of time off work for employees*

or mid-point, is 8.1 weeks. This is due to the small number of very long durations which have a disproportionate effect on the mean. With this in mind, we can break down our sample with a view to explaining the pattern of absence.

On the strength of our discussion in the previous section, we can separate the factors likely to influence the victim's duration of absence into three groups: those which measure the impact of illness or injury on the victim's health; other characteristics of the victim and his family which influence his needs and preferences; and the financial circumstances with which he is faced while out of work, given his expected earnings on return to work. In addition to these influences on the victim's own behaviour, we must also consider the effect of demand conditions in the labour market on the victim's job security and re-employment opportunities, and the effectiveness of the various controls implemented by employers and the State. In this section we shall look at each of these categories in turn, examining the straightforward associations to be observed between each of them and the duration of time off work. This partial view will then be widened in terms of a multi-dimensional causal explanation in which the impact of ill health alone can be separated after controlling for other factors.

First, the impact of illness or injury on health can be examined. We have two useful measures of severity from the survey. The first is a measure of the duration of hospitalization. The respondents were asked how many nights they had spent in hospital because of their illness or injury, and Table 10.2 gives an indication of how this information relates to the duration of their time off work.

Table 10.2 *Time off work by length of stay in hospital for all employees with time off work*

	Time off work (weeks)		
Nights in hospital	Mean	Standard deviation	n̄
0	19.3	52.0	887
1	16.2	30.6	33
2 – 6	31.4	92.5	116
7 –13	51.2	149.4	116
14+	101.7	181.1	360
Total	42.3	113.6	N̄ = 1515*

* Tables exclude missing values from subtotals.

This shows, as expected, that the association between duration of absence from work and time spent in hospital is quite strong. It is, however, interesting to note that victims who spent one night in hospital had a lower mean duration of time off work than those who were not hospitalized at all (16.2 weeks compared with 19.3 weeks). This may be a result of the widespread practice of hospital casualty departments of keeping victims with minor injuries in overnight 'for observation'.

Table 10.3 *Time off work by residual disability for all employees with time off work*

	Time off work (weeks)		
Residual Disability	Mean	Standard deviation	n̄
'Not affected'	8.3	11.4	656
'Never affected a lot'	14.7	21.5	119
'Affected a lot'			
'occasionally'	23.6	42.0	330
'most of the time'	82.1	163.6	205
'all of the time'	158.9	214.7	204
Total	42.3	113.6	N̄ = 1515

A clearer picture of the long-term impact of the illness or injury is given by the survey question on residual disabilities. (It should be recalled that the minimum lapse of time between the illness/injury and the interview is six months (see Chapter 1)). The victims were asked if they were still affected physically *in any way at all* by their illness/injury or its effects. Table 10.3 shows the results. Not surprisingly, there is shown a strong and unambiguous relationship between residual disability reported at the time of interview and duration of time off work. The response to this question therefore represents a powerful indicator of the severity of the individual's injury or illness. It figures prominently in the multivariate analysis of this chapter, particularly as it relates to the *type* of functional impairment which the victim reports. Although this is dealt with more fully in that context, we can here take a partial view of the variation between respondents according to the type of accident or illness from which they suffered (see Table 10.4).

Table 10.4 *Time off work by cause of absence for all employees with time off work*

Cause of absence	Time off work (weeks) Mean	Standard deviation	n̄
Illness	68.4	153.8	670
Road accident	25.5	66.0	176
Work accident	20.7	45.6	409
Other accident	20.5	70.3	260
Total	42.3	113.6	N̄ = 1515

The most significant factor revealed by Table 10.4 is the extent to which illnesses lead to far higher losses of work time on average than injuries. This is presumably due to the physical effects of illnesses having a greater tendency to spread themselves over a considerable period of time (see Table 1.5, indicating the extent of residual disability).

If time off work required a purely medical explanation, there would, of course, be no need to carry our investigation any further. We have stressed in the first section of this chapter, however, that different people will react differently in the labour market to a given illness or injury, depending on the interaction between their ill health and the factors which influence their needs, preferences, and opportunities. The second group of indicators with which we are here concerned is therefore the range of relevant personal and family characteristics of the victim. Table 10.5 shows the age, sex, marital status, and working status of the victim at the time of the illness or injury. This table gives a picture of the type of victim who is likely to be off work for a considerable time, but it must be remembered that these associations are uncontrolled for any other factors. In other words, it is quite possible that the marked relationship between age and time off work is mainly due to a close association between ill health and age (see Table 1.2); it is further possible that part-time workers take less time off work because on the whole they receive less financial support from state benefits whilst ill. Again, widowed, divorced, and separated victims are likely to be older and therefore less healthy than single or married victims, which may explain their longer periods of absence.

Before we attempt to resolve these problems by considering all causal factors together rather than separately, we can briefly look at

Table 10.5 *Time off work by victim's characteristics for all employees with time off work*

	Time off work (weeks)		
	Mean	Standard deviation	n̄
Age: under 25	9.6	13.3	148
25–34	14.2	34.8	307
35–54	41.3	121.5	574
55–64	64.9	121.0	340
65 and over	88.7	187.3	139
Sex: male	38.2	92.1	1057
female	51.8	151.8	458
Marital status:			
married	38.8	106.4	1194
single	33.3	114.5	179
widowed/divorced/ separated	84.3	159.1	135
Work status			
Full time	44.7	119.2	1305
Part time	27.4	66.1	210
Total	42.3	113.6	N̄ = 1515

the third category of influence mentioned above: the degree to which the victim's income is maintained at a level close to his previous earnings. The principal source of income replacement for short-term sickness in the UK is the victim's employer: in 1974 sick pay schemes effectively covered 71 per cent of all males and 68 per cent of all females (DHSS, 1977). This support is separate from that provided by National Insurance benefits. Those who are not covered by an employers' scheme, or who fail to qualify (on contribution grounds, say) for National Insurance benefits, are forced to rely on supplementary benefits. Overall, therefore, sick pay recipients obtain better financial support than non-recipients do during a relatively short absence from work. Table 10.6 shows the difference in mean duration between the two groups.

Table 10.6 simply confirms the difference in the pattern of absence from work which has been demonstrated elsewhere (Denerley, 1952; Buzzard and Shaw, 1952). At first sight, it appears that generous compensation for illness and injury leads to shorter absences. A more careful examination of the data, however, reveals that individuals who are covered by sick pay schemes are more likely to

Table 10.6 *Time off work by receipt of sick pay for all employees with time off work**

Receipt of sick pay	Time off work (weeks) Mean	Standard deviation	n̄
Received	29.8	85.0	874
Not received	60.3	143.2	627
Total	42.3	113.6	N̄ = 1515

*Table excludes cases with unknown duration of absence.

have time off work for non-serious ailments: by which we mean illnesses or injuries which do not lead to permanent residual effects. This is illustrated by Table 10.7, in which the percentage of sick pay recipients is given for each category of residual disability. Out of all individuals who had time off work, almost two-thirds of those who were unaffected by their illness or injury at the time of interview had received some sick pay, whereas fewer than half of those who reported continual residual effects received any sick pay. This is a significant difference, and it appears to show that sick pay recipients are more likely to take time off work for a given severity of illness or injury. Because of this tendency, our sample of sick pay recipients is characterized by a large number of short-term absences, resulting in an apparently lower mean duration of absence, as in Table 10.6. The impact of income replacement on time off work cannot therefore be considered in isolation from the physical effects of ill health.

Table 10.7 *Receipt of sick pay by residual disability for all employees with time off work*

Residual disability	Sick pay entitlement: In receipt of sick pay	Not in receipt of sick pay
	%	%
'Not affected'	64.7	34.3
'Never affected a lot'	53.4	46.6
'Affected a lot'		
'occasionally'	50.9	49.1
'most of the time'	56.5	43.5
'all of the time'	48.6	51.4
Total	57.5	42.5

Moreover, it is probable that sick pay recipients are less likely to turn elsewhere for employment during their period of absence, and are therefore less likely to undergo the process of 'searching' the job market for alternatives. The impact of job opportunities in the local labour market on the probability of re-employment can be examined by comparing regional durations of absence. Table 10.8 shows mean duration of absence for our sample in each of the nine standard regions of England and Wales, together with the average rate of unemployment in these regions between 1970 and 1976. Areas with traditionally high rates of unemployment such as the North and the North-west, are also susceptible to high levels of absence, relative to the Midlands and the South-east. This can be attributed either to a higher likelihood of dismissal following absence from work or to greater difficulty in obtaining employment once dismissed. Moreover, as pointed out above, there is also the possibility of an interaction between sick pay coverage and the propensity to quit employment. The only way to deal with this and similar complicating causal relationships is to consider time off work as a phenomenon to be explained with reference to a number of factors, in order to separate out the independent influences of policy variables such as the level of income replacement and compensation, the local level of unemployment, and certification controls.

Time off work, as reported by the victim, was examined in relation to the victim's health (as measured by self-reported

Table 10.8 *Time off work by region, ranked in order of regional unemployment rate*

Region	Mean duration (weeks)	Unemployment Rate 1970–6	$\bar{n}$
North	70.4	5.05	142
Wales	38.8	4.10	100
North-west	44.5	3.70	240
Yorkshire	44.8	3.22	201
South-west	87.4	3.06	106
West Midlands	37.7	2.60	146
East Midlands	36.4	2.53	138
East Anglia	17.5	2.45	65
South-east	24.2	1.85	377
Total	42.3	2.85	$\bar{N}$ = 1515

residual disability), his age, the rate of unemployment in his area of residence, and the amount of compensation he received in total, as a proportion of his previous earnings. Other factors controlled for were the victim's family circumstances, his skill and work experience. The appropriate statistical technique[2] was used in order to assess the relative contributions of each of these factors to the victim's probability of returning to employment in a given period. In Table 10.9, therefore, a negative coefficient implies that the factor tends to reduce the probability of return and hence *increase* the victim's time off work. Table 10.9 reports the main effects for all full-time employees for whom information was reliably available: that is, excluding cases for which data were missing, and those cases where the illness/injury took place over ten years before the interview. Because of the way in which they are measured, the coefficients on age, unemployment, and compensation can be interpreted as the *proportional* response of time off work to a *proportional* change in these variables. Hence a coefficient of −0.5, say, would indicate that a 10 per cent increase in that variable will be expected to lead to a 5 per cent reduction in the probability of return to work. For all other variables, the coefficients can be interpreted as the proportional change in the probability of return associated with a unit change in these variables. As a rough guide to the statistical significance of these results, a coefficient which is more than twice its standard error indicates a 95 per cent degree of confidence or higher.

The results presented in Table 10.9 generally support the hypotheses generated in the first section of this chapter. Older individuals, those with substantial self-reported residual disablement, or lengthy hospitalization, are generally much less likely to return to work early. Non-manual employees and those with a degree of experience with their employer tend to return sooner, possibly reflecting the greater likelihood that they will be retained by their employer after a long absence. Moreover, the rate of unemployment in the victim's area of residence may be an important determinant of his employment opportunities: the coefficient is statistically significant and implies that a 10 per cent rise in the local unemployment rate will lead to a general reduction in the probability of return to work in that area of around 3.7 per cent.

To the extent that we can control for the health, and other personal and family characteristics of the victim, we can now look at the *independent* effect of the level of income replacement whilst absent

Table 10.9 *Factors influencing the probability of return to work: employees in full-time work at time of illness or injury (N = 586)*

Variable	Coefficient	Standard error
Age[1]	−0.52*	0.13
Local Unemployment Rate[1]	−0.37*	0.15
Income Replacement Rate[1]	−0.06*	0.02
Residual Disability: 'affected a lot'		
'occasionally'	−0.51*	0.11
'most of the time'	−0.93*	0.17
'all of the time'	−2.00*	0.22
Hospitalization over 2 weeks	−0.97*	0.13
Married	0.11	0.12
Number of children	−0.01	0.04
Number of full-time workers in household	−0.04	0.06
Work experience with employer		
6 months – 2 years	0.25	0.20
2 – 5 years	0.36	0.20
Over 5 years	0.34	0.20
Non-manual[2]	0.48*	0.15
Skilled manual[2]	0.19	0.11

An asterisk indicates variable is significant at the 5 per cent level.
[1] Measured as natural logarithm.
[2] The definitions of these categories can be found in Note 6 to Table 1.2. 'Non-manual' comprises Categories 1–3 in that Note, while 'skilled manual' is Category 4.

from work. For absences of less than six months, Table 10.9 demonstrates the existence of a significant reduction in the likelihood of return to work associated with higher rates of income replacement. The coefficient is not high, however, representing only a 0.6 per cent increase in absence duration associated with a 10 per cent increase in the replacement rate. Hence even a doubling of income replacement within the ranges represented in our sample would only add a matter of three to four days to a typical absence of ten weeks. This compares with results from studies of the behaviour of unemployed individuals, which have typically found a considerably larger impact of the income replacement rate on duration of unemployment (Nickell, 1979; Lancaster, 1979). This discrepancy is not surprising, in view of the nature of short-term unemployment as a process of searching for alternative jobs, with a longer search assumed to result in a better job. Hence the incentive to extend this process for an extra week is much greater than the incentive to extend a period of recuperation, where the benefit is simply one of extra leisure time, and where the employee has an interest in maintaining his employer's 'goodwill' towards him.

A further difference between unemployment and sickness absence relates to the established safeguards against 'abuse'. For unemployment benefit, claimants must demonstrate their 'availability' for 'suitable' employment, and not place unreasonable restrictions on such availability. Claimants for sickness benefit, on the other hand, have to show that they are incapable of work through production of a statement of incapacity signed by a general practitioner. There is widespread scepticism, both within and outside the medical profession, as to the efficacy of the certification controls. It is difficult, moreover, to test directly their effectiveness, given the lack of any objective measure of incapacity. However, the evidence of Table 10.9 does appear to reveal some voluntary extension of absence, which could not, of course, take place if certification was working perfectly. Furthermore, we know that the various sick pay schemes differ in their approach to control: some 7 per cent of sick pay recipients in our sample were required to be examined by a works or company doctor, 80 per cent were asked to produce a medical certificate from their GP, and 13 per cent stated that their employer 'took their word for it'. The effect of adding these 'controls' to the explanatory factors in Table 10.9 was not statistically conclusive: there was a slight indication of shorter absences after examination by a company doctor, but the requirement of certification had a negligible effect (Fenn, 1981). The wider problems of medical certification in this context are discussed elsewhere in this volume (Chapter 5, section 3).

(3) Labour market transitions following illness or injury

We have shown in the previous section that the direct losses to the *community* of injury and illness, as measured by the duration of lost productive activity, are related to a wide range of factors other than the strictly medical. The direct loss to the *individual* concerned is, however, mitigated to a certain extent by compensation from various sources which 'replaces' some proportion of previous income. Indeed the existence of compensation may, as we have seen, result in a higher output loss from longer recovery times. What we have not yet considered, however, is the extent to which the immediate, short-term effects of illness or injury lead to more permanent costs to both the victim and the community.

When asked whether they considered that their injury or illness had affected their present job situation, earnings, or educational qualifications, some 290 victims replied 'yes', representing some 20 per cent of all who were at work or in full-time education at the time of the injury or illness. Out of the 196 individuals who had retired from work at the time of the interview (and who had been working before the injury/illness), 113 claimed that because of their illness or injury they had retired earlier than they would have done. Of the sixty employees who changed their employer after their illness or injury, thirty-seven claimed that the change was as a result of the injury or illness. Of those who did not change their employer (830), eighty-four had reduced the number of hours worked, ninety-one had their earnings reduced, and 153 had changed the nature of their duties as a result of their illness or injury. All of this evidence points to a significant degree of transition within the labour market induced by a period of ill health or its after-effects. What it does not show is to what extent we can attribute these transitions to the effects of residual disability and to what extent they are the result of a return to work after a lengthy period of absence, during which time both employer and employee will have changed preferences. In this section we can now examine this problem in the light of our expectations. We consider the three most important transitions in turn – retirement, change of employer, and change of hours worked – and then examine the effect of these transitions on current earnings.

Retirement

Table 10.10 shows the principal determinants of the victim's probability of retirement from work, including a number of self-reported residual effects, or functional limitations, arising from the illness or injury (Question 16a, Appendix II). The results are based on an analysis of 648 male employees. The coefficients can be interpreted as the proportional effects of the relevant factor on the probability of retirement.[3]

Obviously the victim's age is particularly important in determining early retirement, and the non-linear nature of this relationship is revealed by the significance of the coefficient on 'age squared'. Of greater interest is the measured impact of other factors, after having controlled for the effect of age. It was, of course, expected that our

Table 10.10 *Probability of retirement: male employees aged 16+ at the time of illness or injury (N = 648)*

Variable	Coefficient	Standard error
Weeks off work	0.01*	0.003
Age	−0.25	0.16
Age squared	0.005*	0.002
Non-manual	−0.77	0.68
Skilled manual	−1.08*	0.53
Pensionable job	0.69	0.52
Other household income	0.67*	0.13
Residual problems		
Mobility	0.37*	0.16
Bending	0.34	0.27
Gripping	0.21	0.29
Lifting	0.32	0.21
Pain	−0.25	0.21
Respiratory	0.36	0.23
Sight	0.70	0.51
Hearing	−0.41	0.67
Mental	0.05	0.24
Hospitalization (over 2 weeks)	0.32	0.49

An asterisk indicates variable is significant at the 5 per cent level.

measures of the disabling effects of illness and injury should increase the probability of retirement, and this is, on the whole, confirmed by the results, where all but two of the coefficients were positive. Mobility problems were particularly significant, and, to a lesser extent, bending, lifting, respiratory, and sight problems. As far as other personal characteristics are concerned, both non-manual and skilled manual workers, were less likely than unskilled workers to retire prematurely. We might further expect financial considerations to play some part in the retirement decision, and in this respect it is interesting to note the positive coefficients associated with pensionable employment and other family income, both of which might be expected to 'cushion' the impact of retirement. Finally, it seems that the length of time out of work following the injury or illness is a statistically important determinant of the likelihood of early retirement, even after controlling for the disabling effects which remain. This is undoubtedly the result of a gradual reduction in 'employability' over the duration of absence from work: the sparsity of employment offers will eventually discourage the victim's attempt to return and he will drop out of the labour market. This clearly indicates that injury or illness can lead to losses over and above those directly attributable to health effects – the interruption to employment status may permanently reduce the individual's earning capacity, even to the extent of causing him to leave the labour force altogether.

Change of employer

Table 10.11 presents the main determinants of the probability that a given individual will change his employer following a period of absence from work due to injury or illness. The coefficients can be interpreted as the proportional effects on this probability. The impact of health on job changing is interesting. All but one of the coefficients on the residual problems were negative, with respiratory problems significantly so. However, the coefficient on hospitalization (greater than two weeks) is significantly positive. It appears that the acute nature of some illnesses or injuries is sufficient to separate the victim from his employer, although we cannot say on

Table 10.11 *Probability of change of employer: male employees aged 16+ at time of illness or injury (N = 569)*

Variable	Coefficient	Standard error
Weeks off work	0.03*	0.008
Local Unemployment rate	−0.39	0.26
Number of children	0.35*	0.18
Pensionable job	−1.49*	0.53
High wage (over £80 per week)	−0.86	0.52
Residual problems:		
Mobility	−0.18	0.28
Bending	−0.08	0.36
Gripping	−0.06	0.33
Lifting	0.07	0.30
Pain	−0.21	0.21
Respiratory	−1.40*	0.71
Sight	−2.73	7.51
Hearing	−5.48	8.18
Mental	−0.73	0.48
Hospitalization (over 2 weeks)	1.22*	0.48

An asterisk indicates variable is significant at the 5 per cent level.

whose initiative. On the other hand, self-reported chronic limitations which are not severe enough to cause early retirement appear to have the effect of strengthening the employee's attachment to his employer. After controlling for the effect of health, the main determinants of the likelihood of job change appear to be the pensionable nature of existing employment (for obvious reasons) and the number of children in the victim's household. This latter determinant is less obvious and can presumably be explained in terms of the effect of household 'needs' providing an incentive towards labour market mobility in search of higher-paid employment. Financial incentives are also reflected in the negative coefficient on high wages, implying a greater reluctance to leave higher paid employment. There is, moreover, a constraint on job mobility in terms of the number of opportunities available, and this is reflected in the negative coefficient on the local unemployment rate, a proxy for local demand conditions. Finally, the importance of the duration of time off work is shown again here. The explanation in this context is obvious: the longer an individual is off work, the more likely it is that his employer will terminate his contract, or that he will himself find alternative employment.

Hours worked

Table 10.12 presents the main effects on the probability that a given individual will work reduced hours on return to work with his original employer. The 'goodness of fit' of the equation is not as satisfactory as the first two equations and the estimated coefficients are consequently of less significance. It is suspected that this reflects the lack of flexibility over hours worked encountered by many employees. Hence the degree to which hours are reduced following illness or injury depends to a large extent on whether the victim was previously working overtime. This, it is felt, goes a long way towards explaining why skilled-manual, married employees with children are more likely to have reduced their hours on return (although the coefficients, it must be stressed, are not particularly significant). The health measures are predominantly positive as expected, with mobility problems and long-term hospitalization proving to be statistically significant, indicating a greater reluctance to work long hours for those with more severe effects of illness or injury. There is some indication that higher wage earners are less likely to reduce hours, for obvious reasons. The number of weeks off work prior to return is again shown to be a significant factor in the

Table 10.12 *Probability of reduced hours of work on return to previous employers: male employees aged 16+ at the time of illness or injury (N = 529)*

Variable	Coefficient	Standard error
Weeks off work	−0.009*	0.004
Married	0.98	0.60
Number of children	0.22	0.15
Non-manual	−0.40	0.57
Skilled manual	0.42	0.38
High wage (over £80 per week)	−0.29	0.37
Low wage (under £40 per week)	0.41*	0.13
Residual problems:		
Mobility	0.39*	0.14
Bending	0.05	0.23
Gripping	−0.17	0.29
Lifting	0.11	0.17
Pain	0.07	0.15
Respiratory	0.22	0.26
Sight	−2.27	3.25
Hearing	0.23	0.43
Mental	0.25	0.18
Hospitalization (over 2 weeks)	1.14*	0.36

An asterisk indicates variable is significant at the 5 per cent level.

decision to reduce work hours. This factor, together with (but independent from) the effects of ill health, is a consistent feature in all three labour market transitions investigated here. In this context it appears to show the effect of prolonged absence on the victim's preferences for non-work activity relative to income, although it is possible that the explanation lies in the attitude of employers to long term absentees.

Earnings

Illness and injury can lead to a reduction in earnings in a number of ways. The victim may be forced into employment at a lower wage rate, either with his existing employer or another, or he may decide to work fewer hours, as we have seen above. In order to separate as far as possible the impact of health on wage rates from that on hours worked, Table 10.13 presents an analysis of the determinants of the earnings of full-time employees at the time of the interview. The coefficients can again be interpreted as the proportional effect of the relevant factor on the likelihood that the individual is in a higher

Table 10.13 *Determinants of earnings at time of interview of full-time employees (N = 642)*

Variable	Coefficient	Standard error
Sex = male	2.15*	0.23
Age	0.33*	0.04
Age squared	−0.004*	0.0005
Non-manual	0.99*	0.21
Skilled manual	0.51*	0.17
Work experience (>5 yrs)	0.38*	0.16
Residual disability: 'affected a lot'–		
'occasionally'	−0.36	0.19
'most of the time'	0.08	0.26
'all of the time'	−0.03	0.33
Weeks off work	−0.01*	0.004
Unemployment rate	−0.04	0.08

An asterisk indicates variable is significant at the 5 per cent level.

wage band. The results show that for those who return to full-time work, the impact of residual disability is not particularly strong nor significant, after controlling for other factors. It appears that the earnings of full-time workers are better explained by factors other than residual disability. Men are higher earners than women; the relationship between age and earnings is characteristically non-linear; and non-manual, skilled, and experienced workers generally earn more. If injury and illness have any impact on the earnings of those who return to full-time work, it must be indirect, through the effect it has on prolonged absence from employment, which is seen to be a significant factor in reducing earnings in Table 10.13.

(4) Conclusions

We began this chapter by generating a number of hypotheses in relation to the employment behaviour of the victims of illness or injury. The importance of these hypotheses lies in their relevance to any assessment of the costs of illness and injury to the community, by which we mean the productive losses associated with absence from work and subsequent adjustment in the workplace. However, not all of these losses are borne by the victims alone. Because of the development of institutional provision for insurance, employers' sick pay schemes and social security, in addition to common law damages, most developed economies ensure that much of the loss is spread through the community. The mechanisms by which these losses are assessed and compensated are the major concern of this book. This chapter has looked specifically at the 'efficiency' aspects of illness and injury and subsequent compensation: in other words, it has attempted to identify the most important determinants of productive loss, both medical and non-medical, in the light of variations in individual levels of compensation from all sources. Previous chapters have concerned themselves with explaining these variations: this chapter has demonstrated that they have important effects on behaviour in the labour market which are of relevance to a wide area of compensation policy. It will be useful to summarize our findings at this point before discussing their implications.

(1) Out of 1,158 victims in our sample who were employed at the time of their illness/injury, 1,040 had some time off work. The median absence from work was 8.1 weeks for the weighted sample of 1515.

(2) The evidence appears to suggest that employees covered by employers' sick pay schemes are more likely to take short periods of time off work for relatively minor cases – i.e. those where there are no significant residual effects.

(3) The major determinants of increasing absence were age, residual disability, the local unemployment rate, and the level of income replacement while off work. Other influences such as family commitments, training, and job experience were not so significant, but generally operated in the direction expected. The impact of income replacement, although statistically significant, was not particularly large, with a 10 per cent increase in the rate of replacement leading to only 0.6 per cent increase in recovery time.

(4) Some 20 per cent of those who were at work or in full-time education at the time of their injury/illness considered that their present job situation, earnings, or educational qualifications had been affected as a consequence. For those who prematurely retired from the labour force, age and residual disability were important factors influencing the decision, together with the length of time off work and the amount of other household income. For the remainder who did not retire, those who changed employer were likely to be in good health (although they may have spent some time previously in hospital), in low-paid, non-pensionable employment, and with a number of children. Job changing was also more likely after a long

period of time off work, and in areas where the unemployment rate was low. For those who did not change jobs, reduced work hours were characteristic of those with significant residual disability and lengthy absences from work. Other factors were not significant, although the pattern of results appears to suggest that it was victims who were previously accustomed to working overtime who were most likely to reduce hours. Finally, if the victim does manage to return to full-time employment, the evidence suggests that he is unlikely to suffer reduced earnings as a *direct* result of any residual health effects. It is more likely, however, that his earnings will fall if his illness or injury leads to a prolonged absence from work.

These results generally confirm those obtained in other comparable studies relating to the employment of ill or injured individuals. The comprehensive survey of the long-term sick by Martin and Morgan (1975) identified a number of correlates such as age, type of job, and sick pay coverage, but did not attempt to estimate the partial effects of these factors by controlling for the informants' state of health. There have been a number of studies investigating the impact of introducing sick pay or self-certification schemes in given firms, which have tended to suggest that such schemes result in a higher incidence of short-term absences but which are somewhat inconclusive with regard to average duration of absence (Denerley, 1952; Buzzard and Shaw, 1952; Taylor, 1969; Carne, 1969). Recent contributions by Whitehead (1971) and Doherty (1979) have stressed the rising trend in certified sickness absence since the early 1960s in relation to the increase in benefit levels over the same period. A number of studies in the USA have attempted to measure the impact of 'disability' or 'functional impairment' on labour market activity, with broadly similar results to our own (Nagi and Hadley, 1972; Berkowitz, *et al.*, 1976; Scheffler and Iden, 1974; Luft, 1978). Similar work has been done in the UK by Layard *et al.* (1978) but without explicit concentration on the impact of ill health. Closest, perhaps, to the methodology adopted in this chapter, is a recent study by Levy and McManus (1978) which uses US social security data to estimate the likelihood of the various market options following some functional impairment.

What then are the implications of these results for policy in the area of compensation for illness and injury? Firstly, it seems that those who are most prone to labour market disadvantage following illness or injury are those who have suffered prolonged absence from work, irrespective of the extent of residual disability. Hence policy measures directed at more effective recuperation and rehabilitation are important, particularly for older victims, who are most at risk. Compensation to victims is more appropriately based on absence from work *per se* than on measured health impairment, although the latter is more likely to avoid distorting labour market effects (Fenn, 1980). It follows, moreover, that victims of illness, who generally have longer absences, are at a greater risk than victims of accidents – the group who are most likely to benefit from tort awards. Secondly, although there is a demonstrable disincentive effect associated with higher levels of income replacement, it is not large enough to present a serious barrier to policy options which increase levels of replacement. Consequently, an extension of social security provisions in the direction of comprehensive 'no-fault' compensation for illness or injury with a significant element of earnings relationship ought not to be greatly constrained by reference to output loss, particularly if effective controls over eligibility criteria are built into the system. Finally, it seems that the attachment between employer and employee is of considerable importance in relation to the likelihood of permanent disadvantage in the labour market following illness or injury. It appears that the policy-maker must be concerned to balance the requirements of adequate labour mobility with those of adequate security against unanticipated and involuntary loss in earning capacity. Employers' sick pay, occupational pensions, and on-the-job training schemes are all means by which this security can be provided.

Notes

1. See McClements, 1978, for an application of neo-classical labour economics to problems of compensation and social security.
2. Maximum likelihood estimates were obtained for the parameters of a likelihood function based on Cox's proportional hazards model (Cox, 1972). Such estimates are simply those which give the greatest probability of obtaining the observed data, assuming a particular distribution of the error terms. See Kmenta, 1971, for a discussion of the estimates obtained in this chapter. See also Vlachonikolis, 1980.
3. The estimates in Tables 10.10 to 10.13 are maximum likelihood estimates obtained from the fitting of the data to a linear model using the logit transformation. The computer package GLIM was used for this purpose. See Bibby, 1977, for a discussion of the General Linear Model.

References

Berkowitz, M., Johnson, W. G., and Murphy, E.H., 1976, *Public Policy Toward Disability*, New York: Praeger.

Bibby, J., 1977, 'The General Linear Model: A Cautionary Tale', in C. A. Muircheartaigh and C. Payne, eds., *Model Fitting*, London: Wiley.

Buzzard, R. B., and Shaw, W. A., 1952, 'An Analysis of Absence under a Scheme of Paid Sick Leave', 9 *British Journal of Industrial Medicine* 282.

Carne, S., 1969, 'Sick Absence Certification: Analysis of one Group Practice in 1967', *British Medical Journal* 147.

Cox, D. R., 1972, 'Regression Models and Life Tables', 34 *Journal of the Royal Statistical Society*, Series B, 11.

Denerley, R. A., 1952, 'Some Effects of Paid Sick Leave on Sickness Absence', 9 *British Journal of Industrial Medicine* 275.

Department of Health and Social Security (DHSS), 1977, *Report of a Survey of Occupational Sick Pay Schemes*, London: HMSO.

Doherty, N. A., 1979, 'National Insurance and Absence from Work', 89 *Economic Journal* 50.

Fenn, P. T., 1980, 'The Effect of Ex Post Compensation on Absence from Work', Oxford: Centre for Socio-Legal Studies, Wolfson College, *Working Paper No. 7*.

——, 1981, 'Sickness Duration, Residual Disability and Income Replacement: An Empirical Analysis', 91 *Economic Journal* 158.

Kmenta, J., 1971, *Elements of Econometrics*, New York: Macmillan.

Lancaster, T., 1979, 'Econometric Methods for the Duration of Unemployment', 47 *Econometrica* 939.

Layard, R., Piachaud, D., and Stewart, M., 1978, *The Causes of Poverty*, Background Paper No. 5 to the Diamond Commission's Report No. 6, *Lower Incomes*, London: HMSO.

Levy, J., and McManus, L., 1978, 'Functional Limitations and Job Requirements: Effects on Labor Force Choices', in *Policy Analysis with Social Security Research Files*, US Dept. of Health, Education and Welfare, Social Security Administration, pp. 447–60, Washington DC: US Government Printing Office.

Luft, H. S., 1978, *Poverty and Health*, Cambridge: Ballinger.

McClements, L., 1978, *The Economics of Social Security*, London: Heinemann.

Martin, J., and Morgan, M., 1975, *Prolonged Sickness and the Return to Work*, London: HMSO.

Nagi, S. Z., and Hadley, L. W., 1972, 'Disability Behaviour: Income Change and Motivation to Work', 25 *Industrial and Labor Relations Review* 223.

Nickell, S., 1979, 'The Effect of Unemployment and Related Benefits on the Duration of Unemployment', 89 *Economic Journal* 34.

Scheffler, R. M., and Iden, G., 1974, 'The Effect of Disability on Labour

Supply', 28 *Industrial and Labor Relations Review* 122.
Taylor, P. J., 1969, 'Self Certification for Brief Spells of Sickness Absence', *British Medical Journal* 144.
Vlachonikolis, I. G., 1980, 'An Approximation to the Partial Likelihood for the Regression Models of the Analysis of Survival Data', mimeographed, Department of Biomathematics, Oxford University.
Whitehead, F. E., 1971, 'Trends in Certified Sickness Absence', 2 *Social Trends* 121.

11 Household Income

This chapter examines the financial consequences of illness or injury for the household of the victim (see Fenn and Brittan, forthcoming). The focus of the analysis is the total money income of the household: its level and sources, and how these are affected when a member of the household becomes ill or sustains an injury. For some households there may be a direct earnings loss because the victim has time off work as a result of the illness or injury: these effects are reported fully in Chapter 10. However, for many households there is no such loss as the sick or injured person was not contributing to the household income at the onset of his ill health. Nevertheless, in all households an illness or injury may bring about changes in other sources of income (e.g. earnings of non-victims, compensation and transfer payments, and income-earning assets) which will have repercussions on the financial position of the household. Furthermore, these changes may help to ameliorate or they may exacerbate the loss of victim's earnings felt by some households.

(1) The household as a unit of production

Before presenting the analyses of the financial data, let us define the household for our purposes as the group of people who live under one roof and who make, or are subject to others making for them, *joint decisions* about the allocation of household members' time to income-earning labour market activity and to other activities. These other activities may include home duties (such as cleaning and cooking and, especially important in the context of a family unit, child rearing), consumption of goods, sleep and self-care, compulsory and voluntary education and training, recreation etc. (For a rigorous exposition of the economic theory of household production and consumption, see Becker, 1964, 1965.)

We assume that the household aims to make the best use of its members' time by allocating their hours to labour market activity and to other activities, according to the relative productivity of each person in each activity. The age, sex, inborn qualities, health, intensity of work, level of skill, and education of individual members will all be important in determining these relative productivities. Those household members who are relatively more productive at market activity (in the sense that they can command higher earnings for a given level of work), will devote more of their time to work and less to other household activities, and vice versa.

Moreover, a change in the relative productivity of any household member may cause a reallocation of time of *all* persons in the household. Such a change could be brought about by the ill health of one member of the household. The victim who was participating in the labour force at the time of the illness or injury (which suggests that within the household he was then relatively productive at market activity) may now be relatively less able at his job, or even totally unable to compete in the labour market for the reasons explained in Chapter 10. If this is so, we can hypothesize that this member of the household may reduce or even give up some labour market activity and devote more time to other activities such as home duties or self-care, because he is now relatively better at doing these activities than labour market tasks. Depending on the permanency of the ill health, the changed needs of the household, and the earning capacities of its other members, it may now become economically efficient for another member of the household to start a job or to work extra hours to try to maintain the earned income level of the household, or even to increase it to meet extra expenses or debts incurred as a result of the ill health of the one member of the household, which cannot be recouped from unearned sources of income.

An illness or injury within the household may also create additional needs within the household for non-work activities, particularly self-care and care of others. As Oi (1977) has pointed out, a disabled person requires more hours each day for sleep and personal care, and this reduces the hours available for other activities. Depending on the availability and quality of support services and the severity of the victim's handicap, there may also be a need for other members of the household to spend more time at home caring for the victim, and less time at other activities.

Compensation payments made to the victim, a source of unearned income, will also affect household income. The present compensation systems, it has been suggested, are fairly well designed to meet the needs resulting from very short interruptions of normal activity by an accident or illness, but tend to neglect the longer-term implications of ill health. Furthermore, payments differ in amount and type, often quite widely, according to the cause of the ill health and according to the household status of the victim. Consequently, there is reason to suppose that certain categories of victims recover more of their losses than others. The proportion of losses recovered by the victim and the household from a compensation system might affect the degree of adjustment made by the household concerning its division of labour.

An illness or injury may therefore change some or all of the parameters on which the household bases its financial decisions and the allocation of its members' time to labour market and non-labour market activities. In this chapter we look for evidence of the size and directions of adjustments in the level and sources of household income consequent upon an illness and injury and examine the net financial impact of the ill health on the household.

(2) The data used in the analysis

Data were collected in the Compensation Survey on a number of key financial variables. Problems of collecting accurate financial data, in particular the notoriously low response rate, are frequently reported in the literature (e.g. Harris *et al.*, 1971–2, Vols I and III). Questions were selected and framed to elicit as much accurate information as possible about the household's financial standing. Attention was concentrated on obtaining the level of household income *at the time of the interview*. No attempt was made to ask about household income immediately before the onset of the illness or injury nor to impute these values, because respondents might have found it difficult to recall income over long time periods, and because inflation had changed the real value of incomes over the years. In pilot work we explored the possibility of using inflation factors to establish the current value of incomes earned in the past. However, the application of national average inflation factors to individual past incomes, which interviewees recalled with difficulty and probably inaccurately, produced totally unsatisfactory results.

The Family Expenditure Survey (FES) 1976 (Dept. of Employment, 1977) is used to compare our financial data with those of the general population. Despite being primarily an expenditure survey, the FES provides the most comprehensive documentation of the financial position of households in the UK. One problem, however, is that the FES does not use the recognized Social Classes of the

Classification of Occupations (see Classification of Occupations, OPCS, 1970, and Dept. of Employment, 1977, 'Occupation' definition, p. 136); hence for financial comparisons involving socio-economic groups we have to turn to the General Household Survey as our proxy for the general population.

Both the definition of household income and the income brackets were designed to be broadly comparable with those of the 1976 Family Expenditure Survey. The one notable difference is that the Compensation Survey data do not include items of imputed income for households which pay no rent or are owner-occupied (see Dept. of Employment, 1977, definition of household income, p. 138). Respondents to the Compensation Survey were asked: 'Taking all sources of income into account, what is the total gross income of your household *now*, before any deductions for tax, national insurance, etc.?' (Question 97). They were shown a card which identified eight income brackets:

1. Less than £20 per week
2. £20 − < £30 per week
3. £30 − < £40 per week
4. £40 − < £50 per week
5. £50 − < £60 per week
6. £60 − < £80 per week
7. £80 − < £100 per week
8. £100 or more*

*The number of income brackets on the show card was limited to eight and three upper brackets (£100−< £120, £120 − < £140, £140 or more) had to be aggregated into one '£100 or more' category.

If tort damages had been received by the time of the interview and had been invested to give income, the level of household income reported would include such money. A lump-sum payment itself would not be included. However, by the time of the interview only a few victims had received tort damages and the sums involved were usually quite small (see Chapters 2 and 3).

An 87 per cent response rate was obtained for the household income question which compares favourably with response rates of other social surveys. The 13 per cent of households for which income is not recorded, comprise households where respondents did not know the household income and others where they refused to answer the question (see Section 5, 'Non-response and household income').

Data were also obtained on the *sources* of household income both at the time of the interview and immediately prior to the ill health. This was in order to gain an insight into household adjustments consequent upon the illness or injury, and also into the types of recoveries that victims were getting from the various compensation systems.

A series of analyses was undertaken: we begin with a broad comparison of our household income profile with that of FES and then proceed to explore possible explanations for the lower incomes of the Compensation Survey population.

(3) Results and Discussion

The distribution of household income

The weighted distribution of the Compensation Survey household income at the time of the interview (1976/7) together with 1976 FES data, is reported in Table 11.1. Our data have been weighted to take account of the different sampling methods used for different categories of ill health and thus to make the sample broadly comparable with FES national estimates. A chi-square test shows that the distributions of the two populations given in Table 11.1, are significantly different. Moreover, the deviations between the two frequency distributions show a systematic pattern, with the Compensation Survey household income distribution being significantly skewed towards the lower income brackets. The proportions of Compensation Survey households with incomes in each bracket of less than £80 per week are higher than for FES. In fact 30.5 per cent of FES households receive more than £100 per week but only 13.6 per cent of Compensation Survey households have a similar level of income. It is striking to note that whereas the mean household income for Compensation Survey households is about £62 per week, FES households receive, on average, about £82 per week.

The elements of imputed income included in the FES household income but excluded from the Compensation Survey might explain part of the difference between the two income distributions. However, we can infer from the 1976 FES that imputed income accounts for less than 4 per cent (about £3) of the £82 mean household income. Furthermore, the exclusion of imputed income would not significantly change the distribution of income for FES households (see Table 11.1, Note 2). Thus, even allowing for the

Table 11.1 *A comparison between the Compensation Survey and FES populations of the number and percentage of households in each income bracket*

Income bracket	Compensation Survey 1976/77		Family Expenditure Survey 1976[1]	
Gross £ per week	n	(%)	n	(%)
Less than 20	264	8.5	448	6.2
20 – < 30	455	14.6	741	10.3
30 – < 40	399	12.8	584	8.1
40 – < 50	324	10.4	477	6.6
50 – < 60	377	12.1	523	7.3
60 – < 80	518	16.6	1173	16.3
80 – < 100	357	11.4	1062	14.7
100 or more	425	13.6	2195	30.5
Total	3119*	100.0	7203	100.0
Mean household income (to nearest £)	£62		£82[2]	

*Missing observations (Non-respondents) = 467.
$\chi^2 = 460$ d.f. 7 $p < 0.001$
1 Derived from p. 93, Dept. of Employment, 1977.
2 FES Imputed income. The exclusion of imputed income would reduce the mean to about £79 gross per week. Its exclusion is unlikely to change significantly the proportion of FES households in each income bracket. The revised percentages would approximate: 6.7, 10.3, 7.9, 6.6, 7.5, 16.2, 15.0, 29.8. However, it is impossible to identify the exact amount of imputed income for each household from the published tables and hence FES income data reported in this chapter include imputed income.

differences in definition of income, it is clear from the comparison of the Compensation Survey with FES data in Table 11.1 that ill health is associated with relatively low household income.

One obvious possible explanation is that illness or injury directly reduces the income of the victim's household. However, as there is no information about the Compensation Survey household income profile before the onset of ill health, several other possible relationships might contribute to the explanation of the observed association. For example, it could be that ill health is not randomly distributed throughout the income profile of a population but that it is more prevalent among the lower income categories (see Goldberg and Morrison, 1963). Furthermore, the same illness or injury may have a greater effect on lower than on higher income households. Fortunately, data in the survey can help to explain the household income difference in terms of the demographic characteristics peculiar to the Compensation population and can help to identify any residual difference due to health factors. Firstly, we examine a number of demographic variables.

The size and composition of households vary widely: at one extreme there are single persons living alone, at the other, households comprising several generations. Table 11.2 shows that there are more large households and fewer one adult households in the Compensation Survey sample than in FES. As the FES for all years show, household income is usually positively related to household size and other things being equal, we would expect the Compensation sample to have a higher household income profile than the FES population. In fact, the lower mean income of the Compensation sample serves to reinforce the notion of a net household income loss for those households containing a victim of illness or injury. Although the mean household incomes for the Compensation group are considerably lower than those of FES, they do seem to follow a similar pattern to FES when disaggregated

Table 11.2 *A comparison of household types and mean household incomes for the Compensation Survey and for the 1976 FES population.*

			Mean household income of each type (gross £ per week)	
Household type[1]	Compensation Survey households (%)	FES households (%)	Compensation survey (£s)	FES (£s)
1 Adult	13.6	20.4	27	37
1 Adult, 1 or more children	2.3	3.3	34	50
2 Adults	28.3	32.0	52	78
2 Adults, 1 child	8.2	9.4	66	91
2 Adults, 2 children	14.4	13.6	74	94
2 Adults, 3 children	6.7	5.0	73	102
2 Adults, 4 children	4.8	2.4	68	95
3 or more Adults	8.1	7.6	78	133
3 or more Adults, 1 or more children	13.6	6.3	86	145
Total (%)	100.0	100.0	£62	£82
	N̄ = 3563*	N = 7203		

* Missing observations = 23.

[1] Based on FES classification.

according to household type, namely, that household income still tends to be higher the more adults there are in the household.

The mix of socio-economic groups in the Compensation Survey and in the general population as represented by GHS is shown in Table 11.3. Both populations contain roughly similar proportions of 'semi-skilled manual' (19 per cent) and 'unskilled manual' (7 per cent) households. 'Skilled-manual' households are significantly over-represented in the Compensation Survey and one might proffer the explanation that the nature of the work undertaken by 'skilled-manual' heads of households gives rise to more accidents and illnesses than are suffered by other socio-economic groups. This suggestion, however, is not borne out by the data. It appears that this group has relatively more of all types of accident and illness, not only work-related, than other socio-economic groups. Moreover the victim is by no means always the head of the household: he or she is frequently a spouse or a child of a skilled worker. 'Intermediate and junior non-manual' households are clearly under-represented in the survey and there are also very slight, barely significant, under-representations of 'professional' and 'employers and managers' households.

A comparison of populations B and C in Table 11.3 shows that the socio-economic mix of the Compensation sample does not change significantly between the time of the illness or injury and the time of the interview; at this stage we are unable to say whether the few socio-economic group changes that do occur are as a direct consequence of the illness or injury or whether they would have happened anyway. Further investigation of these changes, however, shows that there is no systematic direction of socio-economic group change during the time period. Of those households for which we have a socio-economic code at the time of the illness or injury and at the time of interview ($\bar{N} = 2418$), 2.4 per cent appear to have bettered their socio-economic position, 2.7 per cent seem to have worsened it. These percentages exclude those heads of households who have entered or left the labour market during this time gap. The latter movements can be partly explained by the natural effects of ageing in the population bringing about household adjustments but they may also reflect, to an as yet unknown extent, household adjustments caused by the illness or injury.

Table 11.4 gives the mean household incomes for each socio-economic category for our population and for the general population (GHS). The fact that 'skilled manual' and 'intermediate and

Table 11.3 *Representation of socio-economic groups in the Compensation Survey and the General Household Survey (GHS)*[1]

		S.E.G.[2] of Head of Household						
Source of data		Professional	Employers and managers	Intermediate and Junior non-manual	Skilled manual	Semi-skilled manual	Unskilled manual	Total
A. GHS 1976	(%)	4.1	14.6	21.3	33.4	19.6	7.0	100.0 N = 11585
B. Compensation survey at time of interview, 1976/7	(%)	3.3	13.3	14.0	44.2	18.3	6.9	100.0 N̄ = 2433
C. Compensation survey at time of onset of illness/injury	(%)	2.9	12.4	14.2	44.0	19.1	7.4	100.0 N̄ = 2777

1. Here the GHS is used to provide national estimates as the FES does not have the necessary socio-economic data.
2. The GHS's collapsed version of the Registrar General's socio-economic grouping, 'Classification of Occupations 1970', is used. See Table 1.2, Note 6.

junior non-manual' households receive almost identical levels of income, according to the GHS data, is most important. It suggests that the differential incidence of socio-economic groups in the Compensation Survey when compared with the general population *cannot* explain the lower household income profile of the Compensation Survey. In household income terms, the over-representation in the Compensation Survey of 'skilled manual' households and the under-representation of 'intermediate and junior non-manual' households should cancel each other out, because these two groups actually receive similar levels of income. For example, the mean income for the total GHS sample is £83 gross per week. If we now apply the appropriate GHS mean incomes to the Compensation Survey mix of socio-economic groups we would also expect a mean of about £83 for the Compensation Survey. In fact, the average for those households with economically active heads, which can thus be allocated to one of the six socio-

Table 11.4 *Mean household incomes for Compensation Survey and for GHS in relation to socio-economic group*

Socio-economic group of head of household	Compensation Survey Mean household income at time of interview £ gross per week	Derived from GHS 1977[1] Mean household income £ gross per week
Professional	108	127
Employers and managers	87	119
Intermediate and junior non-manual	70	83
Skilled manual	71	81
Semi-skilled manual	58	64
Unskilled manual	52	48
Mean income for all households with economically active (i.e. SEG categories) heads of households	69	83[2]
Mean income for all households in Compensation Survey	62	

[1] 1977 (rather than 1976) GHS income data are used for this comparison as the GHS concept of income is money received in the last twelve months. The Compensation Survey (and FES) ask for income for the week/month before the interview.

[2] The GHS income figures are not directly comparable with the Compensation Survey or FES because of differences in sampling procedures and income definitions.

economic groups, is £69. The average for the whole Compensation population is £62. Our inference must be that the lower incomes of the Compensation Survey households cannot be attributed to the mix of socio-economic groups in our sample. Further, Table 11.4 demonstrates that in all but one ('unskilled') of the socio-economic groups, Compensation Survey households display lower incomes when compared with their GHS counterparts.

If we now consider the head of household age distribution, as shown in Table 11.5 we find that, overall, the Compensation Survey is quite similar to FES: we do not have significantly more elderly heads of households (which might have been one explanation of the low income profile of our population). It is only when we divide the Compensation population into heads of households who are victims and those who are not that we find the former group having 37.1 per cent heads of households aged 65 or over, compared with 16.4 per cent for non-victim heads of households and 25.5 per cent for FES. Nevertheless, it appears that, age for age, Compensation households receive substantially less in income than their FES counterparts. For the 50–64 age group this loss amounts to 39 per cent of the FES mean income. Even in the 'under 30' group, which appears to be under-represented in the Compensation Survey compared with the general population (9.9 per cent compared with 14.5 per cent) the loss is 5 per cent of the FES mean. Our inference must again be that age alone cannot explain the household loss accruing to the Compensation population.

Table 11.6 compares another characteristic of the Compensation Survey with FES data, namely, work status of the head of the household. Just under 40 per cent of the Compensation heads of households were 'not working' at the time of the interview compared with about 30 per cent of FES. For heads of households who are also victims, this percentage increases to over 52 per cent, compared with about 27 per cent for non-victims. Within the 'not working' category it should be noted that a substantial number of heads of households who are victims, are also housewives. This last table has given us some indication that the work status together with the victim status of the head of household may be important in explaining the lower household income of the Compensation population.

To summarize our first set of analyses: we have demonstrated a significant difference between the household income distribution of the Compensation Survey (mean = £62) and the Family Expendi-

Table 11.5 *Age distribution and mean household incomes in relation to the age of Head of Household for Compensation Survey and for FES*

Age of Head of Household at time of interview	Percentage in each age category Compensation Survey				Mean household incomes Gross £ per week	
	Head of Household is victim (1) (%)	Head of Household is not victim (2) (%)	All heads of households (1) and (2) (%)	FES 1976 (%)	Compensation Survey All heads of household (£s)	FES All heads of household (£s)
Less than 30	9.2	10.5	9.9	14.5	76 n̄ = 952	80 n = 1048
30 – 49	26.7	48.2	37.6	33.5	79 n̄ = 717	103 n = 2410
50 – 64	27.0	24.7	25.9	26.5	60 n̄ = 655	95 n = 1912
65 or over	37.1	16.4	26.6	25.5	35 n̄ = 795	43 n = 1833
Total	N̄ = 1765	N̄ = 1821	N̄ = 3586	N = 7203	62 N̄ = 3119*	82 N = 7203

*Missing observations = 467.

Table 11.6 *Work status of heads of households for Compensation Survey at time of interview and FES*

Work status of head of household	Compensation Survey Head of household is victim (1) (%)	Head of household is not victim (2) (%)	All heads of household (1) and (2) (%)	F.E.S. Heads of house-holds (%)
Working	47.5	73.2	60.5	71.0
Not working				
retired	34.0	19.8	26.8	24.1
housewives	17.0	4.0	10.4 }	4.9
other	1.5	3.0	2.3 }	
Total Ñ	1765	1821	3586	N = 7203

ture Survey (mean = £82) which is used as a proxy for the general population. Further, we have shown that this difference is not adequately explained by the exclusion of 'imputed' income from the Compensation Survey data. Nor is it explained by the differential incidence of a number of household demographic characteristics in the two populations. Even when we control for household type, the socio-economic group, the age distribution, and the work status of the head of the household, we find that Compensation Survey households appear to have lower incomes than their FES and GHS counterparts. It is now appropriate to consider the role of the victim in explaining this lower income: his position in the household and the nature of the ill health.

The victim and household income

Tables 11.7 and 11.8 give an indication of how the household status of the victim affects household income. From Table 11.7 it is clear that where the victim is also the head of the household, which suggests that he or she is the potential main breadwinner for the household, income tends to be lower (mean = £53) than in households where the victim is not the head of the household (mean = £72). However, for both Compensation groups, household income is still lower than in the general population.

Table 11.8 shows that in those households where the victim is working at the time of the interview, which implies that these victims have recovered sufficiently to return to work, incomes tend

Table 11.7 *Household income in relation to household status of victim at the time of the interview compared with FES*

Income bracket Gross £ per week	Victim is head of household (%)	Victim is not head of household (%)	FES 1976[1] All households (%)
Less than 20	14.4	1.8	6.2
20 – < 30	20.4	8.1	10.3
30 – < 40	12.5	13.1	8.1
40 – < 50	10.2	10.6	6.6
50 – < 60	9.6	14.8	7.3
60 – < 80	14.7	18.8	16.3
80 – < 100	8.6	14.6	14.7
100 or more	9.5	18.2	30.5
Total (%)	100.0	100.0	100.0
Total Ñ	1644	1475	N = 7203
Mean household income	£53	£72	£82

Missing observations = 467.
$\chi^2 = 320$ d.f. 7 $p < 0.001$
[1] From Table 11.1

Table 11.8 *Household income in relation to activity status of the victim compared with FES*

	For victims over the age of 16 at the time of the interview*		FES[1] 1976
Income bracket Gross £ per week	Victim working at time of interview (%)	Victim *not* working at time of interview (%)	All households (%)
Less than 20	1	18	6.2
20 – < 30	2	29	10.3
30 – < 40	5	19	8.1
40 – < 50	10	10	6.6
50 – < 60	16	8	7.3
60 – < 80	23	8	16.3
80 – < 100	19	3	14.7
100 or more	24	5	30.5
Total (%)	100.0	100.0	100.0
Total Ñ	1175	1414	N = 7203
Mean household income	£83	£41	£82

* Missing or excluded observations = 997 (492 non-respondents and 505 victims under 16).
1. From Table 11.1

to be higher (mean = £83) than in those households where the victim is not working (mean = £41). In fact, for the former group the incomes are equivalent to those reported for the general population. The 'not working' group will include victims who are still off work as a result of the illness or injury, many old people and also other types of victims who were not working at the time of the illness or injury (e.g. housewives, and those victims over 16 but in full-time education). Let us now turn to some of the health variables to see if they hold any possible explanations of the household income profile for the Compensation population.

Table 11.9 shows the significant difference in income between households where the victim had reported no residual disability at the time of the interview (mean = £70) and those where the victim is experiencing residual disability (mean = £57). Moreover, there appears to be a strong negative relationship between mean incomes and the degree of residual disability: the greater the residual disability, the more depressed the household income. Even the 'no residual disability' group, however, has a mean income (£70) which is significantly lower than FES (£82).

Two further indicators of the severity and residual disability of an illness or injury are the victim's registration as a disabled person with the Local Authority and with the Department of Employment. Table 11.10 shows how this registration is reflected in household income. Only 7 per cent of the households contain victims who are registered with the Local Authority and they display a significantly lower income profile than those containing victims not registered with the Local Authority. The registered victims are primarily handicapped children and the elderly and hence we would expect lower household incomes: the elderly victims, who are heads of households, have relatively lower incomes, whilst handicapped children will probably require the care and attention of other household members, whose time might otherwise have been spent in the labour market. Fewer than 4 per cent of the households contain victims who are registered as disabled workers with the Department of Employment. In these households the victim is trying to contribute to the earned income of the household but the disability is probably responsible, at least in part (see Chapter 10) for the depressed income levels compared with the group where the victim is not registered with the Department of Employment.

Table 11.11 gives the breakdown of household income by the type of illness suffered or injury sustained by the victim. A chi-square test

Table 11.9 *Household income in relation to existence (or not) of self-reported residual disability (at time of interview) in victim compared with FES*

Income bracket Gross £ per week	Residual disability: 'Affected a lot all of the time' (1) (%)	'Affected a lot most of the time' (2) (%)	'Affected a lot occasionally' (3) (%)	'Never affected a lot' (4) (%)	Total experiencing residual disability (1)+(2)+(3)+(4) (%)	No residual disability at the time of the interview[1] (%)	FES 1976 All households (%)
Less than 20	15.5	11.4	9.5	6.4	11.5	4.9	6.2
20 – < 30	29.5	25.6	7.0	9.6	18.9	9.6	10.3
30 – < 40	15.5	12.1	13.6	7.5	13.2	12.3	8.1
40 – < 50	12.3	7.9	11.7	9.1	10.7	10.0	6.6
50 – < 60	8.6	9.2	13.1	11.8	10.6	13.9	7.3
60 – < 80	7.7	12.9	20.5	18.2	14.3	19.3	16.3
80 – < 100	5.1	9.7	10.2	20.3	9.6	13.5	14.7
100 or more	5.8	11.2	14.4	17.1	11.2	16.5	30.5
Total (%)	100.0	100.0	100.0	100.0	100.0	100.0	100.0
Total N̄*	535	403	557	187	1682	1434	N = 7203
Mean household income	£43	£54	£64	£72[2]	£57	£70	£82

* Missing observations = 470.

$\chi^2 = 133$ d.f. 7 $p < 0.001$ when households where the victim is still experiencing residual disability are compared with those where the victim has no residual disability.

[1] By splitting the Compensation Survey sample into these two groups according to whether or not the victim reported any residual disability at the time of the interview, we were able to demonstrate that the overall household income profile is the sum of two lognormal distributions: one for those reporting residual disability and one for those who did not. (The computations involved are fully reported in Brittan and Vlachonikolis, 1981). This result is both interesting and encouraging since many earnings distributions for which information is available (in many countries and periods of time) approximate to a lognormal distribution (see Lydall, 1968, 1979; Horsnell, 1979; Aitchison and Brown, 1969).

[2] This mean (£72) is slightly higher than the mean for the no residual disability group (£70) but no significance should be attached to this due to the huge difference in sample sizes ($\bar{n}$ = 187 and $\bar{n}$ = 1434 respectively).

Table 11.10 *Household income in relation to victims' registered disability with local authority and with Department of Employment*

Income bracket Gross £ per week	Registered disability with local authority*		Registered disability with Department of Employment**	
	Registered (%)	Unregistered (%)	Registered (%)	Unregistered (%)
Less than 20	9.8	8.4	9.8	8.5
20 – < 30	25.4	13.7	23.6	14.2
30 – < 40	22.8	12.1	20.4	12.6
40 – < 50	13.8	10.2	14.6	10.3
50 – < 60	7.6	12.4	14.6	12.0
60 – < 80	12.1	17.0	12.2	16.8
80 – < 100	4.0	12.0	2.4	11.8
100 or more	4.5	14.2	2.4	13.8
Total (%)	100.0	100.0	100.0	100.0
Total Ñ	224	2873	123	2979
Mean household income	£44	£63	£43	£63

* Missing observations = 489
** Missing observations = 484

reveals that, other things being equal, the illness/accident split does significantly affect the profile of household income at the time of the interview. 'Illness households' seem to receive less income (mean = £55) than 'accident households' (mean = £69). Within the 'accident' population there is evidence that households containing victims of road accidents and work accidents generally receive higher levels of income (means = £73 and £77 respectively) than households containing victims of other types of accident (mean = £64). Nevertheless, the mean incomes for all these categories of ill health remain lower than the £82 mean household income of FES.

The wealth of the household

A little information is available from our survey as to how an illness or injury affects the general wealth of the household. Table 11.12 shows that a fifth (20.1 per cent) of the households spent from savings or stopped saving as a result of the illness or injury. The propensity to change savings pattern seemed to be similar for all households, regardless of income group. It should be remembered,

Table 11.11 *Compensation Survey household income in relation to type of accident/illness compared with FES household income*

Income bracket Gross £ per week	Accident type				Illness	
	Road and Work/Road Accidents (1) (%)	Work Accidents (including Industrial Illness) (2) (%)	Other Accidents (Domestic, Leisure, Sport, Criminal Assault, Other) (3) (%)	All Accidents (1)+(2)+(3)	All Illnesses except Industrial Illnesses (%)	FES[1] 1976 (%)
Less than 20	4.6	1.8	9.9	6.6	10.3	6.2
20 – < 30	7.7	4.4	11.2	8.6	20.0	10.3
30 – < 40	9.8	8.6	13.5	11.4	14.0	8.1
40 – < 50	11.0	10.3	9.7	10.2	10.5	6.6
50 – < 60	15.4	11.5	12.2	12.4	11.6	7.3
60 – < 80	18.5	25.1	17.5	19.9	13.6	16.3
80 – < 100	12.1	19.3	10.6	13.4	9.8	14.7
100 or more	20.9	19.0	15.4	17.5	10.2	30.5
Total (%)	100.0	100.0	100.0	100.0	100.0	100.0
Total Ñ	278	434	788	1500	1619	N = 7203
Mean household income	£73	£77	£64	£69	£55	£82

Missing observations = 467.
1. From Table 11.1.

Table 11.12 *Household income in relation to whether any member of the household had to spend from savings or stop saving as a result of the illness or injury*

Income bracket Gross £ per week	Households who spent money from savings or stopped saving	Households with no change in savings pattern	No information on savings	Total $\bar{n}$	Propensity of each income bracket to spend savings or to stop saving (%)
Less than 20	50	214	0	264	18.9 (i.e. 50/264)
20 – < 30	95	354	6	455	20.9
30 – < 40	95	301	3	399	23.8
40 – < 50	64	255	5	324	19.8
50 – < 60	72	303	2	377	19.1
60 – < 80	104	409	5	518	20.1
80 – < 100	82	273	2	357	23.0
100 or more	65	360	0	425	15.3
Total $\bar{N}$	627	2469	23	3119	20.1

Missing observations = 467.

however, that households in the lower income groups are more likely not to have any savings, or to have less savings to spend or smaller amounts to stop saving than those in the higher income groups.

Nearly all of the households (94.4 per cent) in our survey reported that they did not incur debts or have to borrow money as a result of the illness or accident. This finding is supported by the responses to questions in the legal section, which asked victims what they did with lump-sum damages awards: few reported that they used the damages to repay money they had had to borrow (see Chapter 3). Of those who did borrow or incur debts half said the sum involved was £50 or less and only about 8 per cent said the amount was greater than £500. No pattern was discernable when these data were disaggregated by the income group: this is not unexpected. Although we might have expected the lower income households to have borrowed more or incurred greater debts as they are likely to have fewer saved assets to run down, they are less likely to be able to borrow money, being worse risks and less likely to have rich friends and relations or sympathetic bank managers.

Sources of household income

We complete our picture of household income by looking at the sources of income and by examining reports of adjustments in income earning activity by the household. In this way we hope to analyse some of the mechanisms operating within the household, following an illness or injury, which may contribute to, or negate, the depressing effect that an illness or injury has on the level of income for our population.

Table 11.13 gives a picture of all the types of income received by the household, both immediately before the illness or injury and at the time of the interview, other than money earned by the victim or other members of the family. It is noticeable that by the time of the interview the number of households receiving money from each of these sources except Category 3 (regular allowance) had increased although only the increases in Categories 7 (sickness benefit), 8 (invalidity benefit), 9 (disablement benefit), and 12 (attendance allowance) can be directly related to an illness or injury. The sizeable increase in the number of households receiving pension money is probably more attributable to the time-lag between date of onset of ill health and date of interview than to premature retirement due to illness or injury.

Table 11.13 *Percentage of households reporting some income from each of the twelve sources at the time of the onset of the illness/injury and at the time of the interview*

Sources of household income	Households receiving the item at the onset of the illness or injury (%)	Households receiving the item at the time of the interview (%)
1. Interest from stocks, shares, annuities, and other investments	9.0	9.6
2. Rents	1.8	1.9
3. Regular allowance from employer/ relative outside household	2.2	2.2
4. Retirement pension from employer	7.8	10.5
5. Old age or widow's pension	24.4	30.7
6. Unemployment benefit	1.7	3.5
7. Sickness benefit	1.4	2.4
8. Invalidity benefit	2.1	6.9
9. Disablement benefit	1.3	1.9
10. Supplementary benefit	7.5	11.5
11. Family Income Supplement	0.6	1.0
12. Attendance allowance, invalid care, or other special state allowance	1.3	3.2
Total %	100.0	100.0
Total $\bar{N}$	3468*	3467**

* Missing observations = 118.
** Missing observations = 119.

Table 11.14 is perhaps more noteworthy as it reveals the significant change in the *main* source of household income between the time of onset of the illness or injury and the time of the interview: part of the change may be directly attributed to the victim's ill health. The four income sources which we would expect to be more important after an illness or injury are Categories 7, 8, 9, and 12 of Table 11.14. However, their relative position as the *main* source of household income at the time of the interview, although increased, remains small.

The sizeable fall in the importance of Category 13 (wage/salary of the victim) may be due, in part, to the reduced or lost earning power of the victim following the accident or illness. However, the time-lag between the onset of the illness or injury and the date of interview will have been long enough for some victims to give up work quite

Table 11.14 *Percentage changes in the main source of household income from immediately before the onset of the illness or injury to the date of the interview*

	Sources of household income	Households with the item as the main source of income immediately prior to the illness or injury (%)	Households with the item as the main source of income at the time of the interview (%)
1	Interest from stocks, shares, annuities, and other investments	0.3	0.5
2	Rents	0.4	0.2
3	Regular allowance from employer/ relative outside household	0.5	0.6
4	Retirement pension from employer	1.4	1.7
5	Old age or widow's pension	14.4	20.7
6	Unemployment benefit	1.1	1.8
7	Sickness benefit	0.3	0.9
8	Invalidity benefit	0.9	3.8
9	Disablement benefit	—	0.1
10	Supplementary benefit	1.6	2.7
11	Family Income Supplement	—	0.1[1]
12	Attendance allowance, invalid care, or other special state allowance	—	0.1[1]
13	Wage/salary of victim	33.0	24.8
14	Wage/salary of household member other than victim	45.4	41.4
15	Other sources	0.7	0.6
	Total (%)	100.0	100.0
	Total Ñ	3468*	3467**

* Missing observations = 118.
** Missing observations = 119.
$\chi^2 = 192.2$ d.f. 14 $p < 0.001$.
[1] In fact it is impossible for 'Family Income Supplement' to be the main source of household income and if 'Attendance Allowance' ever is, the household must be supported by gifts, income in kind or something similar.

independently of the effect of the ill health. The substantial increase in the percentage of households reporting Category 5 (old age or widow's pension) as the main source of income is one example of how the natural effects of ageing can change the main source of household income. The onset of ill-health may, for some victims, have acted as a catalyst to this process – for example, a few victims are known to have retired prematurely (see Chapter 10).

The reduced percentage of households reporting Category 14 (wage/salary of household member other than victim) as the main source of income at the time of the interview, is probably the net effect of several different kinds of adjustment within the household. Some non-victim household members entered the labour market as a result of the victim's ill health (see Table 11.18), but this increase was overturned by people leaving work both as a result of the natural ageing process and in order to care for the victim.

Household adjustments in the labour market

In the light of our earlier hypotheses about the household's use of its members' time, it is interesting to examine the group of households where the victim of the illness or injury was the main source of household income before the onset of ill health. In particular, it is important to see if there are any differences, in terms of household adjustments and the resulting level of household income, between those households where the victim retains his position as the main source of household income after the illness or injury, and those where something else or someone else takes over as the main source of income for the household by the time of the interview. For this purpose we define two subgroups of our survey population:

Group A – victim no longer main earner: households where at the time of the onset of the illness or injury the main source of income *was* the wage/salary of the victim but at the time of the interview it was something else ($\bar{N}$ = 377).

Group B – victim still main earner: households where at the time of the onset of the illness or injury *and* at the time of the interview the main source of household income *was* and *still is* the wage/salary of the victim (control group, $\bar{N}$ = 767).

Table 11.15 gives an indication of the depressing effect on household income of those illnesses and injuries which cause the victim to lose his position as the prime earner in the household. Whereas the mean income for the 'victim still main earner' group is £81 (roughly equivalent to that of FES), the figure for the 'victim no longer main earner' group is only £39. To account for the large income differential between the two groups we look for evidence of household adjustments which result from the illness or injury.

Nearly a fifth (19.1 per cent) of the Group A households claim

Table 11.15 *Percentage of households in each income bracket for Groups A[1] and B[2], and FES for comparison*

Income bracket Gross £ per week	Victim no longer main earner (Group A) (%)	Victim still main earner (Group B) (%)	FES[3] (%)
Less than 20	12.1	0.8	6.2
20 – < 30	32.8	1.2	10.3
30 – < 40	20.9	5.9	8.1
40 – < 50	14.4	11.2	6.6
50 – < 60	6.5	16.9	7.3
60 – < 80	8.8	28.0	16.3
80 – < 100	1.1	17.8	14.7
100 or more	3.4	18.2	30.5
Total (%)	100.0	100.0	100.0
Total N̄	354*	726**	
Mean household income	£39	£81	£82

* Missing observations = 23.
** Missing observations = 41.
$\chi^2 = 475$ d.f. 7 $p < 0.001$.
[1] Group A – victim no longer main earner: households where at the time of the onset of the illness or injury the main source of income *was* the wage/salary of the victim but at the time of the interview it was something else (N̄ = 377).
[2] Group B – victim still main earner: households where at the time of the onset of the illness or injury *and* and at the time of the interview the main source of household income *was* and *still is* the wage/salary of the victim (control group, N̄ = 767).
[3] From Table 11.1.

that a non-victim had taken over as the main earner by the time of the interview (see Table 11.16). Some of this adjustment may have occurred independently of the accident or illness, for example, through the promotion of a non-victim earner although this should have helped to increase the income of the Group A households. In view of the depressed income levels of these households a more plausible explanation is that a reduction in, or loss of, the victim's earnings following the illness or injury altered the *relative* earnings of the household, so that a non-victim assumed main earner status. Table 11.16 also reveals that almost a quarter (23.3 per cent) of these households rely on Category 8 (invalidity benefit) as the main source of income: this is a change which is directly attributable to the illness or injury and which would lead to low income levels. Another third (32.4 per cent) report Category 5 (old age or widow's

Table 11.16 *Main source of household income, at the time of the interview, for Group A households ('Victim no longer main earner')*

	Number of category as in Tables 11.13 and 11.14	(%)
1	Interest from stocks, shares, annuities and other investments	0.6
3	Regular allowance from employer/relative outside household	0.9
4	Retirement pension from employer	2.7
5	Old age or widow's pension	32.4
6	Unemployment benefit	6.1
7	Sickness benefit	6.1
8	Invalidity benefit	23.3
10	Supplementary benefit	3.3
12	Attendance allowance, invalid care, or other special state allowance	0.3
14	Wage/salary of household member other than victim	19.1
	No information available	5.2
	Total %	100.0

pension) as the prime income source at the time of the interview; this is again probably due to a combination of the natural ageing of the Compensation population together with a few cases of premature retirement of the victim due to ill health (either adjustment resulting in depressed household income levels).

Details of labour market adjustments resulting from the accident or illness, for the two groups under scrutiny, are presented in Table 11.17 (adjustments made by the victim) and Table 11.18 (adjustments made by other household members). For both these groups, victims display more adjustment than non-victims. Over three-quarters (79.0 per cent) of the victims who lost their position as the main income-earner (Group A) had time off work; over 40 per cent claim not to have worked regularly since, and a further 5.9 per cent reported reduced pay on returning to their former employer. Only 12.5 per cent of these households (Group A) reported labour market adjustments by other members of the households (Table 11.18); in the majority of these cases work time was curtailed (probably in order to care for the victim) and household income reduced. In the 'victim still main earner' group (Group B) relatively more victims had time off work (90.6 per cent), but a mere 0.5 per cent have not worked regularly since (see Table 11.17, Note 1), and only 10.2 per cent reported lower wages on returning to their old job. There were few reports of adjustments by other household members (9.3 per

Table 11.17 *Labour market adjustments as a result of the illness or injury made by victims who were previously the main earners.*

Labour market adjustment by victim	*Victim no longer main earner (Group A)* Households where at the time of the onset of the illness or injury the main source of income *was* the wage/salary of the victim but at the time of the interview it was something else (%)	*Victim still main earner (Group B)* Households where at the time of the onset of the illness or injury *and* at the time of the interview the main source of household income *was* and *still is* the wage/salary of the victim (control group) (%)
Time off work but returned to regular work with same employer after interruption caused by illness/injury		
Pay on return not affected	27.0	73.8
Pay on return reduced	5.9	10.2
Pay on return increased	0.0	0.1
Pay on return unknown	0.0	0.5
Time off work, but returned to regular work with new employer after interruption caused by illness/injury	3.7	5.1
Time off work and returned to regular work, but no further information known	0.5	0.4
Time off work and have not worked regularly since illness/injury	41.9	0.5[1]
No time off work (either as sick leave or unemployment)	21.0	9.4
	100.0	100.0
	N̄ = 377	N̄ = 767

[1] Presumably these few victims are able to retain their position as main earner, although they have not yet returned to regular work, because they are in receipt of sick pay.

Table 11.18 *Labour market adjustments made by household members other than the victim as a result of his illness or injury.*

Labour market adjustment by non-victim	*Victim no longer main earner (Group A)* Households where at the time of the onset of the illness or injury the main source of income *was* the wage/salary of the victim but at the time of the interview it was something else (%)		*Victim still main earner (Group B)* Households where at the time of the onset of the illness or injury *and* at the time of the interview the main source of household income *was* and *still is* the wage/salary of the victim (control group) (%)
Adjustment reported as reducing household income:			
Non-victim gave up work	7.2		
Non-victim worked shorter hours	2.9	10.6	3.3
Non-victim changed to less well-paid job	0.5		
Adjustment reported as increasing household income:			
Non-victim started a job	1.4	1.9	6.0
Non-victim worked longer hours	0.5		
No adjustment by non-victim household members		87.5	90.7
Total %		100.0	100.0
		N̄ = 377	N̄ = 767

cent), but two-thirds of those that did take place caused an increase in household income.

Our conclusion from this analysis is that, for those households where the victim was the main earner prior to the accident or illness, the post-accident or post-illness employment behaviour of the victim is of crucial importance in explaining the resulting level of household income. Household income tends to be depressed where the victim is unable to maintain his position as the main earner (usually by failing to return to regular employment after the illness or injury). Adjustments by other household members are fairly rare and do not counter or compensate for the detrimental income and employment effects of the ill health of the victim: in fact, for the 'victim no longer main earner' group (Group A) these adjustments seem to contribute to the depressed income levels.

Examination of the households where 'wage/salary of household member other than victim' is the main income source before the accident or illness (see Table 11.14, $\bar{n}=1575$) produces little evidence of changes in the employment behaviour of non-victims as a result of the victim's ill health. About 10 per cent of these households report adjustments and nearly all are seen as reducing household income: this suggests that 'the need for more care of the victim' prevails over 'the need for more income'. In a few households in this category, by the time of the interview, the non-victim is no longer the main earner: the mean income level of this group is £67, compared with £82 (roughly equivalent to FES) for households where a non-victim continues as the main earner in the household. Again, it seems that labour market adjustments made by household members other than the victim are few and, furthermore, where they do occur, they may depress household income levels.

(4) The contribution of a number of factors in explaining the household income

So far our analyses have told us something about the impact that a number of factors have *individually* on household income when a member of that household suffers an accident or illness. The cross-tabulations gave an indication of how each factor affects household income but without controlling for the influence of the other factors. The information on the sources of income and adjustment showed how different categories of income become more or less important as a result of the illness or injury and suggested a number of ways in which the household income alters in those circumstances. To ascertain the *relative* importance of some of these factors in determining the level of income for households in our sample we used a 'logistic regression model' (see Brittan and Vlachonikolis, 1980).

Table 11.19 lists the explanatory variables considered: seven were found to be of significant importance in explaining household income and they are identified by an asterisk (*). The coefficient (in conjunction with the standard deviation) gives an indication of the

Table 11.19 *Logistic regression results for levels of household income*[1]

	Explanatory variable	Coefficient	Standard deviation	T-value
1	Victim is in full-time work	3.1813	0.17625	18.05*
2	Victim is in part-time work	1.2960	0.24215	5.35*
3	Victim is head of household	– 1.4573	0.14619	– 9.97*
4	Victim is registered as disabled with local authority	0.51399	0.20595	2.50*
5	Victim is registered as disabled with Department of Employment	– 0.019037	0.27756	– 0.07
6	Number of people in household	0.52414	0.068847	7.61*
7	Residual disability - 'affected a lot just occasionally'	– 0.43882	0.19108	– 2.30*
8	Residual disability – 'affected a lot most of the time'	– 0.37108	0.20708	– 1.79
9	Residual disability – 'affected a lot all of the time'	– 0.52675	0.20921	– 2.52*
10	Household adjustment leading to fall in income	0.20280	0.20383	0.99
11	Household adjustment leading to increase in income	0.24271	0.41521	0.58
12	Families with children	0.0094627	0.20786	0.05
13	Accident victim (as compared with victims of illness)	0.012273	0.12661	0.10

* Variable is significant, at 5 per cent level, in explaining household income.
1. The financial data from the survey were adapted for use with the Logistic Regression Model by Ioannis G. Vlachonikolis, who is also responsible for the statistical interpretation of the results.

direction and magnitude of the influence each variable has on household income. Positive coefficients signify positive relationships between variables and levels of household income and vice versa. The larger the value of a coefficient, the stronger the relationship is between a variable and household income. A variable's impact on household income should be seen as negligible if the value of the coefficient, whether positive or negative, is close to zero. The results reported in Table 11.19 are not altogether surprising, and in many cases demonstrate that relationships between certain variables and household income, as suggested by the cross-tabulations, hold even when the influence of other factors is controlled for.

The positive coefficients for the first two variables in Table 11.19

suggest that those households where the victim is working, whether full or part time, at the time of the interview, tend to have higher levels of income than the control groups (non-workers and part-time workers in the one case and full-time and non-workers in the other). This confirms the trend shown earlier in Table 11.8. Furthermore, the relative sizes of the coefficients suggest that this effect is stronger for victims who are in full-time work by the time of the interview, than for part-timers. On the other hand, if the victim is the head of the household (variable 3) the coefficient suggests that household income is depressed compared with those cases where the victim is not the head of the household. (Table 11.7 shows a similar relationship).

As we may expect, incomes tend to be higher the more people in the household (variable 6) but the presence or not of children in the household seems unimportant in determining income levels (variable 12).

All the coefficients referring to residual disability measures (variables 7, 8, 9) have negative signs and, although the coefficients are small, this confirms our earlier results (see Table 11.9) and indicates a slight tendency for victims with residual disability to have lower household incomes than those 'never affected a lot'. In contrast, the coefficient of variable 4 suggests a very slight tendency for household incomes to be higher if the victim is registered as disabled with the Local Authority.

The remaining variables (5, 10, 11, 13) have coefficients close to zero and therefore their impact on household income should be treated as insignificant. In the case of variables 10 and 11 this supports our earlier impression that labour market adjustments made by non-victim household members are infrequent occurrences and far less prevalent than employment changes made by the victim himself: and hence their effect on household income is limited. The difference between accident and illness cases, which seemed important in the cross-tabulation analysis (Table 11.11), also appears insignificant in explaining household income levels when other factors are controlled for. It can be argued that it is through employment effects and residual disability (both significant in the multivariate analysis) that the cause of the ill health affects household income: because illness victims tend to have longer absences from work (see Table 10.4) and more residual disability (see Table 1.5) than accident victims, household income of illness victims tends to be lower than for accident victims (see Table 11.11). The registration (or not) of a victim with the Department of Employment seems equally unimportant in explaining income levels.

For the future, it would be interesting to run a regression on FES data to establish which variables are significant in explaining the level of income for the general population. Our results to date suggest that, of the variables we tested, the crucial factors in determining the household income for the Compensation Survey sample are the work status of the victim, whether the victim is head of household, and the degree of residual disability. The one important variable which does not relate directly to the victim and his state of health is the number of people in the household.

(5) Non-response and household income

One final aspect of the Compensation Survey household income data which has to be considered is whether the 13 per cent of households which did not respond to the income question ($\bar{n} = 467$, see p. 284 above) have different characteristics from those who did ($\bar{n} = 3119$), and whether these differences, if they exist, are likely to have biased the income distribution for the Compensation Survey population. An analysis, therefore, was made to compare the variables which were shown to be significant in explaining household income by the multivariate analysis, for the non-responding with the responding households.

Non-responding when compared with responding households contained proportionally more victims who were not heads of households and proportionally more victims who had no residual disability at the time of the interview; both factors suggest a higher income profile for non-responding compared with responding households. On the other hand there were proportionally fewer victims in work at the time of the interview in the non-responding compared with the responding group which suggests a lower-income profile for the households who did not respond to the income question. Sizes of households were found to be similar for both groups.

The differential characteristics of the two groups suggest that, on balance, there may be a tendency for non-responding households to have slightly higher incomes than the households for which income was recorded. However, bearing in mind the relatively small number of households who failed to answer the income question (13 per cent) it is unlikely that the income levels of the non-responding households, if they were known, would be high enough to increase the mean household income of the whole Compensation Survey population by more than one (or two) pounds.

(6) Conclusions: the impact of illness and injury on household income

In this chapter we have studied the victim in the context of the household unit. Our analysis of the money income of the household has provided one measure, albeit imperfect, of the financial well-being of the household following an accident or illness. Initially, we hypothesized various types of financial adjustment consequent upon the ill health, including changes in the victim's earnings, employment adjustments made by non-victim household members, and the impact of money compensation schemes. The household income profile of the Compensation Survey population describes the net effect of all these adjustments.

The key finding is that the Compensation Survey households report significantly lower incomes than those of the population as a whole: the respective mean incomes are £62 and £82. There are many definitions of the 'poverty line': one of those most frequently used is the rate of ordinary supplementary benefit. Although this rate varies with the type of household, we can deduce from official data that in 1976 the ordinary supplementary benefit rate, even when an allowance for rent is included, for most households was probably less than £30 gross per week (see Supplementary Benefit Commission, 1977). Just over 23 per cent of our households fell below this poverty line; the comparable proportion for the general population was 16.5 per cent.

The next task was to determine whether the low incomes of our population were due to the differential incidence of accidents and illness in low-income groups. Our analysis of the socio-economic group mix of the victims, together with the expected income levels for each group, failed to support the hypothesis that people in low income households are more likely to suffer accidents and illnesses (see Table 11.3 and p. 288 text above) but it confirmed the results of other studies in the UK and USA which have shown the impoverishing effects of illness and injury (see Baldwin, 1977; Luft, 1978; Townsend, 1979).

We therefore looked for reasons why certain types of household in the Compensation Survey had very low incomes after an illness or injury whilst others seemed to escape poverty. Our analysis leads to the conclusion that the prime determinants of the level of household income at the time of the interview relate almost exclusively to the state of recovery of the victim. Where the victim has returned to work by the time of the interview, has kept his position as main earner in the household, and/or suffers no residual disability (i.e. it was a relatively short-term interruption) household incomes tend to be significantly higher (although still sometimes lower than the national FES sample) than in cases of longer-term ill health. The income differences of households containing victims of accidents and illnesses is thus only pertinent if viewed in terms of time off work due to the illness or injury and residual disability measures. It also seems that where adjustments occur in the employment behaviour of non-victim household members, they confirm that the need to care for the victim takes precedence over the need to maintain household income. All these findings support the view that the present array of money compensation schemes are least adequate in coping with the long-term problems of income maintenance which face certain households after accidents and illnesses.

We believe that a multifaceted approach is needed in future policy-making to deal with the economic consequences of illness and injury. The study of household income confirms the importance of a co-ordinated programme to help earner-victims (particularly those most at risk, see Chapter 10) back to work as quickly as possible by improved medical facilities, vocational rehabilitation and, to a more limited extent, by providing more jobs for disabled workers.

For those victims who are unable to work, including those who were not earners at the time of onset of illness or injury, a harmonized programme of short- and long-term income maintenance is required, which takes account of the victim in the context of the household unit, and criteria for entitlements which give higher priority to countering the long-term impoverishing effects of the more serious cases.

References

Aitchison, J., and Brown, J. A. C., 1969, *The Lognormal Distribution*, Cambridge: Cambridge University Press.

Baldwin, S., 1977, *Disabled Children: Counting the Costs*, London: Disability Alliance.

Becker, G. S., 1964, *Human Capital*, New York: Columbia Press.

—— 1965, 'A Theory of the Allocation of Time', 75 *Economic Journal* 493.

Brittan, Y., and Vlachonikolis, I. G., 1980, 'The Effect of Ill-health and Subsequent Compensation and Support on Household Income: A Logistic Regression Approach', Oxford: Centre for Socio-Legal Studies, Wolfson College, *Working Paper No. 6*.

—— 1981, 'The Impact of Residual Disability from Illness and Injury on the Distribution of Household Income: A Lognormal Approach', Oxford: Centre for Socio-Legal Studies, Wolfson College, *Working Paper No. 9*.

Department of Employment, 1977, *Family Expenditure Survey 1976*, London: HMSO (and earlier reports).

Fenn, P., and Brittan, Y., *The Economics of Compensation for Illness and Injury*, (forthcoming).

General Household Survey 1977 (published by Office of Population and Censuses, 1977 and other years), London: HMSO.

Goldberg, E. N., and Morrison, F. L., 1963, 'Schizophrenia and Social Class', 109 *British Journal of Psychiatry* 785.

Harris, A. I., with Cox, E., and Smith, C. R. W., 1971–2, *Handicapped and Impaired in Great Britain*, (3 vols.), London: HMSO.

Horsnell, G., 1979, 'Income Distribution Analysis: U.K. Household Incomes as an Example', Contributed paper to Royal Statistical Society Conference, Oxford.

Luft, H. S., 1978, *Poverty and Health: Economic Causes and Consequences of Health Problems*, Massachusetts: Ballinger.

Lydall, H., 1968, *The Structure of Earnings*, Oxford: Oxford University Press.

—— 1979, *The Theory of Income Distribution*, Oxford: Clarendon Press.

Oi, W. Y., 1977, 'From Disability to Poverty', Rochester, New York: University of Rochester (mimeographed).

OPCS (Office of Population Censuses and Surveys), 1970, *Classification of Occupations*, London: HMSO.

Supplementary Benefit Commission, 1977, *Annual Report 1976*, London: HMSO.

Townsend, P., 1979, *Poverty in the United Kingdom: A Survey of Household Resources and Standards of Living*, London: Penguin.

Part IV SUMMARY AND CONCLUSIONS

12 Review and Prospect

(1) Summary of the main findings of the survey

This section gives a summary of the more important findings of the Compensation Survey reported in this volume.

Part I: Compensation under the damages system

The survey showed that only a small minority of all accident victims initiate legal claims and obtain damages for the losses they have suffered (Chapter 2). For all types of accident taken together, the figure is 12 per cent of cases, but there are important differences in the success rates between different categories of accident. While fewer than one in three of road accident victims, and one in five of work accident victims obtained damages, fewer than one in fifty of all other types of accident victims obtained damages, despite the fact that this represented the largest category of accidents suffered by victims in the sample. Although the chances of obtaining damages were very high once there had been contact with a solicitor about the possibility of making a claim, the vast majority of victims either never considered the question of claiming compensation, or if they did so, failed to take any positive steps to make a definite claim.

Elderly victims and young victims appeared on the whole to be reluctant to claim damages, irrespective of the type of accident suffered, and, for elderly victims at least, irrespective of the degree of residual disability suffered as a result of the accident. Women suffering work accidents claimed less often than men suffering work accidents, although for road and other accidents the proportions were similar. In general, accident victims in full- or part-time employment were considerably more likely to claim damages than those not in employment. Contrary to our expectations, accident victims in lower status socio-economic groups were proportionately *more* likely to obtain damages than victims in professional or managerial groups. The seriousness of injury in both physical terms and the amount of time taken off work was not consistently associated with the likelihood that damages would be obtained, underlining the fact that the tort system is based on the cause of accidents rather than on the consequences.

Detailed analysis of the steps involved in actually perceiving an accident as a problem for which legal advice should be sought indicated that women and the elderly were both less likely to consider the question of compensation, and having done so, were less likely than other groups actually to seek legal advice. For those accident victims who did succeed in obtaining damages it was clear that advice obtained *before* getting in touch with a solicitor was very important in providing or reinforcing the incentive to claim damages. More than two-thirds of those people in contact with a solicitor claimed that the idea of obtaining legal advice *first* came from another person. For victims who have accidents on the road or at work there are normally certain procedures for reporting the accident which have to be followed and during which advice about claiming may spontaneously be offered. For victims who have accidents elsewhere there are no such procedures and the people who disproportionately suffer these types of accidents – women, the elderly, children – are more isolated than those at work from networks of information and advice. Trade union activity in pressing claims for damages provides an important example of both the value of immediate advice and easy access to the legal system.

The reasons given for not proceeding with a claim by those people who had at some time considered the possibility indicate that lack of claims-consciousness, problems about providing evidence, and fear of the legal costs involved in making a claim represent important constraints.

The actual operation of the damages system (Chapter 3) produced relatively low amounts for our sample: a mean of £1135, but a median of only £500. Many pressures on claimants led them to accept amounts which heavily discounted the full award which a court would make. There may be a discount for each risk or uncertainty facing the claimant: the risks that his evidence might not prove fault on the part of the defendent, that he himself might be found partly at fault (contributory negligence), or that the medical reports on his prognosis might be wrong; the uncertainties about whether he could bear the further delay and expense of waiting for a court hearing, and about how much a judge would award for his injuries. The cumulative effect of all these uncertainties was that nearly all claimants agreed to compromise their cases in out-of-court settlements for sums much lower than 'full' legal liability would justify. Every uncertainty and risk is a negotiating weapon in the hands of the insurance company; a particularly powerful weapon is an allegation of contributory negligence, as was shown by solicitors' reports that it was taken into account in nearly half the settlements. The pressures to settle meant that very few cases (five out of 1,177, or 0.4 per cent) actually reached the stage of a contested hearing in court, although formal court proceedings were commenced in about 40 per cent of the claims ultimately settled.

Both solicitors and insurance companies assume that nearly all claims will be settled, and that negotiations will proceed by means of the companies' offers to settle. The data in the survey showed that the first offer was accepted in over half the claims. To the extent that the number of offers rejected indicates the amount of negotiating between the parties, the data provide no evidence that more negotiating takes place in the more serious cases: the data cannot be explained on the hypotheses that more offers are rejected in the relatively serious cases or in the cases with greater residual disability. Nor do the data reveal any simple pattern for the negotiating strategy of insurance companies: their successive offers seem designed to be sufficiently tempting to secure an acceptance rate of 50 per cent or more for each successive category – our data showed that about 60 per cent of claimants accepted the first offer, about 50 per cent the second, and 80 per cent the third. But in individual cases there was substantial variation from these averages, which indicated that insurance companies make assessments of the relative strengths and weaknesses of each claim at each stage.

Delay is an inescapable part of the present tort system. In the survey, the average delay between the date of the accident and the actual receipt of damages was a little over nineteen months; nearly all successful claimants had returned to work before receiving damages. Solicitors had advised delay in 40 per cent of the claims, in order to wait until medical treatment was complete or until the medical condition of the claimant had stabilized. Several trends are clear from the data – the delay is likely to be longer, the longer the victim is off work, and the greater the degree of his residual disability. The data also indicated that the longer the delay before a lawyer is consulted, the worse the chance of obtaining damages: the difficulties of collecting evidence increase with the delay. Two thirds of the solicitors reported difficulties in negotiating with insurance companies, but their clients seemed unaware of many of the difficulties, and reported far fewer. The two main problems for solicitors were to establish liability, and to negotiate the amount of damages. The difficulties led 29 per cent of those who had formally made a claim, or who had consulted a solicitor or trade union about claiming, to decide to abandon it: they reported that they had done so because of problems of obtaining evidence (45 per cent); their own fault (18 per cent); fear of legal expenses (16 per cent); firm denials of liability by the defendants (15 per cent); and problems over trade unions' handling of the claims (15 per cent). (For minor reasons, see Table 3.12.)

Only one in twenty said that they had obtained any advice on how to use the damages. Many bought tangible, durable items; about half saved some for the future; a fifth put some towards a house or house improvements; but only a quarter used some for living expenses. Claimants reported that at first they had had no idea of how much to expect, and so had relied entirely on their lawyers' advice. They explained their acceptance of lower sums than expected by their urgent need for money, or their fear of further trouble and delay, or of going to court. Most solicitors, however, thought that the amounts of damages were 'adequate' in view of all the risks facing their clients. One in twelve (8 per cent) of those obtaining damages did not use a lawyer – they were ignorant of the negotiating process and of the many uncertainties involved, and appeared to assume that the employers, local and transport authorities, and insurance companies (against whom them claimed) could be relied upon to pay whatever sum was appropriate.

The main feature of the solicitor-and-client relationship was the client's almost complete dependence upon the solicitor's knowledge and advice: the process of claiming damages is so complicated, and the legal rules on liability and on the assessment of damages create such uncertainty that the client has no alternative to giving his solicitor the effective control over the decisions to settle or to abandon a claim. The uncertainties surrounding the claim often protect the solicitor from criticism: only 17 per cent of the clients in the survey said that they had any complaint, disagreement, or problem about the way their lawyers handled the claim – mainly complaints about lack of interest shown in them, lack of information about progress, or delay; and disagreements over the amount of damages.

The data showed that claimants did not know the amount of their legal expenses, which were almost always paid by the defendant's insurance company. Over all settlements, these expenses averaged 18 per cent of the damages paid, but they varied considerably between the larger and the smaller cases: they averaged 29 per cent of the smaller claims (damages of £1,000 or under) and 15 per cent of the larger settlements (over £1,000). Although solicitors are charging for work done and not (as in the USA) a percentage of the damages recovered, in the small cases (under £1,000) the amounts of legal expenses were close to the typical US percentage.

Our data showed that it was not victims' attributions of fault which motivated them to make a damages claim (Chapter 4). Fault was not always seen as appropriate grounds for compensation, nor was it necessarily seen as a precondition if a claim was to be made. In only half those cases where the victim took steps to initiate a claim for damages had he also attributed fault to the person against whom the claim would be made. Only about half of those who said their accident was someone else's fault said they had at any time thought that that person should compensate them. Moreover, the pattern of responses for different types of accidents suggested that even in those cases where attributions of fault did coincide with the initiation of a claim, the attribution of fault was a justification rather than a reason for the claim, and that, without the prospect of a possible damages award, fault might have been attributed quite differently, if at all. The question of fault was certainly not unimportant to the victims. In particular, holding someone to blame was clearly seen as threatening to a relationship. However, the factors determining whether or not fault was attributed to someone else, and if so how, were extremely complex, and included many factors besides the causes and circumstances of the accident. Rather than the law reflecting the ordinary man's view of fault and liability, the victims' attributions of fault and liability reflected legal norms and the likelihood of a successful damages claim. The findings also confirmed that the attribution of fault in the context of a particular damages claim is very much a function of that context. It cannot be assumed that the type of attribution of fault generated by the tort system will be appropriate also for purposes of deterrence or accident prevention, where it may be far more effective to focus on quite different causal factors.

Part II: Other systems of compensation and support

The main financial support for victims in the survey came from social security (Chapter 5); but only four out of ten actually received some benefit (averaging £731 up to the time of the interview, but with some future entitlement to benefits which could be worth thousands of pounds (Table 5.3)). About a third of the social security beneficiaries in the survey had to rely on means-tested supplementary benefits, which fact indicates that, for many victims of illness and injury, minimum income levels are not being maintained by the social security benefits specifically designed for illness and injury. A third of the beneficiaries received the long-term invalidity benefits, and a fifth the short-term sickness benefit. In practice entitlement to social security benefit depends largely on previous work status. Nearly three-quarters of those in full-time work before the illness or injury received some benefit but fewer than one in five of other victims received any benefit. This goes some way to explain the fact that many more men than women received support from the social security system.

Data from the survey suggest that difficulties in the administration of social security arise from two factors – the complexity of the criteria for entitlement to some benefits (e.g. means-tested supplementary benefit) and the need for special medical examinations for some benefits (e.g. attendance allowance).

Only seven of the twenty-one victims of criminal injury in our sample obtained an award from the Criminal Injuries Compensation Board (Chapter 6). One person applied for an award but was refused for reasons which were not clear in the account given by the victim. Those people who did not apply were either confused about the regulations regarding awards (for example, they might have thought that it was only possible to apply if the identity of the offender was known) or did not think that they would have been entitled to compensation because the injury was caused in a domestic dispute or in a fight between acquaintances. The criminal injuries reported were generally of a serious nature and in some cases caused long periods off work. The amounts awarded were quite small (mean £245, median £207) and most claims were made direct by the victim to the Board rather than through a solicitor.

Although occupational sick pay is obviously confined to employees, it is an important form of support for those who have lost earnings as the result of illness or injury (Chapter 7). Our data showed that official statistics on membership of sick pay schemes (to the effect that about 80 per cent of full time workers are covered) are not a reliable guide to actual receipts of sick pay. In the survey, of those who had held their employment for less than six months, only 25 per cent obtained some sick pay; for those with six months but less than two years' service, 49 per cent obtained some; and for those with more than five years' service, 62 per cent obtained some. The mean total amount of sick pay received was £248: a typical recipient was someone absent for up to twenty-six weeks being paid £20 to £30 per week. When added to social security benefits, these amounts can provide total compensation equal to full pay for the whole or part of the period of absence, but the longer the absence, the less likely that sick pay will continue to be received: only a relatively small amount of sick pay was received for absences beyond six months.

Our data indicated that private, first-party insurance is an insignificant proportion of present support for illness and injury (Chapter 8). Only 14 per cent of people in the survey held a policy of this type, and they were mainly work and road accident victims (who were also those most likely to obtain some damages). Fewer than half those with policies received a payment, and the mean amount was only £81.

The survey data on social care (Chapter 9) showed that, on average, illness has more serious medical consequences than accidents: those who are ill are more likely to be in hospital for more than a week, and to use the services of general practitioners; they are also more likely to suffer residual disabilities (Tables 9.1–3.) The same holds for local authority and community health services: illness victims (particularly the elderly) make nearly three times as much use of these services as do accident victims (Table 9.4). On the basis of service use, therefore, the 'needs' of illness victims would appear to be greater than those of accident victims, yet the tort system in practice benefits only the latter group.

More than half the victims in the survey received informal care and support from family, relatives or neighbours (Tables 9.5; 9.7; and 9.8). This assistance often continued on a daily basis for more than six months and came largely from family members: it was not dependent on the age of the victim, nor the cause of his incapacity. Informal support is given without payment, and often in addition to, rather than instead of, local authority support.

A comparison of the different combinations of support received by the various categories of victims showed that those who obtain damages (almost exclusively work and road accident victims) are more likely than other victims to receive in addition some social security support, and slightly more likely to receive some private insurance payment.

Part III: Employment and household income

The survey provided new data on incomes and employment (Chapters 10 and 11) and highlighted the issues on which future policy-making should focus. The total income of all households in the survey (after taking account of all sources of income compensation) was found to be only three-quarters of the average incomes of all households in the regular national survey (Table 11.1). When the survey households are subdivided into smaller categories, the reduction in income levels is even more pronounced, as is shown by Table 12.1.

Table 12.1 *Summary of Levels of Household Income (1976–1977)*

	Mean household income[1] gross per week (£s)	Number of households n̄
National sample of all households (FES sample: Table 11.1)	82	
Compensation Survey		
All households in the survey (Table 11.1)	62	3119
Households where the victim is head of the household (Table 11.7)	53	1644
Households where the victim reported the most serious category of residual disability ('affected a lot all the time') (Table 11.9)	43	535
Households where the victim was not working at the time of the Compensation interview (Table 11.8)	41	1414
Households where the victim had previously been the main earner, but could no longer continue that role (Table 11.15)	39	354

[1] The data on household income did not include a lump sum received as damages, but included any income arising from an investment made with the damages.

Multivariate analysis of the data confirms that three of the crucial factors which determine the level of household income after the illness or injury relate directly to the victim himself: whether he can return to work, whether he is the head of the household, and the degree of his residual disability; a fourth factor is the number of people in the household (Table 11.19). As can be inferred from Table 12.1, the most extreme case is the household where the victim of the illness or injury had previously been the main earner within the household, but could no longer continue that role: for this group, the average household income was only £39 (Table 11.15); in nearly a fifth of the households in this group another member of the household had taken over as the main earner (Table 11.16), and in another quarter, invalidity benefit had become the main source of income (Table 11.16). The data also confirm that the greater the degree of residual disability reported by the victim, the lower the household income (Tables 11.9 and 11.10).

The household income data therefore show that the effect of the illness or injury on the victim's status in the labour market is often crucial. The employment data in the survey (Chapter 10) show that many factors, in addition to the purely physical factor of residual disability, affect the employment prospects of sick and injured people. The age of the victim, the local unemployment rate, and the level of income replacement received by him while off work, together with the extent of residual disability, are the main factors affecting the length of the absence from work; less important factors are family commitments, training, and job experience (Table 10.9). Those most likely to suffer more permanent disadvantage in the labour market are those whose illness or injury leads to prolonged absence from work: this factor appears to be more important than the relative degree of residual disability (Tables 10.10–13). About one in five of those in full-time work or education at the time of the illness or injury believed that his job situation, his earnings or his qualifications had been affected as a consequence of his ill-health.

(2) Allocation of compensation by cause of incapacity

Many of the findings of the survey enable comparisons to be drawn between households affected by illness and injury (our survey population) and households generally. Some findings, however, enable a comparison *within* our population between those affected by illness and those affected by injury suffered in accidents. As Table 1.1, Columns 1–3, have shown, some of the existing institutions of compensation draw a rigid distinction between illness and injury as causes of incapacity.

Data from our survey show that illness causes much more incapacity than accident, both in terms of the numbers of people affected, and the length and severity of the consequences. Over the survey population as a whole, the incidence of incapacity lasting two weeks or longer (during the twelve months preceding the screening interview) was 63 per 1,000 for illness, but 40 per 1,000 for accidents (Table 1.2: this Table shows that the incidence of illness increases with age, particularly for those over 54; it is also higher for those who are widowed, divorced or separated than for those who are either married or single; and it tends to be higher for those in the lower socio-economic groups). On average, illnesses cause more serious medical consequences than do accidents; those who are ill are more likely than accident victims to be in hospital for more than a week, and more likely to use the services of general practitioners (Tables 9.1 and 9.3). Those who are ill also make nearly three times as much use of local authority and community health services as do accident victims (Table 9.4). Furthermore, according to the extent of self-reported residual disability, illness is a more frequent cause than accidents of long-term disability (Tables 1.5; 9.2); in this respect, however, *work* accidents – as distinct from accidents generally – cause proportionately almost as much residual disability as illnesses.

Illness, on average, also causes absences from work which last more than twice as long as absences caused by accidents (Table 10.4): as a result it seems likely, on the basis of the analysis in Chapters 10 and 11, that illness leads to more involuntary and unproductive changes in labour market status, and, as a consequence, lower incomes in the long run, than do accidents. Table 11.11 presents data on household income according to the cause of the incapacity. The mean household income in our survey where the cause was accident or industrial illness[1] was £69 a week, whereas for all other illnesses, it was only £55 a week. Multivariate analysis of the data, however, revealed that when a number of health and demographic factors are controlled for, there is an insignificant difference between the income levels of accident households compared with those of illness households. None the less, the analysis also showed that the work status of the victim (at the time of the Compensation Survey interview), and the presence or absence of residual disability, were particularly important in determining the level of household income. Hence, we conclude that it is through changes in work status and through the extent of residual disability that the illness/accident demarcation is significant in determining levels of household income where the incapacity lasts two weeks or more: since, in comparison with accident victims, those who are ill tend to have longer absences from work and greater residual disability, household incomes in cases of illness tend to be lower than in cases of accident.

In practice, compensation under the damages system is virtually confined to accident cases. Illness caused by the fault of another person can rarely be proved: out of the 182 cases where damages were paid in the survey, only two were for illness – both were claims against employers, one for pneumoconiosis suffered by a miner, and one for poisoning from asbestos dust suffered by a factory worker. In a similar way, benefits under the industrial injuries scheme are concentrated almost entirely on accident cases: only one in fifty of the injury benefits commencing in 1976–7 (the year nearest to our survey period) were for diseases prescribed under the scheme (*Social Security Statistics 1977*, Table 20.50). It should be noted, however, that the preference shown by existing compensation systems is not for accident cases in general,[2] but rather for restricted categories of accidents[3] – injuries suffered at work, on the roads, by criminal violence, or through service with the Armed Forces (Table 1.1, Column 1). Our survey data indicate that although those injured in other categories of accident form the vast majority of accident victims (Table 1.2) only one in fifty of them obtains any payment of damages (Table 2.2).

The ultimate abolition of the tort claim and of all cause-based categories

It is a social and political judgment whether accident victims should continue to enjoy this preference. We believe, in the light of the data presented in this volume, that the future policy-maker should plan to phase out all existing compensation systems which favour accident victims (or any category of them) over illness victims.[4] This proposal obviously applies to the damages system, whose deficiences as revealed by the survey (see the summary in section 1 of this chapter) are too deep-rooted to be removed by any modification of the system. Relatively few accident victims recover any damages at all; most amounts recovered are low and therefore can do little to 'compensate'; and the cost of administering the system is very high. Delay and uncertainty are inherent in the system; the adversarial game permits defendants to adopt negotiating strategies which exploit – quite legitimately under the present rules – each uncertainty to defeat a claim, or to reduce the amount paid. The advantages claimed for the system do not, in our opinion, outweigh the disadvantages. Deterrence of carelessness operates in a random way, and accident victims themselves perceive no clear concept of fault or blame underlying the attribution of liability to pay damages. Our data establish that the roles of sick pay and social security in providing income support following illness and injury are now, in the aggregate, of much greater importance than the damages system. Yet the illness/injury demarcation is ignored by sick pay schemes and by all social security benefits introduced since 1946: within social security, only the historically anomalous industrial injuries scheme continues the preference for accident victims. We believe that the damages system for death and personal injury should be abolished as soon as improvements in sick pay and social security provision produce a rational, coherent, and integrated system of compensation for illness and injury.

Our view that we should move towards the abolition of every compensation scheme which is based on a particular category of causation means that we oppose the implementation of many of the recommendations of the Pearson Royal Commission, 1978. The Commission recommended many improvements to the tort claim; a new, no-fault scheme for injuries caused by road accidents; a special benefit for severely handicapped children; and that the criminal injuries scheme should be placed on a statutory basis. In our opinion, these proposals are difficult to justify in social policy terms, and would only increase the complexity of the present web of compensations systems, which are based, not on the relative extent of disabilities, but on the circumstances which give rise to disabilities (Ogus *et al.*, 1978; Harris, 1979).

Our proposals in the next section are designed to permit some of the advantages of the tort system to be retained in any new schemes to replace tort: the individualized assessment of damages to be replaced by better and more flexible types of social security benefits for long-term cases of disability; and deterrence of carelessness through some risk-relationship, by extension of sick pay entitlement, and by new types of risk-related social security contributions. Our proposals would also allow the policy-maker (contrary, however, to our own preference) to choose to implement risk relationship by special, no-fault schemes as part of the overall scheme. The final section of this chapter proceeds to consider the basic structure which we propose for future policy-making in this area; it assumes that the tort system and any cause-based category will not continue as a permanent feature of that structure.

(3) Proposals for future policy-making

Assumptions

In these two paragraphs, we attempt to make explicit the key assumptions which underlie the proposals made later in this section. (Other assumptions are discussed throughout the section.) We first assume that members of society expect that some protection will be provided against the risk that individuals may suffer the financial consequences of illness or injury (e.g. loss of income, or extra costs); and that they also expect that this protection should be above the level of the residual, welfare support intended to provide an income 'floor' for all members of society irrespective of the state of their health (e.g. means-tested supplementary benefits in the United Kingdom). Nearly all the present schemes set out in Table 1.1 make the assumption that special provision — beyond means-tested welfare benefits — is justified in the case of those affected by illness or injury. We further assume that adequate provision for all members of society against the consequences of illness and injury cannot be expected from the private insurance market on its own; that market is not equipped to deal adequately with some problems, e.g. adverse selection by those likely to suffer from illness or injury; or the index relation of income support for the long-term cases (see Chapter 8). Our next assumption is that provision through compulsory or state-organized compensation schemes need not attempt to give a complete indemnity against the full extent of loss or all types of loss caused by illness or injury. We believe that some scope may be left for individual choice to take out private insurance; for trade unions to obtain additional, ill-health benefits through collective bargaining; or for part of the loss to be met by 'self-insurance', viz. by leaving some part of the risk of ill health to be borne by the potential victim or his family, who may use up part of their savings, reduce their expenditure, or rely on the earnings of fit members of the household – which is now the result of waiting periods before benefits are payable, or of ceilings fixed for benefits.

Some further assumptions are needed to support the details of our proposals. We believe that some vestiges of the insurance or contribution principle (viz. that individual benefits should be related to individual contribution records or premiums paid) will be expected by those required to meet the cost of compensation: recognition that earners (or potential earners) have reasonable expectations of maintaining their standard of living, and that as a group they must of necessity be the main contributors to the cost of compensation, may justify higher levels of income support for earners (or potential earners) than for non-earners, e.g. by earnings-related supplements. But our proposals are for social, or group insurance and do not relate individual benefits to individual contributions. Another vestige of the insurance principle which we wish to preserve is the aim that, wherever it is administratively feasible to arrange for it at reasonable cost, differential contributions towards the cost of compensation should be levied on identifiable categories of contributors, so that each category should be under a financial inducement to take care to minimize the risk of illness or injury arising in the course of their activities.

The need for integration

At present, as our survey has shown, many forms of compensation overlap in providing income support for the same person in respect of the same period of time. In particular, as the following outline of the present systems shows (Figure 12.1) sick pay, social security, damages, and private insurance may each independently attempt to provide income support in respect of the same or of overlapping periods of time. Apart from phasing out the damages system (as argued in the previous sections of this chapter), we believe that the major task of the future policy-maker in the United Kingdom must be to rationalize and integrate the other mechanisms of support: since they are already functioning, the feasible approach would be to build on them, rather than to replace them with a completely new scheme of compensation. Although this approach may be pragmatic, it does not mean that our proposals are merely for a tidying-up operation – on the contrary, they involve important changes which reflect our concern with the relative poverty of the long-term victims of illness and injury.

The following section puts forward outline proposals for future policies: for the allocation of benefits (the type of benefits, and the criteria for entitlement); and for the mechanisms for financing the benefits, and the sources of finance. As the purpose of our survey was to collect data on the existing distribution of financial and other support, our proposals on the future types of benefits and the

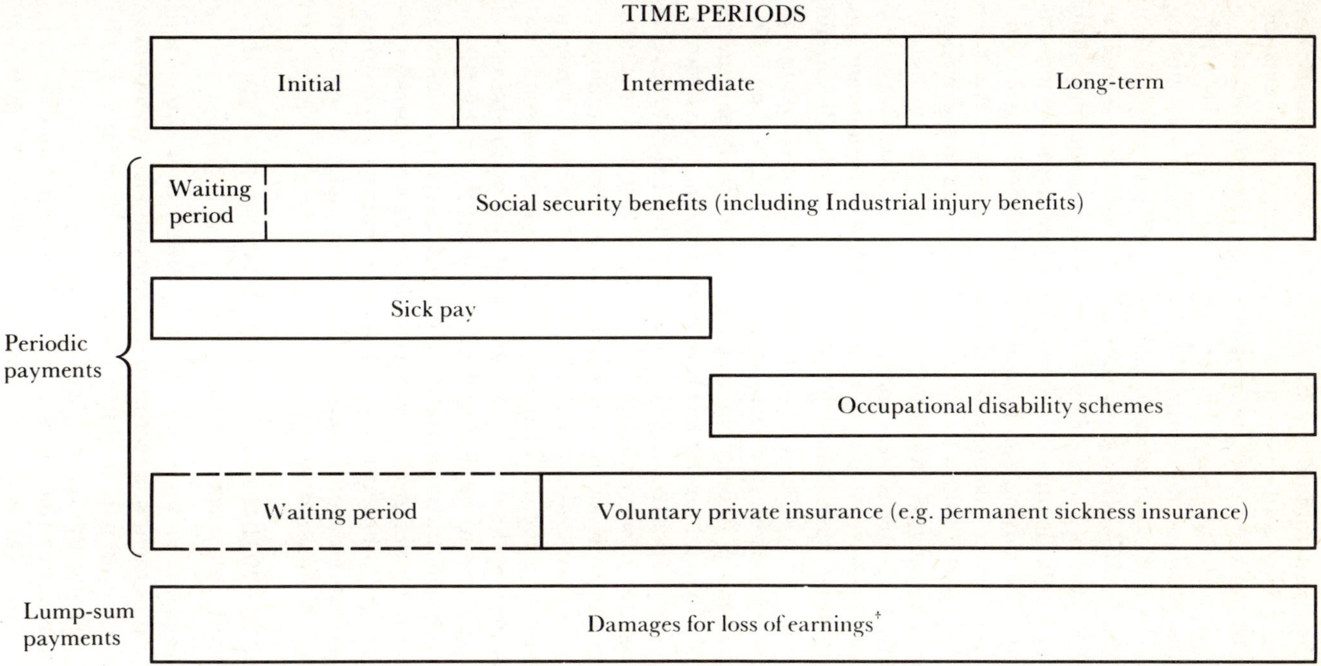

*Retirement pensions are paid throughout to those over working age
†Damages are often paid after long delays: see Figure 3.4

Figure 12.1 *The periods of time in respect of which present systems provide income maintenance for those of working age**

criteria for their distribution are based on our data, in particular those on anomalies and inequities which arise from existing arrangements. They therefore represent our preferred solution to these problems, although we recognize that other proposals might also be derived from the data. Our proposals on financing compensation are more tentative, because our survey was not designed to deal with such issues: but the policy-maker cannot be expected to consider proposals for benefits without some indication as to how they might be financed. Our outline on financing sets out the mechanisms for raising money which we consider feasible, and the sources of finance reached by those mechanisms. We have proposed only broad outlines for future policies, and so leave room for variation in the details of actual schemes.

Our proposals do not assume more than the re-allocation of the resources now devoted to support those who are ill or injured; but we expect that the avoidance of overlapping, through careful integration of the schemes and the resulting saving in administrative expenses, should release considerable amounts for the payment of more, or improved benefits. The levels of benefits must obviously depend on the levels of contributions which can be afforded, but the proposals do not depend on any particular level of benefit; we assume, however, that levels of benefits should regularly be raised in line with improvements in the general standard of living. Since we have assumed that the policy-maker is likely to choose to build on existing arrangements by modifying some and extending others, we have also assumed that the main sources of finance will continue to be those which now contribute directly or indirectly to the cost of compensation for illness and injury, such as employers, contributors to social security, the taxpayer, operators of motor vehicles and other forms of transport, occupiers of premises, manufacturers, and other groups undertaking defined activities involving the risk of accidents.

Entitlement to benefits should not be linked to particular sources of contributions

Under the present common law system, there is a direct link between the entitlement of a victim to damages and the selection by the law of who should pay: in general, only the person proved to be negligent in causing the injuries is compelled to pay and only the victim who can prove that he was injured by that other person's negligence can recover compensation. (In practice, however, the institution of liability insurance, by spreading the risk, softens the impact of the first aspect.) A major feature of our proposals is that there should be no direct link between the criteria for entitlement to benefits (who should get them, and how much they should be) and the criteria under which the money is raised to finance them (who should contribute and how much). In regard to raising the money, we wish to abandon the individualistic approach of the common law, which relies on a particular justification for requiring a specific person to make a special payment to another in respect of a particular event. We believe that the future approach should depend on the group basis of insurance: the rules for contributions should depend on the relative justifications for requiring appropriate *categories* of contributors to support the cost of accidents or illnesses in general. On the other hand, the rules for the allocation of benefits should be based on assessments of the relative needs of victims of illness or injury. If the issues of entitlement and financing are separated in this way the distribution of payments to beneficiaries will not be directly linked to any particular contributor or source of contribution: the compensation will not be distributed by reference to the criteria on which it has been raised, nor by searching for a unique link between a particular victim's need for support and a particular contributor's responsibility to pay.

Our proposals on both entitlement and financing assume (as has been argued in section 2 of this chapter) that the deficiencies and inequities of the existing damages system are so serious that it cannot be incorporated into future compensation schemes for supporting the victims of illness and injury.

The method of integration: division of support into time periods

To avoid wasteful overlapping of financial support from different sources we propose that all schemes for income benefits based on legally enforceable entitlement should be integrated by reference to successive periods of time off work or time off normal activities: for any given period, a person should be entitled to only a single type of income benefit (although the basic entitlement might be supplemented by another type of income support).

This method of integration assumes that some forms of support, such as sick pay and self-insurance, are more appropriate for the short-term cases, while others, such as social security, are better able to deal with the long term. Our proposals use broad bands of time: the 'initial', 'intermediate', and 'long-term' periods. We believe that a clear division into successive time periods will be useful for policy-making on both entitlements to benefits and on mechanisms to finance their cost; it should also permit the progressive integration of existing systems of support into an overall plan. The actual lengths of time fixed for the successive periods will depend on many policy decisions. We are here concerned with the principle of the division of income support into time periods, and our suggestions of the approximate lengths of time which might be fixed are therefore tentative. The initial period could be anything between the first four to eight weeks of incapacity; the intermediate period from then until the beginning of the long term, which might be fixed at any point between six to twelve months from the beginning of the incapacity.

The 'initial' period represents that period in which the bulk of comparatively minor, temporary incapacities fall (see Figure 10.1); the 'long-term' period is that period in which it is felt by policy-makers that sufficient time has elapsed for any incapacity to be considered of a 'permanently' disabling nature. The 'intermediate' period consequently represents the transitional phase between these two references. If we took the dividing lines to be at eight weeks and one year respectively, then for those who were off work in our survey (which excluded many minor cases) 52.4 per cent would return to work within the 'initial' period, 38.7 per cent within the 'intermediate' period, and 8.9 per cent would continue into the 'long-term' period.

Policy goals in the allocation of financial benefits

We would support the following as the policy goals for the allocation of financial benefits to those disabled through illness or injury: these underlie our proposals for allocation of benefits (Figure 12.2). (This section assumes that non-financial support through social and medical care would continue to be provided in addition to financial support.)

(1) No differentiation by cause

As far as the entitlement to benefits is concerned, we should (as argued in section 2 of this chapter) progressively move towards the ultimate abolition of all criteria dependent on the particular cause of the claimant's incapacity. This would mean the abolition of the illness/injury demarcation, as well as the abolition of the fault (tort)

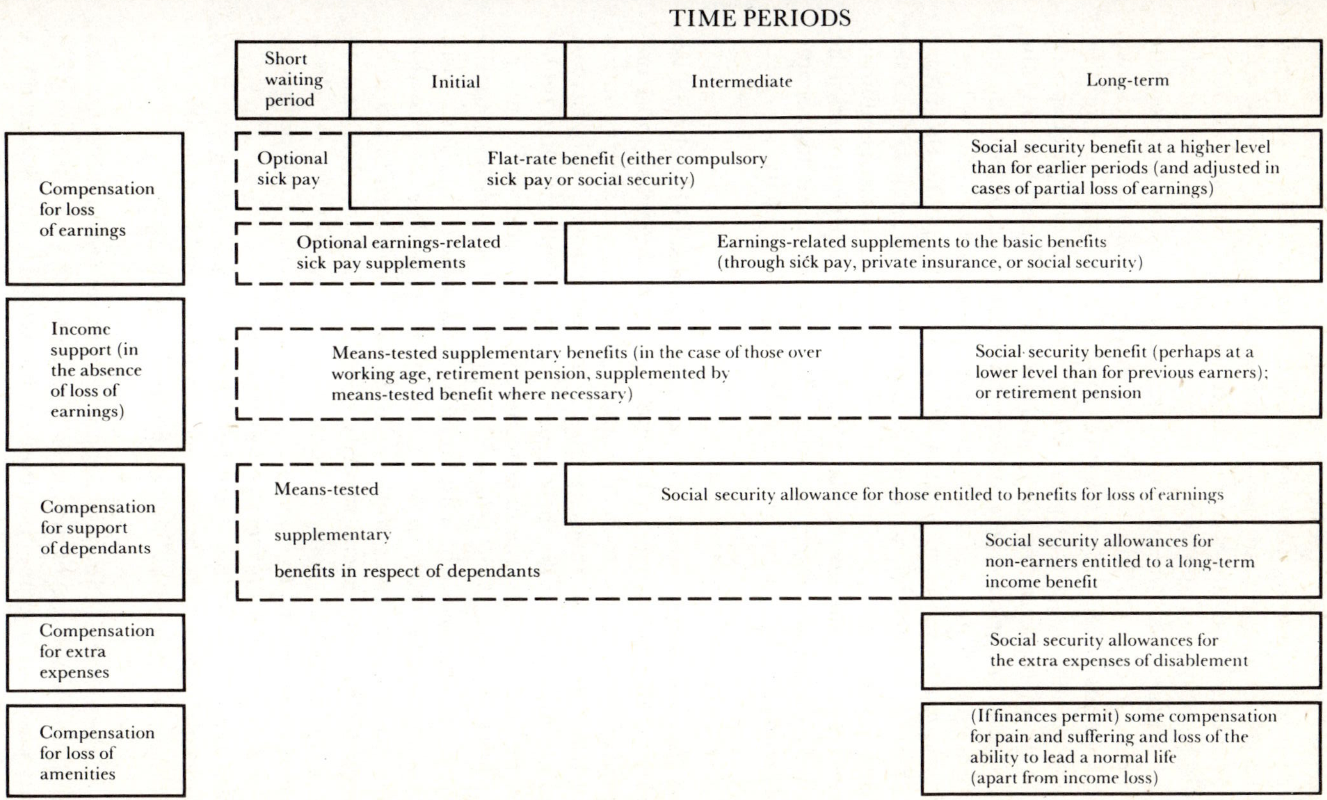

Figure 12.2 *Outline proposals: allocation of financial benefits*

concept and of the differential treatment of some categories of accident (e.g. work accidents or criminal injuries). This result could not be achieved overnight (and we do not attempt here to deal with the transitional arrangements which would be necessary) but it would be possible if all future changes were designed to facilitate the final abolition of all present rules of entitlement which differentiate according to cause or which allow accident victims advantages over illness victims. (The only exception which, in our opinion, might be justified would be battle casualties, that is, the provision of special pensions for those injured in actual armed hostilities, which is the exceptional situation where society may compel citizens to be the front-line of defence against large-scale, organized attack.)

If the cause of the incapacity is to be irrelevant to the future entitlement to benefits, we think it should also be irrelevant to the level of benefits: thus, for instance, we do not think that an employee injured at work should receive a higher level of benefit than if he received the same injury elsewhere, because his need for income replacement is not related to the cause of his incapacity.

(2) Priority to the long-term cases

Although we believe that the cause of the disability should be irrelevant to entitlement to benefits, we nevertheless support one type of differentiation in the allocation of benefits – a differentiation according to the relative length of the period of incapacity. A regular finding in different chapters of this study is that under existing arangements, the long-term case, in relation to the relative length of incapacity, is less well supported financially than the short-term; likewise, the employment prospects of the long-term victim are worse than those of the short-term. We believe that differentiation according to the relative 'need' has been found to be acceptable in many social security benefits (see Table 1.1) and, in our opinion, the least controversial test of relative need is that which depends on the relative length of the incapacity. Our proposals therefore treat the long-term cases separately.

The separation of long-term beneficiaries into a special category enables provision to be made for them which could not be afforded for all those affected by illness and injury, such as:

(i) Higher levels of income support for those still unable to earn their living at the end of the intermediate period. Our data show the relatively poor income position of households which contain a victim with a long-term incapacity.

(ii) Some provision of income support for the long-term, partially disabled who are able to earn, but only at a reduced level (see the (Australian) Woodhouse Report, 1974, Vol. 1, paras 375–405). The fact that this group is largely neglected by existing compensation schemes is not only a source of legitimate grievance, but also could be a disincentive to rehabilitation and return to work. (See discussion of Table 10.9)

(iii) Provision for income support for non-earners below retirement age who are suffering long-term incapacity. Until the long-term period begins, it is reasonable to leave their support to their families (or to whoever was supporting them before the illness or injury), with means-tested supplementary benefits as the 'floor' beneath them; but when their incapacity extends into the long-term, we think that they should be removed from means-testing or from complete dependence on family support. (The non-contributory invalidity pension is already based on this approach, although the present levels do not avoid reliance on supplementary benefits). If allowances for dependants are to continue as a regular feature of social security, it would also be reasonable to introduce them for the dependants of non-earners at the same time, the beginning of the long-term period.

(iv) All long-term cases should be entitled to allowances for the extra expenses of disabled living, i.e. they should not be left to means-tested support, except perhaps during a waiting period. However, for the short-term cases, these extra expenses should be met from savings, family support, or means-tested supplementary benefits. (This approach is already adopted by the attendance and mobility allowances.)

(v) If some financial compensation for non-financial losses is to be paid in future schemes (to replace the function of the disablement benefit for 'loss of faculty' under the industrial injuries scheme, or damages for pain and suffering), it is our view that priority should be given to the long-term cases: in their situation the loss of the ability to lead a normal life (apart from the ability to earn) may justify compensation beyond income support and payment for extra expenses. (We assume that, for the foreseeable future, funds will not be available to provide such compensation for all cases.)

(3) Priorities in the types of benefits

In regard to the types of financial support to be given, we believe that the priorities in the allocation of available resources should be ranked as follows: first, we should provide, up to a reasonable level, income replacement (or income support for non-earners) for all affected by illness or injury; secondly, we should meet the extra expenses of disability, at least in the long-term cases (e.g. attendance and mobility allowances); thirdly, and only when the first two aims have been met, we should make some provision for non-pecuniary loss (e.g. loss of faculty under the industrial injuries scheme, or damages for pain and suffering) again with preference for the long-term cases.

One purpose of giving priority to income support is to restrict the extent to which disabled people are forced to rely on means-tested (supplementary) benefits. Our proposals provide earners with an entitlement to income support viz. without means testing, and leaves them to rely on means-tested supplementary benefit only if, for the initial period, their income is insufficient to maintain their dependants at a minimal level. Our proposals do envisage, however, that non-earners should rely on means-tested entitlement until the period of their incapacity reaches the long term. We therefore do not envisage a situation in which means-tested benefits are unnecessary, but we wish drastically to reduce their role as an ultimate 'net' for disabled people (see Table 5.2).

Our outline includes provision for earnings-related supplements. If the policy-maker wishes to retain any form of earnings-relation for income replacement benefits, we believe that the extra cost should be met by additional, earnings-related contributions from the potential beneficiaries or their employers. The complications of making individual assessments of entitlement to earnings-related supplements would justify not paying them for the initial period of entitlement, unless as part of a sick pay scheme agreed with an employer. A further preference to the longer-term cases could thus be a legal entitlement to earnings-related supplements.

We are not arguing the case for allowances for dependants. The question of adding them to income support benefits should depend on whether they are to remain part of social security benefits in general: if they do, the benefits for the sick and disabled should follow the pattern, so that, on the basis of relative need, a beneficiary with dependants would receive a higher total benefit than one without. Allowances for the dependants of a non-earner should be paid only where the dependants are not supported by another person.

(4) Some preference for earners over non-earners

Our proposals for entitlement to financial support distinguish between compensation for loss of earnings suffered by earners (viz. those who were earning before the illness or injury) and income support for non-earners. Such a distinction is found in nearly all compensation schemes abroad, as well as many of the present compensation systems in Table 1.1. The justifications for giving some preference to earners are that they must, of necessity, be major contributors to the cost of any scheme, and, secondly, that they and their families are almost invariably relying on the earnings to meet their regular living expenses. An illness or injury which incapacitates an earner, causing a loss of earnings, is, in the absence of compensation, therefore very likely to have an immediate and serious financial impact on the household: the same result is unlikely, at least in the short term, for the incapacitated non-earner, whose previous support from earners in the family, or from non-earned income, is likely to continue. Our proposals in Figure 12.2 give some preference to earners in the following ways: (1) earlier entitlement to non-means-tested income support; (2) earlier entitlement to allowances for dependants; (3) long-term income support could, if the policy-maker chose, be at a higher level than for non-earners; (4) potential entitlement to earnings-related supplements; and (5) entitlement to benefits for long-term partial loss of earnings.

We would propose that no contribution record should be necessary for earners (as under the present industrial injuries scheme): benefits should be payable as from the first day of earning. Our proposals would permit the policy-maker to choose to treat as earners those who were only potential earners at the beginning of their period of incapacity e.g. the unemployed, those congenitally disabled, children, students, trainees, and housewives who were then caring for young children or for disabled or elderly relatives, but who could prove (as by previous employment) their intention to return to the labour market when such care was no longer needed. These potential earners could be treated as earners from the times when, in the normal course, they would have started to earn. If the category of earners was widened in this way, it would leave as non-earners only the retired, and those below retirement age whose previous life style had shown that they had no intention of earning in the future, viz. those living entirely on unearned income, or those who had clearly chosen to opt out of the labour market.

(5) Incentives to rehabilitation

Any future scheme should, so far as possible, include incentives to rehabilitation and avoid disincentives to return to work. Provision for long-term, but partial, loss of earnings would partly meet this objective: it would provide an intermediate stage between 'total' incapacity for work, and either full-time work or full capacity to work, and so would encourage a progressive return to full work.

(6) Assessment criteria for entitlement to benefits

We do not put forward any detailed proposals for assessment. We envisage that the basic criteria needed for entitlement to any benefit or financial support set out in Figure 12.2 will be medical; but for loss of earnings in the longer term, some additional social and occupational criteria will be necessary so that the impact of the medical condition on the individual's future ability to earn could be measured in relation to his previous type of job, and to his particular qualifications and experience. The same physical disability may have a catastrophic effect on the earnings of a manual worker, but little or no effect on the earnings of a lawyer (*cf.* 'unable to work' criteria for contributory social security at present). Such additional criteria would be essential for the assessment of long-term partial loss of earnings. Even for income-support benefits for non-earners, some socio-economic criteria for entitlement may be necessary so that the specified medical conditions can be related to the individual's ability to cope with the activities of ordinary living. Purely medical criteria might be feasible for the non-income support envisaged in the proposals (such as allowances for extra expenses or compensation for loss of amenities), but even here some social assessment may also be needed for tests such as 'virtually unable to walk'.

A crucial question for any scheme of benefits is who is to have the authority to interpret and apply the criteria for entitlement to individual cases. In our opinion, for any benefit where many claimants are expected, the initial decision must depend basically on an assessment by the claimant's own general practitioner, with provision for review by appellate panels composed of both medical and non-medical members. For smaller groups of claimants (e.g. for the longer-term benefits), specialist panels may be used for the initial assessment as well as for the appellate review, but we do not believe that their membership should be exclusively medical (see Chap. 5, sections 3 and 4).

Financing

Any proposals for the sources and mechanisms of finance for the benefits outlined in the previous section should be based on explicit policy goals for financing. We accept the following goals:

(1) Clear demarcation of the roles of the private and public sectors

Being based mainly on existing arrangements, our proposals assume that there should continue to be a 'mixed economy' in providing compensation, with some organized through the private sector of the economy, and some through the public sector. Our outline of the mechanisms for financing set out below indicates the order of priority of the different mechanisms for the different time periods: in any given period, only one mechanism should be primarily responsible for supporting a category of beneficiaries, although optional, additional support could come from voluntary insurance or through collective bargaining. If, however, a mechanism of the private sector is primarily responsible, a secondary responsibility on a public mechanism (e.g. social security) may be needed to guarantee the payment of benefits to victims.

(2) Administrative cost

To the extent permitted by the achievement of other policy goals, the methods chosen for raising the cost of benefits should be those with the lowest costs of administration.

(3) Risk relationship

Although our proposals do not preserve the tort action for damages, we believe that future methods of raising the cost of compensation should incorporate mechanisms designed to deter accidents, which is a major objective claimed for the tort action. All future schemes should, as far as administrative cost and convenience permit, incorporate some measure of risk relationship, viz. those who benefit from a particular activity, such as manufacturing or motor transport, should bear much of the costs of accidents arising in that activity.

Sources of finance

We propose that the following categories should be the sources of finance, viz. those who should pay:

1. *Employers*, via (a) sick pay; (b) social security contributions;

(c) general taxation (the Exchequer contribution to the Social Security Fund); (d) levies for any special no-fault schemes; and (e) voluntary insurance premiums.

2. *Employees*, via (a) social security contributions; (b) taxation; and (c) wage-levels will reflect entitlement to sick pay.
3. *The self-employed*, via (a) social security contributions; (b) taxation; (c) levies for any special no-fault schemes (e.g. levies on transport users or manufacturers); and (d) voluntary insurance premiums.
4. *The taxpayer*, via the Exchequer's contribution to the Social Security Fund.
5. *Consumers* of goods and services: prices will reflect any risk-relationship in social security contributions, levies for special schemes, and insurance premiums.

Financing and compensatory mechanisms

These sources of finance should continue (as at present) to be organized through a combination of financing and compensatory mechanisms. We suggest three different combinations, one for each of the three time periods in our scheme (Figure 12.2). For the initial period covering the great majority of claims, the primary source should be sick pay finance from employers: it could be made compulsory, or be adopted by employers on a voluntary, 'opting-out' basis, and employers could choose to finance it through the insurance industry. For compensation not financed through sick pay during the initial period, support must come from social security contributions from employers, employees, the self-employed, and the taxpayer.

For the intermediate period, sick pay finance could still be chosen by those employers who prefer it to social security contributions, or the legislature could choose to impose special 'no-fault' levies on those engaging in particular categories of activities (e.g. employment, road transport, or manufacture). In the absence of either of these, finance must be found through social security contributions, and through voluntary insurance premiums paid by those who want additional protection. Finally, for the relatively few, but expensive cases needing support in the long-term period, we believe that finance must come from social security contributions, with voluntary insurance premiums for extra cover. We proceed to a short discussion of these compensatory mechanisms.

(1) Sick pay

A notable feature of the present mixed system of compensation reported in this volume is the increasing importance of sick pay (Chapter 7). Most employees now receive immediate financial support from this source, irrespective of the cause of the interruption in their ability to work: the money comes to them in the same familiar way as do their normal earnings; and its amount is often sufficient (after taking account of social security payments) to bring their income up to its usual level. Furthermore, for many short-term cases of illness or injury, payments of sick pay already continue for the whole period of absence from work. Thus, up to the present time, the picture has been one of a private 'social security' system, parallel to the official system, but which has not been integrated with it. Since, however, regular improvements in sick pay schemes can be expected in future as the result of collective bargaining, we believe that compensation policy should build on these schemes.

Our proposals in Figure 12.2 give prominence to the role of occupational sick pay as the primary source of support for sick and injured employees during the initial period (see also the Green Paper, 1980.) Since this book has been in the press, the Government has moved in this direction by effectively requiring employers to act as agents for the payment of state benefits. Under the Social Security and Housing Benefits Act 1982, a new statutory sick pay scheme is due to be introduced at a time yet to be fixed (but which is likely to be April 1983). Under the new scheme, after three 'waiting days' employers will be compelled to pay stipulated amounts of sick pay for the first eight weeks of any sickness absence. No sickness benefit under the social security system will be payable to employees for these eight weeks, but the statutory sick pay will be financed by the state system: section 9 of the Act authorizes the making of regulations to permit employers to recoup the cost through deductions from their own social security contributions, and the Government has stated its intention to provide for full reimbursement of all payments of the statutory sick pay.

Our proposals would go further than the 1982 Act: first, we would prefer that employers should bear a substantial part of the cost of statutory sick pay, so as to enforce some 'risk relation' (see below, under (3)); secondly, our suggested voluntary, 'opting out' basis would allow employers and trade unions to choose sick pay as the primary source until the beginning of the long-term period, with a corresponding reduction in the levels of social security contributions.[5] If the opting-out basis were chosen, the decision to opt for a sick pay scheme could either be left to the free choice of the parties, or there could be tax or other incentives to opt for a private scheme, e.g. the reduction in social security contributions for those opting for a private scheme could be fixed at a level designed to induce them to do so (*cf.* the present opting-out arrangements for occupational pensions). Collective bargaining could also deal with the questions whether non-statutory sick pay should be payable for the first three days, and whether earnings-related supplements should be payable under the employers' scheme to 'top up' the entitlement to a flat-rate benefit during any period set out in Figure 12.2.

An advantage of compulsory sick pay is that some of the problems of 'policing' social security benefits so as to prevent their abuse might be avoided when the employer is responsible in all short-term cases. The employer (or one of his managers) is more likely than social security officials to have direct personal knowledge of the employee's circumstances, which would restrict the employee's opportunity to make unjustified claims.[6] But the incentive for the employer is seriously reduced if he is to be reimbursed for all his payments of statutory sick pay.

Our outline of mechanisms for financing represents a considerable shift of responsibility for the short-term cases from the public sector to the private sector of the economy: employers' and employees' social security contributions should therefore be reduced to take account of this relief to the Social Security Fund. However, the proposals for benefits envisage an extension of the role of social security at the other end of the time scale — the support of the relatively few, but socially important, long-term cases; the new level of contributions would need to be calculated by balancing the relief of the cost of the short-term against the increased burden of the long-term cases. We envisage that no contribution record should be necessary for entitlement to sick pay or to any subsequent benefit: an earner should be entitled as from his first day of earning.

Fall-back arrangements for sick pay

At present, any employee unable to work through illness or injury has the assurance of income support through sickness benefit paid from a reliable source, social security. When sick pay from employers replaces sickness benefit (compulsorily for the first eight weeks and possibly longer under our 'opting-out' proposals), some 'fall-back' or 'guarantee' arrangement becomes necessary to protect employees against the risk of default by employers in paying the statutory minimum, or against their insolvency or liquidation.

The 1982 Act does not give an employee an *entitlement* to a social security benefit if, for any reason, his employer fails to fulfil his obligation to pay sick pay, but it does provide for the situation where supplementary or other benefit has been paid to support an employee who has not received the statutory sick pay due to him from his employer: the employer may be compelled to reimburse the amount due as statutory sick pay (Sched. 2, paras. 7–11). However, we would propose that the employee should not be left to rely on means-tested supplementary benefit in these circumstances. The data in our survey show that there is a gap between apparent entitlement under a sick pay scheme and the actual receipt of sick pay when an employee is unable to work (Chapter 5, section 2): efficient policing of employers' obligations, and speedy fall-back arrangements are therefore essential. In order to prevent employers from using the fall-back to avoid their obligations, the Social Security Fund should be entitled to recover from a defaulting employer not only the amount of any benefit paid in lieu of sick pay, but also a penalty designed to discourage employers from avoiding their primary obligation to provide sick pay directly to their employees.

Minimum levels of sick pay

The 1982 Act fixes three minimum levels of entitlement to statutory sick pay, graduated by reference to the employee's normal pay, but with some protection for low earners; the Government must review the levels each year in relation to the general level of prices (section 7; the alternative of fixing a percentage of normal pay had been considered: Green Paper, paras. 24–8). There should be no objection to collective bargaining designed to obtain higher levels of sick pay than the statutory minima: at present, sick pay schemes often pay at levels which, when added to sickness (social security) benefit, produce sums equal to 100 per cent or more of ordinary pay. However, in a properly integrated system, it is very unlikely that agreed levels of sick pay would exceed ordinary pay. (Sick pay, including statutory sick pay, is taxable, but sickness benefit is not.)

Dependants

An important difference between sick pay and sickness benefit is that a higher level of benefit is paid to a man with a dependent wife, and additional allowances for dependent children, whereas sick pay does not vary according to the employee's family responsibilities. Any attempt to integrate sick pay with social security must deal with this inconsistency (Green Paper, paras. 19–23). Statutory sick pay under the 1982 Act follows ordinary pay in ignoring family responsibilities, thus leaving any support for families to child benefit, supplementary benefit, or tax allowances. Complications in sick pay are avoided by this approach, but it increases the numbers who might, as a result of the change, be worse off during the first eight weeks of sickness. Here, as elsewhere, we think that the aim should be to remove as many people as possible from reliance on means-tested supplementary benefit during a period of sickness.

(2) The role of social security

We propose that a major role of social security (see Chapter 5, above) in future should be the exclusive responsibility to support all long-term cases of disability; the increased role proposed for sick pay is partly designed to enable a shift of social security resources from the short- to the long-term cases. The Social Security Fund is able to cope with the needs of long-term victims of illness or injury more efficiently than any other source of support: in particular, the 'pay-as-you-go' method of collecting the contributions to pay for current benefits enables it to cope with the problem of future inflation. No other system, especially those 'funded' on the insurance principle, can provide index-related benefits over a long period. Social security benefits can also (unlike the present system of damages paid in a lump sum) be reviewed from time to time in the light of subsequent changes in the health of the beneficiaries. Some of the advantages which the present damages system enjoys over social security (such as earnings relation in the assessment of lost earnings; provision for the partially disabled person with reduced earnings; or provision for the person who has lost prospects of promotion or of increased earnings) could be built into future social security entitlement rules for the long-term beneficiaries, since a more sophisticated set of entitlement rules would not impose too great a burden on the administration if it were restricted to the relatively small number of long-term cases. Such an improvement in social security might be necessary if it were to be accepted as a reasonable alternative to the existing chances of obtaining damages (which, at least in theory, should be tailored to the individual case).

A secondary role for social security under our outline of financing mechanisms is to provide benefits, during the two earlier periods, for: (i) employees not entitled to (or not actually receiving) sick pay; (ii) those not at work i.e. the unemployed, the congenitally disabled, children, the elderly, and housewives; and (iii) those who fall outside the scope of any special no-fault scheme in force for the intermediate period. A final, residual role for social security would be to provide a means-tested, non-contributory (supplementary) benefit for anyone in need who fails for any reason to qualify for either sick pay or for an 'entitlement' social security benefit.

(3) A possible role for special, no fault schemes: the question of risk relationship

Our outline of mechanisms for financing preserves the opportunity for the policy-maker to choose certain categories of accident where it is desired to link compensation payments directly to the activity in which the accident arose, so that those who benefit from the activity should finance the compensation ('internalizing' the costs of accidents).[7] The same approach could also be used in respect of illnesses associated with defined activities, as with occupational illnesses under the existing industrial injuries scheme. We ourselves would prefer to avoid special schemes, but we wish to indicate how they could be integrated into the overall plan, while maintaining the principle that only one source should be responsible for income support in any given period of time. In our opinion, the main advantage claimed for special schemes, namely, the efficient allocation of resources through risk relationship (e.g. making industry pay for the cost of work accidents and occupational illnesses, or of the injuries caused by defective products), could also be achieved in the way in which contributions are raised, no matter which type of financing mechanism is chosen.

All the different mechanisms we have proposed for financing permit contributions or levies to be related to accident records. Some risk relation could be enforced by compulsory sick pay, if the employer was not reimbursed the full cost from the Social Security Fund (see above under 'Sick Pay'): the employer would then have a direct inducement to minimize the cost of those accidents and illnesses which are caused by work conditions under his control. By the provision of medical services and rehabilitation, the employer can also minimize the effects of illness or injury suffered by his employees. In the case of social security contributions (which have not previously been risk related) we think that, as a consequence of the enhanced future role proposed for social security, contributions from employers should be related to the risks of accidents in their businesses. Wherever it is administratively possible at reasonable cost to internalize the cost of accidents arising in a particular industry, contributions should be based on accident records, using both the frequency and the cost of accidents as the measures. Individual contributors whose accident records were above average (whether judged by the incidence of accidents or their cost) could also be penalized by increased levies. Flat-rate contributions do not encourage those in a position to minimize risks to do so, and would result in the cost of supporting long-term victims of serious accidents being 'externalized' and borne by ordinary contributors to the Social Security Fund. Special no-fault schemes would obviously allow the cost of accidents to be internalized and borne by those taking part in or benefiting from the activity in question. But in our view, the same degree of risk relationship may also be implemented in the way contributions are levied in any general compensation scheme, such as social security. Manufacturers can be made to pay for the cost of accidents caused by defective products, or employers for the cost of work accidents, through the imposition of special contributions to the general compensation fund, without the need for a special scheme for paying benefits to the victims of those accidents. In practice, moreover, there are limits to the possibility of identifying separate 'activities' in respect of which a particular group of contributors or premium-payers can be defined.

Special no-fault schemes may, however, also be justified by the desire to permit some scope for the private rather than the public sector. When the State administers special schemes (as is now the case for work injuries and criminal injuries) there seems little justification for retaining special rules for entitlement to benefits, as well as special methods of raising the finance, but the policy-maker who wishes to retain a large role for the private insurance industry may choose to continue with special schemes because they can be separately financed and administered by insurance companies. If this were done, however, the special schemes should be carefully integrated into the overall compensation plan, and should provide benefits only at the same levels as those available to the victims of other accidents and illnesses. We would also propose that the special schemes should be used to finance compensation for the intermediate period: it would be administratively expensive to use them for the initial period, which could more efficiently be covered by sick pay, and, for the reasons already given, we think that only social security can meet the needs of the long-term cases.

(4) Private insurance

Our proposals permit the private sector (employers and insurance companies) to continue to play major roles in the compensation field. Important political decisions must be made about the relative roles of the public and private sectors in financing and administering those categories of compensation not covered exclusively by social security. For instance, if special no-fault schemes were adopted, either the private insurance industry or a public agency could be given the task of administering them. There would also be considerable scope under our proposals for voluntary private insurance, not only for non-earners during the period before they become entitled to a long-term benefit, but also for the high earner who wishes to top up his basic entitlement during any period. Private insurance could also offer more protection than proposed for the long-term cases for loss of potential earning capacity, or for non-financial losses such as pain and suffering and reduced expectation of life: some of these risks are already covered by personal accident policies. Again, the occupational sick pay schemes of smaller employers (viz. those not sufficiently large to bear all the risk of sick pay entitlement) would often be insured through the private insurance market.

The position of the self-employed in the proposals has been left open: either they could be left to make private insurance arrangements for the period covered by sick pay in the case of employees, so that their social security entitlement would arise at the same time as for employees; or they could be covered from the outset by social security, and pay higher contributions assessed on that basis.

Notes

1. This category was included with accidents because industrial illnesses which are prescribed under the industrial injuries scheme are compensated by that scheme in the same way as industrial accidents.
2. In New Zealand a comprehensive insurance scheme provides compensation for all accident victims, irrespective of the time, location, or cause of the accident: Accident Compensation Act 1972 (as amended), enacted by the New Zealand Parliament. See the Woodhouse (New Zealand) Report, 1967; Blair, 1978; Palmer, 1979; Ison, 1980.

3. 'No-fault' compensation schemes for particular categories of accident victims have often been recommended, and sometimes introduced e.g., Pearson Report, 1978; JUSTICE Report, 1974; Keeton and O'Connell, 1965; Widiss *et al.*, 1977; O'Connell, 1975, 1979.
4. In Australia, a Federal Government Committee recommended a comprehensive social insurance scheme to compensate for both illness and injury: Woodhouse (Australian) Report, 1974; Ison, 1967; Palmer, 1979; Luntz, 1975. On the question of similar treatment for compensation for both illness and injury, see Atiyah, 1980, Chapter 20; Pearson Report, 1978, Vol. 1., paras. 1488–1535, 1711.
5. There would, however, be implications for the funding of such a scheme. Those groups which will 'opt out' will tend to be in a low-risk category, thereby leaving the state sickness benefit scheme to cover only high risk groups. This is an 'adverse selection' problem (see Akerlof, 1970; Wilson, 1977; Rothschild and Stiglitz, 1976; Pauly, 1974). It is likely, therefore, that the funding of the state scheme would shift from a contribution base to a general taxation base.
6. This minimizes the so-called 'moral hazard' problems of insurance by reducing the informational asymmetry which exists between the insurer and the insured (see Arrow, 1963, 1968; Pauly, 1968, 1974; Spence and Zeckhauser, 1971).
7. The use of compensation schemes to reduce the frequency and the cost of accidents is examined in Calabresi, 1970. For UK studies, see Atiyah, 1975; Phillips, 1976; the Pearson Report, 1978, Vol. 1, paras. 900–3, 940–8, 953–4, 1094–8, 1101–2. Further references will be found in Veljanovski, 1979.

References

Akerlof, G., 1970, 'The Market for Lemons: Qualitative Uncertainty and the Market Mechanism', 84, *Quarterly Journal of Economics* 488–500.

Arrow, K. J., 1963, 'Uncertainty and the Welfare Economics of Medical Care', 53 *American Economic Review* 941–69.

—— 1968, 'The Economics of Moral Hazard: Further Comment', 58 *American Economic Review* 537–9.

Atiyah, P. S., 1975, 'Accident Prevention and Variable Premium Rates for Work-Connected Injuries', 4 *Industrial Law Journal* 1, 89.

—— 1980, *Accidents, Compensation and the Law* (3rd edn.), London: Weidenfeld & Nicolson.

Blair, A. P., 1978, *Accident Compensation in New Zealand*, Wellington, New Zealand: Butterworths.

Calabresi, Guido, 1970, *The Costs of Accidents*, New Haven, Conn.: Yale University Press.

Green Paper, 1980, *Income During Initial Sickness: A New Strategy*, London: HMSO, Cmnd. 7864.

Harris, D. R., 1979, Chapter III in D. K. Allen, C. J. Bourn, and J. H. Holyoak, eds., *Accident Compensation after Pearson*, London: Sweet & Maxwell.

Ison, T. G., 1967, *The Forensic Lottery*, London: Staples Press.

—— 1980, *Accident Compensation: A Commentary on the New Zealand Scheme*,

London: Croom Helm.
JUSTICE Report, 1974, *No Fault on the Roads* (Chairman of Committee, Paul Sieghart), London: Stevens & Sons.
Keeton, Robert E., and O'Connell, Jeffrey, 1965, *Basic Protection for the Traffic Victim: A Blueprint for Reforming Automobile Insurance*, Boston: Little Brown & Co.
Luntz, Harold, 1975, *Compensation and Rehabilitation in Australia*, Melbourne: Butterworth.
O'Connell, Jeffrey, 1975, *Ending Insult to Injury: No-fault Insurance for Products and Services*, Urbana, Ill: University of Illinois Press.
—— 1979, *The Lawsuit Lottery: Injuries, Insurance and Injustice*, Urbana, Ill: University of Illinois Press.
Ogus, A. I., Corfield, P., and Harris, D.R., 1978, 'Pearson: Principled Reform or Political Compromise?', 7 *Industrial Law Journal* 143.
Palmer, G. W. R., 1979, *Accident Compensation: A Study of Law and Social Change in New Zealand and Australia*, Wellington, New Zealand: Oxford University Press.
Pauly, M., 1968, 'The Economics of Moral Hazard: Comment', 58, *American Economic Review*, 531–9.
—— 1974, 'Overinsurance and the Public Provisions of Insurance', 88 *Quarterly Journal of Economics*, 44–62.
Pearson, Lord (Chairman), 1978, *Report of the Royal Commission on Civil Liability and Compensation for Personal Injury* (3 vols.), London: HMSO (Cmnd. 7054).
Phillips, Jennifer, 1976, 'Economic Deterrence and the Prevention of Industrial Accidents', 5 *Industrial Law Journal* 148.
Rothschild, M., and Stiglitz, J. E., 1976, 'Equilibrium in Competitive Insurance Markets: An Essay in the Economics of Imperfect Information', 90 *Quarterly Journal of Economics*, 629–49.
Social Security Statistics 1977, (1979) London: HMSO
Spence, M., and Zeckhauser, R., 1971, 'Insurance, Information and Individual Action', 61 *American Economic Review*, 380–7.
Veljanovski, Cento, 1979, *Legal Liability and Negligence*, Bibliography in Law and Economics No. 2, Oxford: Centre for Socio-Legal Studies, Wolfson College, Oxford.
Widiss, A. I., Bovbjerg, R. R., Cavers, D. F., Little, J. W., Clark, R. S., Waterson, G. E. and Jones, T. C., 1977, *No-Fault Automobile Insurance in Action: the Experiences in Massachusetts, Florida, Delaware and Michigan*, New York: Oceana Publications.
Wilson, C., 1977, 'A Model of Insurance Markets with Incomplete Information', 16 *Journal of Economic Theory*, 167–207.
Woodhouse (Australian) Report, 1974, *Compensation and Rehabilitation in Australia*, Report of the National Committee of Inquiry (3 vols.), Canberra: Government Publishing Service.

Woodhouse (New Zealand) Report, 1967, *Report of the Royal Commission of Inquiry on Compensation for Personal Injury in New Zealand*, Wellington, New Zealand: Government Printer.

Appendix I: Questionnaire for the Screening Survey

This questionnaire was used to screen for victims of illness and injury to be followed up with a full interview. See Chapter 1, pp. 26–33 for an explanation of the screening exercise. The show cards referred to in Question 3 are reproduced on p. 396; the Misfortune Sheets (Questions 3.b and 4.a) are not reproduced; they were used to obtain preliminary information about the illness or injury, which was amplified by the information given in the Compensation (recall) questionnaire (Appendix II).

CENTRE FOR SAMPLE SURVEYS LTD. | SOCIAL & COMMUNITY PLANNING RESEARCH

16 DUNCAN TERRACE LONDON N1 8BZ TEL: 01-278-2061

Record No. (1-5)
Card No. (10) (6-7)
Project No. 421 (8-10)

P.421

NATIONAL SURVEY OF MISFORTUNES

March 1976

Area Code ☐☐☐☐ (11-14)

Address Serial No. ☐☐☐ (15-17)

Household No. ☐ (18)

OUO (19-20)

Date of Interview ______ (21-22)

Time Interview Started (WRITE IN) ______

We are carrying out a survey on behalf of the Oxford unit of the Social Science Research Council to find out how many people in the country have had to deal with problems of illness, injury or handicap in the recent past.

1.a) I'd like to check who lives in this household. Please include anyone who normally lives here, but is temporarily away.

Person No	Relationship to H.o.H.	Sex M F	Age last B'day	If under 1 year: 0-5 mths	If under 1 year: 6-11 mths	Marital Status (Persons aged 16 and over only): M	S	W	D	Sep	Working Status: Full-time (31+ hrs. per week)	Part-time (10-30 hrs per week)	NOT WORKING: H/W i f e	F/T E d u c.	O t h e r	
1	Head of H/Hold	1 2		1	2	4	5	6	7	8	1	2	3	4	5	(23-27)
2		1 2		1	2	4	5	6	7	8	1	2	3	4	5	(28-32)
3		1 2		1	2	4	5	6	7	8	1	2	3	4	5	(33-37)
4		1 2		1	2	4	5	6	7	8	1	2	3	4	5	(38-42)
5		1 2		1	2	4	5	6	7	8	1	2	3	4	5	(43-47)
6		1 2		1	2	4	5	6	7	8	1	2	3	4	5	(48-52)
7		1 2		1	2	4	5	6	7	8	1	2	3	4	5	(53-57)
8		1 2		1	2	4	5	6	7	8	1	2	3	4	5	(58-62)
9		1 2		1	2	4	5	6	7	8	1	2	3	4	5	(63-67)

Total number in household ☐☐ (68-69)

Respondent is Person Number ☐ (70)

Housewife is Person Number ☐ (71)

OFFICE USE ONLY (72-74) (75-77)

1.b) IF HOUSEHOLD CONTAINS PERSONS NOT RELATED TO HEAD OF HOUSEHOLD, ASK OF EACH:

How long has ______ been living in your household? IF UNDER ONE YEAR, Q's 3-5 SHOULD BE ASKED PERSONALLY TO SUCH PEOPLE.

PERSON NUMBER	HOW LONG LIVED IN H/HOLD

		Col./Code	Skip to
	ASK Q.2 FOR THE WHOLE HOUSEHOLD	(78)	
2.	Is there anyone whom you have not mentioned who is at present in a hospital, clinic, or residential home, but who would otherwise live with you? No	0	
	Yes - 1 person	1	
	Yes - 2 people	2	
	Yes - 3 or more people	3	

ASK Q.3 SEPARATELY FOR EACH MEMBER OF THE HOUSEHOLD AGED 6 MONTHS OR OVER. USE PROMPT CARDS AS FOLLOWS:-

Record No. (1-5)
Card No (20) (6-7)
Project No. 421 (8-10)

6 months but under 6 years	CARD A
6 years - 16 years or 17-18 & in full-time educ.)	CARD B
All others	CARD C

see p.360

SHOW CARD A, B OR C AS APPROPRIATE

3.a) Over the last 12 months since ____(MONTH) 1975, has ____ (PERSON) had any illness, injury or handicap which made it difficult or impossible to do any of the things on this card?
RECORD ANSWER IN GRID BELOW. IF 'NO' GO TO Q.4a)

	Person No	1	2	3	4	5	6	7	8	9	Skip to
		(11)	(12)	(13)	(14)	(15)	(16)	(17)	(18)	(19)	
a) Illness, injury or handicap over last 12 months.	Yes	A	A	A	A	A	A	A	A	A	
	No	1	1	1	1	1	1	1	1	1	→Q.4a)
IF 'YES' AT a) ASK b)											
b) For how long did this trouble last?	Under 2 weeks	B	B	B	B	B	B	B	B	B	
	2 weeks or more	2	2	2	2	2	2	2	2	2	→SHEET A
IF '2 WEEKS OR MORE' USE MISFORTUNE SHEET VERSION A											
IF 'UNDER 2 WEEKS' AT b) ASK c)											
c) Did ____ (PERSON) have this trouble for a period of 3 days or more during the last 2 weeks?	Yes	3	3	3	3	3	3	3	3	3	
	No	4	4	4	4	4	4	4	4	4	

		Col./Code	Skip to
	ASK Q.4 FOR THE WHOLE HOUSEHOLD		
4.a)	Now I'd like you to think back over the last five years since ____ (MONTH) 1971. (Apart from what we've already talked about) has anyone had an accident on the roads, at work or at home, or been injured by anyone else?	(20)	
	Yes	1	
	No	2	→Q.5a)
	IF 'YES' AT a) ASK b) AND c)		
	b) Who was that? CODE PERSON NO(S) → 1 2 3 4 5 6 7 8 9		
	FOR EACH PERSON CODED USE CARD A, B OR C AND ASK c) — (21) (22) (23) (24) (25) (26) (27) (28) (29)		
	c) Did it make it difficult or impossible to do any of the things on this card, for 2 weeks or more? Yes: 1 1 1 1 1 1 1 1 1		→SHEET B
	FOR EACH 'YES' PERSON USE MISFORTUNE SHEET VERSION B, Q.B1 & B2 — No: 2 2 2 2 2 2 2 2 2		
	ASK Q.5 FOR THE WHOLE HOUSEHOLD		
5.a)	(Apart from all the things we've already talked about) has anyone in the household any long term medical condition, a missing or defective limb or any similar condition?	(30)	
	Yes	1	
	No	2	→Q.6a)
	IF 'YES' AT a) ASK b)		
	b) Who is that? CODE PERSON NO(S) → 1 2 3 4 5 6 7 8 9		(31-39)
	FOR EACH PERSON CODED USE MISFORTUNE SHEET B, Q.B3 & B4		
	ASK ALL		
6.a)	Is anyone in this household at present on a hospital waiting list for any reason?	(40)	
	Yes	1	
	No	2	→Q.7a)
	IF 'YES' ASK b)		
	b) Who is that? CODE PERSON NO(S) → 1 2 3 4 5 6 7 8 9		(41-49)
	OUO: A B (50-51)		

		Col./Code	Skip to
	ASK Q.7 ABOUT DEATHS OF RELATIVES OF HEAD OF HOUSEHOLD. IF RESPONDENT IS NOT HEAD OF HOUSEHOLD, REPEAT QUESTION FOR DEATHS OF RELATIVES OF RESPONDENT.		
7.a)	We are also concerned about the death of relatives aged under 65. Over the past five years, has any relative of ____ died who was aged under 65 and was living with ____ at the time of their death? RECORD ANSWER IN GRID		
	Relative of H.o.H. / Relative of Respondent	(52-53)	
	Yes: 1 / 1		
	No: 2 / 2		
	Respondent is H.o.H.: X / 3		
	IF MORE THAN ONE DEATH HAS OCCURRED ESTABLISH AND CODE THE MOST RECENT → 1 / 2	(54)	
	ASK b)-d) ABOUT THE MOST RECENT OR THE ONE DEATH		
	b) How was the person who died related to ____? WRITE IN ____		
	c) How old was the person when he/she died? WRITE IN AGE IN YEARS [ ][ ] (55-56)	OUO	
	d) What did he/she die of? WRITE IN	(57)	
8.	OCCUPATION (PRESENT OR LAST MAIN PAID JOB) OF HEAD OF HOUSEHOLD	O.U.O.	
	Name/Title of Job ____		
	Description of Activity ____		
	Skill/Training/Qualifications/Experience required for Job ____	(58-60)	
	Supervision/management responsibilities (incl. no. of people supervised) ____		
	No. of employees at establishment: 25 or more A; 24 or fewer B	(61-62)	
	Industry/business/profession (of employer) ____ Employment Status: Employee A; Self-employed B		
	INTERVIEW NUMBER IN THESE BOXES WRITE IN THE NUMBER OF HOUSEHOLD INTERVIEWS YOU HAVE ALREADY CARRIED OUT ON THIS SURVEY, INCLUDING THIS ONE [ ][ ]	(63-64)	
	Time Interview Completed (WRITE IN) ____		
	Length of interview (IN MINUTES) [ ][ ][ ]	(65-67	
	Signature of interviewer ____ INTERVIEWER NO [ ][ ][ ] (68-70)	OUO 1	(71)

Appendix II: Questionnaire for the Compensation Survey

This questionnaire was used at the follow-up (recall) interviews for the main Compensation sample. See Chapter 1, pp. 26, 33–7, for an explanation. The questionnaire is produced in a compressed form (by omitting the larger spaces left for answers) and reduced from A4 size; but the precise wording of all questions, prompts and interview instructions, and all coding numbering, have been retained. Where a show card was used during the interview, it has been reproduced at the end of the questionnaire; but it has not been reproduced where it was embodied in the questionnaire itself. (Not all questions have been analysed in this volume.)

CENTRE FOR SAMPLE SURVEYS LTD. | SOCIAL & COMMUNITY PLANNING RESEARCH

16 DUNCAN TERRACE LONDON N1 8BZ TEL: 01-278 2061

Record No. (1-4)
Card No. (01) (5-6)
P.423 (7-9)

P.423

NATIONAL SURVEY OF MISFORTUNES

Recall Survey

Area Code ☐☐☐☐ (10-13)

Sample Issue No. ☐☐ (14-15)

Special Serial No. ☐☐☐☐☐☐ (16-21)

Type of Misfortune (22)

AA 1
AB 2
AC 3
IA 4
IB 5

Date of Interview ☐☐ (23-24) ☐☐ (25-26)

OUO

Time Interview Started ____________

Earlier this year, we carried out a survey on behalf of the Oxford unit of the Social Science Research Council to find out how many people have had to deal with problems of illness, accident, injury or handicap in the recent past. We are now calling back on some of the people who have had such problems to find out more about how they dealt with them.

PART I NATURE OF MISFORTUNE

1. First I'd like to check some details about you. Then I'd like to check who else belongs to this household. Please include anyone who normally lives here, but is temporarily away.

					Persons aged 16 and over only									
					Marital Status			Working Status						
								Full time	Part time		NOT WORKING			
Person No	Relationship to Named Victim	Sex M	Sex F	Age last B'day	Marr-ied	Sin-gle	Wid/ Div/ Sep	(31 hrs+ per week)	(11-30 hrs per week)	(6-10 hrs per week)	H/ Wife	F/T Educ.	Other	
1	Named victim	1	2		1	2	3	1	2	3	4	5	6	(27-31)
2	HoH (if not victim)	1	2		1	2	3	1	2	3	4	5	6	(32-36)
3		1	2		1	2	3	1	2	3	4	5	6	(37-41)
4		1	2		1	2	3	1	2	3	4	5	6	(42-46)
5		1	2		1	2	3	1	2	3	4	5	6	(47-51)
6		1	2		1	2	3	1	2	3	4	5	6	(52-56)
7		1	2		1	2	3	1	2	3	4	5	6	(57-61)
8		1	2		1	2	3	1	2	3	4	5	6	(62-66)
9		1	2		1	2	3	1	2	3	4	5	6	(67-71)

Total number in household ☐☐ (72-73)

Head of Household is Person Number ☐ (74)

Housewife is Person Number ☐ (75)

Victim is Respondent 1 } (76)

Proxy Respondent, Person No. ☐ }

(77-80)Blank

Record No. (1-4)
Card No. (02) (5-6)
P.423 (7-9)

	Col./ Code	Skip to

CHECK HOUSEHOLD GRID AND SHOW APPROPRIATE CARD. IF NAMED VICTIM IS:

UNDER 6 YEARS OLD - SHOW CARD A
6-16 YEARS OLD
OR 17-18 YEARS AND STILL IN FULL TIME EDUCATION } - SHOW CARD B
ALL OTHERS - SHOW CARD C
} SEE END OF QUESTIONNAIRE

2. I understand that, in the last few years, you have suffered from an accident, injury, illness, handicap or medical condition which at some time made it difficult or impossible for you to do some of the things on this card. MENTION DETAIL OF MISFORTUNE AS GIVEN ON SAMPLE ISSUE SHEET. Can I check what happened? What was the trouble? What was the cause of the trouble? How did it affect you? PROBE FOR FULL DETAILS OF CONDITION AND CAUSE.

FOR OFFICE USE

☐☐☐☐ (10-13)
☐☐☐☐ (14-17)

3. Just as a check, when did your accident/injury happen/when did your illness start?

(18-19) ____________(MONTH) (20-21) ____________(YEAR)

IF MISFORTUNE TYPE ON SAMPLE ISSUE SHEET IS "IB" NOW SKIP TO PART 2,Q.8
ALL OTHERS ASK Q.4-Q.7

ASK ALL WHOSE MISFORTUNE TYPE IS "AA", "AB", "AC" OR "IA"

4.a) Was the accident/injury/illness in any way your fault or the fault of someone else, or was it no-ones fault? RECORD BELOW.

IF IN SOME WAY OWN FAULT AND FAULT OF OTHER NOT MENTIONED

b) Was it wholly your own fault or just partly your own fault? RECORD BELOW.

IF IN SOME WAY OTHER PERSON'S FAULT AND OWN FAULT NOT MENTIONED

c) Was it wholly someone else's fault or just partly someone else's fault? RECORD BELOW

Accident/injury/ilness was:	(22)	
Wholly other person's fault	1	Q.5
Wholly own fault	2 }	Q.7
No-one's fault	3 }	
Partly own, partly other's fault	4 }	Q.5
Partly other's fault but not own	5 }	
Partly own fault but no-one else's	6	Q.7

		Col./Code	Skip to
	IF OTHER'S FAULT IN ANY WAY (CODES 1, 4 OR 5 AT Q.4)		
5.a)	You mentioned that the accident/injury/illness was, at least in part, someone else's fault. Who was that? PROBE FOR RELATIONSHIP TO RESPONDENT	OUO (23-24)	
b)	In what way was it their fault?	(25-26)	
c)	Do you feel _____ (PERSON(S) MENTIONED AT a)) was morally to blame for your accident/injury/illness?	(27)	
	Yes	1	
	No	2	
d)	When you realised what had happened, did you feel angry or annoyed with _____ (PERSON(S) MENTIONED AT a))?	(28)	
	Yes	1	
	No	2	
e)	Do you feel angry or annoyed with _____ (PERSON(S) MENTIONED AT a)) now?	(29)	
	Yes	1	
	No	2	
f)	Did they do it deliberately?	(30)	
	Yes	1	
	No	2	
	IF DONE DELIBERATELY (YES AT Q.5f)) OR IF MISFORTUNE TYPE IS "AC" ASK Q.6 OTHERWISE GO TO Q.7	(31)	
6.a)	Did you tell the police? Yes	1	b) & e)
	No	2	c) & d)
	IF TOLD POLICE		
	b) Why did you tell the police?		
	IF DID NOT TELL POLICE ASK c) AND d)		
	c) Why did you not tell the police?		
	d) Did the police find out anyhow?	(32)	
	Yes	1	
	No	2	(f)

		Col./Code	Skip to
	IF POLICE TOLD OR FOUND OUT (YES AT a) OR d)		
	e) What, if anything, did the police do about it? PROBE FULLY.		
	ASK f) AND g) IN ALL CASES WHERE ACTION WAS DELIBERATE		
	f) Did you yourself try to do anything about it? IF YES: What? PROBE FULLY.		
	g) Has the experience changed your behaviour in any way? IF YES: How?		
	ASK ALL WHOSE MISFORTUNE TYPE IS "AA", "AB", "AC" OR "IA"		
7.a)	Apart from possible faults of particular people, did your accident/injury/illness result in any way from a fault in a manufactured product or thing? This includes possible faults in roads, buildings, vehicles, machinery, equipment, tools, furniture or any other manufactured goods. It includes faults in design, workmanship, production, repair, maintenance or servicing.	(33)	
	Yes	1	
	No	2	PART 2 Q.8
	IF ANY ITEM MENTIONED AT a)		
	b) Can you give me details? (IF A MANUFACTURED ITEM, PROBE FOR TYPE, MAKE AND AGE)		

CARD 02

PART 2 MEDICAL

			Col./Code	Skip to
	ASK ALL			
8.a)	Did you ever go to a hospital because of your illness/injury?		(34)	
		Yes	1	
		No	2	Q.11
	IF YES AT a)		(35)	
	b) How did your first visit to hospital happen? Were you sent there by your GP or some other doctor? Or did you go there yourself? Or did someone else call an ambulance in an emergency?	- sent by GP/other doctor	1	
		- went there yourself	2	
		- someone else called ambulance	3	
	c) Which department of the hospital did you go to on your first visit? Was it the casualty department or some other department? IF OTHER: Which?		(36)	
		Casualty department	1	
		Other (Specify) ______	2	
	d) Did you ever stay in hospital overnight or longer because of your illness/injury?		(37)	
		Yes	1	
		No	2	Q.10
	ASK ALL WHO STAYED IN HOSPITAL OVERNIGHT OR LONGER (YES AT Q.8d)		(38)	
9.a)	How did you first come to stay in hospital overnight because of your illness/injury? Was it that: READ OUT ALL CHOICES.	- you went to the casualty department and they decided you should stay in	1	
		OR - arrangements were made for you to stay in hospital by your GP or by a specialist	2	
		OR - was it in some other way?	3	
	IF 'OTHER WAY' SPECIFY ______			
b)	How many spells in hospital have you had because of your illness/injury?		(39)	
		One	1	
		Two	2	
		Three or four	3	
		Five or six	4	
		Seven or more	5	
c)	In all, how many nights have you spent in hospital because of your illness/injury?		(40)	
		One night	1	
		2-6 nights	2	
		7-13 nights	3	
		14 nights or more	4	
d)	Apart from staying overnight, have you ever attended a clinic or other department of the hospital as an outpatient because of your illness/injury?		(41)	
		Yes	1	Q.10
		No	2	Q.11

CARD 02

			Col./Code	Skip to
	ASK ALL WHO ATTENDED HOSPITAL AS OUTPATIENTS (NO AT Q.8d OR YES AT Q.9d)			
10.a)	You attended hospital as an outpatient because of your illness/injury. What kind of clinic or department did you attend? DO NOT READ OUT LIST. CODE ALL THAT APPLY.		(42)	
		Casualty	1	
		Fracture clinic	2	
		Chest clinic	3	
		Physiotherapy clinic	4	
		Orthopaedic clinic	5	
		Ophthalmic clinic	6	
		Other clinic(s) (SPECIFY) ______		
b)	In all, how many times have you attended a hospital as an outpatient because of your illness/injury?		(43)	
		Once	1	
		Twice	2	
		3 or 4 times	3	
		5 or 6 times	4	
		7-10 times	5	
		11-20 times	6	
		21 times or more	7	
c)	Are you still attending a hospital outpatient clinic because of your illness/injury?		(44)	
		Yes	1	
		No	2	
	ASK ALL		(45)	
11.a)	Have you ever seen your own doctor (your GP) as a result of your illness/injury?	Yes	1	
		No	2	Q.12
	IF GP EVER SEEN ASK b)-d)		(46)	
	b) Did you ever see him for treatment for your illness/injury or its effects?	Yes	1	
		No	2	
	c) Did you ever see him just to get a medical certificate?		(47)	
		Yes	1	
		No	2	
	d) How often in all have you seen your own doctor about your illness/injury? READ OUT		(48)	
		Up to 5 times	1	
		6-10 times	2	
		11-20 times	3	
		OR More than 20 times	4	

CARD 02

	Question	Response	Col./ Code	Skip to
	ASK ALL			
12.a	Apart from your own doctor, were you ever in contact with any of the following about your illness/injury? READ OUT:		(49)	
		A doctor in connection with state benefits	1	
		A doctor in connection with a legal claim	2	
		OR A works or company doctor	3	
		(None of these)	0	
	IF SAW ANY DOCTOR IN CONNECTION WITH STATE BENEFIT		(50)	
	b) What doctors did you see in connection with state benefits? Was it the Regional Medical Officer (RMO) or a medical board or someone else? IF SOMEONE ELSE Who was that?	Saw RMO	1	
		Saw medical board	2	
		Saw other doctor	3	
	(SPECIFY) ______			
	ASK ALL		(51)	
13.a	Have you seen any doctor or received any treatment as a private patient because of your illness/injury?	Yes	1	
		No	2	Q.14
	IF YES TO a)			
	b) Excluding any costs which may have been paid or paid back by medical insurance, what was the total cost to you of private treatment?		(52)	
		Under £50	1	
		£50 but under £100	2	
		£100 but under £200	3	
		£200 but under £500	4	
		£500 or more	5	
	ASK ALL		(53)	
14..	Have you ever asked any of these people for advice about your illness/injury? READ OUT	A chemist	1	
		An osteopath	2	
		A faith healer	3	
		Friends or relations	4	
		(None of these)	0	
	ASK ALL		(54)	
15.a	Are you still receiving any treatment in connection with your illness/injury?	Yes	1	
		No	2	
b	Are you still affected physically in any way at all by your illness/injury or its effects?		(55)	
		Yes	1	
		No	2	Q.18

CARD 02

	Question	Response	Col./ Code	Skip to
	IF STILL AFFECTED BY ILLNESS/INJURY (YES AT Q.15b)			
16.a	What do you find are the main problems you have from your illness/injury or its effects? PROBE FULLY			
	______		OUO (56-57)	
b	Are you ever affected a lot nowadays by your illness/injury or its effects? RECORD BELOW.			
	IF YES AT b)		(58)	
	c) Are you affected a lot all the time, most of the time or just occasionally?	Never affected a lot	1	
		Affected a lot - all the time	2	
		- most of the time	3	
		- just occasionally	4	
d	Does your illness/injury or its effects stop you from doing any hobbies, voluntary work or other leisure activities which you did before?		(59)	
		Yes	1	
		No	2	(f)
	IF YES AT d)			
	e) Which activities? ______		OUO (60)	
f	Does your illness/injury or its effects make it difficult in any way for you to walk or to get about by yourself?		(61)	
		Yes	1	
		No	2	Q.18

CARD 02

	Question	Response	Col./Code	Skip to
	IF MOBILITY AFFECTED AT ALL (YES AT Q.16f)			
17.a	Have you been outside the house in the past week? IF NO: Have you been outside the house in the past month?		(62)	
		Out in past week	1	c)
		Out in past month but not in past week	2	c)
		Not been out in past month	3	
	IF NOT BEEN OUT IN PAST MONTH			
	b) Why have you not been out of the house in the past month?		OUO (63)	
	IF BEEN OUT IN PAST WEEK OR MONTH ASK c) AND d)		(64)	
	c) Did you need any help from someone else to go out?	Yes	1	
		No	2	
	d) Did you need to use any special aids to go out?		(65)	
		Yes	1	
		No	2	
	IF YES AT c) OR d)			
	e) What help or aids did you need? PROBE TO "NONE"		OUO (66)	

CARD 02

	Question	Response	Col./Code	Skip to
	ASK ALL		(67)	
18.a	Do you think your illness/injury affected the health of any other members of your household?	Yes	1	
		No	2	Q.19
	IF OTHERS AFFECTED (YES AT a)			
	b) Whose health was affected? How was it affected? ENTER EFFECTS ON APPROPRIATE LINE.		OUO (68-71)	
	Spouse			
	Parent			
	Child			
	Other (Specify)			
	ASK ALL		(72)	
19.a	Did you have any difficulties in obtaining the medical care that you felt you needed for your illness/injury?	Yes	1	
		No	2	Q.20
	IF YES AT a)			
	b) What difficulties did you have?		OUO (73)	
	ASK ALL		(74)	
20.a	Are you registered as disabled with your local authority social services department?	Yes	1	
		No	2	Q.21
	IF REGISTERED			
	b) Since when have you been registered? MONTH 19 YEAR (75-76)			
	ASK ALL		(77)	
21.a	Are you registered as disabled with the Department of Employment, that is, do you have a green card?	Yes	1	
		No	2	PART 3 Q.22
	IF REGISTERED			
	b) Since when have you been registered? MONTH 19 YEAR (78-79)			
			(80 Blank)	

RECORD NO. (1-4)
CARD NO. 03 (5-6)
P.423 (7-9)

PART 3 LOCAL AUTHORITY AND VOLUNTARY GROUP CARE

ASK ALL

22.a The Local Authority and voluntary groups can provide various kinds of help to people who have suffered an illness or injury; since this time last year have any of these people visited you? READ OUT HEADINGS. CODE 'YES' OR 'NO' FOR EACH ONE. IF ALL CODED 'NO' GO TO Q.23

READ OUT.....	A Social Worker	A Home Nurse	A Health Visitor	A Home Help	Meals on Wheels	A Laundry Help	A Bath Attendant	A Physiotherapist, occupational therapist or home teacher	Col./Code
	(10-14)	(15-19)	(20-24)	(25-29)	(30-34)	(35-39)	(40-44)	(45-49)	
a Visited Yes	A	A	A	A	A	A	A	A	
No	0	0	0	0	0	0	0	0	
FOR EACH PERSON CODED 'YES' AT a) ASK b)-e)									
b) Where were they from? Was it from the Local Authority, a voluntary body or charity, somewhere else or don't you know?									
Local Authority	2	2	2	2	2	2	2	2	
Voluntary body/charity	3	3	3	3	3	3	3	3	
Someone else	4	4	4	4	4	4	4	4	
Don't know	5	5	5	5	5	5	5	5	
c) How did you find out about this service? DO NOT PROMPT									
Own doctor	1	1	1	1	1	1	1	1	
Other doctor/hospital/nurse	2	2	2	2	2	2	2	2	
Other service	3	3	3	3	3	3	3	3	
Friend/relative	4	4	4	4	4	4	4	4	
Media	5	5	5	5	5	5	5	5	
Other	6	6	6	6	6	6	6	6	
(Don't know)	7	7	7	7	7	7	7	7	
d) Did you pay anything towards this?									
Yes	1	1	1	1	1	1	1	1	
No	2	2	2	2	2	2	2	2	
(Don't know)	3	3	3	3	3	3	3	3	
e) How frequently did they visit? SHOW CARD D									
Daily	1	1	1	1	1	1	1	1	
2-4 times a week	2	2	2	2	2	2	2	2	
Once a week	3	3	3	3	3	3	3	3	
Once a fortnight	4	4	4	4	4	4	4	4	
Once every 3 weeks	5	5	5	5	5	5	5	5	
Once a month	6	6	6	6	6	6	6	6	
Less often	7	7	7	7	7	7	7	7	
Came once only	8	8	8	8	8	8	8	8	
UNLESS 'CAME ONCE ONLY' f) For how long did they keep visiting? SHOW CARD E									
One week or less	1	1	1	1	1	1	1	1	
Over 1 week-under 1 month	2	2	2	2	2	2	2	2	
1 month, under 6 months	3	3	3	3	3	3	3	3	
6 months or more	4	4	4	4	4	4	4	4	

CARD 03

ASK ALL

23.a Since this time last year, have you visited .....? READ OUT HEADINGS. CODE 'YES' OR 'NO' FOR EACH PLACE. IF ALL CODED 'NO' GO TO Q.24

READ OUT.....	A Day Centre	A Sheltered Workshop	A Handicapped club	A Lunch club	A Nursery	A Residential Home	Col./Code
	(50-53)	(54-57)	(58-61)	(62-65)	(66-69)	(70-73)	
a Visited Yes	A	A	A	A	A	A	
No	0	0	0	0	0	0	
FOR EACH PLACE CODED 'YES' AT a) ASK b)-e)							
b) Who runs this place? Is it the Local Authority, a voluntary body or charity, someone else or don't you know?							
Local Authority	2	2	2	2	2	2	
Voluntary body/charity	3	3	3	3	3	3	
Someone else	4	4	4	4	4	4	
(Don't know)	5	5	5	5	5	5	
c) How did you find out about it?							
Own doctor	1	1	1	1	1	1	
Other doctor/hospital/nurse	2	2	2	2	2	2	
Other service	3	3	3	3	3	3	
Friend/relative	4	4	4	4	4	4	
Media	5	5	5	5	5	5	
Other	6	6	6	6	6	6	
(Don't know)	7	7	7	7	7	7	
d) Did you pay anything for this? Yes	1	1	1	1	1	1	
No	2	2	2	2	2	2	
e) For how long during the last year were you visiting it?							
Visited Once only	1	1	1	1	1	1	
One week or less	2	2	2	2	2	2	
Over 1 week under 1 month	3	3	3	3	3	3	
1 month under 6 months	4	4	4	4	4	4	
6 months or more	5	5	5	5	5	5	

(Cols 74-80 Blank)

Record No. (1-4)
Card No (04) (5-6)
P.423 (7-9)

CARD 04

ASK ALL

24.a Because of your illness/injury or its effects, have you ever had any special aids or appliances to help in the home, such as .....? READ OUT HEADINGS AND CODE YES OR NO FOR EACH. IF NONE HAD, GO TO Q.25. IF HAD "OTHER SPECIAL AID", SPECIFY TYPE

Col./Code | Skip to: OUO (10-11)

	A Walking Aid, including crutches or Stick	A Wheel chair	A Hoist, Ramp Rail or Handle	A Bath Mat on Commode	A Hearing Aid	A visual Aid Other Than Spectacles	Any Other Special Aid SPECIFY
	(12-14)	(15-17)	(18-20)	(21-23)	(24-26)	(27-29)	(30-32)
a Had Appliance. Yes	A	A	A	A	A	A	A
No	0	0	0	0	0	0	0
FOR EACH CODED YES AT a) ASK b)-d)							
b) Did you pay anything for this? Yes	1	1	1	1	1	1	1
No	2	2	2	2	2	2	2
c) Who provided you with this? Did you get it yourself or was it from the Local Authority, or from a voluntary body or a charity or from someone else or don't you know? Self	1	1	1	1	1	1	1
Local Authority	2	2	2	2	2	2	2
Voluntary body/charity	3	3	3	3	3	3	3
Someone else	4	4	4	4	4	4	4
(Don't know)	5	5	5	5	5	5	5
UNLESS GOT BY SELF ASK d)							
d) How did you find out you could get this? Own doctor	1	1	1	1	1	1	1
Other doctor/hospital/nurse	2	2	2	2	2	2	2
Other service	3	3	3	3	3	3	3
Friend/relative	4	4	4	4	4	4	4
Media	5	5	5	5	5	5	5
Other	6	6	6	6	6	6	6
(Don't know)	7	7	7	7	7	7	7

ASK ALL

25.a Has any group or organisation helped to get or to pay for any of the things on this card? SHOW CARD F AND CODE 'YES' OR 'NO' FOR EACH ITEM

Col./Code | Skip to

READ OUT.....	T.V./radio	Clothing	Holiday	Telephone
	(33-35)	(36-38)	(39-41)	(42-44)
a) Help received Yes	A	A	A	A
No	0	0	0	0
FOR EACH CODED 'YES' ASK b)-d)				
b) Who helped with this? Was it the Local Authority, a voluntary body or charity, someone else or don't you know? Local Authority	1	1	1	1
Voluntary body/charity	2	2	2	2
Someone else	3	3	3	3
(Don't know)	4	4	4	4
c) How did you find out you could get this help? Own doctor	1	1	1	1
Other doctor/hospital/nurse	2	2	2	2
Other service	3	3	3	3
Friend/relative	4	4	4	4
Media	5	5	5	5
Other	6	6	6	6
(Don't know)	7	7	7	7
d) Did you pay anything towards this? Yes	1	1	1	1
No	2	2	2	2

PART 4 INFORMAL CARE

CARD 04

	Col./Code	Skip to
ASK ALL. SHOW CARD G (SEE END OF QUESTIONNAIRE FOR CARD G)		
26.a After an accident or illness some people need extra help with their day-to-day tasks. On this card are a number of things for which people often need help. Leaving aside any time you were in hospital, did anyone help you with any of these tasks after your injury/while you were ill?	(45)	
Yes	1	
No	2	PART 5 Q.29
IF 'YES' AT a)	Helper No.	OUO (46-51)
b) Could you tell me all the people who helped you?		
WRITE IN ONE 'HELPER' PER LINE STATING RELATIONSHIP TO RESPONDENT.	H1	
	H2	
IF 4+ HELPERS ASK FOR THREE WHO HELPED MOST AND LIST THESE ON FIRST THREE LINES.	H3	
LIST OTHER HELPERS UP TO 6 ON LINES 4-6. IF MORE THAN 6 HELPERS WRITE IN NO. OF OTHERS.		
Other helpers ENTER NO.		(52)

ASK ALL WHO RECEIVED HELP (YES AT Q.26a)
START WITH FIRST HELPER LISTED (HELPER NO.1)

	HELPER NO.1's TASKS					
SHOW CARD G AGAIN	(53-55)	(56-58)	(59-61)	(62-64)	(65-67)	(68-70)
27.a With which of these tasks did ____ (REFER TO HELPER NO.1) give you assistance? ENTER APPROPRIATE CODE NO'S FROM CARD. ONE TASK CODE PER COLUMN.						
FOR EACH TASK ASK b) AND c)						
b) Over how long a period did this person help you with this task?						
One week or less	1	1	1	1	1	1
Over 1 week - under 1 month	2	2	2	2	2	2
1 month - under 6 months	3	3	3	3	3	3
6 months or more	4	4	4	4	4	4
c) How often did this person help with this task?						
At least once a day	1	1	1	1	1	1
At least every other day	2	2	2	2	2	2
At least weekly	3	3	3	3	3	3
At least monthly	4	4	4	4	4	4
Less often	5	5	5	5	5	5

CARD 04

	Col./Code	Skip to
ASK IF MORE THAN ONE TASK CODED. OTHERWISE SKIP TO e)		
d) You mentioned that this person helped you with more than one of the things on the card. Over how long a period in all did this person help you?	HELPER NO.1	
	(71)	
One week or less	1	
Over 1 week - under 1 month	2	
1 month - under 6 months	3	
6 months or more	4	
ASK ALL WHO HAD HELP	(72)	
e) Did ____'s (HELPER NO.1's) assistance involve you in any financial cost? Yes	1	
No	2	g)
IF 'YES' AT e)	(73-74)	
f) What was the approximate weekly cost? ENTER COST TO NEAREST £	£____	
ASK ALL WHO HAD HELP	(75)	
g) While ____ (HELPER NO.1) was helping you, was he/she a member of your household? Yes	1	Q.28
No	2	
IF NO AT g) ASK h) AND i)	(76)	
h) How far away did ____ (HELPER NO.1) live? Was it: READ OUT In the same building or next door	1	
Within 5 minutes' walk	2	
Within 10 minutes' walk	3	
OR More than 10 minutes' walk away?	4	
i) Did he/she have others to look after at his/her own home? IF YES Who?	(77)	
No others to look after	1	
Yes - parents only	2	
Yes - children only	3	
Yes - parents and children	4	
Yes - other(s)	5	
IF HELPER NO.1 NOT A HOUSEHOLD MEMBER (NO AT g) AND NOT A RELATIVE (CHECK Q.26b) ASK j) AND k)	(78)	
j) How long have you known ____ (HELPER NO.1)? Under 6 months	1	
6 months - under 1 year	2	
1 year - under 2 years	3	
2 years - under 5 years	4	
5 years or more	5	
k) Did you know ____ (HELPER NO.1) before your injury/before your illness started?	(79)	
Yes	1	Q.28
No	2	
IF NO AT k)	(80)	
l) How did you get to know him/her? DO NOT PROMPT. Through a friend	1	
Through agency/professional	2	
Advertised	3	
Other (Specify) ____		

Record No. (1-4)
Card 05 (5-6)
P.423 (7-9)

IF HAD MORE THAN ONE HELPER ASK Q.28a-1 FOR 2ND HELPER MENTIONED THEN REPEAT FOR 3RD HELPER MENTIONED (I.E. HELPER NO.3) WHERE RELEVANT.

ASK OF SECOND AND THIRD HELPERS AS APPROPRIATE. SHOW CARD G.

28.a With which of these tasks did _____ (HELPER) give you assistance? ENTER ONE TASK CODE PER COLUMN.

	HELPER NO.2'S TASKS						HELPER NO.3'S TASKS					
	(10-12)	(13-15)	(16-18)	(19-21)	(22-24)	(25-27)	(28-30)	(31-33)	(34-36)	(37-39)	(40-42)	(43-45)
FOR EACH TASK ASK b) AND c)												
b) Over how long a period did his person help you with this task?												
One week or less	1	1	1	1	1	1	1	1	1	1	1	1
Over 1 week - under 1 month	2	2	2	2	2	2	2	2	2	2	2	2
1 month - under 6 months	3	3	3	3	3	3	3	3	3	3	3	3
6 months or more	4	4	4	4	4	4	4	4	4	4	4	4
c) How often did this person help you with this task?												
At least once a day	1	1	1	1	1	1	1	1	1	1	1	1
At least every other day	2	2	2	2	2	2	2	2	2	2	2	2
At least weekly	3	3	3	3	3	3	3	3	3	3	3	3
At least monthly	4	4	4	4	4	4	4	4	4	4	4	4
Less often	5	5	5	5	5	5	5	5	5	5	5	5

CARD 05

	Helper No.2	Helper No.3	Skip to
IF MORE THAN ONE TASK CODED			
d) You mentioned that this person helped you with more than one of the things on the card. Over how long a period in all did this person help you?	(46)	(56)	
One week or less	1	1	
Over 1 week - under 1 month	2	2	
1 month - under 6 months	3	3	
6 months or more	4	4	
ASK ALL WHO HAD HELP	(47)	(57)	
e) Did _____ (HELPER NO.2/3's) assistance involve you in any financial cost? Yes	1	1	
No	2	2	g)
IF YES AT e)	(48-49)	(58-59)	
f) What was the approximate weekly cost? ENTER COST TO NEAREST £	£____	£____	
ASK ALL WHO HAD HELP	(50)	(60)	
g) While _____ (HELPER NO.2/3) was helping you, was he/she a member of your household? Yes	1	1	HELPER NO.3 OR PART 5
No	2	2	
IF NO TO g) ASK h) AND i)	(51)	(61)	
h) How far away did _____ (HELPER NO.2/3) live? Was it: READ OUT In the same building or next door	1	1	
Within 5 minutes' walk	2	2	
Within 10 minutes' walk	3	3	
OR More than 10 minutes' walk away?	4	4	
i) Did he/she have others to look after at his/her own home? IF YES Who?	(52)	(62)	
No others to look after	1	1	
Yes - parents only	2	2	
Yes - children only	3	3	
Yes - parents and children	4	4	
Yes - other(s)	5	5	
IF HELPER NOT A HOUSEHOLD MEMBER (NO TO g) AND NOT A RELATIVE (CHECK Q.26b) ASK j) AND k)	(53)	(63)	
j) How long have you known _____ (HELPER NO.2/3)? Under 6 months	1	1	
6 months - under 1 year	2	2	
1 year - under 2 years	3	3	
2 years - under 5 years	4	4	
5 years or more	5	5	
k) Did you know _____ (HELPER NO.2/3) before your injury/before your illness started?	(54)	(64)	
Yes	1	1	HELPER NO.3 OR PART 5
No	2	2	
IF NO TO k)	(55)	(65)	
l) How did you get to know him/her? DO NOT PROMPT Through a friend	1	1	
Through agency/professional	2	2	
Advertised	3	3	
Other (Specify) ______________		(66-80)	Blank

PART 5 VISUAL HANDICAP

Record No. (1-4)
Card (06) (5-6)
P.423 (7-9)

			Col./Code	Skip to
	ASK ALL EXCEPT PROXY RESPONDENTS. IF RESPONDENT IS A PROXY SKIP TO PART 6, Q.35		(10)	
29.	Do you ever nowadays have any difficulty in seeing to read or in seeing to get about?	Yes	1	
		No	2	PART 6 Q.35
	ALL WHO EVER HAVE DIFFICULTY (YES AT Q.29)		(11)	
30.a	Are you registered as blind or partially sighted?	Registered as blind	1	
		Registered as partially sighted	2	
		Neither	3	
b	Because of your sight, do you normally use any aids to help you get about?		(12)	
		Yes	1	
		No	2	d)
	IF YES AT b)		Yes	No
	c) Do you normally use ..... READ OUT ..... CODE YES OR NO FOR EACH.	A guide dog	1	2 (13)
		A sonic aid	1	2 (14)
		A short white cane	1	2 (15)
		A long white cane	1	2 (16)
		An ordinary stick	1	2 (17)
		Another person to guide you	1	2 (18)
	ASK ALL WHO EVER HAVE DIFFICULTY		(19)	
	d) In a room during daytime, can you tell by the light where the windows are?	Yes	1	
		No	2	Q.33
31.	ASK ALL WHO EVER HAVE DIFFICULTY (YES AT Q.29) BUT WHO CAN TELL BY THE LIGHT WHERE THE WINDOWS ARE. (YES AT Q.30d) IF RESPONDENT HAS GLASSES/CONTACT LENSES, THESE MUST BE WORN FOR THIS QUESTION. IF RESPONDENT HAS SEPARATE READING AND DISTANCE GLASSES, DISTANCE GLASSES MUST BE WORN.			
		Respondent wore for this question:	(20)	
		Special distance glasses	1	
		Ordinary glasses	2	
		Contact lenses	3	
		None of these	4	
.a	HOLD UP SNELLEN CHART (LETTER CHART) 10 FEET FROM EYES OF RESPONDENT. Can you see this chart?		(21)	
		Yes	1	
		No	2	Q.32
	IF CAN SEE CHART		(22)	
	b) How far down can you read this chart?	Respondent illiterate	1	Q.33
		Respondent cannot read largest letter	2	Q.32
		Respondent can read all letters correctly down to line :-	(23-24)	
			60	
			36	
			24	
		RING APPROPRIATE NUMBERS	18	
			12	
			09	ASK Q.32, THEN GO TO PART 6
			06	
			05	
			04	
		(Respondent read whole chart correctly)	03	
	IF LOWEST LINE RESPONDENT CAN READ IS LINE 36 (ND) BRING CHART FORWARD 1½ FEET TO 8½ FEET FROM RESPONDENT'S EYES AND ASK:		(25)	
	c) Now can you read the next line down?	Next line (ZHV) read	1	
		Next line not read	2	

CARD 06

			Col./Code	Skip to
32.	ASK ALL WHO EVER HAVE DIFFICULTY (YES AT Q.29), WHO CAN TELL BY THE LIGHT WHERE THE WINDOWS ARE (YES AT Q.30d)) AND WHO ARE NOT ILLITERATE. GLASSES/CONTACT LENSES SHOULD BE WORN. IF RESPONDENT HAS SEPARATE READING AND DISTANCE GLASSES, READING GLASSES SHOULD BE WORN. IF RESPONDENT USUALLY USES MAGNIFIER OR LOW VISION AID THIS SHOULD BE USED.			
		Respondent wore for this question:	(26)	
		Special reading glasses	1	
		Ordinary glasses	2	
		Contact lenses	3	
		None of these	4	
		Respondent used for this question:	(27)	
		Magnifier	1	
		Low vision aid	2	
		Both	3	
		Neither of these	4	
a	HAND TWO CARDS OF TYPEFACES TO RESPONDENT. Can you read any of the words on these cards?		(28)	
		Yes	1	
		No	2	
	IF YES AT a)		(29-30)	
	b) Which is the smallest print you can read?		48	
			36	
		RING APPROPRIATE NUMBERS (ONE PAIR ONLY)	24	
			18	
			14	
			12	
			10	
			08	
			06	
			05	

	Col./ Code	Skip to
CHECK ANSWER TO Q.31 IF RESPONDENT COULD READ DOWN TO LINE 9 OR LOWER ON THE SNELLEN LETTER CHART, SKIP TO PART 6.(Q.35) ALL OTHERS ASK Q.33		
ALL WHO COULD NOT TELL WHERE WINDOWS ARE (NO AT Q.30d)) OR WHO COULD NOT READ DOWN TO LINE 9 ON THE SNELLEN LETTER CHART	(31)	
33.a Have you ever attended hospital for your eyes? Yes	1	
No	2	Q.34
IF YES AT a)		
b) When did you last attend hospital for your eyes? YEAR (WRITE IN) 1 9 _ _	(32-33)	
IF ANSWER TO b) IS 1966 OR EARLIER, SKIP TO Q.34		
ALL LAST ATTENDING HOSPITAL FOR THEIR EYES IN 1967 OR LATER		
c) We are working with Dr. Cullinan, a medical specialist on eyesight at the University of Kent. May Dr. Cullinan write in confidence to the eye specialist at the last hospital you attended?	(34)	
Yes - he may write	1	
No - he may not write	2	PART 6 Q.35
IF HE MAY WRITE, ASK d) - f)		
d) What was the last hospital you attended about your eyes? ______		
e) What was your address at that time? ______ ______		
MARRIED WOMEN ONLY		
f) Was your name then the same as it is now? IF NO What was it? Same name	A	
Other name (WRITE IN) ______		
NOW SKIP TO PART 6, Q.35		

	Col./ Code	Skip to
34. ASK OF ALL WHO HAVE NEVER BEEN TO HOSPITAL FOR THEIR EYES OR WHO HAVE NOT BEEN SINCE 1966.		
IF REGISTERED AS BLIND OR PARTIALLY SIGHTED (Q.30a) ASK (a).		
IF NOT REGISTERED SKIP TO (c)		
IF REGISTERED BLIND OR PARTIALLY SIGHTED		
a) We are working with Dr. Cullinan, a medical specialist on eyesight at the University of Kent. May Dr. Cullinan write in confidence to the Social Services Department with whom you are registered for a diagnosis on your sight?	(35)	
Yes - he may write	1	
No - he may not write	2	PART 6 Q.35
IF YES AT a)		
b) With which social services department are you registered? ______		
NOW SKIP TO PART 6, Q.35		
IF NOT REGISTERED AS BLIND/PARTIALLY SIGHTED		
c) We are working with Dr. Cullinan, a medical specialist on eyesight at the University of Kent. May Dr. Cullinan write in confidence to your family doctor for a diagnosis on your sight?	(36)	
Yes	1	
No	2	PART 6 Q.35
IF YES AT c) ASK d) AND e)		
d) What is the name of your family doctor? ______		
e) What is the address of his surgery? ______ ______		
(37-80 Blank)		

Record No. (1-4)
Card 07 (5-6)
P.423 (7-9)

PART 6 EMPLOYMENT AND EDUCATION

		Col./Code	Skip to
	ASK ALL		
35.	Activity status at time of injury/start of illness.	(10)	
	Working full-time (31+ hrs per week)	1	Q.36 BELOW
	Working part-time (11-30 hrs per week)	2	
	Working part-time (6-10 hrs per week)	3	
	In full-time education	4	SEC.4 Q.51
	Not working - Retired	5	PART 7 Q.60
	Full-time housewife	6	
	Other	7	

Section 1 Work at time of Misfortune

ASK ALL IN FULL OR PART TIME WORK WHEN INJURY HAPPENED/ILLNESS STARTED

		Col./Code	Skip to
36.	OCCUPATION AT TIME OF INJURY/START OF ILLNESS.		
	Name/title of job ______		
	Description of activity ______		
	______	OUO	
	Skill/qualifications/experience required ______	(11-12)	
	______		
	Supervision/management responsibilities (including number supervised)	(13-15)	
	______		
	Industry/business/profession of employer ______		
	______	(16)	
	No. of people employed at place of work: 1 only	1	
	2 - 24	2	
	25 or more	3	
		(17)	
	Employment status: Employee	1	
	Self-employed	2	
37.	How long had you been working for that employer before the injury/before the illness started?	(18)	
	Less than 6 months	1	
	6 months - under 2 years	2	
	2 years - under 5 years	3	
	5 years or more	4	

CARD 07

			Col./Code	Skip to
38.a	On average, what was your total weekly pay, before deductions for tax, national insurance and so on, just before your injury/before your illness began? SHOW CARD H ASK FOR APPROPRIATE LETTER		(19)	
	SEE END OF QUESTIONNAIRE FOR CARD H	J	2	
		K	5	
		M	3	
		N	4	
		P	1	
		R	8	
		S	7	
		T	6	
b	Can I just check again, when was that? (20-21) (22-23)	______ MONTH 19 ______ YEAR		
39.a	Excluding any time off for visits to doctors or clinics, were you off work at all as a result of your injury/illness, whether off work sick or off work unemployed?		(24)	
		Yes	1	
		No	2	SKIP TO SEC. 5, Q.54
	IF YES AT a) ASK b) AND c)		(25)	
	b) How long after your injury/after your illness started did you first have to do this?	Immediately	1	
	(26-27)	______ weeks after	2	
			(28)	
	c) Have you worked regularly at all since then?	Yes	1	
		No	2	

Section 2 Interruption of Work

ASK ALL WHO WERE IN FULL OR PART TIME WORK WHEN INJURY HAPPENED/ILLNESS STARTED AND WERE OFF WORK AT ALL AS A RESULT. (YES AT Q.39a)

			Col./Code	Skip to
40.a	For how long in total were you/have you been off work or out of work as a result of your injury/illness?		(29)	
		3 days or less	1	
		4-6 days	2	
		1 week or more	3	
		WRITE IN NUMBER OF WEEKS		(30-32)

CARD 07

Question	Response	Col./ Code	Skip to
b For how much of that time were you off sick and unable to work as a result of your injury/illness, that is excluding any time you were fit to work but out of work?		(33)	
	No time off sick	0	
	3 days or less	1	
	4-6 days	3	
	1 week or more	3	
	WRITE IN NUMBER OF WEEKS		(34-36)
c Was there any time when you were fit to work but out of work as a result of your injury/illness?		(37)	
	Yes	1	
	No	2	Q.41
IF YES AT c)		(38)	
d) For how long in total were you fit to work but out of work as a result of your injury/illness?	3 days or less	1	
	4-6 days	2	
	1 week or more	3	
	WRITE IN NUMBER OF WEEKS		(39-41)
INTERVIEWER: CHECK TOTAL AT 40.a) AGAINST TOTAL OF 40.b) AND 40.d)			
41.a Apart from holiday pay or any other money already due to you, were you getting any pay from your employer at any time while you were off work as a result of your injury/illness?		(42)	
	Yes	1	
	No	2	Q.42
IF YES AT a) ASK b), c)		(43)	
b) IF GOT SICK PAY AT ALL ASK b) AND c) What evidence of your injury/illness did your employer require before paying you while you were off work? Did he: READ OUT	- Have you examined by a works or company doctor	1	
	- See a medical certificate from your own GP only	2	
	OR - Just take your word for it	3	
c) Was there any time while you were off work when you were getting full pay or when your employer was making up your sickness benefit to full pay?		(44)	
	Yes - got full pay	1	
	Yes - employer made up full pay	2	
	No - never on full pay	3	f)
IF EVER ON FULL PAY OR MADE UP FULL PAY (YES AT c) ASK d) AND e)		(45)	
d) How long did you get this full pay/made up pay?	3 days or less	1	
	4-6 days	2	
	1 week or more	3	
	WRITE IN NUMBER OF WEEKS		(46-48)

CARD 07

Question	Response	Col./ Code	Skip to
e) Was there ever a period while you were off work when you were getting some sick pay from your employer but your total pay was less than full pay?		(49)	
	Yes	1	
	No	2	Q.42
IF EVER ON PART PAY (NO AT Q.41c)) OR YES TO Q.41e)) ASK f) AND g)		(50)	
f) IF EVER ON PART PAY How much was this part pay compared to your usual pay?	Three quarters or more	1	
	Half but under three quarters	2	
	Quarter but under half	3	
	Under a quarter	4	
g) IF EVER ON PART PAY For how long did you get this part pay?		(51)	
	3 days or more	1	
	4-6 days	2	
	1 week or more	3	
	WRITE IN NUMBER OF WEEKS		(52-54)
ASK OF ALL WHO WERE OFF WORK AT ALL			
42. What are your views of your employer's arrangements for sick pay? PROBE FULLY AND RECORD VERBATIM		OUO	
__________		(55)	
ASK ALL WHO WERE OFF WORK AT ALL			
43.a SHOW CARD I While you were off work sick or out of work as a result of your injury/illness, did you get any advice about the sort of work you could do in future from any of these people?		(56)	
	Last employer	1	
	Fellow workers	2	
	Trade union	3	
CODE WHICHEVER APPLY	Disablement Resettlement Officer (DRO)	4	
	Other person from Employment Exchange	5	
	Private Employment Agency	6	
	Employment Medical Advisor (EMA)	7	
	None of these	9	Q.46
IF EMA MENTIONED AT a)		(57)	
b) Who sent you to see the Employment Medical Advisor? Was it: READ OUT	Your own doctor (GP)	1	
	Works or company doctor	2	
	Regional Medical Officer (RMO)	3	
	Disablement Resettlement Officer (DRO)	4	
	or Someone else	5	
IF SOMEONE ELSE: Who sent you? __________			

			Col./Code	Skip to
	IF ANY ADVISOR MENTIONED AT Q.43a) (i.e. ANY CODE RINGED FROM 1-7)		(58)	
44.a	Were you ever offered a place at an employment rehabilitation centre?	Yes	A	
		No	1	Q.45
	IF OFFERED PLACE (YES AT a))			
	b) Did you go to an employment rehabilitation centre?	Yes	2	
		No	3	Q.45
	IF WENT TO ERC ASK c) AND d)		(59)	
	c) Did you go there full-time or part-time?	Full-time	1	
		Part-time	2	
			(60)	
	d) Did you complete the course?	Yes	1	
		No	2	
	IF ANY ADVISOR MENTIONED AT Q.43a)			
			(61)	
45.a	Were you ever offered a place on a training course, to retrain you for different work?	Yes	A	
		No	1	Q.46
	IF OFFERED PLACE (YES AT a)			
	b) Did you go on the course?	Yes	2	
		No	3	Q.46
	IF WENT ON COURSE ASK c) AND d)		(62)	
	c) Who ran the course? Was it READ OUT	your employer	1	
		the government	2	
		a voluntary organisation	3	
		or someone else?	4	
	IF SOMEONE ELSE: Who ran it? ______			
			(63)	
	d) Did you complete the course?	Yes	1	
		No	2	
	ASK ALL WHO WERE OFF WORK AT ALL			
46.a	When you had your injury/illness did you get any money from any of the following? READ OUT		(64)	
		a sick club at work	1	
		a whip round among the people you worked with	2	
		a trade union	3	
		or a friendly society	4	
		(None of these)	0	Q.47
	IF GOT MONEY FROM ANY			
	b) How much money in all did you get from these people? (65-67)	WRITE IN TO NEAREST £ £ ______		

			Col./Code	Skip to
	ASK ALL WHO WERE OFF WORK			
47.a	All in all, setting any sick pay, social security benefits or other benefits you got against any loss of earnings or reduced earnings, how much money do you think you have lost altogether as a result of your injury/illness? PROBE FOR ESTIMATE IF NECESSARY.		(68)	
		None	1	
		Cannot estimate at all	2	
		(69-72) Amount lost £ ______		
b	And, on the same basis, how much money do you think you have lost as a result of your injury/illness over the last twelve months? PROBE FOR ESTIMATE IF NECESSARY.		(73)	
		None	1	
		Cannot estimate at all	2	
		(74-77) Amount lost in past 12 months £ ______		
		(78-80 Blank)		

Record No. (1-)
Card No. 08 (5-6)
P.423 (7-9)

Section 3 The Return to Work

			Col./Code	Skip to
	ASK ALL WHO WERE IN FULL OR PART-TIME WORK WHEN INJURY HAPPENED/ ILLNESS STARTED AND WERE OFF WORK AS A RESULT (YES AT Q.39a) AND HAVE WORKED REGULARLY SINCE (YES AT Q.39c)			
48.a	When did you go back to regular work after your absence because of your injury/illness?	(10-11) ______ MONTH 19 ______ YEAR (12-13)		
b	When you went back to regular work, did you continue with the same employer?		(14)	
		Yes	1	
		No	2	Q.50
	IF CONTINUED WITH SAME EMPLOYER ASK c) AND d)			
	c) Did the average hours you worked in a week, including any paid overtime, change in any way as a result of your injury/illness? IF CHANGED Did they increase or decrease?		(15)	
		Changed - increased	1	
		Changed - decreased	2	
		Did not change	3	
			(16)	
	d) Did your duties or the sort of work you could do change in any way as a result of the injury/illness?	Yes	1	
		No	2	d)
	IF DUTIES CHANGED (YES AT d)			
	e) How did they change? PROBE FULLY.		0U0 (17-18)	
	______			
	______			
	______			

	Question		Col./Code	Skip to
	IF DUTIES DID NOT CHANGE (NO AT d)		(19)	
	f) When you went back to work did you get any help from your employer or the people you work with to make it easier for you to cope with your normal duties?	Yes	1	
		No	2	Q.49
	IF GOT HELP (YES AT f)			
	g) What help did you get? PROBE FULLY. ____________		OUO (20-21)	
49.	ASK ALL WHO CONTINUED WITH SAME EMPLOYER (YES AT Q.48b)			
	When you went back to work was your average total weekly pay affected as a result of your injury/illness? IF YES Was that an increase or a decrease?		(22)	
		Pay affected - increase	1	SEC. 5 Q.54
		Pay affected - decrease	2	SEC. 5 Q.54
		Pay not affected	3	SEC. 5 Q.54
	ASK ALL WHO DID NOT CONTINUE WITH SAME EMPLOYER (NO AT Q.48b)		(23)	
50.a	Did you change your employment because of the injury/illness?	Yes	1	
		No	2	d)
	IF YES AT a)			
	b) Why was that? PROBE FULLY. ____________		OUO (24-25)	
	ASK ALL WHO CHANGED EMPLOYMENT			
	c) DETAILS OF NEXT EMPLOYMENT			
	Name/title of job ____________		OUO (26-27)	
	Description of activity ____________			
	Skill/qualifications/experience required ____________			
	Supervision/management responsibilities (incl. no. supervised) ____________		(28-30)	
	Industry/business/profession of employer ____________		(31)	
	No. of people employed at place of work	1 only	1	
		2-24	2	
		25 or more	3	
			(32)	
	Employment status:	Employee	1	
		Self-employed	2	

	Question		Col./Code	Skip to
	d) On average, what was your total weekly pay, before deductions for tax, national insurance and so on, when you first went there? SHOW CARD H. ASK FOR APPROPRIATE LETTER [SEE END OF QUESTIONNAIRE FOR CARD]		(33)	
		J	2	
		K	5	
		M	3	
		N	4	
		P	1	
		R	8	
		S	7	
		T	6	
	NOW SKIP TO SEC.5 Q.54			
	Section 4 Education			
	ASK ALL WHO WERE IN FULL-TIME EDUCATION AT THE TIME THE INJURY HAPPENED/THE ILLNESS BEGAN (Q.35)			
51.	Were you receiving any grant or scholarship at the time of your injury/the time your illness began?		(34)	
		Yes	1	
		No	2	SEC.5 Q.54
	IF RECEIVING GRANT/SCHOLARSHIP		(35)	
52.a	Was your grant/scholarship stopped completely at any time because of your injury/illness or its effects?	Yes	1	
		No	2	Q.53
	IF GRANT STOPPED ASK b) AND c)			
	b) IF GRANT STOPPED How long after your injury/after your illness began was it stopped?	(36-37) ______ MONTHS		
			(38)	
	c) IF GRANT STOPPED Did it ever start again?	Yes	1	
		No	2	Q.53
	d) IF GRANT STOPPED AND RESTARTED For how many months was it stopped?	(39-40) ______ MONTHS		
	IF RECEIVING GRANT/SCHOLARSHIP		(41)	
53.a	Were you receiving a reduced grant at any time because of your injury/illness or its effects?	Yes	1	
		No	2	SEC.5 Q.54
	IF RECEIVING REDUCED GRANT AT ANY TIME			
	b) How long after your injury/after your illness began did you start receiving a reduced grant?	(42-43) ______ MONTHS		
	IF RECEIVING REDUCED GRANT AT ANY TIME		(44)	
	c) For how long did you receive a reduced grant?	Still receiving reduced grant	1	
		Not now receiving reduced grant, grant was reduced for ______ MONTHS (45-46)		

CARD 08

Section 5 Present Position

		Col./ Code	Skip to
	ASK ALL WHO AT THE TIME OF INJURY/START OF ILLNESS WERE WORKING (FULL-TIME OR PART-TIME OR WERE IN FULL-TIME EDUCATION (CODES 1-4 AT Q.35)		
	IF WORKING THEN - ASK Q.54		
	IF F/T EDUCATION THEN - SKIP TO Q.55		
	ASK ALL WHO AT THE TIME OF INJURY/START OF ILLNESS WERE WORKING FULL OR PART-TIME	(47)	
54.a	Did the job you were doing when your injury happened/ when your illness began carry a pension from your employer? Yes	1	c)
	No	2	
	IF JOB BEFORE INJURY/ILLNESS BEGAN CARRIED NO PENSION	(48)	
	b) Does any job you have done since normally carry a pension from the employer? Yes	1	c)
	No	2	Q.55
	IF IN ANY PENSIONABLE EMPLOYMENT (YES AT a) OR b)	(49)	
	c) Has your injury/illness affected your pension rights or your chances of having a pension from employment in any way? Yes	1	
	No	2	Q.55
	IF PENSION RIGHTS AFFECTED		
	d) How have your pension rights been affected? PROBE FULLY. ________	OUO (50)	
55.a	CHECK PRESENT WORKING STATUS FROM HOUSEHOLD GRID (Q.1)	(51)	
	Working full-time now (31+ hrs per week)	1 }	
	Working part-time now (11-30 hrs per week)	2 }	Q.57
	Working part-time now (6-10 hrs per week)	3 }	
	Not working now - full-time education	4	Q.59
	full-time housewife	5	b)
	- other	6	b)
	b) IF 'FULL-TIME HOUSEWIFE' OR 'OTHER' NOW, CHECK WHETHER:	(52)	
	Permanently retired from work now	1	
	Unemployed and seeking work now	2	Q.59
	Other	3	

CARD 08

		Col./ Code	Skip to
	IF PERMANENTLY RETIRED FROM WORK NOW (CODE 1 AT Q.55b))	(53)	
56.a	Because of your injury/illness, did you retire earlier than you would otherwise have done? Yes	1	
	No	2	Q.59
	IF RETIRED EARLY (YES AT a)) (54-55)		
	b) How many years early? ________ YEARS		
	NOW SKIP TO Q.59		
	IF WORKING FULL OR PART-TIME NOW (CODES 1-3 AT Q.55a))	(56)	
57.a	What is your present occupation: As described at Section 1 Q.36	1 }	Q.58
	As described at Section 3 Q.50b)	2 }	
	Other	3	
	b) IF OTHER THAN PREVIOUSLY DESCRIBED		
	Name/title of job ________	OUO	
	Description of activity ________	(57-58)	
	Skill/qualifications/experience required ________		
	Supervision/management responsibilities (incl. no. supervised) ________	(59-61)	
	Industry/business/profession of employer ________	(62)	
	No. of people employed at place of work 1 only	1	
	2-24	2	
	25 or more	3	
		(63)	
	Employment Status: Employee	1	
	Self-employed	2	
	IF WORKING FULL OR PART-TIME NOW (CODES 1-3 AT Q.55a)		
58.	On average, what is your total weekly pay now, before deductions for tax, national insurance and so on? SHOW CARD H. ASK FOR APPROPRIATE LETTER	(64)	
	SEE END OF QUESTIONNAIRE FOR CARD J	2	
	K	5	
	M	3	
	N	4	
	P	1	
	R	8	
	S	7	
	T	6	
	ASK ALL IN FULL OR PART-TIME WORK OR IN FULL-TIME EDUCATION AT TIME OF INJURY/TIME ILLNESS STARTED.	(65)	
59.a	Had it not been for your injury/illness, do you think that your present job situation, your present earnings or your present educational qualifications would be in any different from what they are? Yes	1	
	No	2	PART 7 Q.60
	b) In what ways would they be different? PROBE FULLY. ________	OUO (66-67)	

PART 7 STATE BENEFITS AND PRIVATE INSURANCE

		Col./ Code	Skip to
	ASK ALL		
60.	SHOW CARD I. This is a list of state benefits which are sometimes available to people who suffer injuries or get ill, providing they were in work at the time or at some time before. Because of your injury/illness, or its effects, did you ever apply for any of these benefits? PROBE: Any others? TO 'NO'	Applied for (10)	
	Industrial injury benefit	1	
	Disablement benefit/lump sum disablement payment	2	
	Sickness benefit	3	
	Invalidity benefit	4	
	Unemployment benefit	5	
	(Applied for none of these)	9	Q.62
	ASK ALL WHO APPLIED FOR ANY (ANY CODE OUT OF 1-5 AT Q.60)		
61.a)	CONTINUE TO SHOW CARD I. Did you ever have any difficulties of any sort with your applications for any of these benefits? IF YES With which benefits? PROBE: Any others? TO 'NO'	(11)	
	No difficulties with any	0	b)
	Difficulties with application for: Industrial injury benefit	1	ASK b) THEN c)
	Disablement benefit/lump sum disablement payment	2	ASK b) THEN c)
	Sickness benefit	3	ASK b) THEN c)
	Invalidity benefit	4	ASK b) THEN c)
	Unemployment benefit	5	ASK b) THEN c)
b)	CONTINUE TO SHOW CARD I. Did you ever have to use the appeals procedure in connection with your applications for any of these benefits? IF YES For which benefits? PROBE: Any others? TO 'NO'	(12)	
	Appeals procedure never used	0	
	Appeals procedure used for:		
	Industrial injury benefit	1	ASK c)
	Disablement benefit/lump sum disablement payment	2	ASK c)
	Sickness benefit	3	ASK c)
	Invalidity benefit	4	ASK c)
	Unemployment benefit	5	ASK c)
	IF ANY DIFFICULTIES (61.a) OR ANY APPEALS (61.b) ASK c). OTHERS GO TO Q.62.		

		Col./ Code	Skip to
c	ASK SEPARATELY FOR EACH TYPE OF BENEFIT WHERE RESPONDENT HAD DIFFICULTIES/HAD TO USE APPEALS PROCEDURE		
	What difficulties did you have with your application for ____? Why did you have to use the appeals procedure over your application for ____? What was the problem? What was the result? PROBE FULLY AND RECORD VERBATIM IN APPROPRIATE SPACE		
	Industrial injury benefit ____________		
	Disablement benefit/lump sum disablement payment ____________		
	Sickness benefit ____________		
	Invalidity benefit ____________		
	Unemployment benefit ____________		
	ASK ALL		
62.	SHOW CARD I Did you ever get any of these benefits as a result of your injury/illness or its effects? (Some of them you can get without applying for them.) IF YES Which? PROBE: Any others? UNTIL 'NO'.	Got (13)	ASK
	Got: Industrial injury benefit	1	Q.63&65
	Disablement benefit/lump sum disablement payment	2	Q.64&65
	Sickness benefit	3	Q.66&68
	Invalidity benefit	4	Q.67&68
	Unemployment benefit	5	Q.69
	(Got none of these)	9	SKIP TO Q.70

Q.	Question	Response	Col./Code	Skip to
	IF EVER RECEIVED INDUSTRIAL INJURY BENEFIT (CODE 1 AT Q.62)			
63.a	When your industrial injury benefit started, how much did you get per week? RECORD TO NEAREST £	£____ per week (14-15)		
b	Did this include any allowance for dependants?		(16)	
		Yes	1	
		No	2	
c	For how long in total did you get industrial injury benefit as a result of your injury/illness?		(17)	
		1-6 days	1	
		1 week or longer	2	
		IF 1 WEEK OR LONGER WRITE IN NO. OF WEEKS	[ ][ ] (18-19)	
	NOTE TO INTERVIEWER PAYABLE NORMALLY FOR 26 WEEKS ONLY PER INJURY/ILLNESS. IF AMOUNT OF BENEFIT INCREASED AFTER 12 DAYS RECORD HIGHER AMOUNT AT a)			
	IF EVER RECEIVED DISABLEMENT BENEFIT/LUMP SUM DISABLEMENT PAYMENT (CODE 2 AT Q.62)			
64.a	You mentioned you got disablement benefit or a lump sum disablement payment. At what percentage was your disability assessed?		(20)	
		100%	0	
		90-99%	9	
		80-89%	8	
		70-79%	7	
		60-69%	6	
		50-59%	5	
		40-49%	4	
		30-39%	3	
		20-29%	2	
		10-19%	1	
		Less than 10%	X	
		Don't know	Y	
b	Did you get a continuous disability pension or a lump sum payment?		(21)	
		Continuous pension	1	d)
		Lump sum payment	2	c)
	NOTE TO INTERVIEWER NORMALLY LUMP SUM IF UNDER 20% DISABLED			
	IF GOT LUMP SUM PAYMENT			
	c) How much was the lump sum payment? RECORD TO NEAREST £	£____ (22-24)		

Q.	Question	Response	Col./Code	Skip to
	IF GOT LUMP SUM PAYMENT. NOW SKIP TO Q.65 IF GOT CONTINUOUS PENSION ASK d)-g)			
	d) When your disablement pension started, did you get any of these special allowances: READ OUT AND CODE WHICH APPLY.		Got (25)	
		Special Hardship Allowance?	1	
		Unemployability Supplement?	2	
		Constant Attendance Allowance?	3	
		Exceptionally severe disablement allowance?	4	
		Hospital treatment allowance?	5	
		(None of these)	0	
	e) When your disablement pension started, how much did you get per week, including any allowances? RECORD TO NEAREST £	£____ per week (26-27)		
	f) For how many weeks in total did you receive or have you received a disablement pension?	RECORD NO. OF WEEKS	[ ][ ][ ] (28-30)	
	g) Are you still receiving a disablement pension?		(31)	
		Yes	1	
		No	2	
	IF EVER RECEIVED INDUSTRIAL INJURY BENEFIT/DISABLEMENT BENEFIT OR LUMP SUM DISABLEMENT PAYMENT (CODES 1 OR 2 AT Q.62)			
65.a	Have you received any money from industrial injury benefit, disablement benefit or a lump sum disablement payment since this time last year?		(32)	
		Yes	1	
		No	2	CHECK Q.66
	IF YES TO a)			
	b) How much have you received in total from these benefits since this time last year? RECORD TO NEAREST £	£____ (33-34)		
	IF EVER RECEIVED SICKNESS BENEFIT (CODE 3 AT Q.62) OTHERWISE CHECK Q.67			
66.a	You mentioned that, at some time, you got sickness benefit as a result of your injury/illness or its effects. When your sickness benefit started, how much did you get per week? RECORD TO NEAREST £	£____ per week (35-36)		
b	Did this include any allowance for dependants?		(37)	
		Yes	1	
		No	2	

		Col./Code	Skip to
c	For how long in total did you get sickness benefit as a result of your injury/illness?	(38)	
	1-6 days	1	
	1 week or longer	2	
	IF 1 WEEK OR LONGER, WRITE IN NO. OF WEEKS	(39-40)	
	NOTE TO INTERVIEWER PAYABLE NORMALLY FOR 28 WEEKS ONLY PER INJURY/ILLNESS. IF AMOUNT OF BENEFIT INCREASED AFTER 12 DAYS RECORD HIGHER AMOUNT AT a)		
	IF EVER RECEIVED INVALIDITY BENEFIT (CODE 4 AT Q.62) OTHERWISE CHECK Q.68		
67.a	You mentioned that, at some time, you got invalidity benefit as a result of your injury/illness or its effects. When your invalidity benefit started, how much did you get per week? RECORD TO NEAREST £ £______per week (41-42)		
b	Did this include any allowance for dependants?	(43)	
	Yes	1	
	No	2	
c	For how many weeks in total did you receive or have you received invalidity benefit? RECORD NO. OF WEEKS (44-46)		
d	Are you still receiving invalidity benefit?	(47)	
	Yes	1	
	No	2	
	IF EVER RECEIVED SICKNESS BENEFIT OR INVALIDITY BENEFIT (CODES 3 OR 4 AT Q.62) ASK Q.68. OTHERWISE CHECK Q.69		
68.a	Have you received any money from sickness benefit or invalidity benefit since this time last year?	(48)	
	Yes	1	
	No	2	CHECK Q.69
	IF YES AT a) b) How much have you received in total from sickness benefit or invalidity benefit since this time last year? RECORD TO NEAREST £ £______ (49-50)		

CARD 09

			NOTE TO INTERVIEWER: IF INCREASED AFTER 12 DAYS, HIGHER AMOUNT AT a)
	IF EVER RECEIVED UNEMPLOYMENT BENEFIT (CODE 5 AT Q.62) ASK Q.69. OTHERWISE SKIP TO Q.70		
69.a	You mentioned that, at some time, you got unemployment benefit as a result of your injury/illness or its effects. When your unemployment benefit started, how much did you get per week? RECORD TO NEAREST £ £______per week (51-52)		
b	Did this include any allowance for dependents?	(53)	
	Yes	1	
	No	2	
c	For how long in total did you receive or have you received unemployment benefit?	(54)	
	1-6 days	1	
	1 week or longer	2	
	IF 1 WEEK OR LONGER WRITE IN NO. OF WEEKS	(55-57)	
d	Are you still receiving unemployment benefit?	(58)	
	Yes	1	f)
	No	2	
	IF NO AT d) e) Have you received any money from unemployment benefit since this time last year?		
	Yes	4	
	No	5	Q.70
	IF STILL RECEIVING UNEMPLOYMENT BENEFIT (YES AT d)) OR ANY MONEY RECEIVED SINCE THIS TIME LAST YEAR (YES AT e)) f) How much have you received in total from unemployment benefit since this time last year? RECORD TO NEAREST £ £______ (59-60)		
	ASK ALL		
70.a	SHOW CARD J. This is a further list of state benefits which are sometimes available to people who are disabled or who are ill for a long time. Because of your injury/illness or its effects, did you ever apply for any of these benefits?	APPLIED FOR (61)	
	Non-contributory invalidity pension	1	Q.71
	Attendance allowance	2	b)
	Mobility allowance	3	Q.71
	(Applied for none of these)	9	Q.72
	IF EVER APPLIED FOR ATTENDANCE ALLOWANCE b) How did you find out you might be eligible for an attendance allowance? DO NOT PROMPT	(62)	
	Own doctor	1	
	Other doctor/hospital/nurse	2	
	Other service/social worker etc.	3	
	Friend/relative	4	
	Media	5	
	Other	6	
	Specify ______		

CARD 09

	Col./Code	Skip to
ASK ALL WHO EVER APPLIED FOR ANY BENEFIT LISTED AT Q.70 (ANY CODE OUT OF 1-3 AT Q.70)		
71.a CONTINUE TO SHOW CARD J Did you ever have any difficulties of any sort with your applications for any of these benefits? IF YES With which benefits? PROBE: Any others? UNTIL 'NO'	(63)	
No difficulties with any	0	b)
Difficulties with application for:		
Non-contributory invalidity pension	1	ASK b) THEN c)
Attendance allowance	2	
Mobility allowance	3	
b CONTINUE TO SHOW CARD J Did you ever have to use the appeals procedure in connection with your applications for any of these benefits? IF YES For which benefits? PROBE: Any others? UNTIL 'NO'	(64)	
Appeals procedure never used	0	
Appeals procedure used for:		
Non-contributory invalidity pension	1	ASK c)
Attendance allowance	2	
Mobility allowance	3	

IF ANY DIFFICULTIES (71.a) OR ANY APPEALS (71.b) ASK c). ALL OTHERS GO TO Q.72.

ASK SEPARATELY FOR EACH TYPE OF BENEFIT WHERE RESPONDENT HAD DIFFICULTIES/HAD TO USE APPEALS PROCEDURE

c) What difficulties did you have with your application for ____? Why did you have to use the appeals procedure over your application for ____? What was the problem? What was the result? PROBE FULLY AND RECORD VERBATIM IN APPROPRIATE SPACE

Non-contributory invalidity pension ____________________

Attendance allowance ____________________

Mobility allowance ____________________

CARD 09

	Col./Code	Skip to
ASK ALL		
72. SHOW CARD J. Did you ever get any of these benefits as a result of your injury/illness or its effects? IF YES Which? PROBE: Any other? UNTIL 'NO'.	Got (65)	
Non-contributory invalidity pension	1	ASK Q73
Attendance allowance	2	ASK Q74
Mobility allowance	3	ASK Q75
(Got none of these)	9	SKIP TO Q.76
IF EVER RECEIVED NON-CONTRIBUTORY INVALIDITY PENSION (CODE 1 AT Q.72)		
73.a For how many weeks in total did you receive or have you received non-contributory invalidity pension? WRITE IN NO. OF WEEKS ☐	(66-67)	
b Are you still receiving non-contributory invalidity pension?	(68)	
Yes	1	
No	2	
NOTE TO INTERVIEWER: NON-CONTRIBUTORY INVALIDITY PENSION ONLY STARTED IN NOVEMBER 1975.		
IF EVER RECEIVED ATTENDANCE ALLOWANCE (CODE 2 AT Q.72)		
74.a When your attendance allowance started, how much did you get per week? RECORD TO NEAREST £ £____ (69-70) per week		
b For how many weeks in total did you receive or have you received an attendance allowance? WRITE IN NO. OF WEEKS ☐	(71-73)	
c Are you still receiving an attendance allowance?	(74)	
Yes	1	
No	2	
IF EVER RECEIVED MOBILITY ALLOWANCE (CODE 3 AT Q.72)		
75.a For how many weeks in total did you receive or have you received a mobility allowance? WRITE IN NO. OF WEEKS ☐	(75-76)	
b Are you still receiving a mobility allowance?	(77)	
Yes	1	
No	2	
NOTE TO INTERVIEWER: MOBILITY ALLOWANCE ONLY STARTED IN JANUARY 1976.		

(78-80 Blank)
Record No. (1-4)
Card (10) (5-6)
P.423 (7-9)

ASK ALL

76. Because of your injury/illness or its effects, did you or any other member of your household ever apply for family income supplement or for supplementary benefit?

	Applied for (10)	
Family income supplement	1	
Supplementary benefit	2	
(Applied for neither)	9	Q.78

ASK ALL WHO EVER APPLIED FOR FAMILY INCOME SUPPLEMENT OR SUPPLEMENTARY BENEFIT (CODE 1 OR 2 AT Q.76)

77.a Did you or any other member of your household ever have any difficulties of any sort with your applications for family income supplement or supplementary benefit? IF YES With which?

	(11)	
No difficulties with either	0	b)
Difficulties with application for:		
Family income supplement	1	ASK b) THEN c)
Supplementary benefit	2	

b Did you ever have to use the appeals procedure in connection with your applications for family income supplement or supplementary benefit? IF YES For which benefits?

	(12)	
Appeals procedure never used	0	
Appeals procedure used for:		
Family income supplement	1	ASK c)
Supplementary benefit	2	

IF ANY DIFFICULTIES (Q.77a) OR ANY APPEALS (Q.77b) ASK c).
ALL OTHERS GO TO Q.78

ASK SEPARATELY FOR EACH BENEFIT WHERE THERE WERE DIFFICULTIES/APPEAL PROCEDURE WAS USED.

c) What difficulties did you have with your application for ____? Why did you have to use the appeals procedure over your application for ____? What was the problem? What was the result? PROBE FULLY AND RECORD VERBATIM IN APPROPRIATE SPACE.

Family income supplement ______________________

Supplementary benefit ______________________

ASK ALL

78. Did you or anyone in your household ever get family income supplement or supplementary benefit as a result of your injury/illness or its effects? IF YES Which?

	Got (13)	
Family Income Supplement	1	ASK Q79
Supplementary benefit	2	ASK Q80
Got neither	9	SKIP TO Q.81

CARD 10

	Col./Code	Skip to

ASK ALL WHO EVER RECEIVED FAMILY INCOME SUPPLEMENT (CODE 1 AT Q.78)

79.a When your family income supplement started, how much did you get per week?

RECORD TO NEAREST £ £______ per week (14-15)

b For how many weeks in total did or has your household received family income supplement?

WRITE IN NO. OF WEEKS [ ] (16-18)

c Is your household still receiving family income supplement?

	(19)
Yes	1
No	2

ASK ALL WHO EVER RECEIVED SUPPLEMENTARY BENEFIT (CODE 2 AT Q.78)

80.a When your supplementary benefit started, how much did you get per week?

RECORD TO NEAREST £ £______ per week (20-21)

b For how many weeks in total did you receive or have you received supplementary benefit?

RECORD NO. OF WEEKS [ ] (22-24)

c Are you still receiving supplementary benefit?

	(25)
Yes	1
No	2

ASK ALL

Now I would like to turn to personal insurance policies.

81.a When the injury happened/when the illness started, did you have any insurance for illness or personal injuries to you or any other personal insurance such as:
READ OUT AND RING WHICH APPLY

	(26)	
Personal accident insurance?	1	
Personal accident cover under a comprehensive motor policy?	2	
Insurance for regular payments during illness or time off work?	3	
Insurance for hospital fees and other medical costs?	4	
Other insurances for personal injury or illness?	5	
(SPECIFY) ______________________		
(None of these)	6	Q.82

IF ANY MENTIONED AT a)

b) Following on your injury/illness, did you receive any money under any of these insurances?

Yes	8	
No	9	e)

IF YES AT b) ASK c) AND d)

c) Up to now, how much money in all have you received for your injury/illness or its effects from these insurances?

RECORD TO NEAREST £ £______ (27-28)

	Col./Code	Skip to
d) Is £______ (AMOUNT AT c) about what you expected to get from these insurances for your injury/illness or its effects or is it more than you expected or less than you expected?	(29)	
About expected amount	1	
More than expected	2	
Less than expected	3	
IF ANY INSURANCES MENTIONED AT a)		
e) Are there any insurances you had under which you expected to get money for your injury/illness or its effects, but in fact have not so far got any money?	(30)	
Yes - there are insurances expected to pay which have not	1	
No such insurances	2	
IF GOT LESS THAN EXPECTED (CODE 3 AT d) OR YES (CODE 1 AT e)		
f) Why have you not got what you expected? PROBE FULLY AND RECORD VERBATIM. ______		
IF ANY INSURANCES MENTIONED AT Q.81a)		
g) You mentioned that at the time the injury happened/the time the illness started, you were covered by ____ (READ OUT INSURANCES MENTIONED AT Q.81a). Since then, has your cover under any of these insurances been cancelled or been reduced?	(31)	
Yes	1	
No	2	Q.82
h) IF YES TO g) Who cancelled or reduced the cover? Was it you or the insurance company? Self	4	
Insurance Co.	5	
ASK ALL		
82.a Since your injury/since your illness started, have you or has anyone else on your behalf taken out any new or extra insurance on your life or against illness or personal injuries to you?	(32)	
Yes	1	
No	2	Q.83
IF YES AT a)		
b) What type of insurance is that? ______	OUO (33)	
ASK ALL		
83.a Since your injury/illness have you had any difficulty in obtaining insurance on your life or against illness or personal injuries to you or any difficulty in obtaining such insurance at normal rates?	(34)	
Difficulty in getting any at all	1	
Difficulty in getting at normal rates	2	
Neither of these	3	Q.84
IF ANY DIFFICULTY MENTIONED AT a)		
b) Can you tell me about these difficulties? PROBE FULLY AND RECORD VERBATIM.		

PART 8 ACCOMMODATION AND HOUSEHOLD INCOME

	Address	District	Col./Code	Skip to
ASK ALL I now want to ask you some questions about your home and the people who live with you.				
84.a How long have you been living at this address? (RING ONE CODE IN FIRST COLUMN)	(35)	(36)		
b How long have you lived in this district? (RING ONE CODE IN SECOND COLUMN) 12 months or less	1	1		
Over 1 year up to 2 years	2	2		
Over 2 years up to 5 years	3	3		
Over 5 years up to 10 years	4	4		
Over 10 years	5	5		
c Have you moved homes since your injury/illness started?			(37)	
Yes			1	
No			2	Q.85
IF YES AT c) ASK d) AND e)			(38)	
d) Was this because of your injury/illness or for some other reason? Because of injury/illness			1	
Other reason			2	
e) Before you moved, how much was your accommodation costing you per week/month/year? Please include any rates and mortgage payments, but deduct any rebates. £______ per ______ (O.U.O.)			(39-41)	
ASK ALL			(42)	
85.a Have you ever thought about moving from this home? Yes			A	
No			1	Q.86
IF YES AT a)				
b) Has your injury/illness had any effect on these plans? Yes			2	
No			3	Q.86
IF YES AT b)			(43)	
c) What effect has it had? Wants to move because of injury/illness			1	
Put off moving because of injury/illness			2	
Other (SPECIFY) ______				

CARD 10

	Question	Response	Col./Code	Skip to
	ASK ALL		(44)	
86.a	What sort of accommodation does your household have here?	Whole house/bungalow	1	
		Self-contained flat/maisonette	2	
		Part of house (not self-contained)	3	
		Single room (not self-contained)	4	
b	Do you or your household own this accommodation or do you rent it? IF RENTED Do you rent it privately or from the council?		(45)	
		Owned/being bought on mortgage	1	
		Rented privately	2	
		Rented from council	3	
		Other (SPECIFY) ______		
c	How much does your present accommodation cost you per week/month/year? Please include any rates and mortgage payments but deduct any rebates. £______ per______	O.U.O.	(46-48)	
	ASK ALL			
87.a	Does this household have the use of any of the following? READ OUT AND ENTER IN GRID BELOW			
	FOR INSIDE FLUSH TOILET AND FIXED BATH OR SHOWER ONLY: IF HAVE USE OF:			
	b) Is it just used by your household or is it shared with other households?			

	(a) Have use of	(a) Do not have	(b) Have sole use	(b) Have shared use
	(49)		(50)	(51)
An inside flush toilet	1	B	1	1
A fixed bath or shower	2	B	2	2
A supply of hot water, that is, a hot tap or geyser	3	B		
Your own telephone	4	B		
A refrigerator	5	B		
A washing machine	6	B		
A car or van for personal use	7	B		

	Question	Response	Col./Code	Skip to
	IF HOUSEHOLD HAS CAR/VAN		(52)	
	c) Do you yourself have a full current driving licence?	Yes	1	
		No	2	Q.88
	IF YES AT c)			
	d) Howadays, do you drive an invacar, an ordinary car, both or neither?	Invacar only	4	
		Ordinary car only	5	
		Both invacar and ordinary car	6	
		Neither	7	

NOTE TO INTERVIEWER

ORDINARY CAR INCLUDES ADAPTED CAR

CARD 10

	Question	Response	Col./Code	Skip to
	ASK ALL			
88.a	Have any alterations been made to this home because of your injury/illness or its effects?		(53)	
		Yes	1	
		No	2	Q.89
	IF YES ASK b) AND c)		(54)	
	b) Who arranged for these alterations to be done?	Self	1	
		Other member of household	2	
		Other relative	3	
		Local authority	4	
		Other (SPECIFY) ______	5	
			(55)	
	c) Did you yourself or your household have to pay anything for these alterations?	Yes	1	
		No	2	Q.89
	IF YES AT c)			
	d) About how much did you have to pay?	RECORD TO NEAREST £ £____ (56-59)		
	ASK ALL			
89.a	Have you been involved in extra household expenses because of your injury/illness or its effects, such as:- READ OUT	Yes (60)		
		Extra heating	1	
		Telephone bills	2	
		Maintenance bills	3	
		Any other household expenses	4	
		(Specify) ______		
		(None of these)	9	Q.90
	IF INCURRED ANY EXTRA EXPENSES			
	b) About how much extra have you spent on these things over the last 12 months?	RECORD TO NEAREST £ £____ (61-64)		

	Col./Code	Skip to
90.a Including yourself, and including any children, how many people were there in your household at the time of your injury/the time your illness started? RECORD IN GRID BELOW.		
b Including yourself, how many of these people were aged 16 or over? RECORD IN GRID BELOW.		
c Including yourself, how many people in your household, if any, were working full-time (i.e. 31 hours a week or more) at the time of your injury/the time your illness started? RECORD IN GRID BELOW.		
d And how many people in your household, if any, were working part-time (6-30 hours a week) at the time of your injury/the time your illness started? RECORD IN GRID BELOW.		

	(a) Total in h'hold	(b) Aged 16+ in h'hold	(c) Working full-time in h'hold	(d) Working part-time in h'hold
	(65)	(66)	(67)	(68)
None	0	0	0	0
1 person	1	1	1	1
2 people	2	2	2	2
3 people	3	3	3	3
4 people	4	4	4	4
5 people	5	5	5	5
6 or more people	6	6	6	6

		Col./Code	Skip to
e Did any member of your household leave home because of your injury/illness or its effects?		(69)	
	Yes	1	
	No	2	g)
IF YES TO e) f) Who was that?	Spouse	4	
	Parent	5	
	Son/daughter	6	
	Other person	7	
(Specify) ______			
g Did any friend or relative move in with you because of your injury/illness or its effects?		(70)	
	Yes	1	
	No	2	
h Did any of your friends or relatives move nearer here because of your injury/illness or its effects?		(71)	
	Yes	1	
	No	2	
i Nowadays, have you any relatives or in-laws who live near here (say within a mile or two)?		(72)	
	Yes	1	
	No	2	

91.a SHOW CARD K Including yourself, was any member of your household receiving income from any of these sources just before your injury/just before your illness started? READ OUT AND RING 'YES' OR 'NO' FOR EACH ON CARD.

b What was the one main source of income in your household just before your injury/just before your illness started? DO NOT PROMPT.

		91(a) Yes	91(a) No	91(b) Main Source
		(73)		(74)
(a)/(b)	Interest from stocks, shares, annuities or other investments	1	A	1
	Rents	2	A	2
	Regular allowance from employer/relative outside household	3	A	3
	Retirement pension from employer	4	A	4
	Retirement (OAP) or widows pension	5	A	5
	Unemployment benefit	6	A	6
	Sickness benefit	7	A	7
	Invalidity benefit	8	A	8
	Disablement benefit	9	A	9
	Supplementary benefit	0	A	0
	Family Income supplement	X	A	X
	Attendance allowance, invalid care or other special state allowance	Y	A	Y
				(75)
(b) only	Wage/salary of victim			1
	Wage/salary of other household member			2
	Other (WRITE IN) ______			3

		Col./Code	Skip to
ASK ALL		Yes (76)	
92.a As a result of your injury/illness or its effects did any member of your household apart from yourself: READ OUT ...	Give up work	1	
	Work shorter hours	2	
	Change jobs to one that was less well paid	3	
	Put off starting a job	4	
	(None of these)	9	Q.93
IF YES TO ANY AT a)		(77)	
b) Did this reduce the income of the household?	Yes	1	
	No	2	Q.93
IF YES AT b) c) By how much per week? RECORD TO NEAREST £	£ ______ (78-80)		

Record No. (1-4)
Card 11 (5-6)
P.423 (7-9)

	Col./Code	Skip to
ASK ALL		
93.a As a result of your injury/illness did any member of your household:	Yes (10)	
READ OUT ..... Start a job	1	
Work longer hours	1	
Change jobs to one that was better paid	1	
(None of these)	1	Q.94
IF YES TO ANY AT a)	(11)	
b) Did this increase the income of the household? Yes	1	
No	2	Q.94
IF YES AT b)		
c) By how much per week? RECORD TO NEAREST £ £______ (12-14)		
ASK ALL		
94.a Because of your injury/illness did you or any other member of your household have to borrow money or run up any debts?	(15)	
Yes	1	
No	2	Q.95
IF YES AT a)		
b) About how much? RECORD TO NEAREST £ £______ (16-18)		
ASK ALL		
95.a Because of your injury/illness, did you or did any other member of hour household have to spend any money from savings or stop saving?	(19)	
Yes	1	
No	2	Q.96
IF YES AT a)		
b) Please tell me the details. PROBE FULLY		

CARD 11

ASK ALL

96.a SHOW CARD K Including yourself, is any member of your household receiving income from any of these sources now? READ OUT AND RING 'YES' OR 'NO' FOR EACH ON CARD.

b What is the one main source of income in your household now? DO NOT PROMPT

	96(a) Yes	96(a) No	96(b) Main Source
	(20)		(21)
a/b) Interest from stocks, shares, annuities or other investments	1	A	1
Rents	2	A	2
Regular allowance from employer/relative outside household	3	A	3
Retirement pension from employer	4	A	4
Retirement (OAP) or widows pension	5	A	5
Unemployment benefit	6	A	6
Sickness benefit	7	A	7
Invalidity benefit	8	A	8
Disablement benefit	9	A	9
Supplementary benefit	0	A	0
Family income supplement	X	A	X
Attendance allowance, invalid care or other special state allowance	Y	A	Y
			(22)
b) Only Wage/salary of respondent victim			1
Wage/salary of other household member			2
Other (WRITE IN) ______			3

ASK ALL

97 Taking all sources of income into account, what is the total gross income of your household now, before any deductions for tax, national insurance etc.?
SHOW CARD H ASK FOR APPROPRIATE LETTER
SEE END OF QUESTIONNAIRE FOR CARD

	(23)
J	2
K	5
M	3
N	4
P	1
R	8
S	7
T	6

IF MISFORTUNE VICTIM IS HEAD OF HOUSEHOLD, NOW SKIP TO PART 9, Q.99

		Col./Code	Skip to
98	OCCUPATION (PRESENT OR LAST MAIN PAID JOB) OF HEAD OF HOUSEHOLD IF OTHER THAN MISFORTUNE VICTIM		
	Name/title of job ______		
	Description of Activity ______		
	Skill/training/qualifications/experience required for job ______	OUO (24-25)	
	Supervision/management responsibilities (incl. no. of people supervised) ______	(26-28)	
	No. of employees at establishment:	(29)	
	1 only	1	
	2-24	2	
	25 or more	3	
	Industry/business/profession (of employer) ______	(30)	
	Employment Status: Employee	1	
	Self-employed	2	

PART 9 LEGAL

ASK ALL WHOSE MISFORTUNE TYPE IS AA AB AC OR IA. IF MISFORTUNE TYPE IS IB, SKIP TO PART 10, Q.155

Section 1 Pre-legal Procedures

		Col./Code	Skip to
		(31)	
99.a	Do you now or did you at any time feel that someone should pay you compensation for your injury/illness? Yes	1	
	No	2	Q.100
	IF YES AT a) ASK b) AND c)		
	b) Who did you think should pay you compensation? ______	OUO (32)	
	c) Why did you think ____ (PERSON MENTIONED AT b) should pay you compensation? PROBE FULLY ______	OUO (33)	

		Col./Code	Skip to
100a	CHECK BACK TO Q.5a) ON PAGE 4. CHECK WHETHER ANY PERSON MENTIONED AT 5a) WHO IS NOT MENTIONED AT Q.99b)	(34)	
	Person mentioned at 5a) but not 99b)	1	b)
	No such person	2	Q101
	IF YES AT 100a)		
	b) You mentioned earlier that your injury/illness was in some way the fault of ____ (PERSON AT 5a). Did you at any time feel that they should pay you compensation?	(35)	
	Yes	1	Q101
	No	2	
	IF NO AT b)		
	c) Why not? PROBE FULLY	OUO (36)	
	ASK ALL		
101a	Did you at any time think it might be possible to make a formal claim for compensation from anyone over your injury/illness? (..... I am not talking about social security, sick pay, claims for damage to property or claims against your own insurance. I mean a claim against some person, company or other body who might be legally responsible for compensating you)	(37)	
	Yes	1	
	No	2	Q.102
	IF YES AT a)		
	b) Against whom did you think it might be possible to make a claim? ______	OUO (38)	
	ASK ALL		
102a	Did you yourself or did anyone else on your behalf talk to, write to or contact a lawyer at any time about the possibility of your making a claim for compensation?	(39)	
	Yes	1	
	No	2	
	IF "YES" AT a) PREFACE b) AND c) BY "BEFORE A LAWYER WAS CONTACTED".		
b	(Before a lawyer was contacted) did you ever discuss the possibility of making a claim with anyone else or do anything to get advice about the possibility of making a claim or do anything to make a claim?	(40)	
	Yes	1	
	No	2	
c	(Before a lawyer was contacted) did anyone else ever talk to you or advise you about the possibility of your making a claim or seek advice on your behalf about the possibility of making a claim or do anything on your behalf to make a claim?	(41)	
	Yes	1	
	No	2	

CHECK ANSWERS TO Q.102

- IF TALKED TO ANYONE OR DID ANYTHING BEFORE SEEING LAWYER (YES AT b) OR c) SKIP TO Q.104
- IF CONTACTED LAWYER AND NO OTHER (YES AT a); NO AT b) AND c) SKIP TO SECTION 2, Q.108
- IF NO DISCUSSION OR ACTION (NO AT a) AND b) AND c) ASK Q.103

	Col./Code	Skip to
103 IF NOTHING DONE ABOUT CLAIM (NO AT 102a), b) AND c) CHECK ANSWERS TO 99a), 100b) AND 101a)		
IF THERE IS NO "YES" ANSWER, SKIP TO PART 10, Q.155		
IF EVER THOUGHT OTHER SHOULD PAY COMPENSATION OR COULD BE CLAIMED AGAINST, ASK:		
You mentioned that at some time you thought ____ should have paid you compensation or that it might be possible for you to make a legal claim against them. Why did you never do anything about it? PROBE FULLY AND RECORD VERBATIM.	000 (42)	
NOW SKIP TO PART 10, Q.155		

ASK ALL WHO DISCUSSED CLAIM WITH OTHER PERSON OR TOOK ANY ACTION BEFORE SEEING A LAWYER (YES AT 102b) OR c)

104a You said that, (before you talked to a lawyer), you talked to someone or were in contact with someone about the possibility of making a claim. Who was that? Any-one else? PROBE TO "NO" AND RECORD IN GRID BELOW.

ASK b) SEPARATELY FOR EACH MENTIONED AT a)

b) How long after the injury/after the illness started was your first contact with ____ about the possibility of getting money as compensation?

	(a) People Contacted	(b) Time of advice: Under 1 week	1 week, under 1 month	1 but under 6 months	6 months	Col./Code
employer	1	2	3	4	5	(43)
insurance co. of employer	7	8	9	0	X	
other representative of employer	1	2	3	4	5	(44)
person responsible (other than employer)	7	8	9	0	X	
insurance co. of that person	1	2	3	4	5	(45)
other representative of that person	7	8	9	0	X	
trade union official	1	2	3	4	5	(46)
Citizens Advice Bureau	7	8	9	0	X	
AA/RAC	1	2	3	4	5	(47)
policeman	7	8	9	0	X	
Own insurance co.	1	2	3	4	5	(48)
doctor at hospital	7	8	9	0	X	
social worker at hospital	1	2	3	4	5	(49)
fellow patient at hospital	7	8	9	0	X	
own doctor (GP)	1	2	3	4	5	(50)
workmate	7	8	9	0	X	
friend	1	2	3	4	5	(51)
relative	7	8	9	0	X	
Other (specify)	1	2	3	4	5	(52)

		Col./Code	Skip to
		(53)	
c Did any of these people say you had a chance of getting some money as compensation?	Yes	1	
	No	2	f)
IF YES AT c) ASK d) AND e)			
d) Who? Anyone else? PROBE TO "NO" AND RECORD IN GRID BELOW.			
e) Who first had the idea you might get some money in compensation? Was it you or one of the other people you have mentioned?		(54)	
	Self	1	
IF OTHER Who was it?	Other person	2	
IF OTHER, RECORD WHO IN GRID BELOW			
f Did any of the people with whom you were in contact (before you talked to a lawyer) say you had little or no chance of getting any money as compensation?		(55)	
	Yes	1	
	No	2	Q.106

IF YES AT f)

g) Who was that? Anyone else? PROBE TO "NO" AND RECORD IN GRID BELOW.

	(d) Said claim possible	(e) First said claim possible	(f) Said no chance	Col./Code
employer	1	2	3	(56)
insurance co. of employer	5	6	7	
other representative of employer	1	2	3	(57)
person responsible (other than employer)	5	6	7	
insurance co. of that person	1	2	3	(58)
other representative of that person	5	6	7	
trade union official	1	2	3	(59)
Citizens Advice Bureau	5	6	7	
AA/RAC	1	2	3	(60)
policeman	5	6	7	
own insurance co.	1	2	3	(61)
doctor at hospital	5	6	7	
social worker at hospital	1	2	3	(62)
fellow patient at hospital	5	6	7	
own doctor (GP)	1	2	3	(63)
workmate	5	6	7	
friend	1	2	3	(64)
relative	5	6	7	
Other (specify)	1	2	3	(65)

CARD 11

		Col./ Code	Skip to
	ASK OF EACH PERSON MENTIONED AT Q.104g) AS SAYING VICTIM HAD LITTLE/ NO CHANCE OF COMPENSATION		
105	You said that _____ said you had little or no chance of getting any money in compensation. What reasons did they give for saying this?		

PERSON CONTACTED (AS PRE-CODED AT Q.104)		REASONS GIVEN	Col./Code
	0U0		0U0
	(66-67)		(68)
	(69-70)		(71)
	(72-73)		(74)
	(75-76)		(77)

(78-80) Blank

Record No. (1-4)
Card (12) (5-6)
P.423 (7-9)

			Col./ Code	Skip to
	ASK ALL WHO DISCUSSED CLAIM WITH OTHER PERSON OR TOOK ANY ACTION BEFORE CONTACTING A LAWYER (YES AT 102b) OR c)		(10)	
106a	(Before a lawyer was contacted IF YES AT Q.102a) did you or did anyone else do anything about claiming compensation from anyone for the injury/illness you had suffered?	Yes	1	
		No	2	CHECK Q.107
	IF YES AT a) ASK b) AND c)			
	b) Who was that?			
	c) What was done?			

106b) Person taking action		106c) What was done	Col./Code
			0U0
Self			(11)
	0U0		
Other (AS PRECODED AT Q.104)	(12-13)		(14)
	(15-16)		(17)
	(18-19)		(20)

			Col./ Code	Skip to
d)	(Before a lawyer was contacted) was any offer of money to settle your claim for your injuries/disabilities made as a result of these actions?		(21)	
		Yes	1	
		No	2	CHECK Q.107
	IF YES AT d)		0U0	
e)	Who made the offer?		(22-23)	

CARD 12

			Col./ Code	Skip to
	IF EVER CONTACTED LAWYER (YES AT 102a) SKIP TO SECTION 2, Q.108			
	IF NEVER CONTACTED LAWYER (NO AT 102a) ASK Q.107			
	IF CLAIM DISCUSSED WITH OTHER/ACTION TAKEN (YES AT 102b) OR c) BUT LAWYER NEVER CONTACTED (NO AT 102a)			
107a	**You talked about the possibility of making a claim, but no lawyer was ever contacted. Why not? PROBE FULLY**		0U0 (24)	
b	**Had you ever yourself consulted a lawyer before about any other matter?**		(25)	
		Yes	A	
		No	0	SEC.3 Q.121
	IF YES AT a)			
	c) How often?	**Once**	1	SEC.3 Q.121
		More than once	2	SEC.3 Q.121

SECTION 2 - LEGAL ADVICE AND ACTION

			Col./ Code	Skip to
	ASK ALL WHO CONTACTED A LAWYER OR ON WHOSE BEHALF A LAWYER WAS CONTACTED (YES TO 102a). OTHERS SKIP TO SEC. 3 Q.121			
108a)	You mentioned a lawyer was contacted about the possibility of you making a claim. What this wholly your own idea or did anyone else at any time suggest it?		(26)	
		Wholly own idea	1	
		Other suggested	2	
	IF ANY OTHER MENTIONED AT a) ASK b) AND c)			
	b) Who else thought a lawyer should be contacted? RECORD IN GRID BELOW			
	c) Who first had the idea a lawyer should be contacted? Was it you or one of the others you have mentioned? IF OTHER Who was it? RECORD IN GRID BELOW.			

Card 12

d) ASK ALL IF LAWYER WAS CONTACTED

Who actually first contacted the lawyer? Was it you or someone else?
IF OTHER Who was it? RECORD IN GRID BELOW

	(b) Suggested contact	(c) First idea of contact	(d) First made contact
	(27)	(29)	(31)
Employer	1	1	1
Insurance company of employer	2	2	2
Other representative of employer	3	3	3
Person responsible (other than employer)	4	4	4
Insurance company of that person	5	5	5
Other representative of that person	6	6	6
Trade union official	7	7	7
Citizens Advice Bureau	8	8	8
AA/RAC	9	9	9
Policeman	0	0	0
Own insurance company	X	X	X
	(28)	(30)	(32)
Doctor at hospital	1	1	1
Social worker at hospital	2	2	2
Fellow patient at hospital	3	3	3
Own doctor (GP)	4	4	4
Workmate	5	5	5
Friend	6	6	6
Relative	7	7	7
Other (specify)______	8	8	8
Self		9	9

109. ASK ALL

a) How long after your injury/after your illness started was a lawyer first consulted about the possibility of a claim for compensation?

	Col./Code	Skip to
	(33)	
Under 1 week	1	
1 week, under 1 month	2	
1 month, under 6 months	3	
6 months or more	4	

b) Had you ever yourself consulted a lawyer before about any other matter?

	Col./Code	Skip to
	(34)	
Yes	A	
No	0	(d)

c) IF YES TO b) How often?

	Col./Code	Skip to
Once	1	
More than once	2	

CARD 12

d) ASK ALL Did you choose the lawyer yourself or did someone else recommend him or did the consultation happen in some other way?

	Col./Code	Skip to
Chose personally	4	(g)
Recommended by other	5	(e)
Other method	6	(f)

e) IF RECOMMENDED BY OTHER AT d)

Who recommended him? RECORD ANSWER AS IN PRECODES FOR Q.108 ______ OUO (35-36)

f) IF "OTHER METHOD" AT d) How did it happen that that particular lawyer was consulted? ______ OUO (37)

g) ASK ALL What sort of lawyer was it who was first consulted?

DO NOT PROMPT

	Col./Code	Skip to
	(38)	
A solicitor in private practice	1	
A trade union lawyer	2	
Citizens Advice Bureau lawyer	3	
Neighbourhood Law Centre lawyer	4	
AA/RAC lawyer	5	
Other lawyer (specify)______	6	

110. ASK ALL What advice did the lawyer who was first consulted give? Did he say you should: READ OUT...

	Col./Code	Skip to
	(39)	
Make a claim for compensation	1	Q.111
Drop the idea of making a claim	2	Q.112
OR Do something else	3	Q.113

111. IF ADVISED TO MAKE CLAIM (CODE 1 AT Q.110)

a) How long after the injury happened/after your illness began did the lawyer give you this advice? ____ months (40-41)

b) Against whom did he advise you could claim? ______ OUO (42)

c) Was an insurance company dealing with the claim on that person's behalf?

	Col./Code	Skip to
	(43)	
Yes	1	Q.114
No	2	Q.114

112. IF ADVISED TO DROP CLAIM (CODE 2 AT Q.110)

a) What reasons did he give for advising you to drop the idea of making a claim? PROBE FULLY ______ OUO (44)

b) Did you accept this advice?

	Col./Code	Skip to
	(45)	
Yes	1	Q.114
No	2	

c) IF NO TO b) Why did you not accept this advice? PROBE FULLY ______ OUO (46)

NOW SKIP TO Q.114

Card 12

	Question		Col./Code	Skip to
113.	IF ADVISED TO DO SOMETHING ELSE (CODE 3 AT Q.110 What did he advise you to do? PROBE FULLY __________ __________ __________		OUO (47)	
114.	ASK ALL		(48)	
a)	Did you yourself ever meet a lawyer personally to discuss the possibility of making a claim for compensation for your injury/illness?	Yes	1	
		No	2	Q.115
	IF EVER MET LAWYER (YES AT a) ASK b) - d)		(49)	
	b) The first time you met a lawyer, did you see him by yourself or did someone else go with you to see him? IF ACCOMPANIED Who was that?	Saw alone	1	
		Saw accompanied by:		
	(SPECIFY)__________			
	c) How many times in all did you yourself meet a lawyer or talk to one over the telephone about your claim? RECORD NUMBER OF T MES__________ (50)			
			(51)	
	d) Did you have to spend any money on travelling to see lawyers?	Yes	1	
		No	2	(f)
	e) IF SPENT ANY MONEY ON TRAVEL How much in all did you spend on travelling to see lawyers? RECORD TO NEAREST £ £________ (52-54)			
			(55)	
f)	IF EVER MET LAWYER (YES AT a) Did you lose any wages or other earnings because of your visits to lawyers?	Yes	1	
		No	2	Q.115
	g) IF YES TO f) About how much in all did you lose in wages or other earnings because of your visits to lawyers? RECORD TO NEAREST £ £________ (56-58)			
115a)	Did a lawyer take any action or start any negotiations to make a claim on your behalf?		(59)	
		Yes	1	Q.116
		No	2	
	IF NO TO a)		(60)	
	b) Did you or did anyone else subsequently take any action or start any negotiations to make a claim on your behalf?	Yes	1	
		No	2	Q.117

Card 12

IF YES TO b)

c) Who what that?

d) What was done?

(c) Person taking action	OUO	(d) What was done	OUO
Self			(67)
Other (specify)	(61-62)		(68)
	(63-64)		(69)
	(65-66)	NOW SKIP TO Q.117	(70)

	Question		Col./Code	Skip to
116a)	IF LAWYER EVER TOOK ANY ACTION OR STARTED ANY NEGOTIATIONS (YES AT Q.115a)		(71)	
	Have there ever been any delays or waiting periods of any sort about your claim?	Yes	1	
		No	2	Q.117
	IF ANY DELAYS (YES AT a)		(72)	
	b) Did your lawyer ever advise that you should delay your claim?	Yes	1	
		No	2	d)
	IF LAWYER ADVISED DELAY			
	c) Why did he advise you to do that?__________ __________ __________ __________		OUO (73)	
	IF ANY DELAYS (YES AT a)		(74)	
	d) Were there any other delays?	Yes	1	
		No	2	Q.117
	IF OTHER DELAYS		(75)	ASK
	e) What were the reasons? Were they caused by your own side or by something else? CODE AS MANY AS APPLY	Own side	1	f) & g)
		Other side	2	h) & i)
		Something else	3	(j)
	IF OTHER DELAYS FROM OWN SIDE (CODE 1 AT e) ASK f) AND g)		(76)	
	f) Were the other delays on your own side caused by: READ OUT:	Your lawyer	1	
	CODE AS MANY AS APPLY	OR your insurance company	2	
		OR delays in receiving medical reports	3	
		OR some other reason	4	

Card 12

Question	Response	Col./Code	Skip to
g) Can you give me details of these delays on your own side. PROBE FULLY AND RECORD VERBATIM ____			
IF DELAYS FROM OTHER SIDE (CODE 2 AT e) ASK h) AND i)			
h) Were the delays on the other side caused by:		(77)	
READ OUT:	their lawyers	1	
CODE AS MANY AS APPLY	OR their insurance company	2	
	OR delays in receiving medical reports	3	
	OR some other reason	4	
i) Can you give me details of these delays on the other side. PROBE FULLY AND RECORD VERBATIM ____			
IF DELAYS MENTIONED OTHER THAN DELAYS FROM OWN OR OTHER SIDE (CODE 3 AT e) ASK j)			
j) Can you give me details of the other delays you mentioned which were not caused by your own side or the other side. PROBE FULLY AND RECORD VERBATIM ____		(78-80)	Blank)
	Record No.	(1-4)	
	Card (13)	(5-6)	
	P.423	(7-9)	
117a) ASK ALL Did you ever have any complaints, disagreements or problems of any sort about the way your case was handled by lawyers?		(10)	
	Yes	1	
	No	2	Q.118
b) What complaints, disagreements or problems did you have? PROBE FULLY AND RECORD VERBATIM ____ ____		OUO (11-12)	
118. ASK ALL			
a) At the time you were discussing making a claim, did you know about the legal advice scheme (that is, the green form scheme)?		(13)	
	Yes	1	
	No	2	CHECK Q.119
IF YES TO a) ASK b) AND c)		(14)	
b) How did you learn about it?	From lawyer	1	
	From media	2	
	From other person	3	
(SPECIFY)____			
c) Did you use this scheme?		(15)	
	Yes	1	
	No	2	

Card 13

Question	Response	Col./Code	Skip to
IF LAWYER EVER TOOK ANY ACTION OR STARTED NEGOTIATIONS (YES AT Q.115a) ASK Q.119 — OTHERS SKIP TO Q.120			
119. IF LAWYER EVER TOOK ACTION OR STARTED NEGOTIATIONS		(16)	
a) At the time the lawyer started taking some action on your behalf, did you know about the legal aid scheme?	Yes	1	
	No	2	Q.120
IF YES AT a) ASK b) AND c)		(17)	
b) How did you learn about it?	From lawyer	1	
	From media	2	
	From other	3	
(SPECIFY)____			
c) Did you apply for legal aid?		(18)	
	Yes	1	
	No	2	Q.120
IF APPLIED FOR LEGAL AID (YES AT c) ASK d) AND e)			
d) How long did you have to wait for a decision about whether you got legal aid or not?	____ weeks (19-20)		
e) Were you granted any legal aid?		(21)	
	Yes	1	Q.120
	No	2	
IF NO AT e)		OUO	
f) Why were you not granted legal aid?		(22)	
120. ASK ALL			
a) Overall, did you get the lawyer's services without having to pay anything yourself, or did you have to pay something for them?		(23)	
	Got without payment	1	(c)
	Paid something	2	
b) IF HAD TO PAY SOMETHING Did you have to pay the whole cost of the lawyer's services or did someone else provide some of them or pay some of the cost?		(24)	
	Paid whole cost	1	(e)
	Other provided/paid some	2	(c)
IF GOT WITHOUT PAYMENT (CODE 1 AT a) OR OTHER PROVIDED/PAID SOME CODE 2 AT b) ASK c) AND d)			
c) Who else provided you with legal services or paid some of the cost? ____		OUO (25-26)	
d) What did they provide or pay for? ____		OUO (27)	
IF GOT WITHOUT PAYMENT (CODE 1 AT a) NOW SKIP TO SEC. 3 Q.121			
IF VICTIM PAID SOMETHING			
e) How much did you yourself have to pay? RECORD TO NEAREST £	£____ (28-30)		

Section 3 Present Position of Claim

	Question	Col./Code	Skip to
	ASK - ALL WHO EVER CONTACTED A LAWYER (THOSE ASKED ANY PART OF SECTION 2) - AND ANY OTHERS WHO TOOK ACTION WITHOUT A LAWYER TO GET COMPENSATION (YES AT Q.106a - OR 116b - SEC.2)		
121	Have you ..... READ OUT	(31)	
	- reached agreement with the other party or his insurance company on a sum of money to be paid to you as compensation	1	SEC.4 Q.124 SEC.5
	OR - had the matter decided by a judge in court. (NOTE: CODE EVEN IF APPEAL PENDING)	2	Q.135
	OR - given up the hope of getting compensation	3	Q.122
	OR - is the matter still undecided	4	Q.123
	IF GAVE UP HOPE OF GETTING COMPENSATION (CODE 3 AT Q.121)		
122a	How much money had you hoped to get as compensation? RECORD TO NEAREST £ £____ (32-36)		
b	Who first thought of this as the sum you might get? ____	(37)	
c	Before you gave up the idea of getting compensation, had the other side or his insurance company made any offers to settle your claim? Yes	8	
	No	9	h)
	IF ANY OFFER MADE ASK d)-f)		
	d) How many offers were made? WRITE IN NUMBER____ (38)		
	e) Did any of these offers take the form of a payment of money into court?	(39)	
	Yes	1	
	No	2	
	ASK SEPARATELY OF EACH OFFER MADE		
	f) How much did they offer? When was the offer made? Why did you not accept it? Did anyone advise you not to accept it? RECORD IN GRID BELOW.		
	IF ANY PAYMENTS MADE INTO COURT (YES AT e)		
	g) Which of these offers took the form of payments of money into court?		

Amount £	Date made Month	Year	Reason not Accepted and Advisor (if any)	Payment into court
				1
				1
				1
				1

	Question	Col./Code	Skip to
	ASK h) AND i) FOR ALL WHO GAVE UP HOPE OF GETTING COMPENSATION (CODE 3 AT Q.121)		
	h) What were the main problems you had about getting compensation? Were they problems about:	(40)	
	READ OUT AND CODE WHICH APPLY — Which witnesses should be believed	1	
	What medical evidence should be accepted	2	
	Whether, on the facts of the case, the other side was at fault	3	
	How much the other side should pay you in compensation	4	
	(None of these)	9	
	i) Why did you give up hope of getting compensation? Was it on anyone's advice? PROBE FULLY AND RECORD ____ ____ ____ ____	OUO (41)	
	NOW SKIP TO PART 10, Q.154		
	IF MATTER STILL UNDECIDED (CODE 4 AT Q.121)		
123a	How much money do you hope to get as compensation? RECORD TO NEAREST £ £____ (42-46)		
b	Who first thought of this as the sum you might get? ____	(47)	
c	Has the other party or his insurance company made any offers to settle your claim? Yes	8	
	No	9	h)
	IF ANY OFFER MADE ASK d)-f)		
	d) How many offers were made? WRITE IN NO.____ (48)		
	e) Did any of these offers take the form of a payment of money into court?	(49)	
	Yes	1	
	No	2	
	ASK SEPARATELY OF EACH OFFER MADE		
	f) How much did they offer? When was the offer made? Why did you not accept it? Did anyone advise you not to accept it? RECORD IN GRID BELOW.		

Card 13 | Col./Code | Skip to

IF ANY PAYMENTS MADE INTO COURT (YES AT e)

g) Which of these offers took the form of payments of money into court?

Amount £	Date Made Month	Date Made Year	Reason not Accepted and Advisor (if any)	Payment into court
				1

ASK h) AND i) OF ALL FOR WHOM MATTER IS STILL UNDECIDED (CODE 4 AT Q.121)

h) What are the main problems you are having in trying to get compensation? Are they problems about:
READ OUT AND CODE WHICH APPLY: (50)

	Code
Which witnesses should be believed	1
What medical evidence should be accepted	2
Whether, on the facts of the case, the other side was at fault	3
How much the other side should pay you in compensation	4
(None of these)	9

i) What is the present position of your claim? OUO
PROBE FULLY AND RECORD VERBATIM ________ (51)

NOW SKIP TO PART 10 Q.154

SECTION 4 - SETTLEMENTS OTHER THAN COURT JUDGEMENTS

ASK ALL WHO REACHED AGREEMENT WITH THE OTHER SIDE ON A SUM OF MONEY AS COMPENSATION WITHOUT HAVING THE MATTER DECIDED BY A JUDGE IN COURT (CODE 1 AT Q.121 IN SECTION 3)

124. How much did they agree to pay you as compensation?
RECORD TO NEAREST £ £________ (50-54)

125. When was the agreement reached? MONTH________ (55-56) YEAR 19________ (57-58)

126a) How much had you originally hoped to get? £________ (59-63)
RECORD TO NEAREST £

b) Who first thought of this as the sum you might get? OUO (64-65)
____

CHECK AMOUNT AT 124 AGAINST AMOUNT AT 126a). IF AMOUNT AGREED LESS THAN HOPED FOR ASK c)

c) Why did you accept £____ (AMOUNT AGREED) rather than trying to get more? PROBE FULLY OUO (66)
____

Card 13 | Col./Code | Skip to

127a) Has the money all actually been paid? (67)

	Code	Skip to
Yes	1	
No	2	(e)

IF YES TO a) ASK b) and c)

b) Was it paid as a lump sum or in instalments? (68)

	Code	Skip to
Lump sum	1	
Instalments	2	ASK c), THEN Q.128

c) When did you receive the money/the last instalment?
________ (69-70) MONTH 19________ (71-72) YEAR

d) IF LUMP SUM AT b)
Instead of a lump sum, would you have prefered a regular weekly or monthly payment which increased if the cost of living increased? (73)

	Code	Skip to
Yes	1	Q.128
No	2	Q.128

IF MONEY NOT ALL PAID (NO TO a), ASK e) AND f)

e) Has any of the money been paid? (74)

	Code
Yes	1
No	2

f) When do you expect to receive all the money? (79-80) Blank)
________ (75-76) MONTH 19________ (77-78) YEAR

Record No. (1-4)
Card (14) (5-6)
P.423 (7-9)

ASK ALL

128a) Before you reached an agreement, had the other side or his insurance company made any other offers of money to settle your claim? (10)

	Code	Skip to
Yes	1	
No	2	Q.129

IF ANY OFFER MADE ASK c) - e)

c) How many offers were made? WRITE IN NO. (11)

d) Did any of these offers take the form of a payment of money into court? (12)

	Code
Yes	1
No	2

e) ASK SEPARATELY OF EACH OFFER MADE
How much did they offer? When was the offer made?
Why did you not accept it? Did anyone advise you not to accept it?
RECORD IN GRID BELOW

f) IF ANY PAYMENTS MADE INTO COURT (YES TO d)
Which of these offers took the form of payments of money into court?

Amount £	Date made Month	Date made Year	Reason not accepted and advisor (if any)	Payment into court
				1

Card 14

			Col./Code	Skip to
129a)	Did you have any difficulties of any sort in trying to reach agreement to settle your claim?		(13)	
		Yes	1	
		No	2	
	IF YES TO a)			
	b) What were the main difficulties you had? PROBE FULLY		OUO	
	______		(14)	
130.	Did the other side at any stage argue about:		(15)	
	READ OUT AND CODE WHICH APPLY	Which witnesses should be believed	1	
		Which medical evidence should be accepted	2	
		Whether, on the facts of the case, they were at fault	3	
		How much they should pay you in compensation	4	
	IF LAWYER EVER TOOK ANY ACTION OR STARTED NEGOTIATION ON RESPONDENT'S BEHALF (YES TO Q.115a) ASK Q.131 OTHERWISE SKIP TO Q.152			
131.	Did your lawyer have to file a claim in court to start a court case before the agreement was reached?		(16)	
		Yes	1	
		No	2	Q.152
	IF LAWYER FILED CLAIM IN COURT		(17)	
132a)	In which court did your lawyer file a claim to start a court case?	High Court	1	
		County Court	2	
		Other court	3	
	(SPECIFY) ______			
b)	When did he do this? ______ month (18-19) 19 ______ year (20-21)			
c)	Was a date fixed for a hearing?		(22)	
		Yes	1	
		No	2	Q.152
133.	At what stage was agreement reached?		(23)	
	READ OUT: Was it:	Before the date of the hearing	1)	Q.152
		On the day of the hearing before the case started	2)	
		After the hearing had started	3	
	IF AGREEMENT REACHED AFTER HEARING STARTED (CODE 3 AT Q.133)			
134a)	At what stage of the hearing was agreement reached? Was it: READ OUT:		(24)	
		Before all the evidence had been given	1	
		OR During the case after evidence had been given	2	
		OR Just before judgement was due	3	

Card 14

			Col./Code	Skip to
b)	Why was agreement reached at that stage? PROBE FULLY		OUO	
	______	NOW SKIP TO Q.152	(25)	
	SECTION 5 - COURT JUDGEMENTS			
	ASK ALL WHOSE CASES WERE DECIDED BY A JUDGE IN COURT (CODE 2 AT Q.121 IN SECTION 3)		(26)	
135.	Which court decided your case?	High Court	1	
		County Court	2	
		Other court	3	
	(SPECIFY) ______			
136.	When was the court hearing held? ______ MONTH (27-28) 19 ______ YEAR (29-30)			
137.	How long did it last?		(31)	
		Under an hour	1	
		An hour but not over a day	2	
		One day but not over two days	3	
		Over two days	4	
138a)	Before the hearing, had the other party or his insurance company made any offers of money to settle your claim?		(32)	
		Yes	1	
		No	2	Q.139
	IF ANY OFFER MADE ASK b) - d)			
	b) How many offers were made?	WRITE IN NUMBER	(33)	
	c) Did any of these offers take the form of a payment of money into the court?		(34)	
		Yes	1	
		No	2	
	d) ASK SEPARATELY OF EACH OFFER MADE How much did they offer? When was the offer made? Why did you not accept it? Did anyone advise you not to accept it? RECORD IN GRID BELOW			
	e) IF ANY PAYMENTS MADE INTO COURT (YES TO d) Which of these offers took the form of payments of money into court?			

Amount £	Date made Month	Date made Year	Reason not accepted and adviser (if any)	Payment into court
				1
				1

Card 14

Question		Col./Code	Skip to
139a) Before the court hearing began, were there any agreements between your side and the other side, so that the hearing was limited to just some particular questions? For example, did the other side agree that they should pay you some money in compensation but just disagree about the amount?		(35)	
	Yes	1	
	No	2	
b) Or did the other side disagree with you about whether they were liable to pay you money in compensation, but agree how much money should be paid if they were?		(36)	
	Yes	1	
	No	2	
c) Was there any other sort of agreement between your side and the other side?		(37)	
	Yes	1	
	No	2	Q.140
IF YES AT c) d) What was that? PROBE FULLY ______			
140a) What were the main questions discussed at the court hearing? Were any of the main questions: READ OUT AND CODE WHICH APPLY		(38)	
	Which witnesses should be believed	1	
	Which medical evidence should be accepted	2	
	Whether, on the facts of the case, the other side was at fault	3	
	How much the other side should pay you in compensation	4	
b) Were there any other main questions discussed at the court hearing?		(39)	
	Yes	1	
	No	2	Q.141
IF YES AT b) c) What were they? PROBE FULLY ______			

Card 14

Question		Col./Code	Skip to
141a) How much money had you hoped would be awarded as damages in compensation for your injuries/illness?	£ ______ (40-44)	000	
b) Who first thought of this as the sum you might get? ______		(45)	
142a) Did the judge actually award you a sum of damages in compensation?		(46)	
	Yes	1	
	No	2	Q.144
IF YES AT a) ASK b) - c) b) How much? RECORD TO NEAREST £	£ ______ (47-51)		
c) Were you satisfied or dissatisfied with this amount? Very or fairly satisfied/dissatisfied?		(52)	
	Very satisfied	1	
	Fairly satisfied	2	
	Fairly dissatisfied	3	
	Very dissatisfied	4	
IF AMOUNT AWARDED (YES TO 142a) 143a) Has the money all actually been paid?		(53)	
	Yes	1	
	No	2	(e)
IF YES TO a) ASK b) & c) b) Was it paid as a lump sum or in instalments?		(54)	
	Lump sum	1	
	Instalments	2	
c) When did you receive the money/the last instalment? ______ MONTH (55-56) 19______ YEAR (57-58)			
d) IF LUMP SUM AT b) Instead of a lump sum, would you have preferred a regular weekly or monthly payment which increased if the cost of living increased?		(59)	
	Yes	1	)
	No	2	)Q.144
IF MONEY NOT ALL PAID (NO TO a) ASK e) AND f) e) Has any of the money been paid?		(60)	
	Yes	1	
	No	2	
f) When do you expect to receive all the money? ______ MONTH (61-62) ______ YEAR (63-64)			

Card 14

Question	Col./Code	Skip to
ASK ALL		
144a) Did the judge make any decision about costs? IF NO Then each side was responsible for their own costs? IF NO What was the situation then?	(67)	
Judge made ruling on costs	1	
Judge made no ruling on costs - each side responsible for own	2	(e)
Other situation (SPECIFY)________		
IF JUDGE MADE RULING	(68)	
b) What decision did the judge make?		
Other side should pay all respondent's costs	1	e) THEN Q.145
Other side should pay some of respondent's costs	2	c) & e)
Respondent should pay some of other side's costs	3	d) & e)
Respondent should pay all other side's costs	4	d) & e)
IF OTHER SIDE PAID ANY OF RESPONDENT'S COSTS (CODES 1 OR 2 AT b))		
c) How much was the other side responsible for paying for your costs? RECORD TO NEAREST £ £________ (69-70)		
IF RESPONDENT PAID ANY OF OTHER SIDE'S COSTS (CODES 3 OR 4 AT b)		
d) How much money were your side responsible for paying for the other side's costs? RECORD TO NEAREST £ £________ (71-72)		
ASK e) AND f) UNLESS OTHER SIDE PAID ALL COSTS (CODE 1 AT b)		
e) (Apart from any which the other side had to pay...) how much in all were the costs on your side? RECORD TO NEAREST £ £________ (73-74)		
f) Were you responsible for paying all of these out of your own pocket?	(75)	
Yes	1	Q.145
No	2	
	000 (76-77)	
IF NO AT f) ASK g) AND h)		
g) Who was?________		
h) How much were they responsible for paying? RECORD TO NEAREST £ £________ (78-79)	(80	Blank)

Question	Col./Code	Skip to
Record No.	(1-4)	
Card (15)	(5-6)	
P.423	(7-9)	
ASK ALL	(10)	
145a) Did you or the other side appeal to a higher court? Yes	1	Q.146
No	2	
IF NO APPEAL (CODE 2 AT a) CHECK Q.142a)		
IF JUDGE AWARDED DAMAGES (YES AT 142a) SKIP TO Q.152		
IF JUDGE DID NOT AWARD DAMAGES (NO AT 142a) ASK b)	(11)	
b) Did you get any advice from anyone on whether to appeal or not? Yes	1	
No	2	(f)
	000	
IF ADVISED (YES AT b) ASK c) AND d)	(12)	
c) Who was that?________		
d) Did he advise you to appeal or not to appeal?	(13)	
Advised appeal	1	(f)
Advised no appeal	2	
IF ADVISED AGAINST APPEAL		
e) Why did he advise you not to appeal? PROBE FULLY ________		
IF NO DAMAGES BUT NO APPEAL		
f) Why did you not appeal? PROBE FULLY ________		
NOW SKIP TO PART 10 Q.154		
IF APPEAL MADE (YES AT Q.145a)	(14)	
146a) Who made the appeal? Own side	1	
Other side	2	
b) To which court was the appeal made?	(15)	
Appeal Court	1	
High Court	2	
County Court	3	
Other (SPECIFY)________		
c) Why was the appeal brought? PROBE FULLY ________		

Card 15

		Col./Code	Skip to
147.	Did the appeal court uphold the original judgement and dismiss the appeal or did the appeal court change the original judgement in some way?	(16)	
	Upheld judgement	1	CHECK Q.158
	Changed judgement	2	
	IF APPEAL COURT CHANGED JUDGEMENT CHECK Q.142a). IF DAMAGES AWARDED IN FIRST COURT (YES TO 142a) ASK Q.148. IF NO DAMAGES AWARDED IN FIRST COURT (NO TO Q.142a) ASK Q.149		
	IF APPEAL COURT CHANGED JUDGEMENT GIVING DAMAGES		
148.	Did the Appeal Court:	(17)	
	READ OUT: Decide you were not entitled to any damages	1	Q.151
	OR Increase your damages	2	Q.150
	OR Reduce your damages	3	Q.150
	OR Decide something else (SPECIFY) ______	4	Q.151
	IF APPEAL COURT CHANGED JUDGEMENT GIVING NO DAMAGES	(18)	
149.	Did the Appeal Court: Award you damages	1	Q.150
	OR Decide something else (SPECIFY) ______	2	Q.151
	IF APPEAL COURT AWARDED, INCREASED OR REDUCED DAMAGES		
150.	How much did the Appeal Court award you in damages? RECORD TO NEAREST £ £______ (19-23)		
	IF APPEAL COURT CHANGED JUDGEMENT IN ANY WAY		
151.	On what grounds did the Appeal Court decide to change the original judgement? PROBE FULLY ______		
	ASK ALL WHO: SECTION 6 - DISPOSAL OF COMPENSATION MONEY REACHED AGREEMENT ON A SUM OF MONEY TO BE PAID (THOSE ASKED ANY PART OF SECTION 4) OR HAD CLAIM DECIDED IN COURT AND FINISHED UP WITH DAMAGES i.e. Awarded damages and no appeal (YES AT 142a AND NO AT 145a) or Awarded damages and kept them after appeal (YES AT 142a AND CODES 2, 3 OR 4 AT 148) or Awarded damages only on appeal (CODE 1 AT 149) - OTHERS GO TO PART 10 Q.154		
152	What have you done with the compensation money or what do you intend to do with it? PROBE FULLY ______ ______	OUO (24-25)	

CARD 15

		Col./Code	Skip to
153a	Have you had any advice on what to do with the money?	(26)	
	Yes	1	
	No	2	PART 10 Q.154
	IF YES AT a)	OUO	
	b) Who from? ______	(27-28)	
	c) What advice were you given? ______		
	d) Did you accept or do you intend to accept this advice?	(29)	
	Yes	1	
	No	2	
	PART 10 MISCELLANEOUS		
154	RECORD DETAILS OF ANY VISIBLE SCAR, DISFIGUREMENT OR DISABLEMENT OF MISFORTUNE VICTIM ______	OUO (24-25)	
155	CONSENT FORMS CHECK PART 9 - IF MISFORTUNE VICTIM WAS IN CONTACT WITH LAWYER (ANY PART OF SECTION 2 ASKED) ASK a) - IF MISFORTUNE VICTIM APPLIED FOR LEGAL AID (YES TO 119c) ASK b) - IF MISFORTUNE VICTIM RECEIVED HELP FROM A TRADE UNION OFFICIAL (TRADE UNION OFFICIAL MENTIONED AT 106b) OR 115b)		
a	The Oxford centre of the Social Science Research Council may wish to contact the lawyer with whom you dealt to find out whether he had any difficulties in dealing with your case. Would you have any objection to this?	(26)	
	Yes	1	
	No	2	
	IF NO OBJECTION ASK RESPONDENT TO COMPLETE CONSENT FORM A AND ATTACH TO QUESTIONNAIRE		
b	The Oxford centre of the Social Science Research Council may wish to contact the Law Society to find out whether they had any difficulties in dealing with your application for legal aid? Would you have any objection to this?	(27)	
	Yes	1	
	No	2	
	IF NO OBJECTION ASK RESPONDENT TO COMPLETE THE CONSENT FORM B AND ATTACH TO QUESTIONNAIRE		
c	The Oxford Centre of the Social Science Research Council may wish to contact your trade union to find out whether they had any difficulties in dealing with your case. Would you have any objection to this?	(28)	
	Yes	1	
	No	2	
	ASK RESPONDENT TO COMPLETE CONSENT FORM C AND ATTACH TO QUESTIONNAIRE Time interview completed ______ Duration of interview [ ][ ][ ] minutes (29-31)		

SHOW CARDS

CARD A **CHILDREN UNDER 6 YEARS**

Get around and play like other children of that age

Feed and dress or help feed and dress himself or herself as well as most children of that age

CARD B **CHILDREN 6-16 YEARS**
or 17 and 18 and still in full time education

Wash himself or herself
Dress himself or herself
Get to and use the WC
Eat a meal by himself or herself

Talk to other people
Hear other people talking
See to read or to get about

Climb stairs or steps
Walk 100 yards

Attend school at all
Attend an ordinary school
Join in all school activities

CARD C
Aged 17 or 18 and not in full time education
Anyone 19 or older

Wash himself or herself
Dress himself or herself
Get to and use the WC
Eat a meal by himself or herself

Talk to other people
Hear other people talking
See to read or to get about

Climb stairs or steps
Walk 100 yards
Use a bus or train

Carry shopping
Cook a hot meal
Clean the house
Wash clothes
Look after the children

Do a job at all
Do a full time job

Card G

Looking after yourself
washing - dressing - eating - getting to WC 1

Keeping occupied
bringing magazines - helping with hobbies 2

Getting about INSIDE the house
getting out of bed - moving rooms - up and down stairs 3

Getting about OUTSIDE the house
walking - or using public transport - getting to and from school/work 4

Keeping up with household chores
washing clothes - cleaning house - shopping - cooking 5

Looking after children 6

Card H

Use at Q.38, Q.50, Q.58, Q.97

Gross Weekly Income	*Code*	*Gross Annnal Income*
Under £20	P	Under £1040
£20 - £29	J	£1040 - £1559
£30 - £39	M	£1560 - £2079
£40 - £49	N	£2080 - £2599
£50 - £59	K	£2600 - £3119
£60 - £79	T	£3120 - £4159
£80 - £99	S	£4160 - £5199
£100 or more	R	£5200 or more

Appendix III: Solicitors' (Postal) Questionnaire

This questionnaire was sent to solicitors who were consulted about claims for damages. See Chapter 3, p. 80, for an explanation.

CENTRE FOR SOCIO-LEGAL STUDIES
WOLFSON COLLEGE
OXFORD
Telephone: 52967/8

SOLICITORS' QUESTIONNAIRE 1978

ALL INFORMATION GIVEN IN THIS QUESTIONNAIRE IS CONFIDENTIAL: NO INDIVIDUAL REPLIES WILL BE DISCLOSED TO YOUR CLIENT

Name of Client ....

Address ....

Date of Accident ....

AMOUNT OF SETTLEMENT

1. What was the total amount of the settlement in this case?

Total General Damages £________

Total Special Damages £________

Loss of earnings up to date of settlement: £________

Estimated loss of future earnings: £________

(What was the period of loss taken into account, or number of years purchase?) ________

Out-of-pocket expenses: £________

---

2. On what date was settlement agreed? ________

On what date was the money actually paid? ________

LEGAL EXPENSES

3. Did your client apply for legal aid? YES/NO

IF YES: Was it granted? YES/NO

What was the amount of your client's contribution? £________

---

4. How long was the period between the date of the application for legal aid and the decision of the Committee? ________ (weeks)

---

5. What were the total legal expenses on your client's side (no matter who paid them)?

(All sums inclusive of VAT)

Solicitors' Fees (including petty and general disbursements): £________

Counsel's Fees: £________

Out-of-pocket disbursements, etc.: £________

Total Legal Expenses: £________

---

6. Who discharged these amounts?

Your client £________

Defendant (or his Insurers) £________

Legal Aid Fund £________

Other (Please specify source)

________ £________

DIFFICULTIES AND DELAY IN NEGOTIATIONS

7. Did you experience any difficulties in handling the claim as a result of delay between the date of the accident and your being consulted? YES/NO

IF YES: Please mention the problem

....

....

---

8. Did you consider that there was undue delay (on either side) in settling this claim? YES/NO

IF YES: To which cause(s) would you attribute the delay?

....

....

....

---

9. Did you advise your client at any stage to delay pursuing the claim: for example, because of uncertainty about the medical prognosis? YES/NO

IF YES: For which reasons did you advise delay?

....

....

10. Were there any difficulties in negotiating with the defendant's insurance company (or solicitors)? YES/NO

IF YES: Which issues were in dispute?

i The question of liability YES/NO

ii The medical prognosis YES/NO

iii The quantum of damages YES/NO

iv Other (please specify)

....

Please give brief details of the difficulties

....

....

---

11. Was there any difficulty in pressing the claim on account of lack of evidence? YES/NO

IF YES: Please give details.

....

....

---

12. Was it necessary for you to commence proceedings against the defendant? YES/NO

IF YES: At which stage exactly was settlement reached?

i Before the date of the hearing YES/NO

ii On the day of the hearing, but before the case started YES/NO

iii After the hearing had started YES/NO

---

13. Had there been earlier offers to settle before the time of the final agreement? YES/NO

IF YES: Please enter details below:

DATE OF OFFER MONTH/YEAR	AMOUNT OFFERED	WAS IT A PAYMENT INTO COURT?
		YES/NO
		YES/NO
		YES/NO
		YES/NO

Had any change in relevant circumstances occurred between the offers? YES/NO

IF YES: Please give brief details

....

....

FACTORS RELATING TO SETTLEMENT

14. Was there any reduction in the amount of the settlement to take account of your client's Contributory Negligence? YES/NO

IF YES: What was the percentage or amount of the reduction? ____________

---

15. Did the settlement take into account any permanent disability? YES/NO

IF YES: Please give details.

....

....

---

16. Do you feel that the settlement which your client eventually received was adequate in the circumstances?

Comments: ....

....

....

---

17. Please use the space below for any additional comments or observations you may wish to make, either about this particular case, or about the present system for claiming damages for injuries.

List of Authors and Government Reports Cited

The full reference to the work cited is found at the end of each chapter in which it is cited. In the case of co-authors, the work is listed under the name of the first.

Abel-Smith *et al.* 47, 135
Abrams 244
Abuse of Social Security Benefits (Committee Report) 167, 197
Adler and Bradley 185
Aitchison and Brown 296
Akerlof 350
Alternative Remedies, Committee on 174
Arrow 220, 350
Atiyah 17, 63, 140, 144, 146, 149, 156, 161, 189, 200, 350
Atkinson 171
Austin *et al.* 141

Baldwin 312
Barry 239
Becker 281
Bell 185, 193
Bell *et al.* 185
Berkowitz 142
Berkowitz *et al.* 277
Beveridge Report 14, 21, 169, 232
Bibby 278
Biderman *et al.* 203
Biggs 228
Blair 349
Blaxter 185, 189
Bradshaw 239
Briar 185
Briggs and Rees 197
British Insurance Association (Insurance Facts and Figures) 233
Brittan and Vlachonikolis 296, 308
Burman and Genn 245, 246
Burman *et al.* 155
Buzzard and Shaw 264, 277

Calabresi 162, 169, 350
Calvert 197
Cantley Committee Report 135
Carne 277
Carrier and Kendall 238
Carson 171, 189
Carter 231
Clarke and Ogus 244
Clayton 230
Collingwood 145
Conard *et al.* 41
Consumers Association (Report) 232
Cox 278
Criminal Injuries Compensation Board (Reports) 202
Curran 47, 48

Davies 239
Daw 231
Denerley 264, 277
Department of Employment *Gazette* 215
Department of Health and Social Security
(Survey of Sick Pay Schemes) 213, 214, 215, 218, 264
(Private Medical Care) 221, 223
(Income during Initial Sickness) 215, 216, 218, 343, 345, 346, 350
Deutsch 142
Doherty 257, 277
Dore 244

Ehrenzweig 155
Elston 244

Family Expenditure Survey 224, 233, 283, *et seq*
Fenn 269, 278
Fenn and Brittan 281
Fleming 17
Fulbrook 185

Galanter 68
General Household Survey 32, 36, 37, 216,

241, 243, 284 *et seq*
Genn 77
George 21
Goldberg and Morrison 286
Green Paper (Income During Initial Sickness) 215, 216, 218, 343, 345, 346, 350
Griffiths 48

Hadley *et al* 245
Harris, A. I. *et al.* 25, 185, 283
Harris, D. R. 328
and Hartz 41
Hart and Honoré 140
Hauser and Burrows 231
Horowitz 237
Horsnell 296
Home Office (Review of Criminal Injuries Compensation) 202, 209
Houghton 172

Income Data Services 211, 212
Industrial Injuries Advisory Council 219
Insurance Year Book 223
Ison 41, 128, 349, 350

JUSTICE Report (No Fault on the Roads) 350
(Trial of Motor Accident Cases) 135

Keeton and O'Connell 350
Kemp and Kemp 83
Kish 27
Kmenta 278

Lancaster 268
Latta and Lewis 68, 80
Law Commission 83
Law Society 132
Layard *et al.* 277
Legal Aid (Lord Chancellor's Advisory Committee) 197
Legal Services (Royal Commission) 135
Lerner 142
Levy and McManus 277
Life Insurance Association 223
Linden 41, 140, 143, 144, 155
Lloyd-Bostock 161
Luft 277, 312
Lund 132
Luntz 350
Lydall 296

Macaulay and Walster 141, 160–1
McClements 278
McGahan 244
McGregor 83
MacKinnon 128
Maclean and Genn 26, 27, 28, 29, 41, 228, 236
McManus 277
Mann 244
Martin and Morgan 219, 277
Mauss 245
Mayhew and Reiss 63
Micklethwait 189
Miers 200
Ministry of Labour (Sick Pay Schemes) 217
Mnookin and Kornhauser 137
Moonman 217
Morris and Paul 41
Munkman 83

Nagi and Hadley 277
National Insurance Advisory Committee (Report) 197
Nickell 268

O'Connell 128, 161, 350
O'Connell and Simon 135
O'Connell and Wilson 143
Office of Population Censuses and Surveys (Classification of Occupations) 31–2, 284
Ogus 190
Ogus *et al.* 328
Ogus and Barendt 21, 169, 172, 173, 183, 187, 190, 197
Oi 282

Palmer 349, 350
Pauly 350
Pearson (Royal) Commission 25, 91, 106, 108, 109, 110–1, 112, 120, 132, 134, 135, 136, 137, 140, 169, 174, 183, 189, 197, 225, 232–3, 237, 238–9, 328, 350
Pfennigstorf 222
Phillips 169, 350
Phillips and Hawkins 94, 135, 158
Policy Holder Insurance Journal 233
Pritchard 135

Reid and Robertson 173
Rein 236
Reiss 203
Reynolds 229
Rosenthal 125

Ross 94, 99, 100, 158
Rothschild and Stiglitz, 350

Sainsbury 185
Sampson 142
Scarman 238
Scheffler and Iden 277
Schuyt *et al.* 47, 48
Sentry Insurance (Motor Insurance Survey) 233
Shavell 162
Social Security Statistics 327
Sparks *et al.* 203
Spence and Zeckhauser 350
Stowell 189
Supplementary Benefit Commission (Annual Report) 312

Taylor 216, 277
Tiley 172
Titmuss 227, 237, 245
Townsend 312

US Department of Transportation 41, 144, 227

Veljanovski 350
Vlachonikolis 278, 309

Walker and Townsend 238
Walster *et al.* 141, 142, 153
Walster and Walster 142
Whitehead 277
Widiss *et al.* 350
Wilkinson 135
Williams and Hepple 140, 141, 146
Wilmott and Young 244
Wilson 350
Winfield and Jolowicz 17
Winn Committee (Report) 135
Woodhouse (Australian) Report 337, 350
Woodhouse (New Zealand) Report 349

Zander 128, 135

Index

abandoning claims to damages 113–20
reasons given for,
avoiding trouble 114–5
defendant's denial of liability 117–8
fear of legal expense 115
legal problems 117
preserving relationships 115
problems of evidence 116
solicitor's failure to make progress 118
victim's fault 116
see also failure to claim damages
absence from work, see time off work
accidents
attribution of causes 144–6
of fault by victims 139–61
causes of 144–5, 148, 152–4, 160
to children 149
domestic 60, 151, 154
incidence of 32–3
types, by socio-economic grouping 50
comparison of consequences with those of illness 2–7, 31–3, 37–8, 87, 189, 240–5, 248–53, 263, 298, 325–7
household income 295, 297–8, 309–10
proposed abolition of differences 327–9, 334–6
prevention of, see tort system (deterrence)
shifting of costs by tort system 139, 159
types of 31–3, 37–8, 50–3, 55–7, 62, 66, 72, 87–8, 146, 151–4, 240–5, 248–53, 263, 298
vindication of victim 139, 141–2, 146, 155, 157
see also claims to damages, fault, tort system
accident records, use of 348
administration of compensation 16, 182–97, 341
expense of 183, 341
savings through integration 332
advice to victims
Citizens' Advice Bureaux 80–1
pre-legal advice 60–70, 76–7
trade unions 66–70, 81, 119–20, 154
see also legal services
assaults, see criminal injuries
attendance allowance 171, 173, 176, 179, 184, 189, 196
as source of household income 300–2, 305
attribution of blame, see fault

barristers 100–1, 123, 132
blame, see fault
borrowing by victims 121–2, 181–2, 300

care for victims, see employment (labour market adjustments), medical services, informal care
cause of incapacity 31–3, 37–8, 87–8, 325–7
effect on household income 295, 297–8, 309–10
present systems of compensation 2–7
proposals for future 325–9, 334–6
residual disability 241–2
see also accident (types), illness
Chronically Sick and Disabled Persons Act 1970 235, 236
Citizens' Advice Bureaux 80–1
claims to damages
advice to claimants who do not use lawyers 81–2
from medical personnel 82
anxiety caused to claimants 147, 157, 160, 161
characteristics of successful claimants 49–65, 70
age 51, 52, 61, 63, 64
accident type 46, 50–1, 62
attribution of blame, relation to 70
claims consciousness 47, 61, 68
employment status 56
pre-legal behaviour 139
receipt of sick pay 56, 58
residual disability 56–9, 63–5
severity of injury 56–9
sex 51–2, 56, 61, 63, 73
socio-economic groups, 52–5, 63, 70

time off work 58–60
decision to claim 139, 148, 150, 155, 159
delay in consulting lawyers, 104
initiative on victim, 139, 147–8, 158
motives for seeking, 139, 147–8, 149–51, 153, 159
pre-legal process, 61–5
unrepresented claimants, 81–2
see also abandoning claims, damages, failure to claim, settlement process
commonsense morality
as basis of tort system, 139–46, 157
community health services, 243–4
compensation
and absence from work, 264, 267, 268
and economic theory 257
and no-fault 278
payments, differences in 282–3
and productive loss 276
see also damages, fault, proposals for policy changes, tort system
compensation systems
administration 16
age restrictions 13
anomalies 2–17
allowances for dependants 14–15
ceilings on benefits, 14
complexities, 2–17
confusing to victims, 154
contributions, payment of 3
duration of benefits 13
earnings-relation 14, 23
entitlement based on cause 2–3
non-pecuniary losses 15
periodical payments 13
sources of finance 16
taxation of benefits 15–16
see also proposals for policy changes
contributory negligence 19, 20
information from solicitors to clients 91–2
and negotiating settlements 91–2, 123
difficulties in negotiating 111
and victims' attribution of blame 91–2
cf. discretion in criminal injuries compensation, 202
court proceedings (damages) 112–3
claimants' fear of 125
rules designed for 133
criminal injuries
assaults reported 151
characteristics of victims 204
compensation scheme 200–3
assessment of awards 201–2
awards received 204–5, 208
claims 204–5
discretion to reduce awards 202
eligibility for awards 201
failure to claim 205–6
information to victims 209
reasons for 206–9
procedure 201
data from survey 203–9
response problems 200, 203
domestic violence 201, 203–4
reluctance to report 203–4
and tort claim 200
criminal law, confused with civil 153
Criminal Law Act 1967 222

damages
adequacy 123–5
views of solicitors 123
advice from lawyers 124–5
on the use of damages 123
amounts recovered 86–91
assessment of 83–6
ceiling, none fixed 83
future contingencies 84–5
individualized 83
inflation 83–4
itemization 90
loss of earnings 83, 90
future loss of earnings 83–4, 90
lump-sum award 84, 85, 90
medical prognosis 83, 84
non-pecuniary losses 85–6, 90, 237–8
pecuniary losses, 83, 90
permanent partial disability 84
taxation 85
uncertainties in assessment 84, 85, 89
discounting 85, 89, 123–5
distribution of amounts 89–90
ignorance of law 74, 75
illness, for 327
needs, meeting 45, 238–40, 252–3
proportion of victims recovering, 46–7, 50–66
reasons given for accepting low amounts 89, 123–5
recovered without using lawyers 81–2
relationship to other types of support 248–52
superiority over other types of compensation 19
support in kind, recognition of 236
use of damages by victims 120–2, 300
advice on use 123

as source of household income, 284
see also abandoning claims, claims to damages, settlement process, tort system
data, see research design
debts incurred by victims 121–2, 181–2, 300
delay, see settlement process
Department of Employment, registration with 236
dependants, allowances for, 14–15, 22, 23–4, 338–9
deterrence (of carelessness), 20, 45, 139, 145–6, 148, 161
disability
definitions of 2, 29, 36
partial 13, 23, 170
reform proposals 337, 339, 340, 346
see also residual disability
disablement benefit, see industrial injuries benefits
disincentives to work 23, 278
see also employment (return to work), residual disability, time off work

earnings
determinants 274–5
and household income,
earnings of non-victim 302–4
earnings of victim 301–2
reduced 270
see also employment
earnings-relation 14, 23, 278
in proposals for policy changes 329–30, 338, 346
employers
attachment to employee 278
change of 272–3
fault in regard to accidents 151
financing 341–2
responsibility for safety 152, 153–4
vicarious liability 18
employment
absence from 260–69 (see also time off work)
changes in 258, 270, 272–3, 276
in earnings 274–5
in hours worked 273–4
constraints to choice 257–8
hours of 258–9, 270, 273–4, 277
labour market status of sample 259
adjustments by households 282, 303–10
transitions 269–75
retirement from 259, 270–2, 276
return to work 258–9, 278
incentives to 217, 218, 258, 266
regression analysis of 266–9
equity theory, see psychology
evidence of fault, see settlement process

failure to claim damages 46–77
reasons given for 49, 70–6
effect on continuing relationships 72, 74–5, 154–8
evidence, lack of 71–3
fear of involvement with law 71–3
fear of legal expenses 72–4
ignorance or confusion 72, 74, 75
trouble, unwillingness to undergo 71–3
see abandoning claims
family income supplement 171, 301–2
fault 139–61
attribution of fault 70, 139, 147–61
by accident type 151–2
and obligation to compensate 149–50
in order to justify claim 150–3
relationship between victim and harmdoer 154
and taking steps to claim 150
by type of fault 152–4
legal and everyday concepts compared 143, 148, 156, 159
moral blame, compared with 156–7
obligation in the absence of fault 154
opinion surveys (fault v. no fault) 143–5
principle of 139, 146, 160
psychology of attributing 144–6, 147, 159
related to legal liability
in ordinary thinking 143, 144, 149, 153, 159
in victim's view 147, 149–51, 159
see also contributory negligence, psychology
fees, see legal expenses
Finance Acts 1946, 1979, 1982, 172–3
financial data 283–5
and see household income and wealth
financial loss, as incentive to claim damages 156, 252–3

health services, see medical services
hospitalization 240–1
and time off work 261–2, 267–8
household income 281–313, 324–5
and age of head of household 291–2

attendance allowance 300–2, 305
changes in sources of 300–3
comparative data 283–5, 291, 293
data from survey 283–5
definition of 284
imputed income, 285, 286
distribution of, 285–6
lognormal distribution of 296
and household type 287–8
and socio-economic groups 288–91
earnings of members 301–3
and household status of victim 293–4, 309–11
and inflation 283
logistic regression model 308–11
loss of income (compensation systems) 14
non-response 311
and registration
with Dept. of Employment 295, 297, 309–11
with local authority 295, 297, 310
replacement of income 14, 264, 267–8, 276, 278
and residual disability of victim 295–6, 309–11
response rate 284, 311–2
sources of 285, 300, 301–2
and type of accident and illness 295, 297–8
and work status 309–10
of head of household 291, 293
of victim 293–5, 309–11
where victim ceases to be main earner 303–8, 309–10
household unit 15, 22
adjustments in the labour market
by non-victims 305–8, 309–10
by victims 305–8, 309–10
victim ceasing to be main earner 303–8, 309–10
regression analysis of factors 308–11
definition of 281
financial decisions 281–2, 283
socio-economic grouping 288–91
types of 287
as unit of production 281–3
household wealth
debts/borrowing 181–2, 300
effects of illness or injury 297–9
spending from (or stopping) savings 180–2, 297–300

illness
comparison of consequences with those of accidents 2–7, 31–3, 37–8, 87, 189, 240–5, 248–53, 263, 325–7
household income 295, 397–8, 309–10
proposed abolition of differences 327–9, 334–6
damages recovered 327
see also causes of incapacity
incapacity
for work 3, 217
incidence of 31–3, 325–7
see also accidents, disability, illness, residual disability
income, see household income
Income and Corporation Taxes Act 1970 172
industrial illness 31, 50, 151, 190, 216, 298, 327, 347, 349
industrial injuries benefits 169–70
difficulties with claims 187, 190–1, 196
disablement benefits 169–70, 176, 179, 300–2, 305
injury benefits 169, 176
inflation 14, 83–4
informal support 244–8
duration and frequency of help 246
and local authority services 246
and other support 248–52
relationship of helpers to victims 247–8
injuries (injured person) see accidents
insurance (private) 220–33
brokers 231–2
claims made 224–5
competition 230–3
difficulties in obtaining 227–9
expectations of policy-holders 225–7
group 211
liability 18, 77, 152
limitations of private market 227–32, 329
objectives of 24
and other support 248–52
payments received 229–30
policies held by the sample 223–4
proposals for the future 333, 349
refusals to insure 227–9
shifting of risks by 220, 230–3
for sick pay 211
types of policies available 221–3
health care 223, 231
legal expenses 222
life 221
permanent health 222
personal accident 221–2
reverse liability cover 223
insurance companies

contesting serious claims 65
negotiations with (damages) 81–2, 93, 99–104
offers to settle 98–9
opposing change 161
payments by 128
proposals for future role 333, 349
relationship with accident victim 158
invalidity benefit 168, 176, 179, 300–2, 304–5
invalidity pension (non-contributory) 170, 176, 179

justice, accident victims' perceptions of 139–61

lawyers, see legal services
legal advice, see legal services
legal aid 130–1, 185
knowledge of scheme 67
legal expenses 128–32
amounts 129–32
as percentage of damages 131–2
contingency fees 128, 131
counsel's fees 132
fear of 72–4, 115–6
information to clients 132
insurance company payments 128
offers to settle 98–9
legal rules, impact on victims' perceptions 153–4, 159–61
legal services
access to 47–8, 80–1
advice 123, 125–8, 150, 158, 161
to accept amounts offered 124
barristers, consultation of 100–1, 123
clients' complaints or disagreements 126–8
delay in consulting lawyers 104–5
differential use of 47–8, 61
failure to make progress with claims 118
failure to seek 60–77
legal advice scheme 67
legal aid 67, 130–1, 185
questionnaire to solicitors 80
relationship between solicitor and client 125–8
selection of solicitors 80–1
settlements without legal services 81–2
specialization and experience 100
success in obtaining damages 46, 61–3, 81
trade union lawyers 80
unmet legal need 47–8
see also legal aid, legal expenses, settlement process
liability, victims' perceptions of 139–61
local authority services 235–6, 243–4
in relation to other support 248–52

means-testing 13, 22, 171, 338, 346
medical appeals (social security), 183–4, 187
medical assessment of criteria for benefits 340
medical certification 183, 191, 242, 258, 269, 277
medical problems (damages) 84–5, 88–9, 94, 98, 108–9, 111
reports/prognosis delayed 109
recovery delayed by claiming 161
medical services 240–3
hospital nights 240–1
and time off work 261–2, 267–8
out-patients 242–3
general practitioners 242–3, 248–50
mobility allowance 171, 173, 176, 179, 188–9, 196
moral blame 156–7
morality, see common-sense morality, fault, socialization

National Assistance Act 1948, 235
National Health Service 235
needs, meeting 45, 238–40, 252–3
negligence (tort of) 17–19
see damages, tort system
negligence, see fault
negotiations, see settlement process
no-fault schemes 143–5, 278, 328, 347–9, 350
see risk relationship
non-pecuniary losses 15, 85–6, 90, 237–8, 337
norms, social and legal 142–5, 153–4, 158–60

occupational sick pay, see sick pay
offers to settle, see settlement process
old age pension 300–2
out-of-court settlements, see damages, settlement process

partial disability 13
and damages 84
partial loss of earnings 23, 170
proposals for reform 337, 339, 340, 346
see residual disability
partial loss of earnings 23, 84, 170, 337,

339, 340, 346
pension (occupational) 271–2, 276
periodical payments 13–14, 85
opinions on 90–1
see damages (lump sums), proposals for policy changes
pre-legal advice, see advice
proposals for policy changes
administration 332, 341
allocation of benefits 334–40
allowances for dependants 338–9
for expenses 337
assessment criteria 340
assumptions underlying 329–30
different time-periods for benefits 333–4, 342
earners, preference for 339
earnings-relation 329–30, 338, 346
employment and earnings 277–8
entitlement to benefits 332
financing (general) 341–9
no-fault schemes 347–9
policy goals 341
private insurance 349
sick pay 343–6
social security 346–7
sources of finance 341–2
integration, need for 330–1
method of 333–5
long-term cases, priority to 336–7, 346
non-earners 337, 339
for non-pecuniary losses 337
partial loss of earnings 337, 339, 340, 346
priorities in types of benefits 337–8
rehabilitation 340
risk-relationship 341, 343, 347–9
self-employed 349
supplementary benefit, avoiding reliance on 338, 346
psychology
of accident victim 139–61
attributing fault 149–61
common-sense morality 157
interpretation process 159
moral blame 156–7
attributing responsibility 144–6
equity theory 141–5, 160
punishment of harmdoer, 141–2
as function of tort system 155, 157
re-actions to harmdoing 141–6
reflection of legal norms 159–61
relationship between victim and harmdoer, 154
avoiding trouble with employers 116, 155
socialization 142–3, 153
social relationships 139–41, 146–8, 154–8, 160

reform proposals, see proposals for policy changes
registration (as disabled)
with Dept. of Employment 295, 297, 309, 311
with local authority 295, 297, 309, 310
rehabilitation 278, 340
damages claim as barrier to 161
research design 25–37
Compensation questionnaire, App. II
demographic characteristics of sample 36–7
incidence rates 31–3
interview response rates 32, 34–5
population studied, 3
proxy response 27
residual disability, prevalence of 36, 38
sample design 27–8
sampling 30–2
screening criteria 28–30
questionnaire, App. I
survey 26–33
solicitors' questionnaire 80, App. III
sub-sampling 33–5
weighting of Compensation sample 35
residual disability
by cause of incapacity 241–2
and change of employer 272–3
and change in hours worked 273–4
and damages 56–9, 63–5
definitions of 36
and earnings, 274–5
and household income 295–6, 309–11
prevalence of 36, 38
and retirement 271
and return to work 258, 266–8
and sick pay 265
and time off work 262
see also partial disability
response rates (interviews) 32, 34–5
and household income 284, 311, 312
responsibility (liability) 140, 145, 153–4, 159
see fault
retirement from work 259, 270–2, 276
return to work 258–9, 278
incentives to 217–8, 258, 266
regression analysis 266–9

see residual disability
risk relationship 16, 169
proposals for future 341, 343, 347–9
and sick pay 215–7

savings, stopping or spending 180–2, 297–300
screening, see research design
settlement process (claims for damages) 93–120, 123–5
court proceedings 112–3, 125, 133
delay
complaints about delay 127
in consulting lawyers 104–5
difficulties caused 104
in negotiating settlements 105–9
reasons given for 109–10
as reason for accepting low sums 124–5
as reason for abandoning claims 118–20
and residual disability 108
and time off work 106
discounting of claims 85, 89, 123–5
evidence of fault, problems with 45, 47, 71–3, 89, 97, 104, 111, 116, 120
insurance companies 81–2, 99–104
negotiations 93–112
difficulties in 110–2
pressures on claimants 123–5
release of information 101
strategies 97–104
strategies of claimants 97–8, 101
strategies of insurance companies 99–104
nuisance value of small claims 99
spreading risks 100
offers to settle 93–104
advice on acceptance 94, 126
data on offers 94–104
effect of rejection 93–4, 97–8
successive offers and seriousness of case 95–7
settlements without use of lawyers 81–2
uncertainties facing claimants 94, 97–8, 123–5, 127, 134
see abandoning claims to damages, claims to damages, damages
sick pay
amounts received 212
by sex 215
by time off work 264–5
coverage 213–5
exclusions from 212
and damages 56, 58
dependants 345–6
duration of receipt 212
government policy 215–8
incentives to return to work 217–8, 266
medical certification 258, 269
number of employees receiving 212
objectives of 24
proposals for future 343–6
and residual disability 265
risk relationship 215–7
social security, relation to 217–8
statutory sick pay 343, 345
minimum levels 345
taxation 217, 345
and time off work 264–5, 276–7
sickness benefit 168, 176, 190–1
dependants' allowances and sick pay 218
relationship with sick pay 217–8
as source of household income 300–02, 305
social care 235–53
allocation criteria 237–40
combinations of support 248–52
community health services 243–4
informal support 244–8
local authority services 243–4
meeting need 238–40
objectives of 24–5
social relationships 115, 139–41, 146–8
effect of damages claim 154–8
and rationale of tort system 160
social security 167–97
administration and adjudication 182–97
amounts of benefits obtained 174–9
appeals 184
assessment of administrative standards 192–7
contributory benefits 167–9
dependants 22, 23–4
difficulties with claims 185–97
administrative difficulties, 191–7
complexity 189–91, 196
demarcation problems 189–91
problems of legal interpretation 187–9
disincentives to work 23, 278
earnings-relation 23, 278
and employment status 180
entitlement to future benefits 177–9
future policy-making 346–9
ignorance about relationship with damages 74–5

incapacity for work 167, 187–8
means-testing 13, 22, 171
medical certification 183, 191, 242, 258, 269, 277
non-contributory benefits 170
objectives of 21–4
and other support 248–52
overlap of benefits 173–4
partial loss of earnings 23, 170
and sex 179–80
taxation 171–3
see also under the names of individual benefits
Social Security Act 1975 167, 189, 190–1
Social Security and Housing Benefits Act 1982 215, 218–9, 343–6
socialization 142–3, 158
socio-economic groups 31–2, 37–8, 50, 54–5, 63, 70, 288–91
solicitors, see legal services
supplementary benefit 171, 174, 176, 185, 189, 195, 196, 264, 301–2, 338, 346

taxation 15–16
damages 85
sick pay 345
social security 171–3
time off work 260–9
and age 263–4
and cause of absence 263
and change in employment 273
and demographic characteristics 263–4
distribution of 260–1, 276
duration 260–9
and earnings 275
and hospitalization 261–2
and hours worked 273
and labour market transitions 269–75
and marital status 263–4
multivariate analysis 267–8
and regional unemployment 266
and residual disability 262
and sex 263–4
and sick pay 264–5
and working status 263–4, 305–7
see employment
tort (damages) system
abolition advocated 327–9, 334–6
advantages retained 328–9
vested interests in retaining 161
allocation of resources, means of 237–40
common sense morality 139–46, 157
cost of 132, 142–3, 157, 161
deterrence of carelessness 20, 45, 139, 145–6, 148, 161
divisiveness of 155, 160, 161
fault principle 139–61
functions of 45, 139, 140, 145–6, 159, 160
hostility, feelings of 141
initiative to claim 139, 147–8, 158
justice of, as perceived 139, 140
objectives 17–21
compensation 17–20
deterrence 20, 45, 139, 145–6, 148, 161
need for an inquest 21
preference for accident victims 327–8
retribution or vindication 21, 156, 157
shifting of costs of accidents 139, 159
see also claims to damages, damages, fault, psychology
trade unions
advice on claiming damages 81
claimants' reliance on 119–20
handling claims 68, 105
failure to make progress 119–20
providing pre-legal advice 66–70, 154
referrals to lawyers 80–1
resistance to change 161
trade union lawyers 80–1

unemployment 266, 273, 276–7
unemployment benefit 168, 176, 301–2
unmet legal need 47–8

vicarious liability 18

wage/salary 273–5
as source of household income
of victim 301–2
of non-victim 302–4
see earnings
wealth, see household wealth
work, see employment
work illness, see industrial illness